Dictionary of Multicultural Education

Edited by Carl A. Grant
and Gloria Ladson-Billings

ORYX PRESS
1997

*The rare Arabian oryx is believed to have inspired the myth of the unicorn. This desert
antelope became virtually extinct in the early 1960s. At that time several groups of
international conservationists arranged to have 9 animals sent to the Phoenix Zoo
to be the nucleus of a captive breeding herd. Today the oryx population
is over 1,000, and over 500 have been returned to the Middle East.*

Published simultaneously in Canada
Printed and bound in the United States of America

∞ The paper used in this publication meets the minimum requirements of
the American National Standard for Information Sciences—Permanence
of Paper for Printed Library Materials, ANSI Z39.48-1984.

Library of Congress Cataloging-in-Publication Data

Dictionary of multicultural education / edited by Carl A. Grant and
    Gloria Ladson-Billings.
        p.   cm.
    Includes bibliographical references and index.
    ISBN 0-89774-798-4 (alk. paper)
    1. Multicultural education—Dictionaries.   I. Grant, Carl A.
II. Ladson-Billings, Gloria, 1947–
LC1099.D53   1997
370.117'03—dc21   97-15019
                                                            CIP

In Memory of
James E. Browne, Jr.
1951–1995

CONTENTS

LIST OF TERMS

CONTRIBUTORS

Martha Adler
University of Michigan-Ann Arbor

Susan Matoba Adler
University of Wisconsin-Madison

Peggy J. Anderson
Wichita State University

Vernon Andrews
University of Wisconsin-Madison

Michael W. Apple
University of Wisconsin-Madison

Cherry A. McGee Banks
University of Washington-Bothell

James A. Banks
University of Washington-Seattle

H. Prentice Baptiste, Jr.
Kansas State University

Percy Bates
University of Michigan-Ann Arbor

Deborah A. Batiste
Anti-Defamation League,
*   A World of Difference Institute*

Jean T. Belkhir
Towson State University

Christine I. Bennett
Indiana University

Jane Bernard-Powers
San Francisco State University

Marilynne Boyle-Baise
Indiana University

Carin M. Bringelson
University of Wisconsin-Madison

Hank Bromley
State University of New York at Buffalo

James E. Browne, Jr.
University of Wisconsin-Madison

Patricia L. Browne
Indianapolis Public Schools

Edward Buendia
University of Illinois at Urbana-Champaign

Philip C. Chinn
California State University, Los Angeles

Harold Chu
George Mason University

Ellen Riojas Clark
University of Texas at San Antonio

Elizabeth G. Cohen
Stanford University

Mary Carol Combs
University of Arizona

Catherine Cornbleth
State University of New York at Buffalo

Carlos E. Cortés
University of California, Riverside

Warren E. Crichlow
University of Rochester

Kathleen Densmore
San Jose State University

Nadine Dolby
University of Illinois at Urbana-Champaign

Karen B. McLean Donaldson
Iowa State University

Donna Elam
New York University

Liba H. Engel
University of Wisconsin-Madison

Yen Le Espiritu
University of California, San Diego

Walter C. Farrell, Jr.
University of Wisconsin-Milwaukee

Lynn Fendler
University of Wisconsin-Madison

Susan Stanford Friedman
University of Wisconsin-Madison

Laurie Fuller
University of Wisconsin-Madison

Mary Lou Fuller
University of North Dakota-Grand Forks

Michael Fultz
University of Wisconsin-Madison

Jesus Garcia
University of Illinois at Urbana-Champaign

Sara S. Garcia
Santa Clara University

Geneva Gay
University of Washington-Seattle

Kristin Gilbert
*U.S. Department of Education
Office of Migrant Education*

Maureen Gillette
College of Saint Rose

Gloria F. Gilmer
*International Study Group on
Ethnomathematics*

Donna M. Gollnick
*National Council for Accreditation of Teacher
Education*

Mary Louise Gomez
University of Wisconsin-Madison

Beverly M. Gordon
Ohio State University

Carl A. Grant
University of Wisconsin-Madison

M. Elizabeth Graue
University of Wisconsin-Madison

Jill Moss Greenberg
*National Association for Multicultural
Education*

Richard E. Gross
Stanford University

Dawnene Hammerberg
University of Wisconsin-Madison

Robert G. Hanvey
Bloomington, Indiana

Annette Henry
University of Illinois at Chicago

Hilda Hernández
California State University, Chico

Asa G. Hilliard
Georgia State University

Etta R. Hollins
Washington State University

Tonya Huber
Wichita State University

Allen Hunter
*University of Wisconsin-Madison
A.E. Havens Center*

Rhonda Baynes Jeffries
University of Wisconsin-Milwaukee

Contributors

Elizabeth Kean
University of Nebraska-Lincoln

Joe L. Kincheloe
Pennsylvania State University

Joyce E. King
University of New Orleans

Milton Kleg
Center for the Study of Ethnic and Racial Violence

Jeanne Lacourt
University of Wisconsin-Madison

Gloria Ladson-Billings
University of Wisconsin-Madison

James G. Ladwig
University of Newcastle

Stacey J. Lee
University of Wisconsin-Madison

Joy L. Lei
University of Wisconsin-Madison

Amy Ling
University of Wisconsin-Madison

Kofi Lomotey
Louisiana State University

Wilma S. Longstreet
University of New Orleans

Frances A. Maher
Wheaton College

Monica Miller Marsh
University of Wisconsin-Madison

Renée J. Martin
University of Toledo

Cameron McCarthy
University of Illinois at Urbana-Champaign

Peggy McIntosh (PM1)
Wellesley College

Peter McLaren (PM2)
University of California, Los Angeles

Rubén Medina
University of Wisconsin-Madison

Merry M. Merryfield
Ohio State University

Lori Mestre
University of Massachusetts at Amherst

Mary Haywood Metz
University of Wisconsin-Madison

Barbara D. Miller
George Washington University

Luis C. Moll
University of Arizona

Alberto M. Morales
University of Massachusetts at Amherst

Sonia Nieto
University of Massachusetts at Amherst

Michael R. Olneck
University of Wisconsin-Madison

Valerie Ooka Pang
San Diego State University

Walter C. Parker
University of Washington-Seattle

Nancy Pauly
University of Wisconsin-Madison

Brenda G. Plummer
University of Wisconsin-Madison

Charlene Pope
University of Rochester

Thomas S. Popkewitz
University of Wisconsin-Madison

Gary G. Price
University of Wisconsin-Madison

Evelyn M. Reid
University of Toledo

Fred Rodriguez
University of Kansas-Lawrence

Richard Ruiz
University of Arizona

Janet Ward Schofield
University of Pittsburgh

Ann Scott
University of Massachusetts at Amherst

James T. Sears
University of South Carolina-Columbia

Rosa Sheets
University of Washington-Seattle

Mwalimu J. Shujaa
State University of New York at Buffalo

Christine E. Sleeter
California State University, Monterey Bay

Marion Smiley
University of Wisconsin-Madison

G. Pritchy Smith
University of North Florida

Geneva Smitherman (GS1)
Michigan State University

C. Matthew Snipp
University of Wisconsin-Madison

Elizabeth Spalding
National Council of Teachers of English

George Spindler (GS2)
Stanford University

Louise Spindler (LS1)
Stanford University

Joel Spring
State University of New York at New Paltz

Shirley R. Steinberg
Adelphi University

Lynda Stone (LS2)
University of North Carolina at Chapel Hill

Beth Blue Swadener
Kent State University

William F. Tate
University of Wisconsin-Madison

Beverly Daniel Tatum
Mount Holyoke College

Jacqueline B. Temple
University of Wisconsin-Madison

Mary Kay Thompson Tetreault
California State University, Fullerton

Carlos Alberto Torres
University of California, Los Angeles

Michael Tucker
University of Wisconsin-Madison

John Tyler
University of Massachusetts at Amherst

Alice Udvari-Solner
University of Wisconsin-Madison

Gajendra K. Verma
University of Manchester

Howard Winant
Temple University

John F. Witte
University of Wisconsin-Madison

Shelley D. Wong
University of Maryland at College Park

Sylvia Wynter
Stanford University

Kenneth M. Zeichner
University of Wisconsin-Madison

FOREWORD

The western tradition since the eighteenth century has been partly defined by dictionaries—philosophical, historical, critical. There were, for instance, Voltaire's *Philosophical Dictionary* (1741), Samuel Johnson's dictionary (1755), as well as an atheist dictionary, a Christian dictionary, and Gustave Flaubert's semi-comic *Dictionary of Received Ideas* (first published in 1913). Like the present work, each one went far beyond the mere definition of terms. They were intended to clarify beliefs and concepts, to expose clichés and mystifications, to educate. Voltaire, for all his skepticism, hoped that his dictionary would play a part in eliminating prejudice, which he thought to be a "scourge," not the least among "the evils which afflict man." Like others who compiled dictionaries, he was concerned about the reciprocal obligations that ought to develop among human beings and about what was required to nurture a sense of justice. Looking back upon them now, viewing the present volume in the contexts they created and they create, we may see them all as efforts to map the landscapes of their time, to invent the kinds of geographics that might help their contemporaries pay closer heed to one another as they tried (usually in the midst of crisis) to find their ways.

This dictionary of multicultural education revises and at once advances the tradition as it opens windows in the Eurocentric and the predominantly western canons to Africa, the south, and the east. Like the best of its predecessors, it avoids prescriptions and certainties. Multiple perspectives are provided here, not only on race and ethnic distinctions, but also on gender considerations, postmodernism, critical theory, and the meanings of all this for curriculum. The orientation towards expanded dialogue and an ideal of social justice makes it far more than an academic exercise; it may become not only a resource for multicultural scholarship, but also an aid in the efforts to combat chauvinism, nativism, and nationalist rivalries, as well as the ever-lingering damage done by racism.

The wonder of this work is partly to be found in its reconciliation of scope and diversity, something with which today's educators must be concerned. The editors have gathered scholars qualified to probe this history of ideas, cultural studies, identity politics, legal precedents, and equity issues in a manner that can only restructure the field, interdisciplinary as it is. The "received ideas" about multiculturalism and multicultural education are laid to rest in this book: no longer will teachers believe they have solved the problem by varying their menus, instituting "brotherhood" weeks, or incorporating "native" arts festivals. The dictionary makes it clear that the scope of the field is much, much wider, that it must respond to some of the most far-reaching demographic and cultural changes ever seen in history.

The expansion of the field, however, has not meant an overlooking of diversity and, indeed, particularity in this book. In part because the editors have paid attention to the importance of situated vantage points, in part because none of the old abstract categories are appropriate any longer, many points of view are visible here, as are many of the long-ignored nuances of cultural and human diversity. Clifford Geertz, in his book called *Local Knowledge* (1983), has written about the "ethnography of modern thought." That thought, he said, "is spectacularly multiple as product and wondrously singular as process. . ." and this is made dramatically evident in the dictionary with which we are concerned. Like many other modern scholars, and certainly like the editors of this volume, Geertz is interested in the relation between thought and action, as he is in the achievement of some kind of reciprocity. This dictionary may well become a resource for precisely such an ethnography.

In her introduction to *Fires in the Mirror* (1993), Anna Devere Smith wrote about the negotiation of identity in America. She said:

> There is an inevitable tension in America. It is the tension of identity in motion, the tension of identity which is in contest with an old idea, but a resonant idea of America. It was developed initially, or so we are told, by men, by White men, but an idea which has in fact been adopted by women and people of color. Can we guide that tension so that it is, in fact, identity in motion, identity which like a train can pick up passengers and take them to their destination? Or is this tension always going to be derailed onto a sidewalk where some innocents are waiting to be struck down? (p. xxxiv)

The dictionary before us must have arisen from a recognition of this tension. And surely, readers will lay it down with a consciousness of open questions like those posed by Anna Devere Smith. A work suffused with a concern about derailment must necessarily be a concern for social justice—for the innocent, the silent, the misunderstood, the oppressed. This dictionary is worthy of its great tradition. It opens gateways, places in which its readers (and perhaps its future contributors) can begin.

Maxine Greene
Teachers College, New York

PREFACE

he notion of a dictionary is an overwhelming one. The notion of a *multicultural* dictionary is both overwhelming and frustrating. Despite its burgeoning popularity and use, *multicultural education* and the vocabularies associated with it have suffered from a lack of clarity (Sleeter & Grant, 1987). Thus, our focus in the compilation of this dictionary is to help explicate the meanings and perspectives of various terms that are used in multicultural education. But this dictionary is more than a strict definitional one. Instead, the contributors have often addressed both the literal meanings of words and terms as well as the contextual meanings and exemplars that help create those meanings.

Our reasons for compiling this dictionary are twofold. The more obvious reason is to have it serve as a resource for scholars, students, education practitioners, and lay people as they read, write, and study in a multicultural education framework. We intend for this dictionary to be a reliable and dependable companion for multicultural educators.

Our second reason for compiling this dictionary is more complex. As we move into the twenty-first century, we recognize the attention being paid to the increasing demographic diversity throughout the world. In the United States, states like California, Texas, New York, and Florida have seen a remarkable change in the numbers of people of color over a relatively short period. California's Anglo or European American population has gone from more than 70 percent of the population in the late 1970s to about 57 percent in the 1990s. Throughout the world, destabilizing and shifting economic and political situations have precipitated major migrations. Thus, economically and technologically more prosperous nations in the industrialized West are playing host to displaced peoples from Asia, Africa, and South and Central America.

At the same moment that these demographic shifts are creating an awareness of a richly diverse world, the flames of racism, xenophobia, neonativism, and anti-immigrant hysteria are being fanned. In the United States we see mean-spirited and vitriolic challenges to any notion of diversity and multicultural education—in the workplace, in college and university admissions, in the content of the curriculum, and in the substance of research and scholarship. In Europe we see open hostilities toward immigrants and people of color in a resurgence of Nazism and other hate group activities.

This dictionary cannot serve as a panacea to these worldwide concerns. Its function is to make dialogue across differences possible and likely. We operate from a perspective of "knowing more" as a necessary—but not sufficient—condition for promoting the principles of equity and social justice. Our work as scholar-activists is always partially as writers and editors. Its completion comes only as we and others participate in systematic practices to support the ideals for which we stand.

The process of compiling and editing this dictionary required us to solicit entries from a variety of sources. In many instances we called upon those whose work already has made an impact on the field. Additionally, we solicited entries from a broad range of professionals and graduate-level students at professional meetings such as the American Educational Research Association and the National Association of Multicultural Education. Responses from these colleagues helped us to refine and rethink both the quantity and quality of the entries.

As editors, it was our job to read and review each entry and to contact authors for feedback and editorial changes. Together with our editorial assistant, Joy Lei, we were able to sift through scores of definitions and make critical decisions about what to include in the dictionary. We edited this dictionary in the spirit of multicultural education; that is, we included both supporters and critics of the field to demonstrate our commitment to including multiple perspectives.

This dictionary, like others, is arranged alphabetically. But that is where the similarities end. This dictionary comprises a variety of entries. Some are terms such as *Culture* or *Race*. Here authors have attempted to define what they mean in relation to current thinking in multicultural education and to provide meaningful examples. Other entries are court cases and legal precedents that have influenced our thinking about issues of diversity and multicultural education. Examples of such entries include *Brown v. Board of Education* and *Lau v. Nichols*. A third set of entries are methodological and theoretical-conceptual. Terms such as *Ethnography* or *Critical Theory* are included, not because they are the sole purview of multicultural education, but because they are often-used tools for the research and scholarship of multicultural educators. The entries vary in length because they vary in complexity and significance. Some entries, such as *Neo-Marxism*, require extensive elaboration and discussion, while others do not.

What readers will not find in this dictionary are biographical entries. One reason is the constraint of space, but a more significant reason is the fact that so many people have contributed (and continue to contribute) to multicultural education. A dictionary of this scope and size could not do them justice. Instead, we have called upon many of the contemporary multicultural education scholars to serve as contributors to this effort.

We also have elected not to include terms that describe groups of people such as *African Americans*, *Asian Americans*, or *Native Americans*. Instead, we have included the intellectual traditions that have emerged from the struggles of such groups, for example, *African American* or *Black Studies*, *Asian American* and *American Indian Studies*. However, we have included an entry on *Naming* to discuss the contested nature of identity and identity struggles. We made that decision because any attempt to define particular groups is likely to result in our omitting other groups. For example, a naming category such as *Asian Americans* covers a vast group of people without revealing the complexity and diversity within that category. The name connotes not only Chinese Americans and Japanese Americans but also Korean Americans, Filipino Americans, Laotian Americans, Vietnamese Americans, Cambodian Americans, Hmong Americans, Native Hawaiians, and Asian Indians, to name some of the members of this group. Any entry under the name Asian American will lose the richness and within group diversity that is a part of Asian American life and experiences. Asian American Studies as an entry, however, can be described historically, intellectually, and curriculum-wise. We can better "fix" the intellectual traditions rather than the names.

Some of the conventions we have adopted in this volume are the use of the term *people of color* instead of *minority* wherever possible. We recognize that the term *minority* has multiple and complex meanings. Thus, we avoid a situation when a community like East Los Angeles, where Latinos are the numerical majority, is termed a *minority community*. This designation is used by the dominant culture to signify the community's subordinated political status—that is, their superior numbers do not translate into greater social, economic, or political power.

Each entry is followed by the initials of the contributor. This identification is done as both an acknowledgment of the work of the scores of individuals who worked hard to make this effort possible and to identify for readers individuals whose work they may choose to research for further reading. Where necessary we have provided cross-references. As we struggle with new language and knowledge constructions, we find that some terms are used interchangeably. Thus, *Black Studies* may be used by some contributors, while *African American Studies* is used by others.

Finally, we devoted time and energy to compiling this dictionary because it is emblematic of the way in which the United States continues to remake itself. That we might need to search for a new language to explain our relationships with difference and diversity indicates that there continues to be hope and progress toward equity and social justice. It is our hope that as scholars and students use this dictionary, they will find themselves asking new questions and seeking new solutions to the conflicts and contestations of our histories and cultures. It also is our hope to inspire scholars and students to continue what we see as a new scholarly tradition that will call for subsequent editions of the dictionary. Our job was to begin this work. We trust that our colleagues—present and future—will continue it.

References

Sleeter, C. E., & Grant, C. A. (1987). An analysis of multicultural education in the United States. *Harvard Educational Review, 57*(4), 421–44.

Acknowledgements

First and foremost we wish to acknowledge the authors of the entries. We are pleased with their enthusiastic response to our requests to write entries. Our colleagues reported that, because of the importance of the dictionary, they wanted to contribute and would make time to meet the deadline. Our gratitude is extended to the individuals and organizations who helped circulate information about the dictionary and who offered suggestions about the entries.

A special thanks is given to Dr. Cherry McGee Banks for her initial work on developing the dictionary. We benefited greatly from her work and wanted to publicly acknowledge Cherry's contribution.

Chris Kruger deserves high praise for keying in the entries and organizing the material on computer disks.

Finally, we would never have finished this project without the magnificent support, organization, editorial assistance, and all-around management of Joy Lei. Thanks Joy, we sincerely appreciate you!

Carl A. Grant
Gloria Ladson-Billings
University of Wisconsin-Madison

INTRODUCTION

The creation of this dictionary is a major step in the field of multicultural education. It affirms that the subject has evolved to the point where it has its own distinctive vocabulary. Vocabulary, more than any other part of language, is about power and control. Those who define our words control our worlds. Ironically, however, vocabulary is the most mutable and the most constantly changing aspect of language. Old words may take on new meanings over time and perhaps, as a result, find themselves displaced or abandoned. New words are also being added to our vocabularies, often at an astonishing rate. Although science, with its breakthroughs and discoveries, is a substantial contributor of new words and definitions, so too are other fields such as politics, art, and education.

While scientific definitions usually strive for precision, we know that even the most rudimentary terms are subject to change. The definition of the atom, for instance, has continued to change and evolve as we learn more about the nature and characteristics of this tiny building block.

In attempting to produce and publish a dictionary of multicultural education, we acknowledge the conflicts often created by the issues of control and change. We also recognize the urgent need to define the terms of the debate—the terms of engagement in the struggle to make multicultural education a real and viable part of the way we educate the people of this nation.

Multicultural education has become more than a topic of discussion, and more than a dream about what should be. It has become an important educational movement with strong momentum and committed adherents. At the same time, however, multicultural education has been the target of scorn and derision, proffered by those who disagree with its tenets, fear its goals, or simply do not understand it.

In publishing this dictionary, we are attempting to wrest control of the vocabulary of multicultural education and, in so doing, further establish it as a serious field of scholarship. Standardization of its vocabulary is necessary for communication both within the academy and across the many political and social boundaries that must be spanned to make multicultural education a reality.

The Evolution of Multicultural Education

In one sense, multicultural education in the United States, as defined here, began when African American enslaved people began to educate themselves about their history in Africa and the United States, their role and participation in these histories, and how their racial identity dictated their treatment in U.S. society (Banks, 1994; Ladson-Billings, 1994). Multicultural education began when members of Native American tribes began to educate themselves on how to survive, resist, and get along with White, European colonizers and other cultural groups, including other tribes. This point of beginning for multicultural education also includes the time when Asian Americans, particularly the Chinese, communicated with their families and communities in their native land about life in the United States, and when they learned to resist, survive, and get along with White Americans and other people of color. Similarly, it can be said that in the U.S. Southwest, as Mexicans engaged in various interactions with Native Americans, African Americans, Asian Americans, and White Americans, multicultural education began. In other words, the beginning of multicultural education in the Untied States occurred during the early years of this country when the people who lived here began interacting with people outside of their cultural groups.

Multicultural education as philosophy and practice continued its early development as these different groups (African American, Asian American, Latino, Native American, and European American) began to learn (both formally and informally) about how race, class, and gender influence their presence in society, and how their group and other groups contributed to the growth and development of the United States.

In this century, two social movements were particularly important forces in shaping our present understanding of multicultural education—the Civil Rights Movement and the Ethnic Studies Movement that grew out of it.

The Civil Rights Movement consists of the actions of several marginalized groups to gain equality and equity. A pivotal moment in this movement occurred when Rosa Parks, an African American woman refused to give up her seat to a White person and move to the back of the bus in Montgomery, Alabama, in 1955. Other groups, including women, people with disabilities, the poor, and gays and lesbians and bisexuals were inspired by the actions of African Americans and their supporters, and similarly began to increase their efforts to make society equal and equitable for members of their groups.

The Ethnic Studies Movement that grew out of the Civil Rights Movement of the 1960s and 1970s was also central to the development of multicultural education. During this movement, African Americans and many other groups of color demanded equity and equality in the policies and practices of schooling. At numerous high schools and colleges, ethnic studies courses became a part of the curriculum, and at a number of universities, ethnic studies departments and programs were established.

It was coming out of these periods of action for equality and equity that the multicultural education movement began. In the 1970s this movement, energized by scholarship and participation by groups of color, women, and people with disabilities, began to capture the attention of K-12 and university educators. From that time to the present day, multicultural education has developed to become the educational vision and idea advocated by an increasing number of people, but also objected to by others.

Growing Problems

The coming together of the different groups and the varied interests they represented brought with them conceptual confusion and ambiguity regarding the meaning of multicultural education. Additionally, during the early days of multicultural education, those championing this movement saw benefit in not having a narrow or particular definition of multicultural education. Grant recalls writing in 1975:

> I think it would be wrong to posit a rigid and inclusive definition of multi-cultural education. I would prefer to describe multi-cultural education as a concept, because a concept embodies process—movement— and as such its contours are flexible. (p. 2)

Although the definition of multicultural education was still inchoate during these early years, those who adopted multicultural education as a topic of scholarly investigation and work were united in their demand for school policies and practices that would prepare students to work actively toward social structural equality and the promotion of cultural pluralism. For example, James Banks (1979) argues, "Ethnic studies instruction should help students develop the ability to make reflective decisions on issues related to ethnicity and to take personal and public action to help solve the racial and ethnic problems in our society" (p. 20). In *The Journal of Negro*

Education, Gwendolyn Baker (1979), one of the first proponents of multicultural education, asserts a definition she had advanced earlier:

> To this writer, a multiethnic education, in 1972, implied the utilization of a multiethnic approach to the curriculum. This approach was defined as a method of teaching that integrated into all aspects of the curriculum the influences and contributions of Blacks, Indian, Japanese, Jewish, and Mexican American culture to the culture of American Society. This approach means planning and organizing the learning experiences for children in the classroom so that these experiences reflect cultural diversity. (p. 254)

Educational associations and organizations also offered support to the multicultural education movement. The American Association of Colleges for Teacher Education's Commission on Multicultural Education (1977) produced one of the most quoted statements during the mid-1970s to early 1980s on multicultural education:

> Multicultural education is education which values cultural pluralism. . . . Multicultural education reaches beyond awareness and understanding of cultural differences. More important than acceptance and support of these differences is the recognition of the right of these different cultures to exist. The goal of cultural pluralism can be achieved only if there is full recognition of cultural differences and an effective program that makes cultural equality real and meaningful. (pp. 21-23)

The Association for Supervision Curriculum Development (ASCD) (1976) also produced a statement:

> Multicultural education is a humanistic concept based on the strength of diversity, human rights, social justice, and alternative life choices for all people. It is mandatory for quality education. It includes curriculum, instructional, administrative, and environment efforts to help students avail themselves of as many models, alternatives, and opportunities as possible from the full spectrum of our culture. . . . Multicultural education is a continuous, systematic process that will broaden and diversify as it develops. It views a culturally pluralistic society as a positive force that welcomes differences as vehicles for understanding. (Cited in Grant, 1977, p. 3)

During the nascent period of the multicultural education movement, scholars advocating multicultural education were united in their belief that the concept needed to promote structural equality. However, there was concern about the inclusion of other ascribed characteristics and experiences in addition to race in the definition of multicultural education. Some scholars, for example, believed that race alone should be the focus of multicultural education; others contended that the focus should be broadened to include many other groups that were and are similarly oppressed. Socioeconomic class, gender, religion, and disability are the characteristics that received the most attention.

To add to this confusion, some multicultural education scholars often used different terms to discuss concepts and issues of diversity. Banks (1973) and Garcia (1979), for example, wrote about *ethnic studies* or *multiethnic education;* H. P. Baptiste, Jr., and M. L. Baptiste (1979), Gollnick and Chinn (1983), and Suzuki (1980) used the term *multicultural education* in their writings. Grant and Sleeter (1986) used *education that is multicultural and social reconstructionist.*

Many authors writing about multicultural education adopted the terms and definitions most acceptable to educational journals because, during the early days of multicultural education, it was difficult to get articles on this subject published. Consequently, writers concerned with multicultural education often felt compelled to lessen or modify the complete meaning and full exposition of their ideas about multicultural education in order to spread the concept of multicultural education to a wider audience.

Many journal editors were stubborn about terminology and used their positions of power to determine the terms used. Therefore, if an invitation was issued to a scholar of multicultural education to write an article on the topic and the journal was using the term *ethnic*, usually *ethnic* was the term used in the article, instead of the term desired by the author, which may have been more appropriate for the essay.

Early scholars (1970s and early 1980s) of multicultural education believed that it was more important to get the "word" out and meet the "publish or perish" requirement for tenure than to put their careers and multicultural education in academic jeopardy. To be sure, they had concerns about this position and recognized that they were participating in the perpetuation of conceptual ambiguity about multicultural education. Nevertheless, these writers kept the discussions on multicultural education alive in the academic discourse and contributed, despite the obstacles (editorial and otherwise), to the development of one of the major themes in the educational reform movement.

Despite the disagreement among these early scholars of multicultural education with respect to which oppressed groups to include and which terms to use, they were united in espousing a common objective for multicultural education. They believed it should have at its core a curriculum and mode of instruction that would enable students (1) to learn the history and contributions to society of the diverse groups who comprise the population of the United States; (2) to respect the culture and language of these diverse groups; (3) to develop knowledge, understanding, and appreciation of one's multiple group characteristics and how these characteristics can privilege or marginalize the individual and others; and (4) to learn how to bring about social and structural equality and work toward that end.

Unfortunately, in the mid-1980s, this trend was interrupted. As the conceptual framework for multicultural education was finding common consent among advocates, it begin a rapid rise in popularity in part because many saw a sterile version of multicultural education as a possible way to placate the increasingly racially, linguistically, and ethnically diverse student population. This more superficial version did not change or changed only slightly the status quo in society and schools, but even this slight change threatened some people. On several university campuses scholars and public officials began to portray multicultural education as an unwanted intruder and challenger to the Western civilization canon in the colleges of letters and science.

With the increased attention toward multicultural education, educators and others began to ask: What is it? What does it mean? Is there a definition of multicultural education? The frequency of such queries, along with the conceptual ambiguity surrounding multicultural education in the academic and popular media, strongly implies that a definition is needed and that a dictionary of multicultural education is needed. Thus, the confusion in the field and society over the meaning of multicultural education and the demand from scholars in the field to provide conceptual clarity have produced a strong rationale to comply and include a definition in this dictionary.

A Definition of Multicultural Education

Multicultural education is a philosophical concept and an educational process. It is a concept built upon the philosophical ideals of freedom, justice, equality, equity, and human dignity that are contained in documents such as the Constitution, the Bill of Rights, and the Declaration of Independence. It recognizes, however, that equality and equity are not the same thing: equal access does not necessarily guarantee fairness. Multicultural education is also a process that takes place in schools and informs all subject areas and policies and practices of the school. It prepares all students to work actively toward structural equality in the organizations and institutions of the United States. It helps students to develop accurate self-concepts and accurate conceptions of others, to discover who they are, particularly in terms their multiple group memberships. Multicultural education does this by providing knowledge about the history, culture, and contributions of the diverse groups that have shaped the history, politics, and culture of the United States.

Introduction

Multicultural education acknowledges and affirms the belief that the strength and richness of the United States is in its human diversity. It demands a school staff that is multiracial, multiculturally literate, including some staff members who are fluent in more that one language. It demands a teaching staff that reflects gender and race diversity across subject matter areas. It demands a curriculum that organizes concepts and content around the contributions, perspectives, and experiences of all the groups that are a part of U.S. society. It confronts current social issues involving race, socio-economic status (SES), gender, sexuality, and disability. It accomplishes this by providing instruction in a social-cultural context that students understand and are familiar with, and builds upon students' learning styles. It teaches critical thinking skills, as well as democratic decision making, social action, and empowerment skills. Finally, multicultural education is a total process—it cannot be truncated—all the components of its definition must be in place for multicultural education to be genuine and viable.

Like a living and growing thing, multicultural education is constantly changing its outward appearance. While it retains its fundamental identity— its DNA structure, if you will—its appearance does and will change as it matures and is affected by external forces, including the environment in which it exists and hopes to survive. Also, no definition of multicultural education, including the one we offer above, should be so broad or so inclusive that it can be mistaken for something else or misappropriated by those who would misuse its energy, directing it away from the goal of equality, equity, and social justice for all.

Carl A. Grant
Gloria Ladson-Billings
University of Wisconsin-Madison

References

American Association of Colleges of Teacher Education Commission on Multicultural Education. (1973). No one model American. *Journal of Teacher Education, 24*(4), 264-65.

Baker, G. (1979). Policy issues in multicultural education in the United States. *Journal of Negro Education, 48*(3), 253-66.

Banks, J. A. (1994). *An introduction to multicultural education.* Boston: Allyn and Bacon.

Banks, J. A. (1979). *Teaching strategies for ethnic studies* (2nd ed.). Peabody, MA: Allyn and Bacon.

Banks, J. A. (Ed.). (1973). *Teaching ethnic studies: Concepts and strategies.* Washington, DC: National Council for the Social Studies.

Baptiste, Jr., H. P., & Baptiste, M. L. (1979). *Developing the multicultural process in classroom instruction.* Washington, DC: University Press of America.

Garcia, R. L. (1979). *Teaching in a pluralistic society.* New York: Harper & Row.

Gollnick, D. M., & Chinn, P. C. (1983). *Multicultural education in a pluralistic society*. St. Louis: Mosby.

Grant, C. A. (1977). Encouraging multicultural education: The ASCD Multicultural Education Commission. In C. A. Grant (Ed.), *Multicultural education: Commitments, issues, and applications* (pp. 1-5). Washington, DC: Association of Supervision Curriculum Development.

————. (1975). Exploring the contours of multi-cultural education. In C. A. Grant (Ed.), *Sifting and winnowing: An exploration of the relationship between multi-cultural education and CBTE*. Madison, WI: Teacher Corps Associates.

Grant, C. A., & Sleeter, C. E. (1985). The literature on multicultural education: Review and analysis. *Educational Review, 37*(2), 97-118.

Ladson-Billings, G. (1994). *The dreamkeepers: Successful teachers of African American children*. San Francisco: Jossey-Bass Publishers.

Suzuki, B. H. (1979). Multicultural education: What's it all about? *Integrated Education, 17*(1-2), 43-50.

Ablism *See* Disability Studies

Access

In relation to education and other human agencies, access addresses one's opportunity to enter into social institutions and agencies with all rights and privileges. Access also enables one to obtain services by being included in, and therefore accepted by, social institutions whose purpose is to provide information, along with other resources. This process ultimately develops and increases a person's and community's quality of life.

Equal access in the United States has been and continues to be marred by a number of policies and procedures. Racist policies, such as those of the Jim Crow era of the late 1800s, continue to play a detrimental role in the education and development of people of color, women, children, and their communities in the late 1900s. Jim Crow laws, although judged unconstitutional in the 1950s, have had a lasting effect on poor and underserved communities throughout the United States. Jim Crow laws and other similar laws have created a society that practices de jure segregation, which acts as the major obstacle for underserved students to gaining access to greater opportunities.

De jure segregation leads to unbalanced, underfinanced school districts, which have to compete with school districts that have twice the amount of monies to invest in their students. This imbalance in our educational system is the greatest example of access being unequal in education. This unequal access provides a perfect breeding ground for more unequal opportunities for underserved students throughout the United States. Unequal opportunities perpetuate more denied access to higher education and other postsecondary employment opportunities. Access to equal opportunity in education is the first in a series of barriers that must be torn down if the United States is to be truly a democratic nation for all of its people. *AMM*

Acculturation

In the broadest sense acculturation refers to a process of cultural change and adaptation that occurs when groups with different cultural norms come into contact and that progresses with each succeeding generation (Banks, 1991; Gibson, 1988; Tamura, 1994). In this context acculturation would be considered politically neutral and bidirectional between two cultures. Each cultural group might adapt to the traditions and beliefs of the other cultural group without losing its own cultural integrity.

In the context of U.S. society where a power differential exists between minority and dominant middle-class White cultures, acculturation can be better defined as a process by which immigrants or racial and ethnic groups outside of the mainstream culture adapt to that culture in order to fit in. They integrate values, beliefs, and patterns of behavior while also maintaining many of their own family or ethnic group beliefs and traditions (Banks, 1988; Gordon, 1964; Kiefer, 1970; O'Brien & Fugita, 1991).

Acculturation, also referred to as *cultural assimilation* (Gordon, 1964), is therefore determined in part by individuals who decide how much they want to dress, speak, and behave like members of the dominant group (Gollnick & Chinn, 1990). Over the generations, immigrant populations and their offspring have become *Americanized*, that is, have adopted mainstream Euro-American cultural habits and traditions to different degrees. The rate of acculturation of an ethnic group is influenced by a number of factors, such as the degree of isolation from the immigrant or native culture, and by societal prejudice and discrimination, which may heighten or lessen the desire of individuals to acculturate.

Lebra and Lebra (1974) differentiate between nonlinear acculturation models and linear acculturation models in the following way: In a nonlinear model the new culture is added to the old one, while in linear models partial replacement of the old culture by the new one occurs. In a nonlinear model acculturating people are free to choose from different cultural alternatives according to a given situation, while those using a linear model accept one cultural standard, thereby rejecting the others. Therefore, the acculturation process is contingent upon context and is a function of social relationships, roles, audiences, or reference groups.

An example of the nonlinear model of acculturation would be the following: A third generation Japanese American might focus upon collective responsibility to family and elders and on subtle communication in the presence of other Japanese Americans in the ethnic community, but he or she might demonstrate a competitive individualism with Euro-American peers in the dominant society. Thus, they have added a more assertive behavioral style to their Japanese American communication repertoire.

In contrast, immigrants using a linear model would accept one cultural standard as the preferred norm and perhaps diminish or even reject parts of their native culture. Linear models are individually oriented so that personal decisions are made to shape one's behavior around a particular cultural framework. For example, after World War II and the internment of Japanese Americans, many second generation Japanese Americans chose to develop their American side with the expectation that they could more easily integrate into mainstream society if they did so. As a result for some, their dress, patterns of speech and communication, and their perspectives on individual freedom replaced traditional Japanese views held by their immigrant parents. This led to cultural discontinuity and generational as well as cultural conflict.

In a school setting an example of nonlinear acculturation is the behavioral shifts of African American students who accommodate to the mainstream classroom behavior expectation of reserve turn-taking and individualized study, but in the context of the Black community interact more overtly, combining physical responses and verbal expressiveness. American Indian students might use a more observational and collective style of learning based upon attentive listening to family elders and then private mastering of the skill. In a school setting these same students might adapt to the more verbal, interactive approach of mainstream classrooms where critique is freely offered by teachers and peers (Hirschfelder, 1995).

An example of the linear model in the school context is reflected in the choice of some African American parents to move their families to suburban school districts in order to inculcate mainstream behavioral patterns, to have access to wealthier and more prestigious schools, and to develop mainstream contacts for the purpose of upward mobility. Another example is the opposition of Punjabi parents to bilingual education in school in order for their children to adapt to an all-English environment (Gibson, 1988). Punjabi would be taught at home. In both cases partial replacement of a native culture is deemed necessary and desirable as a means for integration into mainstream society. *SMA* • *See also* **Assimilation**

References

Banks, J. A. (1988). *Multiethnic education: Theory and practice* (2nd ed.). Boston: Allyn & Bacon.

———. (1991). *Teaching strategies for ethnic studies* (5th ed.). Boston: Allyn & Bacon.

Gibson, M. A. (1988). *Accommodation without assimilation: Sikh immigrants in an American high school.* Ithaca, NY: Cornell University Press.

Gollnick, D. M., & Chinn, P. C. (1990). *Multicultural education in a pluralistic society* (3rd ed.). Columbus, OH: Merrill.

Gordon, M. M. (1964). *Assimilation in American life: The role of race, religion, and national origins.* New York: Oxford University Press.

Hirschfelder, A. (1995). *Native heritage: Personal accounts by American Indians 1790 to the present.* New York: Macmillan.

Kiefer, C. W. (1970). The psychological interdependence of family, school and bureaucracy in Japan. *American Anthropologist, 72,* 66–75.

Lebra, T. S., & Lebra, W. P. (1974). *Japanese culture and behavior: Selected readings.* Honolulu: University Press of Hawaii.

O'Brien, D. J., & Fujita, S. S. (1991). *The Japanese American experience.* Bloomington, IN: Indiana University Press.

Tamura, E. H. (1994). *Americanization, acculturation, and ethnic identity: The nisei generation in Hawaii.* Urbana, IL: University of Illinois Press.

Action Research

Action research is a process of inquiry by which educators systematically and collaboratively study their own educational practice in order to improve their practices, their understandings of their practice, and the situations in which their practices exist (Kemmis & McTaggart, 1988). Action research has been viewed as a vehicle for the professional development of educators, for school reform, and as a means of knowledge production about education that challenges conventional knowledge and power relationships between academics and school practitioners. It has also been used as a vehicle for improving school-community relations (e.g., Burch, 1993) and as a strategy for community empowerment (e.g., Gaventa, 1993).

There are many different ideas about the nature of the action research process in the literature. Some have emphasized the similarities between action research and conventional academic research, both of which include the collection of data about specific research questions using common research methods and reporting formats (e.g., Myers, 1985). In some cases action research looks no different from the research published in academic journals and conducted by academic researchers about other educators' practices. Others have stressed the ways in which action research is different from conventional forms of academic research and have sought to push the boundaries about what counts as research in the doing and reporting of action research. Here the argument is made that, because action research generates insider and local knowledge about a situation, it should be evaluated with criteria that are different from those used to assess the quality of academic research (Anderson, Herr, & Nihlen, 1994).

For example, two criteria often used to determine the quality of academic research are the degree to which a study is strongly grounded in public academic theories and the degree to which a report of research thoroughly documents the external academic literature related to the issue(s) under study. Anderson, Herr, and Nihlen (1994) make the argument that with action research these criteria are less important than those that reflect the action orientation of practitioner research, such as the clarity and coherence of the presentation of the research, the degree to which all parties affected by the research have been involved, and the degree to which the research empowers people to act or provides new insights to researchers and readers.

There is a long history of action research by teachers and other school-based educators in the United States dating back to at least the 1940s (Noffke, 1994). Although it has not been a dominant vehicle for professional development or educational research, action research is consistent with an emerging consensus regarding good professional development that recognizes the knowledge and expertise of accomplished educators (e.g., Corcoran, 1995), and it is increasingly being viewed as a source of new knowledge about teaching and learning that is unavailable from the research of outsiders (Cochran-Smith & Lytle, 1993). Research on educational reform has clearly demonstrated the importance of involving teachers and other school practitioners as active participants in the creation and adaptation of school reforms and of giving educators more control over the design and implementation of their own professional development (Little, 1994).

Although the process of action research can be used for a variety of purposes, some of them contrary to the goals of multicultural education, it has been used in some cases by individual educators and by entire schools to improve the quality of multicultural teaching—teaching that is sensitive to the different cultural elements in our society and that honors and builds upon the experiences and cultural resources that pupils bring to school and that exist in communities (e.g., Stanford-Taylor, 1992; Streib, 1985; Sylvester, 1994). It has also been used by educators as a tool for promoting greater equity in schooling (e.g., Krater, Zeni, & Cason, 1994).

From a professional development perspective, teachers find the experience of doing action research highly rewarding. The literature is filled with accounts by teachers of how the process has increased their confidence and helped them to narrow the gap between their aspirations and realizations, to understand their own practices and their students more deeply, to revise their personal theories of teaching, and to internalize the disposition to study their teaching practice over time (Zeichner, 1994). Action research can also be used, however, as a vehicle to manipulate teachers to implement some externally conceived reform under the guise of empowerment (Griffiths, 1990). While it offers much potential for furthering the goals of multicultural education, it is not necessarily tied to the promotion of multicultural education or to greater equity and social justice in schooling and society (Weiner, 1985). *KMZ*

References

Anderson, G., Herr, K., & Nihlen, A. (1994). *Starting your own school*. Thousand Oaks, CA: Corwin.

Burch, P. (1993). Circles of change: Action research on family-school-community partnerships. *Equity and Choice, 10*(1), 11–16.

Cochran-Smith, M., & Lytle, S. (1993). *Inside-outside: Teacher research and knowledge*. New York: Teachers College Press.

Corcoran, T. C. (1995). *Transforming professional development for teachers: A guide for state policymakers*. Washington, DC: National Governor's Association, Center for Policy Research.

Gaventa, J. (1993). The powerful, the powerless, and the experts: Knowledge struggles in an information age. In P. Park, M. Brydon-Miller, B. Hall, & T. Jackson (Eds.), *Voices of change: Participatory research in the United States and Canada*. Westport, CT: Bergin & Garvey.

Griffiths, M. (1990). Action research: Grassroots practice or management tool? In P. Lomax (Ed.), *Managing staff development in schools*. Clevedon, PA: Multilingual Matters.

Kemmis, S., & McTaggart, R. (1988). *The action research planner*. Geelong, Australia: Deakin University Press.

Krater, J., Zeni, J., & Cason, N. (1994). *Mirror images: Teaching writing in Black and White*. Portsmouth, NH: Heinemann.

Little, J. (1994). Teacher's professional development in a climate of educational reform. *Educational Evaluation and Policy Analysis, 15*, 129–52.

Myers, M. (1985). *The teacher-researcher: How to study writing in the classroom*. Urbana, IL: National Council of Teachers of English.

Noffke, S. (1994). Action research: Toward the next generation. *Educational Action Research, 2*, 9–22.

Stanford-Taylor, C. (1992). Increasing the involvement of African-American parents in the school. In C. Caro-Bruce & J. McCroadie (Eds.), *Principals-action research* (pp. 7–18). Madison, WI: Madison Metropolitan School District.

Streib, L. (1985). *A Philadelphia teacher's journal*. Grand Forks, ND: North Dakota Study Group Center for Teaching and Learning.

Sylvester, P. S. (1994). Elementary school curricula and urban transformation. *Harvard Educational Review, 64*(3), 309–31.

Weiner, G. (1985). Professional self knowledge versus social justice. *British Educational Research Journal, 15*(1), 41–51.

Zeichner, K. (1994). Action research: Personal renewal and social construction. *Educational Action Research, 1*(2), 199–220.

Affirmative Action

Enacted September 24, 1965, Executive Order 11246, dubbed affirmative action, outlines equal opportunity employment standards and is a legal statement to implement nondiscrimination in government employment. This order pledges government contracting agencies to nondiscrimination against any employee or applicant for employment because of race, color, religion, sex, or national origin. This pledge includes the commitment to fair treatment of workers during employment, in opportunities for advancement, demotion, transfer, recruitment and advertising, layoff or termination, rates of pay and other forms of compensation, and in training and apprenticeships. Furthermore, it states that government contracting agencies will post, in conspicuous places, the provisions of this nondiscrimination pledge for employees and applicants for employment.

The use of such provisions became apparently necessary during the 1960s and 1970s after years of presumed commitment to affirmative action proved inadequate. Highly desirable apprenticeships and various positions in industry were gained almost exclusively through networking until the introduction of affirmative action incentives. Resolutions such as the Philadelphia Plan, the *Weber* case, the *Griggs* decision, and the Steel Industry Settlement are examples of successful affirmative action legislation in response to such acts of exclusion. These cases demonstrated the need for timetables and specific numerical goals in hiring and employment practices. Additionally, they brought to bear the implications of Title VII of the 1964 Civil Rights Act which empowers the courts to order "affirmative action as may be appropriate" for relief of past discrimination (Ezorsky, 1991).

Affirmative action measures suffered a dramatic decline in enforcement during the 1980s as new Supreme Court decisions weakened compliance guidelines. Currently, affirmative action is under even greater scrutiny. The conservative politics of the 1990s have threatened to make affirmative action a thing of the past due to the emerging notion of diminished discrimination in U.S. society (Chavez, 1995). Regardless of evolving trends, affirmative action and equal employment opportunity standards ensure people outside of the mainstream favorable circumstances to enter and excel in their employment endeavors. *WCF & RBJ*

References

Chavez, L. (1995). Demystifying multiculturalism. In J. W. Noll (Ed.), *Taking sides: Clashing views on controversial educational issues* (8th ed.) (pp. 94–98). Guilford, CT: Dushkin.

Ezorsky, G. (1991). *Racism and justice: The case for affirmative action*. Ithaca, NY: Cornell University Press.

African American Language

Also known as *Black vernacular English* or *Ebonics* (ebony for Black, phonics for sounds), African American Language (AAL) is a mixture of European American English and the Niger-Congo family of African languages, such as Yoruba, Wolof, Efik, and Twi, which are spoken throughout West Africa. Although most of the words in AAL can readily be identified as European American English words, it is the nuanced meanings, the pronunciation, the linguistic practices, and the ways in which the words are combined into statements that distinguish it from European American English.

AAL forms can be found in all the domains of language and speech: syntax, pronunciation, lexicon, discourse practices, and rhetorical and semantic strategies. For example, consider the statement, "The Brotha be lookin' good; that's what got the Sista nose open!" *Brotha* is AAL for an African American man, *lookin' good* refers to his attractive appearance, *Sista* is AAL for an African American woman, and her passionate love for the man is conveyed by the phrase *nose open*. The use of *be* indicates that the quality of *lookin' good* is not limited to the present moment, but reflects the man's past, present, and future essence. Thus, as is the case in Efik and other Niger-Congo languages, AAL uses a verb pattern to convey habitual events. Note also in this statement that the grammatical integrity of AAL denotes the possessive by context and does not require the redundancy of an "'s," that is, "Sista nose," not "Sista's nose."

Some of the richest expressive forms of AAL can be found in the various Black verbal traditions—signification/signifyin', storytelling, toasts, jokes, proverbs, and lies. For example, in *signifyin'*, the speaker deploys clever language, exaggeration, irony, and indirection in an artistic expression of verbal social critique. It is commonly played as a game of ritualized insult, as in *yo' momma jokes* (referred to as *playin' the Dozens* or *snappin'*); as with certain other aspects of AAL, analogues have been located in West African rhetorical practices. However, signification can also be appropriated for serious, instructive purposes. Malcolm X once began a speech with these words: "Mr. Moderator, Brother Lomax, brothers and sisters, friends and enemies." Malcolm's ironic statement, his signifyin', signalled to the audience that he knew inimical forces were out there.

About 90 percent of African Americans speak or have spoken AAL at some point in their lives. At the same time, many—particularly middle-class professionals—also speak the language of wider communication in the United States (that is, European American English). That is, many African Americans are adept at code-switching—changing from one language to another to fit the speech situation.

AAL reflects the transformation of ancient elements of African linguistic forms and practices into a new language, which was forged in the crucible of enslavement, Southern-style apartheid, racism, and the struggle to survive and thrive in the face of this domination. From its beginning as a *pidgin* (a mixture of two or more languages) during the Slave Trade, this Pidgin English served both as a transactional language between captors and captives, neither of whom could speak the other's language, and as a *lingua franca* among enslaved Africans of diverse ethnic backgrounds. (A *lingua franca* is a common system of communication used by people of different language backgrounds.) Although *Ole Massa* would combine groups of Africans from different linguistic backgrounds on his plantation in order to foil communication and thwart escape, the Africans appropriated the foreign tongue and reconstructed it as a counter language by superimposing their own linguistic practices upon the White man's speech. When an enslaved African said "Eveybody talkin bout Heaben ain goin dere," it was a double-voiced form of speech which signified on slaveholders who professed Christianity but practiced slavery. Thus, AAL provided a code for Africans in America to talk about Black business, publicly or privately, and even to talk about *Massa* himself right in front of his face.

On the one hand, AAL continues to enrich the everyday language of the United States through such African linguistic survivals as the *cola* of *coca cola*, through the practice of assigning Black meanings to Euro-American words, as in *bad* to signify *good*, and through linguistic crossover into public culture via mass media—advertising, popular singing, comedy, and current Hip Hop culture. On the other hand, AAL historically represents a linguistic tool in the continuing struggle to affirm Black culture and fight White racism. Thus, the absorption of AAL into American public language is viewed with a great degree of ambivalence in the African American community.

Scholars of AAL include Molefi K. Asante, Beryl Bailey, John Baugh, David Dalby, J. L. Dillard, Ralph Fasold, Joseph Holloway, Patricia Jones-Jackson, Thomas Kochman, William Labov, Clarence Major, Claudia Mitchell-Kernan, Salikoko Mufwene, John Rickford, Jerrie Cobb Scott, Arthur Spears, Lorenzo Turner, Winifred Vass, and Walter Wolfram. *GS1* •
See also **Code-Switching**

Afro-American Studies

The emergence of Afro-American studies, also called African American studies or Black studies, at predominantly White and leading historically Black institutions in the midst of the social struggles of the 1960s, represented a stunning break with the dominating social construct and Euro-American cultural hegemony. Struggles against institutional racism permeated educational systems as Black students enrolled in college in higher numbers and challenged the role and function of higher education. They demanded a relevant education related to the needs of Black communities. Student-led movements, which established the first formal Black studies program at San Francisco State College (now called San Francisco State University) in 1968, grew out of Black student involvement and leadership in the Civil Rights, Anti-War, and the Black Power movements.

From its inception, Afro-American or Black studies, as a mode of critical interdisciplinary and applied investigation, distinguished itself from Negro history and evolved beyond Black history. Following the tradition of social theorizing and scholarly activism epitomized by W. E. B. DuBois and Carter G. Woodson, among others, this discipline addresses academic and social concerns for the betterment of society and the well-being of Black people. Its scholarship, curricula, cultural production, research, and social action repudiate the presumed neutrality of knowledge, the separation of art from life, and the complicity of universities with societal injustice. Black studies encompasses a particular epistemological, axiological, and ontological mission across the disciplines. By asking new questions from a Black perspective or worldview concerning the Black experience and the human experience as well, this paradigm also dispenses with the specious question of whether non-Blacks can teach Black studies. Compared to ethnic studies and multicultural education approaches that expand or multiculturalize knowledge, Afro-American or Black studies theorizing and research stress a deciphering role for knowledge in order to address societal obstacles to Black people's development and to expose and reinterpret the American past and the encounter between the peoples of Africa, Europe, and the Americas.

The field includes seven basic subject areas or core courses: Black–history, religion (spirituality and social ethics), arts (music, art, literature, and theater), sociology (or social organization), psychology, politics, and economics. The National Council for Black Studies and the African Heritage Studies Association are the discipline's two major professional organizations. The National Council for Black Studies' constitution states that the discipline "include[s] any subject area that has the Black Experience as the principle object and content of study" (Karenga, 1993, p. 22). Maulana Karenga (1993) defines the discipline as "the systematic and critical study of the multidimensional aspects of Black thought and practice in their current historical unfolding" (p. 21).

Important contributors to the field include Lerone Bennett, John Henrik Clarke, Harold Cruse, St. Clair Drake, John Hope Franklin, Vincent Harding, Nathan Hare, Henry Louis Gates, Abdul Al-Khalimat (Gerald McWhorter), Joyce Ladner, Manning Marable, Charshee McIntyre, Claudia Mitchell-Kernan, Lynda James Myers, Wade Nobles, Sterling Stuckey, and Sylvia

Wynter. African and African Caribbean scholars, including Cheikh Anta Diop, C. L. R. James, and Frantz Fanon, have influenced Black studies, as have the tenets of both Marxism and cultural nationalism. Recent developments that have contributed to the discipline, to African-centered knowledge, and to curriculum transformation include Molefi Asante's articulation of the concept of Afrocentricity; Black women's studies, including theorizing and critical writing from Black feminist and womanist perspectives (bell hooks, Patricia Hill-Collins, Barbara Christian, and Joy James) and reflecting the legacy of educators like Mary McLeod Bethune; and research in classical African civilizations (e.g., the Nile Valley, Zimbabwe). Afro-American (or Black, African, African-American, or Africana) studies has survived both retrenchment and absorption, and 43 degree-granting programs emphasize classical African, Afro-American, and diasporic studies, including the Caribbean, the African presence in Asia and Europe, student and faculty involvement in community service, study of African languages, African study abroad, and faculty exchange programs. Finally, public schools in several major cities, including Berkeley, California, and New Orleans, Louisiana, have African and African American curriculum departments or studies programs. *JEK*

References

Karenga, M. (1993). *Introduction to Black studies* (2nd ed.). Los Angeles: Sankore Press.

Afrocentrism

Afrocentrism is a theory of personal and social transformation. Its proponents have made important contributions toward countering the negative effects of White supremacist ideologies on postenslavement, postcolonial African thinking, and generally, on ways of thinking about Africa and its people. Afrocentrism concomitantly addresses the interpretation or reinterpretation of reality from perspectives that are centered by and within the processes that maintain and perpetuate African life and culture.

Afrocentrism wholly corellates to the African worldview (Asante, 1980, 1987, 1990; Azibo, 1992; Carruthers, 1980; Ekwe-Ekwe & Nzegwu, 1994); Cheikh Anta Diop's ([1959] 1978) theory of African cultural unity is generally regarded as foundational to both of these concepts. Diop's work is credited with beginning a movement that extended the thinking of African intellectuals worldwide and beyond the limitations of racial analyses by demonstrating the existence of particular qualities of African history, linguistics, and psychology, all of which have endured as aspects of African culture since antiquity (Ekwe-Ekwe & Nzegwu, 1994; Spady, 1978).

While the Afrocentric worldview has existed from antiquity, Afrocentrism as a construct has not. Carruthers (1980) defines the concept of worldview and distinguishes it from ideology. Unlike ideology, which he associates with class interests, worldview "includes the way a people conceived of the fundamental questions of existence and organization of the universe" (p. 4). The Afrocentric worldview, according to Carruthers, rests on two basic truths: it is distinct and universal among African people throughout the world, and its restoration is the only viable foundation for African liberation. Conceptions of the Afrocentric worldview consistent with that put forth by Carruthers have been articulated by Ani (1994), Azibo (1992), Nobles (1974), and Richards (1989, 1990). Afrocentrism, as a concept, enables the strengths of enduring African cultural unity to serve as weapons for liberation and as tools for building new social realities in which Africans understand themselves as subjects of their own experiences (Asante, 1980).

Asante (1980) offers that Afrocentricity is a "transforming agent" for the restoration of the Afrocentric worldview. He argues that the personal transformation process enables an individual to transcend a consciousness born out of Otherness and realize Afrocentricity. It is precisely this possibility of individual transformation that makes an Afrocentric collective consciousness viable.

Azibo (1992) argues that restoring the African worldview requires an understanding and use of three approaches: deconstructionist, reconstructionist, and constructionist. Non-African concepts, variables, and formulations must be deconstructed and reconstructed. The deconstructionist approach employs critical analysis in a fashion that corresponds to Ani's (1994) notion of "de-Europeanization." The reconstructionist approach "revises, revamps, and otherwise alters alien-centered formulations to better fit or jibe with African reality" (Azibo, 1992, p. 86). Lastly, the constructionist approach "proceeds with formulations and concepts derived from the African cultural deep-structure" (p. 86).

Ani (1994) focuses on personal transformation facilitated by the "de-Europeanization" of the culture concept. She argues that the ideological function of culture can be understood through a systematic analysis of European culture's deep structure and the uses of its logic. This essentially means learning how to demystify the universalistic claims of Western cultural imperialism by treating them as manifestations of ideology. *MJS & KL*

References

Ani, M. (1994). *Yurugu: An African-centered critique of European cultural thought and behavior.* Trenton, NJ: Africa World Press.

Asante, M. K. (1980). *Afrocentricity.* Buffalo, NY: Amulefi.

———. (1987). *The Afrocentric idea.* Philadelphia: Temple University.

———. (1990). *Kemet, Afrocentricity, and knowledge*. Trenton, NJ: Africa World Press.

Azibo, D. A. (1992). Articulating the distinction between Black studies and the study of Blacks: The fundamental role of culture and the African-centered worldview. *The Afrocentric Scholar, 1*(1), 64–97.

Carruthers, J. H. (1980). Reflections on the history of the Afrocentric worldview. *Black Books Bulletin, 7*(1), 4–7, 13, 25.

Diop, C. A. ([1959] 1978). *The cultural unity of Black Africa: The domains of patriarchy and of matriarchy in classical antiquity*. Chicago: Third World Press. Originally published as *L'unite culturelle de l'Afrique noire* (1959).

Ekwe-Ekwe, H., & Nzegwu, F. (1994). *Operationalising Afrocentrism*. Reading, UK: International Institute for Black Research.

Nobles, W. W. (1974). Africanity: Its role in black families. *The Black Scholar, 5*(9), 10–17.

Richards, D. M. ([1980] 1989). *Let the circle be unbroken: African spirituality in the diaspora*. Trenton, NJ: Red Sea Press.

———. (1990). The implications of African spirituality. In M. K. Asante & K. W. Asante (Eds.), *African culture: The rhythms of unity* (pp. 207–31). Trenton, NJ: Africa World Press.

Spady, J. (1978). Afterword. In C. A. Diop, *The cultural unity of Black Africa: The domains of patriarchy and of matriarchy in classical antiquity* (pp. 209–35). Chicago: Third World Press.

Alterity

The term *alterity* is crucial to an understanding of the cultural system in which we live, not only in the United States, but globally. According to the *Oxford English Dictionary* (1971), *alterity* derives from the Latin *ateritat-em*, a being otherwise, and from *alter*, meaning other. The primary meaning is "the state of being otherwise." Looked at transculturally, alterity defines through negation the criterion of being or of what each specific culture requires to be a "good man or woman of one's kind" (Davis, 1992). Alterity, therefore, refers to the alter-ego category of otherness that is specific to each culture's "metaphor of the Self" (Pandian, 1985).

The anthropologist Jacob Pandian points out that in the Judeo-Christian local culture of the West (Geertz, 1983) the *True Christian* was the medieval religious metaphor of the *Self*. Its category of alterity was the *Untrue Christian* and by extrapolation the *Heretic, Infidel, Idolater*. With the transformation of the identity of True Christian to that of *Man*, two population groups came to constitute the postreligious category of *Otherness* or alterity. As *Rational Man* became the first sixteenth-century secular metaphor of the Self, the indigenous peoples of the Americas were made to occupy the place of the *Untrue Self* as the stigmatized Irrational, or "Savage" Other (Pandian, 1985).

The transported African slave (the *negro*) was associated with the extreme form of this category, of the Irrational, "Savage" Other. In the wake of the abolition of slavery in the nineteenth century, however, the cultural category of the Self changed again, this time in terms of eugenic or genetically selected criteria. Thus, as *Biogenetic Man* replaced being *rational*, all people of

African hereditary descent were made to reoccupy the position of the stigmatized category of Otherness or alterity.

As a result of this transformation, the cultural system of the United States instituted itself on the basis of a White/Black, self/alterity metaphor of the Self. "One of the many immutable prescriptive rules of America," Asmarom Legesse, an Eritrean anthropologist, points out "is the classification of human beings into Blacks and Whites." Legesse (1973) continues:

> These are mutually exclusive categories in the sense that one cannot be both Black and White at the same time. One cannot help but be impressed by the extreme rigidness of this native model. It denies the fact that Blacks and Whites do intermarry and enter into elaborate, illicit sexual liaisons. The myth of the two races is preserved by the simple rule that all the *offspring of interracial unions are automatically classified as Black*. (p. 258)

Because the premise of this cultural system, however, in its North American and global expression, is that its reality is not that of a culture *at all*, the role of alterity imposed upon the population group of African hereditary descent, wholly or partly, i.e., Black, is not easily recognizable.

The Negritude Movement in the Caribbean offers one example. Aimé Césaire's Negritude Movement (Toumson & Henry-Valmore, 1993) called for the reinvention of what has now become the globalized "local culture" of the West, in whose cultural terms we have all been socialized. Césaire's Martinican definition of Negritude was against the alterity role imposed upon Black people and was a call for a cultural revolution. This *radical alterity* position has been recently challenged by the *acultural* movement of Creolite, which calls, instead, for a reformist multicultural definition of the reality of Martinique. This Creolite definition emphasizes the "exoticism of the diverse" or of ethnicity. A clash, therefore, exists between a reformist movement of ethnicity-multiculturalism and the call for cultural transformation implicit in the radical conception of alterity (Wynter, 1992). *SW*

References

Davis, J. (1992). *Exchange*. Minneapolis: University of Minnesota Press.

Geertz, C. (1983). *Local knowledge: Further essays in interpretive anthropology*. New York: Basic Books.

Legesse, A. (1973). *Gada: Three approaches to the study of an African society*. New York: The Free Press.

Oxford English Dictionary. (1971). Glasgow, England, and New York: Oxford University Press.

Pandian, J. (1985). *Anthropology and the Western tradition: Towards an authentic anthropology*. Prospect Heights, IL: Waveland Press.

Toumson, H., & Henry-Valmore, S. (1993). *Aimé Césaire: Le nègre inconsolè*. Paris: Syros.

Wynter, S. (1992). *Do not call us "negros": How "multicultural" textbooks perpetuate racism*. San Francisco: Aspire Books.

The American Dilemma

> The American Negro problem is a problem in the heart of the American. It is there that the interracial tension has its focus. It is there that the decisive struggle goes on . . . . The "American Dilemma," referred to in the title of this book is the ever-raging conflict between, on the one hand, the valuations preserved on the general plane which we shall call the "American Creed," where the American thinks, talks, and acts under the influence of high national and Christian precepts, and, on the other hand, the valuations on specific planes of individual and group living, where personal and local interests; economic, social, and sexual jealousies; considerations of community prestige and conformity; group prejudice against particular persons or types of people; and all sorts of miscellaneous wants, impulses, and habits dominate his outlook. (Myrdal, 1944, p. lxxi)

The goal of Myrdal's historic study, *An American Dilemma,* funded by the Carnegie Corporation, was a "comprehensive study of the Negro in the United States, to be undertaken in a wholly objective and dispassionate way as a social phenomenon" (Myrdal, 1944, p. li). No mean task. Andrew Carnegie and the foundation that bore his name had a strong record in the early twentieth century for donations to Negro institutions (e.g., Hampton and Tuskegee Institutes), causes, and research. In addition to funding this study of the Negro for the general "advancement and diffusion of knowledge and understanding" (Myrdal, 1944, p. xlvii), the Carnegie Corporation saw, as a secondary factor, "the need of the foundation itself for fuller light in the formulation and development of its own program" (Myrdal, 1944, p. xlvii) of grant giving to various individuals and institutions concerned with Negro affairs. They sought a researcher and eventually chose Gunnar Myrdal, who "could approach his task with a fresh mind, uninfluenced by traditional attitudes or by earlier conclusions" (Myrdal, 1944, p. xlviii). Further, they sought someone outside the United States—and from a country with no background or traditions of imperialism—in order to gain "the confidence of the Negroes in the United States as to the complete impartiality of the study" (Myrdal, 1944, p. xlviii).

Gunnar Myrdal, social economist at the University of Stockholm, and his wife Alva, social scientist, civil servant, and eventual Nobel Prize winner, came to the United States intent upon studying its racial problem. They concluded that the American Dilemma was the contradiction between the American creed of justice, equality of opportunity, fairness, "civil rights, civil liberties, a free press, and democratic decision making" (May, 1991, p. 1185), and America's immoral racial segregation, economic deprivation, and discriminatory treatment of its Negro population. Myrdal enlisted the expertise of a wide variety of top scholars with various social and political perspectives to write many of the book's chapters on topics such as population and migration, race, economic and social inequality, and justice. His solutions, primarily institutional, called for federally sponsored full employment, government aid for education and housing, and migration of Blacks to less-hostile northern states. Myrdal asserted that better treatment of Blacks would be consistent with an advanced, technologically sophisticated economy. Without this level of Black inclusion, the American economy would not perform to its capacity.

Myrdal is not without his critics, who commented that he was naive to think America—once realizing its moral contradiction of creed versus behavior toward Blacks—would institute positive changes affecting social conditions. For many southern Whites, no dilemma existed. Perhaps he was too optimistic, some said.

Critics aside, many hailed the book as a bold attempt by Black and White social scientists to comprehensively assess the racial problem in America and to attempt socially engineered change. Indeed, the social impact and influence of this 1,500-page volume lasted 20 years. For example, in the 1954 Supreme Court decision for *Brown v. Board of Education* (which ruled against school segregation), the key passage that overturned *Plessy v. Ferguson* of 1896 (which stated that separate but equal facilities for Whites and people of color are constitutional) cited *An American Dilemma* as a "modern authority" in support of the proposition that segregation did indeed harm Black people. (Blumer, 1993). *VA* • *See also* **Brown v. Board of Education; Plessy v. Ferguson**

References

Bulmer, M. (1993). The apotheosis of liberalism? An American dilemma after fifty years in the context of the lives of Gunnar and Alva Myrdal. *Ethnic and Racial Studies, 16*(2), 345–57.

May, A. M. (1991). Gunnar Myrdal and America's conscience: Social engineering and racial liberalism, 1938–1987. *Journal of Economic Issues, 25*, 1184–86.

Myrdal, G. (1944). *An American dilemma*. New York: Harper and Brothers.

Pressman, S. (1994). An American dilemma: Fifty years later. *Journal of Economic Issues, 28*, 577–85.

American Indian Studies

American Indian studies is a highly interdisciplinary area of study ranging across the social sciences and humanities. The development of American Indian studies coincided with the development of other ethnic studies programs in the late 1960s, largely in response to the demands of Native American students who wanted to learn more about the history, culture, and social concerns of their people. However, as this area has developed into coherent academic programs, it has attracted the attention and participation of a wide variety of scholars, Native and non-Native, who publish their work in journals such as the *American Indian Quarterly*, *American Indian Culture and Research Journal*, and *Akwekön*.

In the humanities American Indian studies is most prominently represented by the visual arts, literature, and music. Some of this work is devoted to the preservation of traditional tribal culture by documenting teachings, songs, and stories historically communicated through oral traditions. Crafts and artwork produced using traditional techniques and indigenous materials also reflect this effort to maintain tribal culture. However, in recent years, a number of American Indian artists and writers have branched out to use traditional cultural motifs in ways that reflect the contemporary lives of modern American Indians. Leslie Silko and Louise Eridrich, for example, have been acclaimed by Native and non-Native critics for their novels about reservation life. N. Scott Momaday received the Pulitzer Prize for his book *House Made of Dawn*. A burgeoning market also exists for distinctively American Indian art produced with non-Indian media such as oil paints or bronze sculpture.

There is an equally diverse array of activities in the social sciences connected with American Indian studies. Much of this work is concentrated in history and anthropology. Predictably, much of this work consists of historical studies of tribal social life and culture. There is also a small group of scholars, notably archaeologists, demographers, and others, who are concerned with understanding the structure and organization of Native societies before the arrival of Europeans. Contemporary studies of American Indians deal with a variety of issues ranging from political behavior such as the spread of pan-Indian movements to studies of economic conditions and models for economic development. *CMS*

American Studies

The emergence of American studies coincided with the recognition by an increasing number of scholars that the study and teaching of various aspects of American life—past and present—were often incomplete and fragmented when approached as a whole through a single academic discipline, such as history. Persons interested in American literature, American history, sociology, anthropology, political science, philosophy, fine arts, linguistics, and other disciplines found interrelationships between these previously separate disciplines to be of high value in their work. Librarians, museum directors, and government officials found that interdisciplinary insights enriched their own responsibilities. The results of recent research and writing in the field makes it clear that joint studies and cooperative activities between individuals in these different areas merit increased emphasis.

By mid-century a number of colleges and universities began to offer concentrations and majors in this area. The University of Wisconsin, for example, introduced a broad field undergraduate major in American studies in the 1940s, entitled American Institutions. In 1951, the American Studies Association, which offers individual and institutional memberships, was founded. It sponsors the journal *American Quarterly,* which is published by the Johns Hopkins University Press.

The breadth of American studies allows for numerous subareas of attention, such as the factors affecting immigrant and diverse groups and the roles of women. The association includes regional chapters where attention may be paid to specific local or statewide aspects of American society, as well as broader topics. American studies offerings have appeared frequently in foreign universities and often are taught by visiting scholars. *REG*

Antibias Curriculum

Antibias curriculum was popularized in the mid-1980s by Louise Derman-Sparks and a task force of early childhood educators in Pasadena and Los Angeles, California. This multiracial group of practitioners formed in response to the lack of early childhood curricula that went beyond issues of representation and the celebration of diversity. As teacher, parent, and activist, Derman-Sparks recognized that the institutionalized nature of racism, classism, sexism, and ablism influenced and affected the identity formation and attitude development of young children. Derman-Sparks looked towards the child development literature for support as she attempted to develop strategies that help young children deal proactively with the prejudice, stereotypes, and discriminatory behaviors that are threaded through their experiences. Although a strong research base had been built concerning older children, antibias research in the realm of child development was virtually nonexistent. Drawing on the antiracist and antisexist work of the Council on Interracial Books for Children, Derman-Sparks began laying the foundation for child development-based research. *Anti-bias Curriculum: Tools for Empowering Young Children* (Derman-Sparks, 1989) evolved out of this work and was published in collaboration with the Anti-Bias Curriculum Task Force. Currently, the book is being revised to include a culturally relevant component which emphasizes the need for congruence between the child's cultural context and learning.

The philosophy behind antibias curriculum maintains that if young children are encouraged to discuss, explore, and think critically about issues of race, ethnicity, gender, sexual orientation, religious diversity, socioeconomic status, and physical ableness, they will become empowered to recognize and take action against bias. According to Derman-Sparks and the Anti-Bias Task Force, the goals of the curriculum are to "enable every child to construct a knowledgeable, confident self-identity; to develop comfortable, empathetic, and just interaction with diversity; and to develop critical thinking and the skills for standing up for oneself and others in the face of injustice" (Derman-Sparks, 1989, p. ix).

Antibias curriculum is an integrated curriculum that emerges from the needs, thoughts, and experiences of young children. Educators choosing to employ an antibias approach infuse antibias lessons and activities into their existing curricula. Antibias curriculum takes on a variety of forms as it is shaped to meet the needs of individual students. By directly addressing the diverse needs of students, teachers help every child develop to his or her full potential.

Activism and social change are central to antibias education. As children begin to question and challenge the status quo in their immediate surroundings, they take the first step towards breaking down social barriers and achieving social transformation. An antibias approach to teaching extends beyond the scope of multicultural education and into the realm of "Education that is Multicultural and Social Reconstructionist" (Sleeter & Grant, 1987). Antibias curriculum is one of the few curricula for young children that promotes an understanding of social problems and provides children with strategies for improving social conditions. *MMM*

References

Derman-Sparks, L. (1989). *Anti-bias curriculum: Tools for empowering young children*. Washington, DC: National Association for the Education of Young Children.

Sleeter, C. E., & Grant, C. A. (1987). An analysis of multicultural education in the United States. *Harvard Educational Review, 57*(4), 421–44.

Antiracist Education

Antiracist education is a critical pedagogy that seeks to take a stand against racial injustice and oppression. In the United States many scholars of multicultural and non-Eurocentric education, or others with these perspectives, have sought to develop antiracist education as part of their projects. In the United Kingdom the antiracist movement has been described as a development of multicultural education and a reaction to it (Verma, Zec, & Skinner, 1994). It grew out of a realization that simply focusing on cultural diversity did not ensure that more subtle forms of racism, particularly at the institutional level, would be addressed. Central to the concept of antiracist education is the need to deal with racial discrimination and to develop a more critical approach to all teaching methods and materials. As Rex (1989) puts it, "anti-racism has a moral purpose going beyond multi-cultural education."

Attempts to "bridge the gulf" between antiracist and multicultural models by Grinter (1985) and others produced a concept of *antiracist multiculturalism*. In his later writing Grinter argues that the gulf is unbridgeable and "the philosophies do not meet" (Grinter, 1990). In practice, Grinter argues, terminology is perhaps less important than the practical responses of teachers.

However, in the United States many theorists-practitioners have used the framework of multicultural education to address the ills of racism in U.S. schools, seeing antiracist education as an integral component of multicultural education. Whether standing alone or in conjunction with multicultural education, antiracist education seeks to combat the racial intolerance that is evident in schools in numerous educational biases.

These biases are apparent in standardized testing, curriculum that excludes or minimizes various cultural contributions, student organization that promotes tracking and ability grouping, high suspension and detention rates for students of color, inequalities in school financing, and lower teacher expectations of students of color. Racism in schools is also manifested in school policies such as the failure to hire people of color at all levels and the omission of antiracist regulations in faculty and student handbooks. Racism also surfaces in schools through individual acts of bigotry and lack of understanding.

Antiracist education practice begins with educating administrators and teachers to understand racial oppression and racial identity issues, as well as racist conditioning and internalized oppression. Antiracist education challenges the total school environment to understand the ways in which racism is manifested in schools and society. It encourages educators to integrate antiracist concepts into all subject areas. Through recent research studies with students, antiracist education attempts to reveal the adverse effects of racism on student learning and development (Donaldson, 1996; Lee, 1996; Murray & Clark, 1990). Furthermore, a number of studies of antiracist–education teachers have been conducted, and some teacher preparation programs now offer antiracist–education courses. Tatum (1992) has researched and designed psychology of racism and racial identity development theory models for undergraduate students.

In an antiracist program at the elementary level students are taught to appreciate the contributions and experiences of all racial groups and to become aware of racial injustices. At the secondary level students may explore issues of racism and seek solutions for reducing it.

The challenge of accepting antiracist education as viable pedagogy is dealing with fear and resistance. Schools often refuse to use the term *antiracist education*. Many schools, in an attempt to feel safe, choose the term *multicultural education* because they assume that antiracist education is not a major characteristic of multicultural education. This misunderstanding frequently causes a wedge between antiracist and multicultural education in practice. For many students antiracist education is a high priority. As cultural diversity and curriculum reform take shape in our schools, all indications point to the emergence of antiracist education as an important educational approach. *KBMD & GKV*

References

Donaldson, K. (1996). *Through students' eyes: Combatting racism in United States schools.* Westport, CT: Greenwood.

Grinter, R. (1985). Bridging the gulf: The need for an anti-racist multi-culturalism. *Multi-cultural teaching.* Warwick: Trentham Books.

————. (1990). Developing an anti-racist national curriculum: Constraints and new directions. In P. D. Pumfrey & G. K. Verma (Eds.), *Race relations and urban education: Contexts and promising practices.* London: Falmer Press.

Lee, S. J. (1996). *Unraveling the model minority stereotype: Listening to the voices of Asian American youth.* New York: Teachers College Press.

Murray, C., & Clark, R. (June, 1990). Targets of racism. *The American School Board Journal* 177, 22–24.

Rex, J. (1989). Equality of opportunity, multi-culturalism, anti-racism and education for all. In G. K. Verma (Ed.), *Education for all—A landmark in pluralism.* Lewes: Falmer Press.

Tatum, B. D. (1992). Talking about race, learning about racism: The application of racial identity development theory in the classroom. *Harvard Educational Review, 62,* 1–24.

Verma, G., Zec, P., & Skinner, G. (1994). *The ethnic crucible: Harmony and hostility in multi-ethnic schools.* London: Falmer Press.

Anti-Semitism

Anti-Semitism is a term coined by the German Wilhem Marr in 1879, originating from the Greek *anti-* and *Semite*, to designate the anti-Jewish campaigns taking place in Europe at that time. Anti-Semitism is now accepted as a general term to denote all forms of hostility manifested toward Jews from ancient times to the modern era including opposition, prejudice, and intolerance. The first *pogrom*, or officially santioned massacre, took place in Egypt in 38 A.D. During the Middle Ages the blood libel or ritual murder incorrectly accused Jews of murdering Christian children to obtain blood for the Passover ritual. For example, the allegation of the Simon of Trent blood libel in 1475 led to the extermination of the Jewish community in Trent, Italy. As late as 1791 French revolutionaries purported "obnoxious" Jewish traits to include homelessness as in the image of the Wandering Jew condemned to roam from country to country; physical aberrations such as a tail and horns (attributes of the devil) and a distinctive odor. They were called "Christ-killers" and "Christ-rejecters." Christian theology sealed the most ancient of all anti-Semitic themes: Jews were a uniquely alien element within human society.

It was not until the work of Leo Pinsker and Theodor Herzl, the founders of modern *Zionism*, the re-establishment of a Jewish national homeland, particularly in Palestine, that anti-Semitism was identified as a form of xenophobia or hatred of the stranger, thereby making it one of the oldest and most complicated examples of such hatred. In Europe the twentieth century brought the most violent anti-Semitism in history: six million Jews, including one million children, perished in the Holocaust. The newest forms of anti-Semitism include a stereotype of the Jew as arrogant, victorious, and ruthless toward Arab people.

In summary, the existence of the Jews, the Jewish community, and Jewish identity as *a people apart* provides a unique opportunity for attack by anti-Semites. The hatred of the unlike or different is all too common a response. Although a minority group within most societies (except for Israel), Jews have experienced and continue to experience great hatred from the majority. *LHE*

References

Almog, S. (Ed.). (1988). *Anti-Semitism through the ages.* Translated by N. H. Reisner. New York: Pergamon Press.

Cohen, S. S. (Ed.). (1987). *Anti-Semitism: An annotated bibliography* (Vols. 1–3). New York: Garland.

Poliakov, L. (1974). *The history of Anti-Semitism* (Vols. 1–2). London: Routledge & Kegan Paul.

Reinharz, J. (1987). *Living with Anti-Semitism.* Hanover, NH: University Press of New England.

Asian Pacific American Studies

Asian Pacific American studies was created, along with other ethnic studies programs, as a result of the Third World Students strike at San Francisco State University (formerly called San Francisco State College) in 1969. It is an interdisciplinary area of study focused on the histories, experiences, and concerns of Americans from a host of Asian countries of origin. Although geographically Asia extends as far west as the Ural Mountains, in practice the western border of Asian Pacific American studies generally ends at Pakistan. Even so, encompassing such vastness and diversity, the term is unwieldy and somewhat contested. Although their countries of origin may have been at war in Asia, Asians in the United States have a shared history of economic exploitation, racial stereotyping, and discrimination.

Despite a more-than-hundred-year-long presence in the United States beginning with the Gold Rush in 1849, Asians were denied the vote and full citizenship until 1954. They were the last diverse group to be enfranchised. Today, Asian Americans are still perceived as foreigners and are asked, "Where do you come from?" or are complimented on their "good English." On the other hand, the media has represented them as a model minority that is more highly educated and better paid than Whites, creating resentment and scapegoating. Asian Pacific American studies comprises issues such as assimilation, acceptance, stereotyping and misrepresentation, the literature and culture produced by Asian Americans, the specific histories, and the educational, sociological, political, and psychological concerns of Asian Americans.

Insecure in their sense of belonging, Asian Americans had been silent about their own history of exploitation and discrimination, silent about the fact that the preponderance of humble Chinese hand laundries was the result of legal exclusion from other means of employment, and silent about the uprooting of 110,000 Japanese Americans from their homes on the West Coast and their containment in barbed-wire relocation camps. However, since the creation of the field of Asian Pacific American studies, the scholarship and the speaking up have virtually exploded. Asian American literature, for example, has reached backward, as scholars retrieve such forgotten pioneers as late nineteenth century writers Sui Sin Far and Lee Yan Phou, and forward as young writers, such as Gish Jen and Fae Myenne Ng, produce new work. In the past two decades Asian American writers have won national attention with such awards as the National Book Critics Circle Award (Maxine Hong Kingston's *The Woman Warrior* in 1976), the Yale Younger Poet's Competition (Cathy Song's *Picture Bride* in 1982), the Lamont Poetry Prize (poets Garrett Hongo for *The River of Heaven* in 1988 and Li-Young Lee for *The City in Which I Love You* in 1991); and Broadway's Tony Award (David Henry Hwang for *M. Butterfly* in 1988). The major motion picture adaptation (1993) of Amy Tan's best-selling novel, *The Joy Luck Club* (1989), has brought a few of the numerous and diverse Asian American experiences to the attention of large audiences.

In academia the Asian American Studies Association draws 500 people to its annual conventions. Asian Pacific American studies courses and programs flourish on many campuses throughout the nation, including the University of Washington; several campuses of the University of California; San Francisco State University; University of Colorado—Boulder; University of Michigan; University of Wisconsin—Madison; Cornell; Queens College of CUNY; Tufts; and Brown. University presses such as those of Illinois, Temple, and Washington have Asian American studies series. UCLA offers a master's degree in Asian American studies, and U.C. Berkeley offers a doctorate in ethnic studies with a focus on Asian American studies. *AL* • *See also* **Model Minority**

References

Hongo, G. (1988). *The river of heaven*. New York: Alfred A. Knopf.

Hwang, D. H. (1989). *M. Butterfly*. New York: Plume.

Jen, G. (1991). *Typical American*. Boston: Houghton Mifflin.

Kingston, M. H. (1976). *The woman warrior: Memoirs of a girlhood among ghosts*. New York: Alfred A. Knopf.

Lee, Li-Young. (1990). *The city in which I love you*. New York: BOA Editions.

Lee, Y. P. (1887). *When I was a boy in China*. Boston: D. Lothrop.

Ling, A., & White-Parks, A. (Eds.). (1995). *Sui Sin Far: Mrs. Spring and other writings*. Champaign-Urbana: University of Illinois Press.

Ng, F. M. (1993). *Bone*. New York: Hyperion.

Song, C. (1983). *Picture bride*. New Haven, CT: Yale University Press.

Sui, S. F. (1912). *Mrs. Spring fragrance*. Chicago: A. C. McClurg.

Tan, A. (1989). *The Joy Luck Club*. New York: G. P. Putnam's Sons.

Assimilation

Assimilation is the process by which a person or group is absorbed into the social structures and cultural life of another person, group, or society. Assimilation is considered an important and integral component of any analysis of race and ethnic relations. For example, Robert E. Park, one of the earliest sociologists on race relations in the United States, proposed a "race relations cycle which takes the form, to state it abstractly, of contacts, competition, accommodation and eventual *assimilation* [and which] is apparently progressive and irreversible" (Park, 1950, p. 150, emphasis added).

In his analysis of the processes of assimilation Milton M. Gordon (1964) outlines seven types or stages of assimilation: (1) *cultural* or behavioral, that is, acculturation (change of cultural patterns to those of the host society); (2) *structural* (large-scale entrance into cliques, clubs, and institutions of the host society on a primary group level); (3) *marital* (large-scale intermarriage); (4) *identificational* (development of a sense of peoplehood based exclusively on the host society); (5) *attitude receptional* (absence of prejudice); (6) *behavior receptional* (absence of discrimination); and (7) *civic* (absence of value and power conflict) (p. 71). Gordon's typology is useful in examining the assimilation processes of individual groups. However, while he sees the different types of assimilation as occurring in sequential stages (where the process could end at cultural assimilation), an examination of the current conditions of race relations in the United States suggests that the different types of assimilation do occur out of Gordon's proposed sequence. For example, while cultural, marital, and identificational assimilation may have occurred for an individual or a group, structural assimilation may be denied or allowed only to a nonthreatening degree. Thus, the types and stages of assimilation can be as varied as the individual racial and ethnic groups. Also, individual assimilation experiences vary for each member of a racial or ethnic group, depending on individual characteristics (e.g., socioeconomic class background, group identification).

According to Gordon, the U.S. as a host society has been dominated by the White, Anglo-Saxon, Protestant (WASP) culture since colonial times. He also recognizes that different philosophies or goal-systems of assimilation exist which could be synthesized into three main ideologies:

> (1)[T]he "Anglo-conformity" theory demand[s] the complete renunciation of the immigrant's ancestral culture in favor of the behavior and values of the Anglo-Saxon core group; (2) the "melting pot" idea envisage[s] a biological merger of the Anglo-Saxon peoples cultures into a new indigenous American type; and (3) "cultural pluralism" postulate[s] the preservation of the communal life and significant portions of the culture of the later immigrant groups within the context of American citizenship and political and economic integration into American life. (Gordon, 1964, p. 85)

In the United States *Anglo-conformity*, in its more moderate form, has been the most prevalent ideology of assimilation throughout the nation's history (Gordon, 1964, p. 89). In addition, racial and ethnic groups that are not a part of the WASP culture have been consistently denied attitude receptional, behavioral receptional, and civic assimilation. Cultural, structural, marital, and identificational assimilation do occur, but in varying degrees for different groups and individuals.

Historically, schools were thought to serve an assimilation purpose, that is, students of all racial and ethnic backgrounds are taught the language, values, and norms of the dominant group in order to maintain the common culture and keep the nation unified. Within this ideology cultural differences are considered to be deficits and disadvantages. Critics of assimilationist ideology, including multicultural educators, see this ideology as undemocratic, ethnocentric, and unrealistic. Instead, multiculturalists argue for a society and education that value and include the languages and cultures of the diverse racial and ethnic groups in the United States equally rather than treating them as inferior, exotic, and/or deviant from the socially constructed norm. Furthermore, multiculturalists argue that in order to truly unify the nation we need to redefine the common culture to reflect the nation's diverse citizenship.

While assimilation is often written about in reference to racial and ethnic groups, it can also be discussed and examined within the context of the experiences of gender, class, sexual orientation, and disability cultures. *JLL* • *See also* **Acculturation; Common Culture**

References

Gordon, M. M. (1964). *Assimilation in American life: The role of race, religion, and national origins.* New York: Oxford University Press.

Park, R. E. (1950). *Race and culture.* Glencoe, IL: Free Press.

Ringer, B. B., & Lawless, E. R. (1989). *Race-ethnicity and society* (pp. 119–50). New York: Routledge.

At Risk Versus At Promise

Implicit in the growing use of labels such as children and families *at risk* is the assumption that such children and families are at risk for failure—failure to achieve academically or stay in school, failure to successfully raise healthy children, failure to learn English, failure to be employed, or even failure to stay out of prison. In her foreword to Swadener and Lubeck's book *Children and Families "at Promise,"* Sleeter (1995) states that "the discourse over children at risk can be understood as a struggle for power over how to define children, families, and communities who are poor, of color, or native speakers of languages other than English. The dominant discourse attempts to frame such children and their families as lacking the cultural and moral resources for success in a presumed fair and open society and as in need of compensatory help from the dominant society" (p. ix). Several researchers have argued that the discourse of risk is merely a reshaping of earlier labels applied to oppressed groups (Fine, 1990; Swadener, 1990) such as *culturally deprived* or *disadvantaged*. These labels are often used to make broad generalizations serving to pathologize the poor (Reed, 1992; Polakow, 1993) and dismiss their potential for future success. This self-fulfilling prophecy of *at risk for failure* can be viewed as lacking in respect for those it identifies and serves—a view shared by many parents and youth to whom this label has been increasingly applied.

Deconstructions of the *at risk* label include the critique that it is essentialist, reductionistic, dogmatic, and fraught with contradictions. On a global scale the notion of risk has been reframed as "children in difficult circumstances," emphasizing the environmental factors versus assumed internal or personal-cultural-class attributes. The huge literature on "children in difficult circumstances" has also been quite lacking in "success stories," or documentation of both contradictions and resistance to the label and its implicit and explicit assumptions.

A metaphor that has been applied as a reframing of the discourse is children and families *at promise* (Arnold & Swadener, 1993; Ford & Harris, 1991; Swadener, 1990; Swadener & Lubeck, 1995). Rather than merely a semantic substitution for *at risk*, this perspective is meant to convey the potential of *all* children. By emphasizing an "at promise" perspective, an opening or space is created in which more attention can be focused on institutionalized oppression and injustice and on the individual lives, needs, and future possibilities of children and their families. Supporters of this perspective argue that when educators, policy makers, and the public see a more balanced portrayal of all children's potential, the resources now spent on more sophisticated ways of identifying and intervening with children "at risk" can be spent investing in their future promise in appropriate and respectful ways. In other words, how can children be supported in reaching their full potential if that potential is dismissed and clouded in a discourse of risk, which often overlooks individual strengths? Viewing children and families as "at promise" has many implications for curriculum, instruction, full inclusion, and substantive or nontrivial parent involvement, and certainly for education that is multicultural. *BBS* • *See also* **Culturally Deprived**

References

Arnold, M. S., & Swadener, B. B. (1993). Savage inequalities and the discourse of risk: What of the White children who have so much green grass? *Educational Review, 15,* 261-72.

Fine, M. (1990). Making controversy: Who's "at risk?" *Journal of Cultural Studies, 1*(1), 55–68.

Ford, D. Y., & Harris, J. J., III. (1991). Black students: "At promise" not "at risk" for giftedness. *Journal for Human Behavior and Learning, 7*(2), 21–29.

Polakow, V. (1993). *Lives on the edge: Single mothers and their children in the other America.* Chicago: University of Chicago Press.

Reed, A., Jr. (1992). The underclass as myth and symbol: The poverty of discourse about poverty. *Radical America, 24*(1), 21–40.

Sleeter, C. E. (1995). Foreword. In B. B. Swadener & S. Lubeck (Eds.), *Children and families "at promise": Deconstructing the discourse of risk.* Albany: State University of New York Press.

Swadener, E. B. (1990). Children and families "at risk:" Etiology, critique, and alternative paradigms. *Educational Foundations, 4*(4), 17–39.

Swadener, E. B., & Lubeck, S. (eds.). (1995). *Children and families "at promise": Deconstructing the discourse of risk.* Albany: State University of New York Press.

Bicultural Education

A definition of *bicultural education* must first begin with the underlying problem that faces many diverse groups of students: a lack of *voice* in the current mainstream curriculum. As Antonia Darder (1991) points out in her book *Culture and Power in the Classroom*, "[S]tudents of color are silenced and their bicultural experiences negated and ignored" (p. 68). One must also look at a definition of *multicultural education* in order to define bicultural education. According to Perry and Fraser (1993), "[M]ulticultural education is the process that honors the multicultural nature of the society in which we live and, as an agent of change, examines the connection between power and knowledge" (p. 48). This definition is expanded by adding another element essential to the learning process, the *bicultural voice*. Darder (1991) suggests that the process of development of a bicultural voice is an interactive one. In this process, students are actively involved in considering critically all curriculum content, texts, classroom experiences, and their own lives for the emancipatory as well as oppressive and contradictory values that inform their thoughts, attitudes, and behaviors. Ultimately it is a critical pedagogy for both student and teacher and is at the foundation of bicultural education.

Using this definition, Darder shows that critical pedagogy and development of a bicultural voice are the tools bicultural students need in the ongoing process of mediating in their bicultural world. But as a process bicultural education engages teachers while requiring them to be willing to deviate from their own need to control knowledge and to be willing to listen to students. For example, instead of transmitting knowledge to students in a didactic way, teachers must use students' background and experiential knowledge as a basis for teaching and learning. *ERC* • *See also* **Multicultural Education**

References

Beardsmore, H. B. (Ed.). (1993). *European models of bilingual education*. Philadelphia: Multilingual Matters.

Butler, J. E., & Walter, J. C. (Eds.). (1991). *Transforming the curriculum: Ethnic studies and women's studies*. Albany: State University of New York Press.

Byram, M., & Leman, J. (Eds.). (1990). *Bicultural and trilingual education: The Foyer model in Brussels*. Philadelphia: Multilingual Matters.

Darder, A. (1991). Culture and power in the classroom: A critical foundation for bicultural education. Westport, CT: Bergin & Garvey.

Perry, T., & Fraser, J. (Eds.). (1993). *Freedom's plow: Teaching in the multicultural classroom*. New York: Routledge.

Biculturality/Biethnicity *See* Biraciality

Bilingual Education

Bilingual education can be defined simply as the use of two languages as the media of instruction. While *bilingualization* (the development of bilingual proficiency in students) may or may not be the goal of bilingual education, this definition implies that the issue of language proficiency development is secondary to the learning of subject matter through language. In other words, bilingual education is an approach to teaching that uses two languages; it is not primarily an approach to the teaching of languages. It should be distinguished from English as a second language (ESL), the purpose of which is to teach English. Nevertheless, the connection between subject matter learning and language development, especially that of the first language, has been shown by various researchers to be extremely strong. The relatively early work of Wallace Lambert, Richard Tucker, and Lily Wong Fillmore is still being developed; more recent work by Kenji Hakuta, Virginia Collier, David Ramirez, Eugene Garcia, Barry McLaughlin, Catherine Snow, Stephen Krashen, Jim Cummins, and others has further extended our knowledge of basic language development processes in bilingual contexts.

Bilingual education in the United States has been controversial because it has been linked with the political and ideological conflicts stereotypically associated with liberals and conservatives, especially since 1968 when Congress passed Title VII of the Elementary and Secondary Education Act of 1965, commonly known as the Bilingual Education Act (BEA), allowing federally sponsored public school bilingual programs. Because bilingual education is most often associated with the education of culturally diverse populations (in the United States it is frequently labeled *bilingual-bicultural education*), its definition has generally included a cultural dimension, as in the following: "The term 'program of bilingual education' means a program of instruction . . . in which . . . there is instruction given in, and study of, English and, to the extent necessary to allow a child to progress effectively through the educational system, the native language of the children of limited English-speaking ability, and such instruction is given with appreciation for the cultural heritage of such children" (PL 93-380, Sec. 703a4A). This is seen as both reasonable and natural; language is part of culture, and language behaviors and proficiency should be developed in a cultural context, rather than divorced from it. This theoretical and pedagogical point is lost in the debate about whether public school programs should encourage cultural and ethnic maintenance in diverse populations.

The classic legislative conceptualization of bilingual education is that of *transitional bilingual education,* first codified into federal law by the 1974 revision of the BEA. According to the law, the purpose of a bilingual program should be to teach the non- or limited-English-proficient student enough English to allow a transfer into the all-English classroom as soon as possible and to use only enough of the native language to ensure that he or she does not fall behind peers in subject matter learning. This version of bilingual education was reinforced in the 1984 and 1988 reauthorizations, which allowed that a certain amount of money appropriated for bilingual programs could fund approaches that used nothing but English as a medium of instruction—the so-called special alternative instructional programs. This provision was based on a largely intuitive sense that children learn English fastest and best in an environment that gives it maximum exposure by excluding all other languages from the classroom. While this intuition is disputed by all the major researchers in second language acquisition, bilingualism, language development, and bilingual education (see e.g., Collier, 1995; Snow and Hakuta, 1992; McLaughlin, 1987; Ramirez, et al., 1991), these programs continue to be allowed in the 1994 reauthorization of the BEA. However, it should be noted that the latest enactment removed much of the old language surrounding bilingual education that portrayed bilingualism as a deficit or a problem to be solved, promoting instead the view that it is a national resource that must be cultivated, not merely for the benefit of ethnic communities, but for the good of the nation as a whole (Stanford Working Group, 1993). It remains an open question whether a policy that portrays bilingualism and bilingual education positively will remain in force for long, and, if it does, whether it will make any real programmatic and pedagogical difference. *RR* • *See also* **Bicultural Education; Code-Switching; Limited English Proficiency (LEP)**

References

Collier, V. P. (1995). *Promoting academic success for ESL students: Understanding second language acquisition for school*. Elizabeth, NJ: New Jersey TESOL/Bilingual Educators.

Cummins, J. (1989). *Empowering minority students*. Sacramento, CA: California Association for Bilingual Education.

Garcia, E. (1994). *Understanding and meeting the challenge of student cultural diversity*. Boston: Houghton Mifflin.

Hakuta, K. (1986). *Mirror of language: The debate on bilingualism*. New York: Basic Books.

Krashen, S. (1991). *Bilingual education: A focus on current research*. Washington, DC: National Clearinghouse for Bilingual Education.

Lambert, W. E., & Taylor, D. M. (1990). *Coping with cultural and racial diversity in urban America*. New York: Praeger.

Mackey, W. F. (1978). The importation of bilingual education models. In J. Alatis (Ed.), *Georgetown University round table: International dimensions of education*. Washington, DC: Georgetown University Press.

McLaughlin, B. (1987). *Theories of second language learning*. London: Edward Arnold.

Ramirez, D., Yuen, S. D., Ramey, D. R., & Pasta, D. J. (1991). *Final report: National longitudinal study of structured-English immersion strategy, early-exit and late-exit transitional bilingual education programs for language minority children (Vol. 1–2). Technical Report*. San Mateo, CA: Aguirre International.

Snow, C., & Hakuta, K. (1992). The costs of monolingualism. In J. Crawford (Ed.), *Language loyalties: A source book on the official English controversy* (pp. 384–94). Chicago: University of Chicago Press.

Stanford Working Group. (1993). *Federal education programs for limited-English-proficient students: A blueprint for the second generation*. Stanford, CA: Stanford Working Group.

Tucker, G. R. (1990). Second language education: Issues and perspectives. In A. Padilla, H. Fairchild, & C. Valadez (Eds.), *Foreign language education: Issues and strategies*. Newbury Park, CA: Sage.

Wong Fillmore, L. (1991). Second language learning in children: A model of language learning in social context. In E. Bialystok (Ed.), *Language processing in bilingual children* (pp. 49–69). Cambridge: Cambridge University Press.

Biraciality

The concept of biraciality is a particularly sensitive and misunderstood issue in U.S. society. Much of the confusion surrounding race and biraciality stems from the traditional classifications for racial groups as well as judgments about race. Classifications that ignore biraciality and judgments about race are often based upon visible physical features such as skin color and above-the-neck-characteristics such as hair, eyes, ears, and so forth.

Biracial people are the offspring of an interracial parental lineage. These unions were made legal when the United States Supreme Court in *Loving v.*

Virginia (1967) struck down antimiscegenation laws, which had previously prohibited interracial marriages. While such legal mandates provided equality and due process for interracial couples, their biracial offspring still fight for their civil rights and psychological freedom in society.

Clinical psychology literature (e.g., Gibbs, 1974; Gibbs, Huang, et al., 1989; McRoy, et al., 1984) points to identity formation as one of the major issues for biracial people. This literature asserts that while *racial definition* is externally imposed and focuses on differences, *racial identity* is formed internally and focuses on personal characteristics. This distinction is crucial in understanding the dilemmas of biracials because racial identity, unlike racial definition, need not necessarily consist of a mutually exclusive choice. However, some biracial Americans still do accept a socially imposed racial identity, thus eliminating the individual's necessity to choose.

Two concepts related to biraciality are *biculturality*, which refers to individuals who have successfully and harmoniously identified and adopted two cultural group characteristics, and *biethnicity*, which refers to individuals who have acquired knowledge, understanding, and acceptance of two ethnic group rules, rituals, traditions, customs, and belief systems and have effectively negotiated crossing group boundaries. In addition, *multiraciality* refers to persons who identify with and who have successfully negotiated multiple racial boundaries and their connecting history, geography, migration patterns, and social, economic, and political realities. Multiracial citizens have acquired knowledge, understanding, and acceptance of multiple ethnic group rules, rituals, traditions, customs, and belief systems.

Biracial Americans come from parental lineages representing two racial backgrounds (e.g., Mexican vs. Anglo American, Chinese vs. African American, Puerto Rican vs. Anglo American). Demographic data on biracials are inaccurate because many interracial families fail to respond to federal forms that ignore biraciality. Researchers approximate the biracial population to be at 500,000 to 650,000. The exclusion of biracials in society is the result of longstanding beliefs regarding racial purity held by many U.S. Americans. These beliefs evoke conceptions of norm/deviant, good/evil, or superior/inferior; grant privileges to Whites; and deny privileges to anyone who is non-White.

The notion of biracials having to choose one race over the other has ushered in the notion of *passing*, which has been documented in the popular media, in the literature of psychology on interracial families, and in the literature of education. For instance, in the 1954 movie *Imitation of Life*, a young Black/White girl faced the harsh physical consequences from some White youth when they recognized that she had passed for White. In the 1960s, Neila Larson's book, *Passing*, chronicled the dilemmas of a Black/White girl who struggled with whether or not to pass for White. Gordon

(1964) documented that "[often] well-intentioned intermarried Black/White parents find it difficult to provide their children with the security that comes from 'knowing who I am and what I am'" (p. 317). These well-intentioned parents often leave their children to decide their racial background on their own, and due to pressures from society, they often choose the dominant White group.

However, many interracial couples actively oppose societal constraints and provide supports to meet their children's needs. In fact, biracial youth, along with the protection of their parents, have actively opposed societal constraints that exclude their needs. Recent opposition to laws and policies can be seen in the case of eight-year-old James McCray who challenged the Cincinnati public school system for failing to provide a specific designation for biracial students (Ramsey, 1991, 1992). In opposition to Wedowee (Alabama) High School Principal Hullond Humphries' exclusion of biracial couples from the high school prom and his derogatory statements about them, Revonda Bowen, a young 16-year-old biracial student, and her parents challenged Humphries' statements that her parents "had made a mistake" by having her and that "he didn't want anyone else to make the same mistake" (Reed, 1994). Opposition to societal constraints and the exclusion of biracials has prompted many interracial unions and other sensitive adults to build support systems.

Recently, interracial couples and their biracial children have established periodicals written by and for biracials that address their specific needs (e.g., *The Northwest Ethnic News*, a monthly periodical sponsored by the Ethnic Heritage Council, and *Interracial Books for Children*, a periodical published eight times annually and sponsored by the Council on Interracial Books for Children). Intermarried couples and their biracial children meet nationally (e.g., annual Children of Interracial Families conferences) and locally (e.g., Biracial Family Network, Chicago, Illinois; Interracial Club of Buffalo, New York; Interracial Families, Inc., Tarentum, Pennsylvania) to share experiences and offer support.

These grassroots movements serve as a reminder that the government, school systems, and other societal institutions exclude, and therefore ignore, the specific needs of biracial students. *EMR*

References

Gibbs, J. T. (1974). Patterns of adaptation among Black students at a predominantly White university. *American Journal of Orthopsychiatry, 44*, 728–40.

Gibbs, J. T., Huang, L. N., et al. (1989). *Children of color*. San Francisco: Jossey-Bass.

Gordon, A. I. (1964). *Intermarriage*. Boston: Beacon Press.

Loving v. Virginia, 388 U.S. 1.

McRoy, R., et al. (1984). The identity of transracial adoptees. *Social Casework: The Journal of Contemporary Social Work, 65*(1), 34–39.

Ramsey, K. (1991). A box for the "other" kids. *Cincinnati Inquirer,* September 9.
————. (1992). Biracial student offered a new designation. *Cincinnati Inquirer.*
Reed, S. (1994). Heat of the night. *People Weekly, 42*(8), 40.
Thomas, A. (1994). Racism is alive in America. *Jet, 86*(1), 14.

Black Studies *See* Afro-American Studies

Black Vernacular English *See* African American Language

Border Studies

Border studies refers to a relatively new, interdisciplinary area of study that focuses on the United States-Mexican border. Since the 1980s the border between the United States and Mexico has become an extremely appealing area of study for those interested in theorizing about culture, identity, modernity, migrations, writing, postmodernity, and First and Third World crossings and interdependencies.

Two scholarly and critical trends have shaped the development of United States–Mexican border studies. The first was the study of the systematic linkages between the two nations in the border region from the perspective of the social sciences, an approach pioneered in the 1950s by Charles Loomis and Julián Zamora. These scholars revealed the unique character and the socioeconomic and cultural dynamics of the border, and they developed methodologies for its study. They also established the study of Mexican American communities as fundamental "to a solid grasp of Border reality" (Driscoll, 1993). The second trend is the collective and individual work of artists, writers, anthropologists, and literary and cultural-studies scholars who have focused on border cultural life in an attempt to explore cross-cultural situations, oppositional and nonhegemonical cultural practices, *mestizaje* (cultural mixing), and *deterritorializations* (when someone enters into an alien space or engages in social practices different than one's own). The work of these intellectuals and artists has broadened the meaning of the word *border* from a primarily geographical term to one that holds social, cultural, gender, linguistic, political, and epistemological significance. Thus, the border is seen as a space of cultural intersection and blending, providing a context for the development of new forms of understanding, cultural expression, and identity.

Although border studies is relatively new as a discipline (booming within the past 15 years), the border between the United States and Mexico has long been a topic in the imagination and political agenda of Chicanos and Chicanas. In feminist writer Gloria Anzaldúa's articulation the border refers both to the geographical juxtaposition of the U.S. Southwest and Mexico and metaphorically to a space of encounter between the self and the Other, the familiar and the alien, the heterosexual and gay-lesbian, and the White and people of color. For Anzaldúa (1987) borders are "physically present whenever two or more cultures edge each other, where people of different races occupy the same territory, where under, lower, middle, and upper classes touch, where the space between two individuals shrinks with intimacy" (p. ix).

Part of the political significance of the border concept comes from the idea that the border has the virtue of serving as a model for understanding the multiracial and multicultural character of the country as a whole. This paradigm is proposed in contrast to the traditional *melting pot* model, which is seen as negating or aggressively erasing the culture of immigrants and indigenous peoples in a process of acculturation and transculturation. In the borderlands formation there is a daily process of multicultural exchange and a hybridization of behaviors, values, symbols, and languages, which creates a plural and shifting identity. In the borderlands it is supposed that Anglo-American culture is only one of the many interpolations and experiences. Thus, the border is seen as a site for contesting dominant paradigms and articulations. *RM*

References

Anzaldúa, G. (1987). *Borderlands/La Frontera: The new Mestiza*. San Francisco: Spinsters/ Aunt Lute.

Calderón, H., & Saldívar, J. (Eds.). (1991). *Criticism in the borderlands*. Durham, NC: Duke University Press.

Driscoll, B. A. (1993). *La Frontera and its people: The early development of Border and Mexican American Studies*. East Lansing, MI: Julian Samora Research Institute.

Gómez-Peña, G. (1993). *Warrior for Gringostroika*. Minneapolis, MN: Graywolf Press.

Hicks, E. (1991). *Border writing: The multidimensional text*. Minneapolis, MN: University of Minnesota Press.

Rosaldo, R. (1989). *Culture and truth: The remaking of social analysis*. Boston: Beacon Press.

———. (1993). Border of fear, border of desire. *Borderlines, 1*(1), 36–70.

Brown v. Board of Education

The 1954 United States Supreme Court decision *Brown v. Board of Education* reversed the *Plessy v. Ferguson* (1896) ruling as it pertained to public schools by declaring that in the field of education the doctrine of "separate but equal" had no place. This landmark reversal by the Supreme Court held de jure public school segregation to be unconstitutional. Since this decision courts have had a veritable stream of cases brought before them in which they have had to determine whether alleged segregative policies in southern schools, nonsouthern schools, and private schools were unconstitutional.

Chief Justice Warren wrote for the opinion of the Court:

> These cases come to us from the States of Kansas, South Carolina, Virginia, and Delaware. They are premised on different facts and different local conditions, but a common legal question justifies their consideration together in this consolidated opinion.
>
> In each of these cases, minors of the Negro race, through their legal representatives, seek the aid of the courts in obtaining admission to the public schools of their community on a nonsegregated basis. In each instance, they had been denied admission to schools attended by White children under laws requiring or permitting segregation according to race. This segregation was alleged to deprive the plaintiffs of the equal protection of the laws under the Fourteenth Amendment . . . .
>
> Today, education is perhaps the most important function of state and local governments. Compulsory school attendance laws and the great expenditures for education both demonstrate our recognition of the importance of education to our democratic society. It is required in the performance of our most basic public responsibilities, even service in the armed forces. It is the very foundation of good citizenship. Today, it is a principal instrument in awakening the child to cultural values, in preparing him for later professional training, and in helping him to adjust normally to his environment. In these days, it is doubtful that any child may reasonably be expected to succeed in life if he is denied the opportunity of an education. Such an opportunity, where the State has undertaken to provide it, is a right which must be made available to all on equal terms.

The Court posed the following question:

> Does segregation of children in public schools solely on the basis of race, even though the physical facilities and other "tangible" factors may be equal, deprive the children of groups of color of equal educational opportunities? We believe that it does. . . . Whatever may have been the extent of psychological knowledge at the time of *Plessy v. Ferguson*, this finding is amply supported by modern authority. Any language in *Plessy* contrary to this finding is rejected. . . . We conclude that in the field of public education the doctrine of "separate but equal" has no place. Separate educational facilities are inherently unequal.

Over a generation after *Brown* judicial decisions are still required to settle social and legal issues emanating from the circumstances surrounding desegregation. Full realization of the complexities brought on by the decision was probably, to a degree, unforeseen by the Supreme Court when it first rendered its decision in 1954.

In 1955 after due consideration of courses of action for implementation, the Court ruled that consideration should be given to "the public interest," as well as the "personal interests of the plaintiffs." In viewing this dichotomy the Court directed lower courts to fashion remedies that would permit desegregation "with all deliberate speed." This second Court decision has become known as *Brown II*.

Today some maintain that the implementation decision, *Brown II*, allowed too much flexibility; others claim it did not allow enough. From the Supreme Court's perspective the wisest course was to allow the local federal district courts to settle the individual complaints on a case-by-case basis with due regard to equity for all concerned, and during the periods of transition the lower courts were to retain jurisdiction to see that desegregation was properly implemented. The Supreme Court sought to avoid unreasonable delays by requiring specifically that the lower courts "will require that the defendants make a prompt and reasonable start toward full compliance with our May 17, 1954 ruling." *FR* • *See also* **Desegregation; Plessy v. Ferguson**

References

Brown v. Board of Education of Topeka, 347 U.S. 483 (1954).
Brown v. Board of Education of Topeka, 349 U.S. 294 (1955).

Busing *See* Desegregation

Chicano and Chicana Studies

Chicano and Chicana studies refers to an academic discipline dedicated to the study of people of Mexican origin in the United States. It is an area of inquiry that emerged in the late 1960s as a product of the oppositional politics created by the Civil Rights, Black Power, student, community, and cultural pride movements. Chicano studies programs were established throughout the nation, particularly in the Southwest where a high percentage of the population is Mexican American. In opposing assimilation into the dominant culture of U.S. society and in organizing against poverty and racism, Chicanos and Chicanas demanded space—both physical and intellectual—in institutions of higher education dedicated to the systematic study of the Chicano experience.

Chicano studies programs and departments were originally envisioned, as Carlos Muñoz, Jr., has indicated, with various expectations: (1) to develop meaningful academic alternatives to traditional departments in order to overcome a tradition of exclusion and exclusionary discursive practices, (2) to address students' cultural identity crises caused by the assimilation process and racial oppression, and (3) to serve as a training ground for community organizers. Given this history, Chicano studies programs have focused on a number of distinct directions: efforts to legitimize areas of research and knowledge; advocacy for and provision of student services to Chicano and Chicana students; documentation of the contributions of Mexicans and Mexican Americans in the development of U.S. society; and development of an academic curriculum and the creation of paradigms for interdisciplinary analysis as ways to overcome academic ghettoization and indifference.

At times these goals have coexisted; at other times an academic focus has dominated. However, as a second generation of scholars emerges in the field of Chicano studies, a more rigorous academic approach has developed as well as a reformulation of Chicano studies through the specific inclusion of Chicanas and feminist revisioning. Although Chicana feminist writings are heterogenous and articulate diverse ideologies, most writings tend to speak against the double oppression of their experiences in the larger society and within their culture and households. Chicanas have engaged in a revision of cultural myths such as La Malinche, La Llorona, and La Virgen de Guadalupe, in an exploration of relationships among women and between men and women, and in constructions of Chicana subjectivity and epistemologies. They have pointed out the limitations of the early Chicano (male) discourses and questioned them for not addressing the issues of gender oppression and sexual orientation; they have also questioned the White feminist discourses for not addressing issues of race and ethnicity. These efforts have contributed to the creation of Chicana studies and to increased involvement by male scholars in gender issues.

In addition, there has been a resurgence of student activism at universities with the goal of strengthening the administrative and financial foundations of Chicano studies programs. In some institutions Chicano studies has been successful in maintaining or establishing distinct departmental status, which has opened the possibility of training graduate students in the field. In others, different models, including ethnic studies and Latino studies departments, have emerged. *RM* • *See also* **Latino Studies**

References

Alarcón, N., Pérez, E., Pesquera, B., et al. (1993). *Chicana critical issues*. Berkeley, CA: Third Woman Press.

Chabram-Dernessesian, A. (1992). I throw punches for my race but I don't want to be a man: Writing US-Chica-nos (girl, us)/ Chicanas-into the movement script. In L. Grossberg, C. Nelson, & P. Treichter (Eds.), *Cultural studies*. New York: Routledge.

García, E., Lomelí, F., & Ortiz, S. (1984). *Chicano studies: A multidisciplinary approach*. New York: Teachers College Press.

Muñoz, C., Jr. (1989). *Youth, identity, power: The Chicano movement*. London: Verso.

Sánchez, G. J. (1993). *Becoming Mexican-American: Ethnicity, culture, and identity in Chicano Los Angeles*, 1900–1945. Oxford: Oxford University Press.

Citizenship Education

Citizenship education is wedded to politics; therefore, it is a contested concept. Very generally it is education aimed at preparing individuals for a particular relationship to the state or polity—that is, for the role of citizen. Sociologists and political scientists call it *political socialization*. In many democracies, parents, professional educators, and scholars disagree about the nature of the relationship of the individual to the state. Whether citizens mainly should be compliant or critical is an old polarity in this debate; whether citizenship education should emphasize knowledge about government or participatory skills is another.

The meaning of state or polity in this definition is flexible. In ancient Greece it was the city; in modernity it is a nation state or other civil order. In American constitutional democracy, citizenship refers to an individual's relationship to the nation state (the United States), state (e.g., Washington), and local jurisdictions (e.g., King County, City of Seattle). For modern Canadians, there is also the commonwealth of Great Britain. According to the U.S. Constitution, "All persons born or naturalized in the United States, and subject to the jurisdiction thereof, are citizens of the United States and of the state wherein they reside."

In the citizen role one typically owes allegiance to the polity, is entitled to its protection, enjoys rights and liberties, and has obligations. These obligations can range from paying taxes and voting in elections to helping develop public policy, recycling waste, and sacrificing one's life for the polity as a soldier or police officer.

Citizenship, and therefore citizenship education, is not always defined in relationship to a polity per se. Some individuals consider themselves to be world citizens, though there is no world civil order with which a formal relationship can be struck; some members of aboriginal groups have *first nation* identities (e.g., the Sioux Nation); and members of some ethnic or faith-based groups define relationships that border on citizenship (e.g., Serbians, Amish, the Nation of Islam).

There is a general consensus in constitutional democracies that citizens should be educated to understand and participate in majority rule, to protect civil liberties, and to limit the size and scope of government. Still, wide leeway is left to educators. If they conceptualize the citizen role mainly as one of compliance and cooperation, they may only reward these behaviors and teach about law and government; if they define the role in more participatory terms, however, educators might teach students how to influence public affairs and deliberate public policy. Both viewpoints are plentiful in U.S. citizenship education literature. *WCP*

Civil Rights Movement

The United States has been the locus for many civil rights movements in which diverse groups, women collectively, or other disadvantaged groups have struggled to achieve full citizenship. The most common use of the term Civil Rights Movement in the U.S. context, however, and its most widely understood definition, refers to the social movement of twentieth century African Americans in the pursuit of civil equality and the elimination of all forms of discrimination.

The Supreme Court decision *Plessy v. Ferguson* of 1896 ruled that the social separation of Black citizens did not compromise their civil rights as long as facilities available to them equaled in quality those obtainable by Whites. The decision ignored the handicaps that Afro-Americans faced, particularly in the South, where the vast majority of Black Americans lived. A racist and harshly exploitative political and economic system made the notion of Black equality under segregation an illusion. Segregation, now with the force of national law, spread throughout the country.

The Civil Rights Movement emerged initially as a response to the clearly inferior status of Afro-Americans following the collapse of Reconstruction. Black people resisted the Jim Crow laws that had become pervasive by the turn of the century, but Black disfranchisement and other forms of political repression enfeebled early efforts at boycotts and protest. By the 1930s, however, civil rights activity achieved some modest successes. Early civil rights campaigns rarely made a direct challenge to the fiction that the separate-but-equal doctrine rested on, but instead used the courts to enforce equality within the realm of segregation. Virginia's successful teacher-salary equalization cases brought to court in the 1930s, for example, resulted in equitable pay for Black school teachers without altering the state's racially segregated school system.

Civil rights activity in the first four decades of the twentieth century also focused substantially on the problem of lynching with the objective of securing federal antilynching legislation. Liberal representatives introduced several bills in Congress during this era. The presence in Congress of powerful White southern lawmakers who saw lynching as a method of social control, however, continued to thwart efforts to make lynching a federal crime.

With the onset of the Great Depression, the growing political influence of organized labor, and the partial economic recovery due to increased defense spending (1929–1941), protest against employment discrimination played an increasing role in civil rights work. Civil rights proponents wanted the federal government, which, under the stimulus of the economic crisis had become more activist than ever before, to help ensure that Afro-Americans had fair access to jobs. Labor leader A. Philip Randolph planned to lead a protest march to Washington, D.C., if action was not taken. President Franklin D. Roosevelt responded by issuing an executive order that established a Fair Employment Practices committee charged with overseeing the hiring practices of defense contractors. Similar bodies were organized on the local level during and after World War II in northern cities and states where the Black vote could be determinative.

World War II promised to accelerate the pace of reform. Widespread revulsion against Nazi racism, acknowledgement of Black wartime contributions, and the new position of global leadership that the United States enjoyed helped discredit the White supremacist values undergirding segregation. The development of Cold War competition with the Soviet bloc further accentuated the need to make changes in race relations. Ironically, fear of subversion and the opportunistic conflation of racial reform with Communism neutralized the thrust of the reform impulse and delayed progress on civil rights for nearly a decade.

The Supreme Court decision *Brown v. Board of Education* in 1954 overturned the *Plessy* decision and opened the door for full racial integration. The decision was a product of years of preparatory work by the National Association for the Advancement of Colored People (NAACP) Legal Defense Fund, which brought cases to court that built precedent for eroding and finally toppling segregation. The following year, the widely publicized Montgomery, Alabama, bus boycott brought Martin Luther King, Jr., to center stage as a national leader and put the South in focus as the arena in which many of the most important civil rights battles would be fought.

The early 1960s were the high point of mass mobilization as protesters, using the method of nonviolent direct action, mounted sit-ins, boycotts, and freedom rides. The movement was successful in gaining worldwide support and in breaking down formal segregation in American institutional life. Its achievements culminated in passage of the Civil Rights Act of 1964 and the Voting Rights Act of 1965.

Black civil rights insurgency served as a model, though not the only one, for other aggrieved populations. Mexican Americans as a racial-ethnic group, for example, faced many of the same problems as did African Americans. Due to the historically specific character of their presence and participation in national society, however, civil rights activism among different groups varied in character and timing. The Mexican American experience owed much to the circumstances under which the United States acquired the Southwest, a region where Mexican culture and the Spanish language remain deeply ingrained. The redrawing of the border as a result of the 1848 Treaty of Guadalupe-Hidalgo made immigration questions significant. Ambivalence toward Mexican immigration reflected the conflict between the needs of the regional economy on the one hand and notions of racial and cultural hegemony on the other. The widespread treatment of migrant labor as cheap and expendable and a desire to repress Mexican and Mexican American political demands created the climate for the emergence of a civil rights movement among Mexican Americans.

Immigration and, in particular, exclusion policies have been features of the civil rights concerns of Asian Americans and Americans of Caribbean descent. In 1915 the NAACP successfully lobbied to defeat a bill that would have specifically barred entry into the United States to persons of African descent. Almost 30 years later Congress repealed discriminatory exclusion laws directed against Chinese and East Indians. The United States sought the cooperation of people of these nationalities as allies against Hitler.

Tribal sovereignty long displaced and disguised civil rights issues for Native Americans. Although federal policy makers historically shifted between a preference for acculturation or separatism for indigenous peoples, issues associated with Native American citizenship tended to link them to particular communities with which authorities had concluded specific agreements. The increasing urbanization of aboriginal peoples in recent decades and the growing acquaintance among some with practical ethnic politics has helped erode tribal distinctions as Native Americans confront the common urban problems of the poor as members of a racial-ethnic group rather than as members of discrete national entities. Federal officials, in efforts to tabulate racial-ethnic identity for distributive purposes, have compressed and standardized these identities for all groups of color.

Civil rights movements mounted by other disadvantaged groups include the Gay Rights Movement and the Disabled Persons' Movement. In both cases the emergence of insurgency followed upon the creation of a collective self-identity. The Gay Rights Movement developed only when significant numbers of gay people were prepared to acknowledge their sexual orientation and identify common interests. Similarly, the Disabled Persons' Movement was a product of medical advances that created a constituency by producing higher rates of survival for critically injured war veterans, victims of chronic disease, and survivors of crimes and accidents. Large numbers of people with disabilities and their families and associates provided the political pressure necessary for passage of the Americans with Disabilities Act in 1990. People with disabilities enjoyed greater political success than gay rights adherents, whose fight against discrimination has met more formidable social prejudice.

The Women's Movement has also been a civil rights movement insofar as it has involved itself actively in political struggles to secure specific rights such as suffrage. The suffrage movement was the longest sustained civil rights campaign within the Women's Movement culminating in passage of the Nineteenth Amendment in 1920 granting women the right to vote. Beginning in 1923 feminists lobbied for an equal rights act for women. In the past 20 years women as a group have benefited from antidiscrimination laws, but no constitutional amendment specifically guaranteeing the civil equality of women has ever been adopted. The failure of 38 states to ratify the most recent Equal Rights Amendment, passed by Congress in 1972, suggests that the issue of equality for women remains tied to deeply held cultural, religious, and social beliefs.

Although the African American Civil Rights Movement is often seen not only as a parent and exemplar to the others, but also as a completed project, a right-wing trend in U.S. politics has reopened debate about the meaning of the movement and cast a shadow over the permanence of its achievements. State and federal challenges to diverse group entitlement and diverse group voting districts threaten to reverse the gains of the past. *BGP*

Class

Class refers to the economic, social, and political relationships that govern life in a given social order. Class relationships reflect the constraints and limitations individuals and groups experience in the areas of income level, occupation, place of residence, and other indicators of status and social rank. Relations of class are those associated with surplus labor: who produces it and who is a recipient of it. Surplus labor is that labor undertaken by workers beyond that which is necessary.

Class relations also deal with the social distribution of power and its structural allocation. Today there are greater distinctions within the working classes, and it is now possible to talk about the new class groupings within the American social structure consisting of Black, Latino/a, and Asian class factions, together with the White aged, the unemployed and underemployed, large sections of women, people with disabilities, and other marginalized economic groups. *PM*

Reference

McLaren, P. (1994). *Life in schools: An introduction to critical pedagogy in the foundations of education* (2nd ed.). New York: Longman. This definition originally appeared in this reference. Reprinted by permission of Longman.

Code-Switching

Code-switching is a term used to describe the systematic shifting or alternation between languages in discourse among bilinguals sharing common language codes. It is a complex sociolinguistic phenomenon found in areas in which languages are in contact and conditions favor rapid social change. Among bilinguals, alternating from one language to another may take place within sentences through the use of selected words and phrases or across larger stretches of discourse involving sentences. Elements involved in code-switching retain their own meaning and adhere to the rules of pronunciation and grammar that govern the language of origin. Grosjean (1982) provides us with this example in French and English: "*Va chercher Marc* ('go fetch Marc') and bribe him *avec un chocolat chaud* ('with a hot chocolate') with cream on top" (p. 145). From Sánchez (1983) we get this example of code-switching from Chicano discourse in Spanish and English: *"Me dio un* ride *pa'l pueblo"* ("S/he gave me a ride to town") (p. 140).

Research reveals that code-switching occurs in response to a number of factors (Grosjean, 1982; Peñalosa, 1980; Sánchez, 1983; Valdes-Fallis, cited in Ovando & Collier, 1985). In general, code-switching is influenced by age, gender, degree of proficiency, education, domain, geographical region, and degree of formality (McMenamin, cited in Peñalosa, 1980). Individual speakers are influenced by external factors such as social role, situation, topic, and group identity. When quoting, bilinguals will often choose to keep the original language used by the individual whose words are being conveyed. Certain topics or situations may be associated with one language rather than the other. In school young children will switch codes to favor the language they perceive to be the teacher's dominant language. While at home parents may code-switch to keep children out of their conversation.

Among bilinguals, code-switching is more widely used in informal than formal situations. Code-switching is also motivated by internal factors— frequently used elements, formulaic items, stylistic preferences, and the need for specific terminology or vocabulary. As illustrated by Chicano writers and poets, for example, code-switching may reflect different attachments to each language—personal feelings and the realm of home and culture as opposed to impersonal feelings and matters typically American (Timm, cited in Peñalosa, 1980). At the individual level complex code-switching demands proficiency in both of the languages used (Valdes, 1988). At the societal level code-switching may represent an intermediary step in the process toward eventual loss of a language that is in a subordinate relationship to one that is dominant. This happens over time as the dominant language—the language of literacy—assumes more and more of the functions once within the domain of the other (Sánchez, 1983).

In the United States code-switching must also be considered in relation to use of the vernacular. A dialect is "a variety of a language distinguished according to the use: different groups of people within the language community speak different dialects" (Halliday, McIntosh, & Strevens, 1982, p. 149). There are different dialects of Spanish spoken across the United States. (See Valdes, 1988, for a discussion of the language situation of Mexican Americans; see García & Otheguy, 1988, for Cuban Americans; and see Zentella, 1988, for Puerto Ricans). In addition, while educated bilingual members of Hispanic communities may control both standard and vernacular forms of Spanish and English, many Hispanic bilinguals have limited proficiency in the standard forms of one or both languages (Keller, 1982).

Grosjean (1982) notes that monolinguals have always held strongly negative attitudes toward code-switching, perceiving the mixture of languages as a jargon lacking rules and structure. This has affected bilinguals' perceptions of code-switching as well: "[S]ome bilinguals never switch, while most others restrict it to situations in which they will not be stigmatized for doing so" (p. 147). Attitudes within bilingual communities are mixed. Though central to the Chicano sociolinguistic experience, among many Chicanos code-switching "is generally stigmatized" (Peñalosa, 1980, p. 67). Nobel (1982), however, suggests that many English-Spanish bilinguals see it as a positive affirmation of their allegiance to their Hispanic heritage and American culture.

For students from language minority backgrounds, code-switching is a natural and creative process with important implications. Ovando and Collier (1985) advise bilingual teachers to recognize student patterns of language use in the classroom when the curriculum is delivered in two languages. They encourage acceptance of students' use of code-switching but advise teachers not to code-switch within sentences in their own speech. When feasible, teachers are advised to develop individual language profiles of language use for individual students and become familiar with the functions, if any, assumed by code-switching. Zentella (1988) also emphasizes the importance of teacher awareness of the factors that determine language choice within a community: "Classroom norms may be in conflict with community norms if students are never allowed to code-switch in any part of a lesson or a school day. The feelings of insecurity that negative labels such as 'Spanglish' foster serve only to obstruct important educational objectives" (p. 158). Huerta-Macías and Quintero (1992) contend that when code-switching is accepted as part of a whole language approach, it enhances children's oral and written communication and facilitates development of bilingualism and biliteracy. While Keller (1982) supports use of the vernacular in transitional bidialectal education and for initial language arts instruction, he also encourages teachers to ensure that "bilingual students be taught to read and write the standard registers of both English and Spanish" (p. 83). In the final analysis, the appropriateness and use of code-switching in a particular setting is dependent on community goals, program design, classroom organization, bilingual proficiency, and the nature of communicative and academic tasks. *HH* • *See also* **Bilingual Education**

References

García, O., & Otheguy, R. (1988). The language situation of Cuban Americans. In S. L. McKay & S. C. Wong (Eds.), *Language diversity: Problem or resource? A social and educational perspective on language minorities in the United States* (pp. 166–92). Cambridge: Newbury House/Harper Row.

Grosjean, F. (1982). *Life with two languages.* Cambridge, MA: Harvard University Press.

Halliday, M. A. K., McIntosh, A., & Strevens, P. (1982). The users and uses of language. In J. A. Fishman (Ed.), *Readings in the sociology of language* (pp. 139–69). The Hague: Mouton.

Huerta-Macías, A., & Quintero, E. (1992). Code-switching, bilingualism, and biliteracy: A case study. *Bilingual Educational Journal, 16*(3&4), 69–90.

Keller, G. D. (1982). The ultimate goal of bilingual education with respect to language skills. In J. A. Fishman & G. D. Keller (Eds.), *Bilingual education for Hispanic students in the United States* (pp. 71–90). New York: Teachers College Press.

McMenamin, J. (1973). Rapid code-switching among Chicano bilinguals. *Orbis, 22,* 474–87.

Nobel, B. L. (1982). *Linguistics for bilinguals.* Rowley, MA: Newbury House.

Ovando, C. J., & Collier, V. P. (1985). *Bilingual and ESL classrooms.* New York: McGraw-Hill.

Peñalosa, F. (1980). *Chicano sociolinguistics.* Rowley, MA: Newbury House.

Sánchez, R. (1983). *Chicano discourse.* Rowley, MA: Newbury House.

Valdes, G. (1988). The language situation of Mexican Americans. In S. L. McKay & S. C. Wong (Eds.), *Language diversity: Problem or resource? A social and educational perspective on language minorities in the United States* (pp. 111–39). Cambridge: Newbury House/Harper Row.

Valdés-Fallis, G. (1978). *Language in education series, No. 4: code switching and the classroom teacher.* Arlington, VA: Center for Applied Linguistics.

Zentella, A. C. (1988). The language situation of Puerto Ricans. In S. L. McKay & S. C. Wong (Eds.), *Language diversity: Problem or resource? A social and educational perspective on language minorities in the United States* (pp. 140–65). Cambridge: Newbury House/Harper Row.

Colonialism

Colonialism is a policy and practice of a nation to impose its control over other nations or peoples in foreign lands. Several of these policies and practices are directly related to education. Domination and control of others through colonization has involved cultural destruction, destruction of history, destruction of ethnic identity, and the prevention of cultural practices such as language. It involves re-education and teaching the genetic supremacy of dominating nations especially of their ruling population. Education and other communication systems must be used in order to achieve full domination, because ideas may be more powerful than military force.

Many countries throughout Asia, Africa, the Americas, and the West Indies have been colonized primarily by European nations, in particular England, France, Spain, and Portugal. Thus, it is not uncommon in former colonial nations for schooling, form of dress, language, and many aspects of culture to show the imprint of the colonizer.

Although U.S. history describes its colonial period in romantic terms, colonialization involves asymmetrical power relations that exploit resources—both human and material—for the benefit of the colonizer. Multicultural education provides an opportunity to study history and cultures from the perspective of the colonized or subjugated. *AGH*

Common Culture

The concept of common culture in the United States is a myth whose history dates to the nation's founding and is well-documented in Appleby's (1992) presidential address to the Organization of American Historians, "Recovering America's Historical Diversity." The myth of America's common culture gives the appearance of national social and cultural unity as long as it is not scrutinized too closely, and it serves to privilege those who subscribe to it and have been accepted by earlier adherents and self-appointed gatekeepers.

A *myth* is a widely held belief with tenuous connections to pertinent evidence or circumstance (Eliade, 1963). Although moderns tend to think of myth as false belief and to assume they have rid themselves of such vestiges of a pre-scientific age, all cultures have their guiding myths. Like the ancients, moderns see their beliefs as *truths*—as common sense, empirically established fact, or natural law (Toulmin, 1982). Whereas ancient myths were particular, modern myths such as common culture tend to be abstract and transhistorical. Through repetition and reification the abstraction comes to be treated as *real* or natural. (See, e.g., Barthes, [1957] 1972.)

In textbook histories and other national self-presentations, the purported elements of common culture substitute for the actual lived cultures of individuals and groups. Betsy Ross, for example, has long exemplified the "All American" woman. The myth is taken for the histories, cultures, experiences, and perspectives of those who have made and constitute the United States (Cornbleth & Waugh, 1995). Then, ironically, whoever does not reflect or abide by the mythic common culture is treated as deviant.

Related to the abstract quality and sometimes scientific veneer of modern myth is the appearance of universalism. What is created in particular social and historical circumstances (such as the notion of common culture constructed in the early national period of U.S. history in an effort to meld 13 British colonies into the nation envisioned by the Constitution) is taken out of context and made to seem universal—a common culture for all times. Myth "transforms history into nature," thus "giving an historical intention a natural justification, and making contingency appear eternal" (Barthes, [1957] 1972, pp. 129, 142).

If there were to be a common culture or national identity that distinguished the new American nation from its Native American, European, and African precursors, such a culture and identity would have to be created. (See, e.g., Anderson, 1991.) Given the various peoples who constituted the United States, it would have to be a civic culture and community, not one that is based on ethnicity. Thus, the United States democratic civic culture (Almond & Verba, 1963) is characterized by political principles and institutions and by ideals yet to be realized. These include government by consent, due process and equality before the law, minority rights, and majority rule.

U.S. civic culture is based historically, following Fuchs's (1990) compelling analysis, on the principles that "ordinary men and women can be trusted to govern themselves through their elected representatives, who are accountable to the people" (p. 5), that all adult citizens are eligible to participate as equals in public life, and that citizens are "free to differ from each other in religion and in other aspects of their private lives" (p. 5).

When civic culture is reified as a tangible common culture, problems arise. What constitutes this rarely specified common culture? (Is it McDonald's, jeans, or sneakers?) Problems also arise when a putative common culture intrudes into the private sphere as a coercive morality. It appears that common culture is used as a rallying cry in defense of a dominant, or would-be dominant, culture and the political and economic status quo—and in opposition to those who would renegotiate the *unum* to include more of the United States' peoples and share the nation's bounty more equitably. (See, e.g., Banks, 1993.) *CC*

References

Almond, G. A., & Verba, S. (1963). *The civic culture*. Princeton, NJ: Princeton University Press.

Anderson, B. (1991). *Imagined communities*. London and New York: Verso.

Appleby, J. (1992). Recovering America's historic diversity: Beyond exceptionalism. *Journal of American History, 79*(2), 419–31.

Banks, J. A. (1993). Multicultural education: Development, dimensions, and challenges. *Phi Delta Kappan, 75*(1), 22–28.

Barthes, R. ([1957] 1972). *Mythologies*. Translated by Annette Lavers. New York: Hill and Wang.

Cornbleth, C., & Waugh, D. (1995). *The great speckled bird: Multicultural politics and education policymaking*. Mahwah, NJ: Erlbaum.

Eliade, M. (1963). *Myth and reality*. New York: Harper & Row.

Fuchs, L. H. (1990). *The American kaleidoscope: Race, ethnicity, and the civic culture*. Hanover, NH: Wesleyan University Press.

Toulmin, S. F. (1982). *The return to cosmology: Postmodern science and the theology of nature*. Berkeley: University of California Press.

Content Integration *See* Multicultural Education, Dimensions Of

Cooperative Learning

Cooperative learning is a strategy for classroom instruction in which small groups of students work interdependently on academic tasks. The tasks range from work on a mathematics problem that has a right answer to an open-ended discussion, a long-term investigation, creative problem solving, or development of a physical model or role play. Students learn how to take responsibility for their own learning and to manage interpersonal relations.

Heterogeneous cooperative groups, mixed as to achievement, language, and ethnicity, are widely recommended for interracial, multilingual, and multicultural classrooms because they provide a structured basis for interaction between class members who would ordinarily ignore or avoid each other. As early as 1954 Gordon Allport recommended cooperative interaction: "Prejudice may be reduced by equal status contact between majority and minority groups in the pursuit of common goals" (p. 281). Slavin (1995) concludes that the results of studies of cooperative learning meeting Allport's conditions clearly indicate that when students work in ethnically mixed cooperative learning groups, they develop more cross-ethnic friendships that are strong and long lasting. Moreover, cooperative learning has positive effects on student achievement in a wide variety of subjects. Researchers such as David and Roger Johnson have repeatedly found prosocial effects on students of cooperative learning, whether in segregated or mixed ethnic settings. (See Johnson, Johnson, & Maruyama, 1984.) These effects include interpersonal liking, attraction, trust, sense of being accepted by teachers and peers, and liking for school and the learning situation.

There are a variety of models of cooperative learning. In a study that specifically compared the effects of Slavin's model (called STAD—Student Teams Achievement Divisions), Sharan's Group Investigation model, and traditional whole-class instruction, Sharan, et al. (1984), found that both STAD and Group Investigation increase general friendliness and helping behaviors in comparison to whole-class instruction. However, Group Investigation was significantly more likely to stimulate cross-ethnic cooperation than either traditional methods or the STAD model of cooperative learning. It is not clear from this study whether these favorable effects of cooperative learning would take place without teaching the students how to work in groups or without providing rewards for helping each other.

Cooperative learning efforts in multiethnic classrooms that include a wide academic range will confront status problems in which some students will dominate and others will withdraw or be pushed out because their contributions are ignored. Students who have high academic or peer status are likely to be more active and influential than those who are not seen as good students or who are not popular. When diverse ethnic and cultural students are not as academically successful as dominant group students, this unequal participation is undesirable from the perspective of intergroup relations. In addition, less interaction is likely to result in less learning (Cohen, 1994). In order to change this situation, teachers must raise expectations for competence for the low-status student. There are several status treatments developed by Cohen and her colleagues that have been shown to be effective in boosting the participation of low-status students (Cohen & Lotan, 1995). *EGC* • *See also* **Social Contact Theory**

References

Allport, G. (1954). *The nature of prejudice.* Cambridge, MA: Addison-Wesley.

Cohen, E. G. (1994). *Designing groupwork: Strategies for the heterogeneous classroom* (2nd ed.). New York: Teachers College Press.

Cohen, E. G., & Lotan, R. A. (1995). Producing equal-status interaction in the heterogeneous classroom. *American Educational Research Journal, 32,* 99–120.

Johnson, D. W., Johnson, R., & Maruyama, G. (1984). Goal interdependence and interpersonal attraction in heterogeneous classrooms: A metanalysis. In N. Miller & M. B. Brewer (Eds.), *Groups in contact: The psychology of desegregation* (pp. 187–212). Orlando, FL: Academic Press.

Sharan, S., Kussell, P., Hertz-Lazarowitz, R., Bejarano, Y., Raviv, S., & Sharan, Y. (1984). *Cooperative learning in the classroom: Research in desegregated schools.* Hillsdale, NJ: Erlbaum.

Slavin, R. E. (1995). Cooperative learning and intergroup relations. In J. Banks & C. A. McGee Banks (Eds.), *Handbook of research on multicultural education* (pp. 628–34). New York: Macmillan.

Critical Theory

Critical theory generally refers to the theoretical response to Marxist thought developed by the Frankfurt School, a group of writers connected to the Institute of Social Research at the University of Frankfurt, Germany. Max Horkheimer, Theodore Adorno, and Herbert Marcuse initiated a conversation with the German tradition of philosophy and social thought from their vantage point in post–World War I Germany. Perceiving that the world was in need of reinterpretation, they focused their attention on the ways that injustice and subjugation shaped the lived world (Bottomore, 1984; Held, 1980; Jay, 1973; Kincheloe, 1993, 1995; McLaren, 1994, 1995). Looking at the ever-changing nature of capitalism, the early critical theorists analyzed the mutating forms of domination that accompanied this change. In so doing, they analyzed the production of consciousness and the role of human agency in effecting radical social change. Reflecting the practical intent of fostering a critique of the existing social order—the repressive, alienating, and exploitative social reality—in order to advance the struggle for human freedom and social justice, critical theory utilizes a negative dialectic. In other words, critical theory reveals how the given facts of our ordinary, everyday reality, which appear as the positive index of truth, are really the negation of truth, such that truth can only be revealed through the destruction of facts (i.e., determinate negativity).

Many scholars who came of age in the political atmosphere of the 1960s directed their scholarly attention to critical theory. These scholars, frustrated by the forms of domination emerging from post-Enlightenment modernism nurtured by an evolving capitalism, saw in critical theory a method of freeing their lives and their scholarly work from these forms of power. Taken by critical theory's concern with the way everyday experience is socially shaped, these scholars viewed their fields of study as manifestations of the power relations of the social and historical forces that produced them. The hope and the possibility implicit within this recognition of social construction served to entice these scholars with a sense of moral purpose.

Human agency, the promise that men and women can determine their own existence despite the constrictions and contradictions of power, moved these young scholars to believe that their life work actually mattered. Radical educational theory had traditionally been controlled by orthodox forms of Marxism with its iron laws of history and the market. Arguing that schools were simply agencies that reproduced the economic disparity of the larger society, orthodox Marxists were criticized by critical educators as determinists who offered little hope for educational transformation (Giroux, 1985, 1988). Viewing schools as venues of hope, critical educators maintained that schools can become institutions where forms of knowledge and values are taught for the purpose of educating young people for democratic empowerment rather than conformity and subjugation (Britzman, 1991; Giroux, 1994; Kincheloe, 1991; Kincheloe & Steinberg, 1993; Lather, 1991; McLaren, 1986; Pagano, 1990; Wexler, 1991).

In recent years critical theory's interaction with poststructuralist, postmodernist, cultural studies, neo-Marxist, and feminist discourses has moved traditional critical theory onto a new cultural terrain. The conversation between critical theory and these compelling traditions illustrates critical theory's elastic clause, or its self-critical evolutionary orientation. Such postdiscourses admit to the cultural and pedagogical conversations previously forbidden evidence derived from previously excluded voices such as those of women, African Americans, the poor, and Native Americans (Apple, 1986; Aronowitz & Giroux, 1991; Butler, 1990; Derrida, 1976; Fehr, 1993; Fiske, 1993; Foucault, 1980; Gresson, 1995; Grossberg, 1995; Haymes, 1995; King & Mitchell, 1995; Pinar, 1994). *PM2 & JLK* • *See also* **Cultural Studies; Feminism; Neo-Marxism; Postmodernism**

References

Apple, M. (1986). *Teachers and texts*. New York: Routledge.

Aronowitz, S., & Giroux, H. (1991). *Postmodern education: Politics, culture, and social criticism*. Minneapolis: University of Minnesota Press.

Bottomore, T. (1984). *The Frankfurt school*. London: Tavistock.

Britzman, D. (1991). *Practice makes practice: A critical study of learning to teach*. Albany: State University of New York Press.

Butler, J. (1990). *Gender trouble*. London: Routledge.

Derrida, J. (1976). *Of grammatology*. Translated by G. Spivak. Baltimore, MD: Johns Hopkins University Press.

Fehr, D. (1993). *Dogs playing cards: Powerbrokers of prejudice in education, art, and culture*. New York: Peter Lang.

Fiske, J. (1993). *Power plays, power works*. New York: Verso.

Foucault, M. (1980). *Power/knowledge: Selected interviews and other writings*. Edited by C. Gordon. New York: Pantheon.

Giroux, H. (1985). *Theory and resistance in education: A pedagogy for the opposition*. South Hadley, MA: Bergin & Garvey.

———. (1988). *Schooling and the struggle for public life*. Minneapolis: University of Minnesota Press.

———. (1994). *Disturbing pleasures: Learning popular culture*. New York: Routledge.

Gresson, A. (1995). *The recovery of race in America*. Minneapolis: University of Minnesota Press.

Grossberg, L. (1995). What's in a name? (One more time). *Taboo, 1*(1), 1–37.

Haymes, S. (1995). *Race, culture, and the city: A pedagogy for Black urban struggle*. Albany: State University of New York Press.

Held, D. (1980). *Introduction to critical theory: Horkheimer to Habermas*. Berkeley: University of California Press.

Jay, M. (1973). The dialectical imagination: A history of the Frankfurt School and the Institute of Social Research, 1923–1950. Boston: Little, Brown.

Kincheloe, J. (1991). *Teachers as researchers: Qualitative paths to empowerment*. New York: Falmer.

———. (1993). *Toward a critical politics of teacher thinking: Mapping the postmodern*. Westport, CT: Bergin & Garvey.

———. (1995). *Toil and trouble: Good work, smart workers, and the integration of academic and vocational education*. New York: Peter Lang.

Kincheloe, J., & Steinberg, S. (1993). A tentative description of post-formal thinking: The critical confrontation with cognitive theory. *Harvard Educational Review, 63*, 296–320.

King, J., & Mitchell, C. (1995). *Black mothers to sons*. New York: Peter Lang.

Lather, P. (1991). *Getting smart: Feminist research and pedagogy with/in the postmodern*. New York: Routledge.

McLaren, P. (1986). *Schooling as ritual performance: Toward a political economy of educational symbols and gestures*. London: Routledge & Kegan Paul.

———. (1994). *Life in schools: An introduction to critical pedagogy in the foundations of education*. White Plains, NY: Longman.

———. (1995). *Critical pedagogy and predatory culture: Oppositional politics in a postmodern era*. New York: Routledge.

Pagano, J. (1990). *Exiles and communities*. Albany: State University of New York Press.

Pinar, W. (1994). *Autobiography, politics, and sexuality: Essays in curriculum theory, 1972–1992*. New York: Peter Lang.

Wexler, P. (1991). *Critical theory now*. New York: Falmer.

Cross-Cultural Competency

If culture is defined in terms of "standards of perceiving, evaluating, believing, and doing" (Goodenough, 1976), then cross-cultural competency is the ability to use the standards for perceiving, evaluating, believing, and doing that are associated with one or more cultures beyond one's native culture. Cross-cultural competency is the ability to interpret and evaluate intercultural encounters with a high degree of accuracy and to show cultural empathy.

Gudykunst and Kim (1984) define the cross-culturally competent person as "one who has achieved an advanced level in the process of becoming inter-cultural and whose cognitive, affective, and behavioral characteristics are not limited but are open to growth beyond the psychological parameters of any one culture. . . . The inter-cultural person possesses an intellectual and emotional commitment to the fundamental unity of all humans, and at the same time, accepts and appreciates the differences that lie between people of different cultures" (pp. 229–30). While culturally competent people understand and respect different cultures, they do not necessarily adopt new cultural ways, nor must they remain neutral about cultural practices they find abhorrent.

Given that we live in a multicultural society and world, cross-cultural competence is an essential goal of multicultural education. This goal recognizes that communication between people from different cultural backgrounds can be hindered by culturally conditioned assumptions they make about each other's behavior and beliefs. It is also based on the assumption that persons can achieve a psychological balance between cultural pride and identity on the one hand and appreciation of cultures very different from their own on the other. It is assumed that increased intercultural contact will not necessarily lead to assimilation of microcultures into the mainstream culture.

Hanvey (1976) explains that to develop cross-cultural competency, people must first understand their own worldview and realize that every person's perception of reality is shaped by his or her own experience. Once people understand how their own language, experience, and current modes of cognition relate to their own culture, contrasts may be made with the cultural experience and modes of cognition of others who are culturally different. Ultimately, they are able to move to a level of *transpection*, what Hanvey describes as "the capacity to imagine oneself in a role within the context of a foreign culture" (p. 12).

Teachers who are cross-culturally competent are comfortable with their students' cultural styles. They understand their students' verbal communication and body language, preferred modes of discussion and participation, time and space orientations, social values and religious beliefs, and preferred styles of learning. Interculturally competent teachers are aware of the diversity within racial and cultural groups, they know that cultures are in perpetual change, and they are aware of the dangers of stereotyping. At the same time they know that if they ignore their students' cultural attributes, they are likely to be guided by their own cultural lenses, unaware of how their culturally conditioned expectations might cause learning difficulties for some children. Although most schools primarily reflect the mainstream culture, some degree of cross-cultural competency among educators is needed to ensure that *all* students have the opportunity to develop their highest potential. *CIB* • *See also* **Perspective Consciousness**

References

Goodenough, W. (1976). Multiculturalism as the normal human experience. *Anthropology & Education Quarterly*, 7(4), 4–6.

Gudykunst, W. B., & Kim, Y. Y. (1984). Communicating with strangers: An approach to intercultural communications. New York: Addison-Wesley.

Hanvey, R. G. (1976). *An attainable global perspective*. New York: Center for War/Peace Studies.

Cultural Assimilation *See* Assimilation

Cultural Capital

Recognized as one of the unique conceptual contributions of the French sociologist Pierre Bourdieu, cultural capital has come into very wide usage in sociological analyses of education and curriculum. Bourdieu and his colleagues originally employed the concept of cultural capital in the 1960s analyses of French higher education, where the focus was on the reproduction and production of social and economic inequality (Bourdieu & Passeron, [1970] 1977). The concept was imported into sociological analyses of educational inequality in nearly all English-speaking countries. In England and subsequently in the United States the term was first used in the 1970s within the so-called new sociology of education, where the specific focus was analyzing class inequalities in education (Apple, 1978; Young, 1971). Since then, the term has gained very wide use in sociocultural analyses of educational inequality.

There are three economically informed sociological and anthropological premises on which the concept of cultural capital is based. First, seeing culture as capital implies that the value of any one piece of capital is culturally arbitrary, i.e., determined by sociocultural convention, whether conscious or unconscious. Second, in any one society the exchanges of cultural capital with other, more generally recognized, forms of capital (economic and social) are set within an overall hierarchal distribution of capitals. Third, like economic and social capital, cultural capital is time dependent. That is, over time both accumulation and loss of cultural capital are possible.

Culture is here taken to be represented in various forms. Bourdieu himself delineates three states in which cultural capital exists: the *embodied*, *objectified*, and *institutionalized* (Bourdieu, 1986). In its embodied state cultural capital takes the form of durable dispositions of mind and body (knowledge, cultivated appearances, etc.). In its objectified state cultural capital takes the form of specific, material cultural goods (books, paintings, etc.); and in its institutionalized state cultural capital takes the form of official credentials such as educational qualifications.

While these background premises and the various forms of cultural capital are quite general, it is important to see that the value and currency of any cultural capital is highly context specific. The value of one form of culture will depend on the specific social field in which it is exchanged, and these social fields are themselves subject to the overall societal hierarchy of power (e.g., while a master of business administration degree might be quite valuable in the business field but less valuable in the artistic field, the artistic field may itself be less valued than business—all depending on which society and specific social context one examines, of course). The exchanges possible between cultural capital and other forms of capital are evident in the process of using an educational credential to secure employment, in this case, exchanging cultural capital for economic capital. Because the concept of cultural capital is applicable at many levels of social analysis, it can be said that the various debates which circulate around multicultural education are fundamentally about just which forms of culture are to be consecrated as cultural capital. *JL*

References

Apple, M. W. (1978). The new sociology of education: Analyzing cultural and economic reproduction. *Harvard Educational Review*, *48*, 495–503.

Bourdieu, P. (1986). The forms of capital. In J. G. Richardson (Ed.), *Handbook of theory and research for the sociology of education* (pp. 241–57). New York: Greenwood Press.

Bourdieu, P., & Passeron, J. C. ([1970] 1977). *Reproduction in education, society, and culture.* Translated by. R. Nice. Beverly Hills, CA: Sage.

Young, M. F. D. (Ed.). (1971). *Knowledge and control.* London: Collier-Macmillan.

Cultural Identity

Cultural identity is based upon personal traits and values learned as part of an individual's membership in various microcultures such as ethnic or national origin, religion, gender, age, class (socioeconomic status), primary language, geographical region, place of residence (urban, suburban, or rural), and exceptionality (Gollnick & Chinn, 1990). In the United States (a macroculture) membership in the various microcultures is determined by shared cultural traits, discourse patterns, ways of learning, values, and behavior characteristics. Individuals can be members of many microcultures, and membership in one microculture can influence the characteristics and values inherited from other microcultures. The interaction of these microcultures begins to determine an individual's cultural identity and is most dynamic across race, class, and gender lines (Gollnick & Chinn, 1990).

The relationship of racially distinguished or diverse groups like African Americans, Hispanics (Latinos), Asian Americans and American Indians with the dominant group can impact an individual's cultural identity. In addition, different ways of thinking and behaving are differentially rewarded in the society at large (Lubeck, 1988). Nieto (1992) distinguishes *deep culture* or the values and worldview of an ethnic group from superficial aspects of culture like food, dress, and music preferences. It should not be assumed that cultural identity has been lost because outward behavior appears to be mainstream or assimilated and does not reflect these superficial aspects of culture or ethnic traditions. Values and interpretation of the world may inconspicuously reflect the culture of the family or community.

Identity is both *self-ascribed* and *appropriated*, meaning socially defined by others, and it can change in order to adjust to different contexts (Thornton, 1992; Root, 1992). Identity by race, class, gender, ethnicity, age, or religion intersect and hold different priorities at different times and in different situations. Cultural identity, therefore, follows the same pattern in which individuals may embrace particular cultural aspects of their lives while other members of one's family or community may select different cultural traits as more personally relevant. *SMA*

References

Gollnick, D. M., & Chinn, P. C. (1990). *Multicultural education in a pluralistic society* (3rd ed.). Columbus, OH: Merrill.

Lubeck, S. (1988). Nested contexts. In L. Weis (Ed.), *Class, race, and gender in American education*. Albany: State University of New York Press.

Nieto, S. (1992). *Affirming diversity: The sociopolitical context of multicultural education*. White Plains, NY: Longman.

Root, M. P. (1992). Loyalty, rootedness and belonging: The quest for defining Asian American identity. In L. C. Lee (Ed.), *Asian Americans: Collages of identities* (pp. 175–83). Ithaca, NY: Cornell University Press.

Thornton, M. (1992). Finding a way home: Race, nation and sex in Asian American identity. In L. C. Lee (Ed.), *Asian Americans: Collages of identities* (pp. 165–74). Ithaca, NY: Cornell University Press.

Cultural Knowledge

Cultural knowledge is the *lieux de memorie* ("collective memory") of a people. When speaking of African American cultural knowledge, the emphasis is on *African* and *knowledge*. *Knowledge* is a socially constructed system of meanings and understandings, a philosophy, if you will, that frames our living, values, worldview, and belief systems. It is a collective wisdom that gives guidance about living, seeing, and being in the world. African American cultural knowledge is unique because it is *autochthonous* to the African diaspora in the Americas. Cultural knowledge is manifested in artifacts of the African American existential condition, reflecting the cultural, social, economic, historical, and political experience disseminated through the academic, folk, and popular forms of literary arts, dance, film, spirituality and/or religion, music meanings, philosophy, athletics, organizations, activism, and style.

The concept of African American cultural knowledge may be best understood through songs, sayings/proverbs, gestures, imagery, and stories, all of which are rich with meaning. For example, African American cultural knowledge includes the following:

- calling upon the ancestors and God at all moments from giving praise and thanks to beseeching help, strength, and guidance
- dawning awareness of one's spirituality—the kind of spirituality that comes through living, meditation, and inspiration
- understanding that knowledge, interwoven with wisdom, is handed down from one generation to the next
- smile of recognition at Richard Pryor's saying: "Old people don't get old bein' stupid"
- listening to old folk talk—of meanings and understandings of the world
- deep and abiding understanding of Langston Hughes's phrase: "Life ain't been no crystal stair"
- being overwhelmed at having lived and seen James Weldon Johnson's words: "God of our weary years, God of our silent tears, Thou who hast brought us thus far on the way"
- living every day with the awareness that, in the minds of some, people of African descent were property taken away from Whites by the federal government
- not needing the approval of the White world to acknowledge the contributions of ancient and modern Africans to the advancement of world civilization
- a worldview whose very existence defies Western hierarchical structuring of humanity in racial categories
- both the antithesis of racism and hatred and, simultaneously, the insistence on the successful pursuit of dreams; it is the persistence to uplift in the face of living under siege every day of your life because you are of African descent

For people of the African diaspora in the Americas, cultural knowledge has its roots and *lieux de memoire* in Africa and has both transcended and continued to transform the American experience.

King (1995) argues that cultural knowledge includes "forms of knowledge, that is, thought, perceptions, and belief structures that—by making certain ways of knowing oneself and the world possible—function in behalf of integrating the extant (or envisioned) social framework" (p. 270). She further asserts that "to acknowledge that individuals enculturated within a common group experience share a distinct mode of social thought and a shared body of cultural knowledge is not to imply an essentialized, romantic, biocentric ethnorationality" (p. 271). Thus, when Mexican Americans rely on *dichos* (proverbs or sayings) to guide their children or when Chinese Americans urge family members to behave in particular ways to *save face*, those behaviors have particular meanings within those cultures that do not necessarily mean the same thing outside of their culture; i.e., they cannot be easily appropriated by other groups and cultures. However, not every member of the culture will know or participate in its shared cultural knowledge. How fully one is immersed in a culture can vary according to socioeconomic status, geographic region, cultural dispersion, intergenerational contact, and other factors.

The specifics of a group's cultural knowledge are difficult to capture for analytical purposes. These ways of knowing are subtle and tacit. Attempts to delineate them often result in a trivialization of their meanings and import. Perhaps the best we can do is attempt to understand the ways in which our own culture functions to structure our thoughts and actions. By recognizing that culture informs everything human beings do and acts as a "design for living" (Nobles, 1985), we can come to understand that people who are members of cultures other than our own have ways of knowing and being different from our own. *BMG*

References

King, J. (1995). Culture-centered knowledge: Black studies, curriculum transformation, and social action. In J. A. Banks & C. A. M. Banks (Eds.), *Handbook of research on multicultural education* (pp. 265–90). New York: Macmillan.

Nobles, A. W. (1985). *Africanity and the Black family*. Oakland, CA: Black Family Institute.

Cultural Literacy

The term cultural literacy was coined by E. D. Hirsch in his book *Cultural Literacy: What Every American Needs to Know* (1987). Hirsch was alarmed by a general decline in literate knowledge in the United States. According to Hirsch, verbal skills, as indicated by scores on national standardized tests, were diminishing, and the amount of shared knowledge that served as the basis for nationwide communication was decreasing. These trends demanded a refocusing of education on the achievement of universal literacy. This goal necessitated renewed emphasis on written language and cultural knowledge in schools. Hirsch argued that the language and culture emphasized in schools should be national in character. He defined this as traditional material from our Greco-Roman, European heritage; common myths, tales, and events from our American story; Standard English; and shared attitudes such as national loyalty and pride. Hirsch and several colleagues attempted to capture the essence of cultural literacy by determining a list of 5,000 essential names, phrases, dates, and concepts that every American needs to know (Hirsch, Kett, & Trefil, cited in Hirsch, 1987).

Proponents of multicultural education were alarmed by Hirsch's thesis for a number of reasons, some of which were delineated by Simonson and Walker in *Multicultural Literacy: Opening the American Mind* (1988). Simonson and Walker derided Hirsch's conceptualization of culture as static, shallow, and biased toward a "White, male, academic, eastern U.S., Eurocentric" view (p. 2). These authors attempted to define the concept of multicultural literacy by developing a more culturally pluralistic list of things Americans needed to know.

Multicultural advocates were also alarmed by Hirsch's misinterpretation of multicultural education, negative perception of changes in literacy, and limited views of educational change. Hirsch perceived multicultural education as *supplanting* and *interfering* with children's mastery of American literate culture (p. 18). From a multicultural perspective, it is *traditional* culture that excludes, denigrates, or misrepresents much of the American story and interferes with the education of all children. Hirsch portrayed literacy as in decline. From a multicultural perspective, literacy is in transition and there is a need for a more truthful, complex, diverse version of the cultural knowledge taught in schools (Banks, 1991–92). For Hirsch, increased literacy was a fundamental goal. From a multicultural perspective, increased literacy is not, by itself, seen as a substantive challenge to the status quo.

These two stances represent radically different worldviews. Hirsch's ideas reflect an essentialist stance toward schooling. For essentialists, the primary responsibility of schools is passing on the cultural heritage deemed essential to the continued functioning of our national society; education functions as a form of cultural conservation (Longstreet & Shane, 1933). Proponents of multicultural education represent a reconstructionist perspective. For reconstructionists, the primary responsibility of schools is preparing students for a better life in the future; education functions as form of societal change (Sleeter & Grant, 1994). While Hirsch perceives the promotion of multicultural literacy as tinkering with a time-tested national story, multicultural educators see the notion of cultural literacy as a return to biased definitions of knowledge. They are apt to ask: cultural literacy for whom and for what ends? *MBB*

References

Banks, J. A. (1991). Multicultural education: For freedom's sake. *Educational Leadership, 49*(4), 32–6.

Hirsch, E. D. (1987). *Cultural literacy: What every American needs to know.* New York: Random House.

Longstreet, W., & Shane, H. (1993). *Curriculum for a new millennium.* Boston: Allyn & Bacon.

Simonson, R., & Walker, S. (1988). *Multicultural literacy: Opening the American mind.* St. Paul, MN: Graywolf Press.

Sleeter, C. E., & Grant, C. A. (1994). *Making choices for multicultural education: Five approaches to race, class, and gender* (2nd ed.). New York: Merrill.

Culturally Congruent Pedagogy *See* Culturally Relevant Pedagogy

Culturally Deprived

In 1962 Frank Riessman wrote *The Culturally Deprived Child.* This book made famous the term *culturally deprived*, which was soon used as a label to describe poor and low-achieving students, mainly African American students living in urban areas. The home environment of the students was seen as the reason they were not achieving academically in school. Sociologists argued that these children were from homes where they did not receive the same social, economic, and academic advantages to succeed in school and life as middle-class children. Also, during the 1960s and 1970s some educators used the terms *culturally disadvantaged* or *disadvantaged* to refer to this group of students.

The use of the term culturally deprived to refer to African American students was not readily accepted by a good number of educators and parents, especially African Americans. In 1976 in the preface of his new book, *The Inner-City Child*, Riessman acknowledged poor judgment in using the term: "When I began to write this book, I believed that I was preparing a new edition of the *Culturally Deprived Child*, which first appeared in 1962. I realized shortly that not only was the old title inappropriate, but so much new material and thinking had evolved in the last decade and a half that it made more sense to write a new book" (p. ix).

In 1994 DeMarrais and LeCompte further repudiated the culturally deprived thesis by stating, "What was documented was not so much a culture per se, but a response to oppressive conditions of racial isolation, powerlessness, and poverty. Anthropologists [now] argue that growing up in one culture does not mean being deprived of another and that the children described as 'culturally deprived' actually function[ed] quite well in their own milieu" (pp. 238–39). *RJM*

References

DeMarrais, K. B., & LeCompte, M. D. (1994). *The ways schools work: A sociological analysis of education.* White Plains, NY: Longman.

Riessman, F. (1962). *The culturally deprived child*. New York: Harper & Row.
————. (1976). *The inner-city child*. New York: Harper & Row.

Culturally Relevant Pedagogy

Culturally relevant pedagogy is an approach to teaching and learning that empowers students intellectually, socially, emotionally, and politically by using cultural referents to impart knowledge, skills, and attitudes (Ladson-Billings, 1994). Unlike sociolinguistically grounded approaches such as *culturally appropriate* (Au & Jordon, 1981), *culturally congruent* (Mohatt & Erickson, 1981), and *culturally responsive* (Cazden & Leggett, 1981; Erickson & Mohatt, 1982), the cultural referents in this pedagogical perspective are not merely vehicles for bridging or explaining the dominant culture; they are aspects of the curriculum in their own right. Three dimensions of culturally relevant pedagogy are its emphases on academic achievement, maintaining and supporting cultural competence, and engendering a sense of sociopolitical critique.

Teachers who might be regarded as *culturally relevant* educators demonstrate broad pedagogical understandings in three areas: conceptions of themselves and others, conceptions of social relations, and conceptions of knowledge. In their conceptions of themselves and others culturally relevant teachers

- believe that all students are capable of academic success,
- see their pedagogy as art—unpredictable and always in the process of becoming,
- see themselves as members of the community,
- see teaching as a way to give back to the community, and
- believe in the Freirean notion of "teaching as mining" or pulling knowledge out, not putting it in.

In their conceptions of social relations, culturally relevant teachers

- maintain fluid student-teacher relationships,
- demonstrate a connectedness with all students,
- develop a community of learners among students, and
- encourage students to learn collaboratively and be responsible for each other.

In their conceptions of knowledge, culturally relevant teachers

- understand that knowledge is not static—it is shared, recycled, and reconstructed,
- understand that knowledge must be viewed critically,
- recognize the need to be passionate about knowledge and learning,

- *scaffold* or build bridges to facilitate learning, and
- believe that assessment must be multifaceted, incorporating multiple forms of excellence.

Multicultural education must address issues of pedagogy. In addition to what we teach students, how we teach them is equally important. Culturally relevant pedagogy attempts to help teachers focus on the totality of the teaching-learning experience. Rather than focus on fragmented pieces, culturally relevant teaching asks teachers to consider their underlying beliefs and ideologies as they attempt to teach all students successfully. *GLB*

References

Au, K., & Jordan, C. (1981). Teaching reading to Hawaiian children: Finding a culturally appropriate solution. In H. Trueba, G. Guthrie, & K. Au (Eds.), *Culture and the bilingual classroom: Studies in classroom ethnography* (pp. 139–52). Rowley, MA: Newbury House.

Cazden, C., & Leggett, E. (1981). Culturally responsive education: Recommendations for achieving Lau remedies II. In H. Trueba, G. Guthrie, & K. Au (Eds.), *Culture and the bilingual classroom: Studies in classroom ethnography* (pp. 69–86). Rowley, MA: Newbury House.

Erickson, F., & Mohatt, G. (1982). Cultural organization and participation structures in two classrooms of Indian students. In G. Spindler (Ed.), *Doing the ethnography of schooling* (pp. 131-74). New York: Holt, Rinehart & Winston.

Ladson-Billings, G. (1994). *The dreamkeepers: Successful teachers for African American children.* San Francisco: Jossey-Bass.

Mohatt, G., & Erickson, F. (1981). Cultural differences in teaching styles in an Odawa school: A sociolinguistic approach. In H. Trueba, G. Guthrie, & K. Au (Eds.), *Culture and the bilingual classroom: Studies in classroom ethnography* (pp. 105–19). Rowley, MA: Newbury House.

Vogt, L., Jordan, C., & Tharp, R. (1987). Explaining school failure, producing school success: Two cases. *Anthropology and Education Quarterly, 18*, 276–86.

Culturally Responsive Pedagogy *See* Culturally Relevant Pedagogy

Cultural Pluralism

Cultural pluralism implies cultural diversity, equality among groups, and a commitment to the value of diversity in society. The supporting values include belief in the freedom of association, belief that there is no single best way of life, belief that society must allow for many competing ways of life, and acknowledgement that different ways of life can interact and compete without changing each other (Green, 1966). Cultural pluralism promotes a group's right to preserve and develop its own cultural patterns. Individual and group differences are valued and not viewed as inferior to others; as a result, no single group rules over or exploits another. It extols the value of *e pluribus unum* in which many groups exist while supporting and developing a "cohesive society whose culture is enriched by sharing widely divergent ethnic [and cultural] experiences" (Pai, 1990, p. 97).

Often cultural pluralism is used simply to describe the existence of diversity—ethnic, racial, economic, religious, or political; or in gender, language, ability, or age—within the United States and the world. At the same time it refers to a theory and an ideology that explain how diverse groups function and are treated in society.

Horace Kallen introduced the term *cultural pluralism* in a 1915 article on democracy and the melting pot in *The Nation*. He believed that almost everyone in the United States could identify themselves as a member of an ethnic group, that cultural pluralism was essential to democracy, and that society could be diversified and unified. John Dewey presented the same concept to educators in a 1916 speech to the National Education Association in which he discussed the education of immigrants. In 1920 Isaac Berkson argued that ideal cultural pluralism allowed people to identify with cultural communities that were compatible with their own preferences.

Discussions early in the twentieth century focused on the diversity of the immigrants at that time. The 1970s saw a rebirth of discussions on cultural pluralism by sociologists, philosophers, anthropologists, educators, and politicians. This *new pluralism* grew out of the Civil Rights Movement, in which African Americans celebrated their ethnic heritage. Many individuals, including those with ties to European countries, renewed their association with their ethnic groups during this period. Soon cultural pluralism expanded to include more than identity with an ethnic group; it embraced women, economic ability, and homosexual and age groups. By the end of the twentieth century, debates related to cultural pluralism focused on the rights of groups in a democracy, on diversity versus one right way of life, and on the meaning of social equality. The acceptance and appreciation of diversity and the commitment to equality across groups continued to be a major challenge for societies around the world.

The 1972 publication *No One Model American* by the American Association of Colleges for Teacher Education called for education for cultural pluralism that included four components: (1) the teaching of values that support cultural diversity and individual uniqueness; (2) the encouragement of the qualitative expansion of existing ethnic cultures and their incorporation into the mainstream of American socioeconomic and political life; (3) the support of explorations in alternative and emerging lifestyles; and (4) the encouragement of multiculturalism, multilingualism, and multidialectism. Twenty-five years later cultural pluralism, along with equality, remains one of the tenets that undergirds multicultural education.

Cultural pluralism requires that the diversity of students and communities be understood, valued, and integrated in all aspects of the educational process. The curriculum must reflect the diversity of the nation and the world; it cannot be centered in a single culture. Students must see themselves in the pages of their textbooks. Representations used by teachers to help students learn must be drawn from students' own cultural backgrounds. At the same time students should be introduced to multiple perspectives and ways of perceiving the world. *DMG*

References

Appleton, N. (1983). *Cultural pluralism in education: Theoretical foundations*. New York: Longman.

Banks, J. A. (1988). *Multiethnic education: Theory and practice* (2nd ed.). Boston: Allyn & Bacon.

Green, T. (1966). *Education and pluralism: Ideal and reality*. Twenty-Sixth Annual J. Richard Street Lecture, Syracuse University School of Education.

No one model American. (1972). Washington, DC: American Association of Colleges for Teacher Education.

Pai, Y. (1990). *Cultural foundations of education*. Columbus, OH: Merrill.

Pratte, R. (1979). *Pluralism in education: Conflict, clarity, and commitment*. Springfield, IL: Charles C. Thomas.

Cultural Relativism

Cultural relativism is the principle that cultural traits are best understood in the context of the cultural system of which they are a part and, therefore, not subject to external or absolute standards. Cultural relativism became a central tenet of cultural anthropology, particularly as anthropologists sought to dispel notions of racism and ethnocentrism in the early twentieth century. Cultural relativism asks us to engage in a *suspension* of our values so that we might interpret other people's customs in the context of their cultures. To do otherwise—to judge other peoples' customs from our own culture's viewpoint—often leads to *ethnocentrism*, or the belief that one's own culture and its values are superior to that of others.

Many anthropologists still hold to some form of *absolute cultural relativism* by which anything that is acceptable in any one culture has to be viewed as acceptable by an outsider seeking to understand the practice.

An alternative conceptual option is what Miller (1994) terms *critical cultural relativism*. This perspective is situated within the general framework of cultural relativism, whereby we try to view all cultures empathetically from the inside. But it is more specific. It prompts us to understand the plural interests within any society—whether it is between Nazis and Jews, the old and the young, the rich and the poor, men and women, the able and the less able—and to understand the power relationships between these interest groups. We must critique the behavior of these groups from the standpoint of some set of more or less generally agreed upon human rights.

The French anthropologist Claude Lévi-Strauss commented that "no society is perfect" even when considered in light of what that society claims as its moral values. He pinpoints the difficult position of the anthropologist who looks from one culture to another. The predicament is how to maintain what could be called scientific objectivity. Lévi-Strauss claims that the task of the anthropologist is to study the other culture without passing judgment. Other anthropologists claim, to the contrary, that since one cannot ever achieve true objectivity, the best we can do is examine and expose our own biases and then try to treat all cultures equally, or be equally critical of all cultures—one's own and others. Critical cultural relativism tries to do this in terms of a set of universal human rights.

However, cultural anthropologists following a path of critical cultural relativism face the challenge of what might be considered universal human rights, that is, rights that should be guaranteed to all people everywhere regardless of their culture.

Critical cultural relativism helps us better understand which cultural practices and actions are desirable, given certain norms of universal moral behavior and universal human rights. *BDM* • *See also* **Ethnocentrism**

Reference

Miller, B. D. (1994). A case of missing persons: Cultural relativism in today's world. *AnthroNotes*, *16*(3), 1–8.

Cultural Studies

Cultural studies is an interdisciplinary, transdisciplinary, and sometimes counterdisciplinary field that functions within the dynamics of competing definitions of culture. Unlike traditional humanistic studies, cultural studies oftentimes dramatically unsettles the equation of culture and high culture. Cultural studies asserts that myriad expressions and representations of cultural production should be analyzed in relation to other cultural dynamics and social and historical structures and practices. Such a position commits cultural studies to a critical engagement with a potpourri of artistic, religious, political, economic, and communicative discourses. It is important to note that while cultural studies is associated with the study of popular culture, it is not primarily about popular culture. Cultural studies interests are much broader and tend to generally involve the production and naturalization of the rules of inclusivity and exclusivity that guide issues of academic evaluation and legitimation—in particular, the way these rules shape and are shaped by relations of power.

Cultural studies is not one subject—it perseveres as a multidimensional, multicultural, and fragmented constellation of disciplines that addresses a variety of questions. By no means is its future predictable or subject to the control of one ideological perspective. Work in cultural studies examines cultural practices from a perspective that positions them in relation to the dynamics of history, power, and the social relations of both signification and capitalist production. Such a characteristic implies that scholarship in the field will, on some level, grapple with the interrelationship between cultural production, distribution, and reception as relational historical forces.

Cultural studies is concerned with its application to the world existing outside the academy. Proponents maintain that the project of cultural studies is to address the most urgent social questions of the day in the most rigorous intellectual manner available. Thus, the everyday concerns of cultural studies are contextually bound—indeed, the work of the interdisciplinary discipline is constantly being articulated and re-articulated around new social, cultural, and political conditions. Its engagement with the ever-evolving historical context subverts any tendency on the part of cultural studies scholars to become complacent about the field's contributions, both inside and outside the academy. So important is this notion of context that some scholars maintain that the primary role of cultural studies involves providing insight into new and ever-changing contexts by looking at the issues of race, class, gender, and power within that context.

Cultural studies traces its beginnings to the field of education, adult education in particular. Raymond Williams, one of the architects of the field, developed ideas that would help map the concerns of cultural studies and those of an adult educator integrating academic knowledge into the lived context of working students. *PM2 & SRS*

References

Bakhtin, M. (1981). *Dialogic imagination.* Austin: University of Texas Press.

Barthes, R. ([1957] 1972). *Mythologies.* Translated by Annette Lavers. New York: Hill and Wong.

Baudrillard, J. (1968). *Le systeme des objets.* Paris: Gallimard.

Bourdieu, P. (1986). *Distinction: A social critique of the judgment of taste.* Translated by R. Nice. Cambridge: Harvard University Press.

Fiske, J. (1993). *Power plays, power works.* New York: Verso.

Fiske, J., & Hartley, J. (1978). *Reading television.* London: Methuen.

Foucault, M. (1980). *Power/knowledge: Selected interviews and other writings, 1977–1984.* Edited and introduced by L. Kritzman. London: Routledge.

———. (1988). *Politics, philosophy, culture: Interviews and other writings, 1977–1984.* Edited and introduced by L. Kritzman. London: Routledge.

Gates, H. L., Jr. (Ed.). (1986). *"Race," writing, and difference.* Chicago: University of Chicago Press.

Giddens, T. (1979). *Central problems in social theory: Action, structure, and contradiction in social analysis.* Berkeley: University of California Press.

Giroux, H. (1993). *Living Dangerously: Multiculturalism and the politics of difference.* New York: Peter Lang.

———. (1997). *Channel surfing: Race talk and the destruction of today's yuth.* New York: St. Martin's Press.

Gramsci, A. (1985). *Selections from cultural writings.* Edited by D. Forgacs & G. Nowell-Smith. London: Lawrence and Wishart.

Grossberg, L. (1986a). History, politics, and postmodernism: Stuart Hall and cultural studies. *Journal of Communication Inquiry, 10*(2), 61–77.

———. (1986b). *Teaching the popular.* In C. Nelson (Ed.). Theory in the Classroom. Urbana: University of Illinois Press.

———. (1989a). The formations of cultural studies: An American in Birmingham. *Strategies, 2,* 114–49.

———. (1989b). The circulation of cultural studies. *Critical Studies in Mass Communication, 4*(4), 413–20.

———. (1995). What's in a name? (One more time). *Taboo, 1*(1), 1–37.

Hall, S., Grossberg, L., & Slack, J. D. (1993). *Cultural studies.* London: Macmillan.

Hutcheon, L. (1989). *The politics of postmodernism.* London: Routledge.

Kincheloe, J. (1996). The new childhood: home alone as a way of life. In N. Denzin (Ed.), *Cultural Studies: A research value.* Volume I. Middlesex, England: JAI Press.

Lyotard, J. (1986). *The postmodern condition: A report on knowledge.* Minneapolis, MN: University of Minnesota Press.

McLaren, P. (1993). *Schooling as a ritual performance.* New York and London: Routledge.

———. (1994). *Life in schools.* White Plains, NY: Longman.

———. (1995). *Critical pedagogy and predatory culture.* New York and London: Routledge.

Minh-ha, T. T. (1989). *Woman, native, other: Writing postcoloniality and feminism.* Bloomington: Indiana University Press.

Morris, M. (1988). Banality in cultural studies. *Discourse, 10*(2), 3–29.

Ross, A. (1989). *No respect: Intellectuals and popular culture.* London: Routledge.

Shelton, A. (1995). Where the Big Mac is king: McDonalds' USA. *Taboo: The Journal of Culture and Education, 1*(2), 1–38.

Steinberg, S., & Kincheloe, J. (Eds.). (1997). *Kinderculture: The corporate construction of childhood.* Boulder, CO: Westview.

Williams, R. (1958). *Culture and society:* 1780–1950. Harmondsworth: Penguin.

———. (1989a). *The politics of modernism: Against the new conformists.* London: Verso.

———. (1989b). *"Adult education and social change." What I came to say* (pp. 157–66). London: Hutchinson-Radus.

———. (1989c). *Resources of hope: Culture, democracy, socialism.* In R. Gable (Ed.). London: Verso.

Willis, P. (1977). *Learning to labour: How working class kids get working class jobs.* New York: Columbia University Press.

Cultural Styles

Research from a wide range of disciplines, including anthropology, psychology, biology, and sociology, documents that individuals learn in different ways. These differences may be related to culture and ethnicity, religion, social status, economic level, gender, sexual orientation, home environment, experiences, voluntary/involuntary immigrant status, genetic and biological factors, cognitive skills, and a host of other related factors, the sum of which define the parameters of the domain of culture.

In education the term *styles* refers to sensory perceptions impacted by such external stimuli as time of day, lighting, position, or noise (Guild & Garger, 1985). The term *modalities* generally refers to the sensory channels through which we give and receive messages and which are shaped by sensation, perception, and memory. The most important sensory channels for learners are the auditory, visual, and tactile-kinesthetic. The work of Ramirez (1973), Shade (1989), Tafoya (1982), More (1987), and others extends the definition beyond the sensory styles identified by cognitive modality theorists to explore the full range of cultural characteristics—talking styles, walking styles, interaction styles, styles of dress, and questioning styles. Because the research is imbedded in cultural contexts, educators refer to these distinct elements of culture as *cultural modalities* or cultural styles. An exhaustive and growing body of research establishes these cultural styles as significant factors impacting the learning process. Since people who share a common cultural and experiential background often share common patterns of intellectual abilities and thinking styles, misuse of cultural styles research may create stereotypes. Caution must be used to ensure that the unique way in which each individual constructs his or her version of the larger culture is respected (Garcia, 1994).

While many educators-theorists lump all of the concepts discussed so far into a broadly defined styles category, *intelligences* remains a distinct descriptor in the professional literature because it deals with a cognitive model that seeks to describe how individuals use their intelligences to solve problems and fashion products—how the human mind operates on the contents of the world, rather than how the contents are received. This makes intelligences theory very different from the visual-auditory-kinesthetic model, the most common styles theory. Gardner's (1983, 1991) multiple intelligence theory is related to that of the learning styles, cultural modalities, and style theorists, but it is not synonymous. Styles are often the manifestation of our intelligence(s), but are equally the result of our cultural identity and experiences. (See Huber & Pewewardy, 1990, for a more extensive review of the professional literature.)

Understanding the different ways of knowing and learning present in each classroom empowers teachers to move beyond easily stereotyped surface culture characteristics and elements to respond responsibly to the uniquely diverse learners. As Hilliard (1989) advises, "Educators need not avoid addressing the question of style for fear they may be guilty of stereotyping students. Empirical observations are not the same as stereotyping, but the observations must be empirical and must be interpreted properly for each student" (p. 69). *TH*

References

Garcia, E. (1994). *Understanding and meeting the challenge of student cultural diversity*. Boston: Houghton Mifflin.

Gardner, H. (1983). *Frames of mind*. New York: Basic Books.

———. (1991). *The unschooled mind*. New York: Basic Books.

Guild, P. B., & Garger, S. (1985). *Marching to different drummers*. Alexandria, VA: Association for Supervision and Curriculum Development.

Hilliard, A. G., III. (1989, January). Teachers and cultural styles in a pluralistic society. *NEA Today. Special Edition: Issues 89*, 65–69.

Huber, T., & Pewewardy, C. D. (1990). *Maximizing learning for all students: A review of literature on learning modalities, cognitive styles and approaches to meeting the needs of diverse learners* (ERIC Clearinghouse on Teacher Education). U.S. Department of Education, Office of Educational Research and Improvement. ERIC Document Reproduction Service No. ED 324289.

More, A. J. (1987). Native Indian learning styles: A review for researchers and teachers. *Journal of American Indian Education, 27*(1), 17–29.

Ramirez, M. (1973). Cognitive styles and cultural democracy in education of Mexican Americans. *Social Science Quarterly, 53*, 895–904.

Shade, B. J. R. (Ed.). (1989). *Culture, style, and the educative process*. Springfield, IL: Charles C. Thomas.

Tafoya, T. (1982). Coyote's eyes: Native cognitive styles. *Journal of American Indian Education, 21*(2), 21–33.

Cultural Therapy

Cultural therapy is associated with the work of George and Louise Spindler as developed in their edited book *Pathways to Cultural Awareness: Cultural Therapy with Teachers and Students* (1944). Cultural therapy as presented by the Spindlers is a process of raising an individual's awareness of his or her own culture as well as that of others. There are several layers to this awareness: the first is one's specific values, the second is more generalized and pervasive value orientations, and the third is assumptions and concepts that are not verbalized or only partially verbalized. Since all three levels directly affect perceptions, the process of cultural therapy involves examining one's perceptions of one's own behavior in relation to one's perceptions of others' behaviors as well as acquiring an understanding of others' perceptions of one's own behavior. This may be done in several ways. An antecedent concept *anthropotherapy,* is developed by Theodore Brameld. (See Spindler, 1966.) A related concept, *conscienceization,* is presented and practiced by Paulo Friere in *Pedagogy of the Oppressed* (1974).

George Spindler started cultural therapy in the 1950s with a case study of a young male teacher whom he named "Roger Harker" in subsequent publications. Roger Harker was regarded as a very successful teacher headed for an administrative post by the administrators in the school system and by himself. Careful ethnography of his classroom revealed that he was actually teaching only those students who were like himself culturally—White and middle class—and that he was leaving about 40 percent of the class out in the cold. Though there was no active rebellion in the class—he was a well-liked teacher—it was apparent that his communication with the 40 percent who were not like him was poor to nonexistent. His cultural therapy consisted of showing him, step by step, that this was the case and how his communications were culturally biased. This was difficult for him to accept, but a patient processing of the case data collected on his class and on his behaviors brought him to a new level of awareness concerning the sources of his perceptions and behaviors and the responses of others to him.

Also, another approach is developed by the Spindlers in their recent work in the Schonhausen and Roseville schools where they present videos of classrooms in the German school and the American school to teachers in each school and thus stimulate reflective, comparative analyses by the teachers of their behaviors in relation to those of the others being viewed. (See Spindler, 1993a). *GS2 & LS1*

References

Friere, P. (1974). *Pedagogy of the oppressed*. New York: Seabury Press.

Phelan, P., & Davidson, A. L. (Eds.). (1993). *Renegotiating cultural diversity in American schools*. New York: Teachers College Press.

Spindler, G. (1966). Comment by George Spindler. *Human Organization, 24*(4), 293–95.

Spindler, G., & Spindler, L. (1944). *Pathways to cultural awareness: Cultural therapy with teachers and students*. Thousand Oaks, CA: Corwin Press.

———. (1993). Cross cultural, comparative, reflective interviewing in Schonhausen and Roseville. In M. Schwartz (Ed.), *Qualitative voices in educational research* (pp. 106–25). London: Falmer Press.

———. (1993b.) The process of culture and person: Cultural therapy and culturally diverse schools. In P. Phelan, & A. L. Davidson (Eds.), *Renegotiating cultural diversity in American schools*. New York: Teachers College Press.

Cultural Transformation

Cultural transformation is a process by which the culture of a specific group is partly inherited, partly modified, and partly invented as it is passed from generation to generation. It is not a mere vertical transmission of traits, values, beliefs, and behavior but a dynamic process by which new cultural forms are created through the interpretation and re-interpretation of original cultural content and its interaction with a new society (Lowe, 1991). Espiritu (1992) points out that new forms of ethnic cultures are always being created based on cultural traditions that are symbolic or mythical and may no longer exist. Aspects of native culture are retained, modified, reinserted into contemporary environments, and reissued so that they will be workable in a new society (Nieto, 1992). For example, the break-dancing movement of the 1980s was a unique blend of African American and Latino music transported to the U.S. urban scene (Nieto, 1992). Sonia Nieto (1992) describes American culture itself as a process of transformation: "What is 'American' is neither simply an alien culture imposed on dominated groups nor an immigrant culture transposed to new soil. Neither is it an amalgam of old and new. What is 'American' is the complex of interactions of old, new, and created cultures. These interactions are not benign or smooth. Often characterized by unavoidable tension and great conflict, the creation of new cultures takes place in the battlefields of the family, the community, and the schools" (pp. 232–33). *SMA*

References

Espiritu, Y. L. (1992). *Asian American panethnicity: Bridging institutions and identities*. Philadelphia: Temple University Press.

Lowe, L. (1991). Heterogeneity, hybridity, multiplicity: Marking Asian American differences. *Diaspora, 1*(1), 24–44.

Nieto, S. (1992). *Affirming diversity: The sociopolitical context of multicultural education*. White Plains, NY: Longman.

Culture

Culture is often defined as the underlying phenomenon guiding humanity. For example, John Barrett (1984) defines culture as "the body of learned beliefs, traditions, and guides for behavior that are shared among members of any human society" (p. 54). Edward Hall (1977) describes the function of culture in the following statement:

> Culture is a man's medium; there is not one aspect of human life that is not touched and altered by culture. This means personality, how people express themselves (including shows of emotion), the way they think, how they move, how problems are solved, how their cities are planned and laid out, how transportation systems function and are organized, as well as how economic and government systems are put together and function. However, like the purloined letter, it is frequently the most obvious and taken-for-granted and therefore the least studied aspects of culture that influence behavior in the deepest and most subtle ways. (p. 16)

These descriptions of culture capture the essence of definitions provided by many researchers and scholars. Yet, they seem insufficient for describing the deep meaning of culture in school learning.

A more precise definition of culture related to school learning must address factors associated with culturally mediated cognition, culturally valued knowledge, and culturally appropriate social situations for learning. These factors influence the efficiency and potential effectiveness of specific instructional approaches, curriculum designs, and social arrangements for learning for those from different cultural and experiential backgrounds (Hollins, 1996).

Culturally mediated cognition can be defined as the mutuality of the relationship between cognitive development (including the formation of memory structures and mental operations for information processing) and the cultural context in which it is embedded. This means that cognition and culture are mutually constructed during a child's growth and development. School practices that build upon and extend this process of child development are likely to be more efficient and productive than in situations where this is not the case (Dewey, 1902, 1938).

Culturally valued knowledge is an aspect of culturally mediated cognition. The enculturation process involves selective attention and particularly framed perceptions of the world into which the child is socialized and about which specific understandings are developed. This suggests that the quality and quantity of attention awarded a phenomenon and the framing of perception related to it are important in determining what constitutes culturally valued knowledge. Incorporating culturally valued knowledge into curriculum content occurs more naturally when the learner and those who design school practices share the same culture (Au, 1980; Lipka, 1991; Philips, 1972, 1983). Including culturally valued knowledge requires a more conscious effort when this is not the case.

Culturally appropriate social situations for learning are directly related to culturally mediated cognition and culturally valued knowledge. During the enculturation process, as part of understanding the world into which an individual is socialized, attention is given to social relationships and social interactions with other individuals in specific situations, for specific purposes, and under specific conditions. The understandings acquired through this socialization process direct individual social behavior, as well as what is anticipated in the behaviors and responses of others. When culturally appropriate social situations are employed, school learning is likely to be more efficient and productive than when this is not the case (Au, 1980; Lipka, 1991; Philips, 1972, 1983).

An example of the importance of culturally mediated cognition, culturally valued knowledge, and culturally appropriate social situations for learning is in research described by Michael Cole (1974). According to Cole most researchers have found that conducting a valid and reliable study of cognitive development and memory structures in cross-cultural situations requires the use of familiar cultural content that is presented through usual social practices found within the particular culture of which the subjects are members. Cole references a study conducted by Lennenberg and Roberts (1956) in which monolingual Zuni Indians, bilingual English-speaking Zuni Indians, and monolingual English speakers were compared on their ability to recall colors in the yellow-orange section of the color spectrum. The Zuni language does not differentiate colors in this range, thus it is not a part of the social practice among the Zuni Indians. As would be suspected, monolingual Zuni speakers made the most errors in recall, and bilingual English-speaking Zuni Indians made the fewest. The significance of culturally mediated cognition, culturally valued knowledge, and culturally appropriate social situations for learning are made explicit in this example.

In summary, in relationship to school learning, culture can be defined as those values and practices that shape the content, process, and structure of initial and subsequent intellectual, emotional, and social development among members of a particular group. Culture provides the conditions under which human growth and development most naturally occur. School learning is most efficient and productive when it is borne of the cultural value and practices of the learners. *ERH*

References

Au, K. H. (1980). Participation structures in a reading lesson with Hawaiian children: Analysis of a culturally appropriate instructional event. *Anthropology and Education Quarterly, 11*(2), 91–115.

Barrett, J. A. (1984). *Culture and conduct: An excursion in anthropology.* Belmont, CA: Wadsworth.

Cole, M. (1994). *Thought and culture: A psychological introduction.* New York: Wiley.

Dewey, J. (1902). *The child and the curriculum.* Chicago: University of Chicago Press.

————. (1938). *Experience and education.* New York: Macmillan.

Hall, E. T. (1977). *Beyond culture.* Garden City, NY: Anchor Books.

Hollins, E. R. (1996). *Culture in school learning: Revealing the deep meaning.* Mahwah, NJ: Erlbaum.

Lipka, J. (1991). Toward a culturally based pedagogy: A case study of one Yup'ik Eskimo teacher. *Anthropology and Education Quarterly, 22,* 203–23.

Philips, S. (1972). Participant structures and communicative competence. In C. B. Cazden, et al., (Eds.), *Functions of language in the classroom.* New York: Teachers College Press.

————. (1983). *The invisible culture: Communication in the classroom and community on the Warm Springs Indian Reservation.* White Plains, NY: Longman Press.

Culture Shock

Culture shock is the second stage in the adjustment process when a person is suddenly transplanted abroad and totally immersed in a new culture. Both new immigrants and visitors (short- and long-term) can experience culture shock unless they are well acculturated and bilingual. New immigrants and visitors may be anxious because they do not speak the language, know the customs, or understand people's behavior in daily life. In addition, they may find that "yes" may not always mean "yes," that friendliness does not necessarily mean friendship, or that statements that appear to be serious are really intended as jokes. Furthermore, new immigrants and visitors may be unsure as to when to shake hands or embrace, when to initiate conversations, or how to approach a stranger. The notion of culture shock helps explain feelings of bewilderment and disorientation. Language problems do not account for all the frustrations that people feel. When one is deprived of everything that was once familiar, such as understanding a transportation system, knowing how to register for university classes, or knowing how to make friends, difficulties in coping with the new society may arise.

When an individual enters a strange culture, he or she is like a fish out of water. New immigrants and visitors feel at times that they do not belong and consequently may feel alienated from the native members of the culture. When this happens, they may want to reject everything about the new environment and may glorify and exaggerate the positive aspects of their own culture. Conversely, new immigrants and visitors may scorn their native country by rejecting its values and instead choosing to identify with, if only temporarily, the values of the new country. This may occur as an attempt to overidentify with the new culture in order to be accepted by its people.

Reactions to a new culture vary, but experience and research have shown that there are distinct stages in the adjustment process of new immigrants and visitors to a foreign land. When leaving the comfortably secure environment of home, a person will naturally experience some stress and anxiety. The severity of culture shock depends on the person's personality, language ability, emotional support, and duration of stay. It is also influenced by the degree of difference, actual or perceived, between the two cultures.

Visitors coming for short periods of time do not always experience the same intense emotions as visitors who live in foreign countries for a longer period. The adjustment stages during prolonged stays may last several months to several years. The following "w" shaped diagram (Levin & Adelman, 1982) illustrates periods of adjustment in a second culture and might apply to a one-year stay (approximately) in a foreign culture. Although the stages in the cycle do not always occur in the same order and some stages may be skipped, the following pattern is a common one:

The Adjustment Process in a New Culture

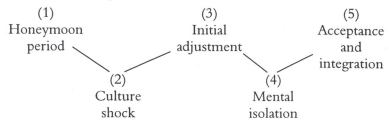

(1) Honeymoon period	(3) Initial adjustment	(5) Acceptance and integration
	(2) Culture shock	(4) Mental isolation

Each stage in this process is characterized by *symptoms* or outward signs typifying certain kinds of behaviors:

1. Honeymoon period: Initially many people are fascinated and excited by everything new. The individual is elated to be in a new culture.
2. Culture shock: The individual is immersed in new problems such as housing, transportation, shopping, and languages. Mental fatigue results from continuously straining to comprehend the foreign language.
3. Initial adjustment: Everyday activities such as housing and shopping are no longer major problems. Although the individual may not yet be fluent in the language spoken, basic ideals and feelings in the second language can be expressed.
4. Mental isolation: Individuals have been away from their family or good friends for a long period of time and may feel lonely. Many still feel they cannot express themselves as well as they can in their native language. Frustration and sometimes a loss of self-confidence result. Some individuals remain at this stage.
5. Acceptance and integration: A routine (e.g., work, business, school) has been established. The individual has accepted the habits, customs, foods, and characteristics of the people in the new culture. They feel comfortable with friends, associates, and the language of the country (Levin & Adelman, 1982). *HC*

References

Levin, D. R., & Adelman, M. B. (1982). *Beyond language: Intercultural communication for English as a second language.* Englewood Cliffs, NJ: Prentice Hall.

Obeng, K. (1979). Culture shock and the problem of adjustment. In E. C. Smith & L. F. Luce (Eds.), *Toward internationalism.* Rowley, MA: Newbury House.

Rhinesmith, S. H. (1975). *Bring home the world: A management guide for community leaders of international programs.* New York: Amacon.

Curriculum Change

Curriculum change is best understood within the context of a continuum of actions involving instructional planning. For purposes here, *curriculum* is defined as a systematic plan for the education of students. It can be as simple as an individual lesson plan or as complicated as a districtwide schemata for educating students in all grades and subjects, K–12. Regardless of its magnitude, the fundamental components of a curriculum are rationale, goals, objectives, content, learning activities, evaluation strategies, and related resources and materials. The extent and kinds of efforts made to modify these determine whether they are considered curriculum change or something else.

Some curriculum specialists distinguish between *curriculum change* and *curriculum improvement*. One frequently referenced distinction, according to Taba (1962), is that improvement occurs when relatively minor modifications are made in some select components of the curriculum but not in its underlying assumptions or its overall organizational structure. Zais (1976) adds that curriculum improvement "essentially involves only a refinement of the status quo with minimal alterations of value orientation" (p. 19). Thus, if a chronological approach to U.S. history which begins with European exploration and settlement were improved, it might include contemporary Asian and Caribbean immigration as modern extensions of these concepts. A language arts curriculum that replaces sentence diagramming with some other technique for teaching grammar is another example of curriculum improvement. A math curriculum that uses the lived experiences of poor urban dwellers as the content of word problems (rather than the conventional preference for middle-class, suburban orientations) is only an improvement because assumptions about the value and validity of word problems are unaffected.

By comparison, *curriculum change* means transforming all design components and altering the values and beliefs upon which they are based. Taba (1962) suggests that, "to change a curriculum means, in a way, to change an institution" (p. 454). This is so because it involves major alterations in "values, people, society and culture, and basic assumptions, therefore . . . curriculum change . . . occurs only very gradually . . . [and is] almost always vehemently resisted" (Zais, 1976, p. 19). Any educational plan that places cultural diversity at the core of the teaching-learning process and treats it as a valuable attribute of social and personal life to be actively promoted constitutes curriculum change.

Curriculum change is far more comprehensive and encompassing than curriculum improvement. It transforms the ideological and methodological centers of the instructional planning process. For example, rather than perpetuating the belief that national unity is contingent upon all ethnic groups in the United States conforming to European American cultural norms, a changed curriculum would promote pluralism as a valid foundation for unity. Curriculum change in a course or unit of study entitled "Classics in American Literature" might critically examine the meanings of "classics, American," and "literature" to reveal that they actually have multiple cultural meanings that are all socially constructed. Curriculum change for teaching reading appropriately to diverse students incorporates explicit references to and examples of cultural diversity throughout its rationale, or justification, for learning to read; sources and samples of materials to be read; learning activities provided for students to practice different reading skills; and the tools and techniques used to determine students' mastery of various reading skills. Curriculum change comprises approaches to education that teach students to deconstruct policies and practices that ignore, denigrate, exploit, or oppress diverse ethnic, racial, and social groups and to develop social action skills to transform society and secure greater freedom, equality, and justice. Sleeter and Grant's (1994) conceptualization of "Education that is Multicultural and Social Reconstructionist" and Banks' (1993) "social action" and "transformation" approaches to multicultural education epitomize curriculum change for dealing with diversity. As Sleeter and Grant explain, it extends explorations of cultural pluralism "into the realm of social action and focuses at least as much on challenging social stratification as on celebrating human diversity and equality of opportunity" (p. 35). GG • See also **Multicultural Education, Approaches To; Curriculum Inclusion**

References

Banks, J. A. (1993). Approaches to multicultural curriculum reform. In J. A. Banks & C. A. M. Banks (Eds.), *Multicultural education: Issues and perspectives* (2nd ed.) (pp. 195-214). Boston: Allyn & Bacon.

Sleeter, C. E., & Grant, C. A. (1994). *Making choices for multicultural education: Five approaches to race, class, and gender* (2nd ed.). New York: Merrill/Macmillan.

Taba, H. (1962). *Curriculum development: Theory and practice.* New York: Harcourt Brace Jovanovich.

Zais, R. S. (1976). *Curriculum: Principles and foundations.* New York: Thomas Y. Crowell.

Curriculum Inclusion

Curriculum inclusion is a form of *curriculum improvement* rather than *curriculum change*. It is more of a refinement of existing frameworks than a transformation or replacement of them. Within the arena of multicultural education, curriculum inclusion occurs when information about the cultural artifacts, experiences, and contributions of ethnic and social groups other than middle-class European American males is added to the content of educational plans. It is distinguished by the purpose, place, quality, and consistency of the new content.

Multicultural curriculum inclusion is motivated by the need to correct errors of omission and commission related to ethnic and cultural diversity. Its goals are twofold: (1) to present information about groups who traditionally have been oppressed and marginalized in U.S. society and have been excluded from the instructional agendas of schools; and (2) to replace incomplete, distorted, or stereotypical portrayals of marginalized groups with accurate information. For example, the image of ethnic groups of color and women as passive spectators of sociopolitical activity and cultural creations is replaced with one showing them as active contributors to the development of society. These efforts, however, are highly selective, restricted, and fragmentary. Information about these groups and individuals is not placed at the core of educational plans, nor is it very significant or presented with dependable regularity. Instead, content about the experiences and contributions of marginalized groups is marginalized *itself* in the curriculum in several ways. It tends to be about exotic historical customs, highly stylized celebrations, and exceptional individuals. The emphasis is on artifact, ritual, entertainment, and individual dimensions of culture (such as costumes, cuisine, arts and crafts), to the virtual exclusion of political and economic issues and group dynamics. The heroes and heroines selected to represent their ethnic, cultural, and social groups closely approximate Eurocentric heroes in attributes, achievement, and persona. As Banks (1993) explains, "The criteria used to select ethnic heroes for study and to judge them for success are derived from the mainstream society and not from the ethnic community" (p. 198). These individuals are *safe* choices of minimum threat to the status quo who represent only one view of their cultural group. The "more radical and less conformist individuals who are heroes only to the ethnic community tend to be ignored" (Banks, 1993, p. 198). This selective information is presented as a supplement, addendum, or appendage to what already exists, is often reserved for special occasions and events (e.g., Black History month, Asian American Heritage month, Women's Celebration month), restricted to a few subjects taught in schools (e.g., social studies, language arts, fine arts), and assumed to be only for students who are members of the groups whose contributions are targeted (e.g., Asian Americans, Latinos, African Americans, Native Americans, females). It is also decontextualized in that the diverse facts, individuals, and events included in the curriculum are isolated from their broader historical, political, social, and cultural backgrounds and experiential frameworks.

Different conceptual models of approaches to multicultural education that illustrate features of curriculum inclusion have been developed by several scholars in the field. Among them are Banks' (1993) "contributions" and "additive" approaches, Lynch's (1989) "folkloric multicultural education," Nieto's (1996) "tolerance" level, and Sleeter and Grant's (1994) "single group studies." GG • *See also* **Multicultural Education, Approaches To; Curriculum Change; Curriculum Infusion**

References

Banks, J. A. (1993). Approaches to multicultural curriculum reform. In J. A. Banks & C. A. M. Banks (Eds.), *Multicultural education: Issues and perspectives* (2nd ed.) (pp. 195–214). Boston: Allyn & Bacon.

Lynch, J. (1989). *Multicultural education in a global society*. London: Falmer Press.

Nieto, S. (1996). *Affirming diversity: The sociopolitical context of multicultural education* (2nd ed.). New York: Longman.

Sleeter, C. E., & Grant, C. A. (1994). *Making choices for multicultural education: Five approaches to race, class, and gender* (2nd ed.). New York: Merrill/Macmillan.

Curriculum Infusion

According to Taba's (1962) distinctions between *curriculum improvement* and *curriculum change* for curriculum modifications to qualify as change, they have to revise the underlying organizational structures and assumptions of existing instructional priorities and educational value orientations. While infusion approaches to multicultural education make significant modifications in the content taught about ethnic, cultural, racial, and social diversity, they do not challenge the core assumptions, values, or patterns of traditional curricula. Therefore, multicultural education infusion, like inclusion, is more a form of curriculum improvement than curriculum change. But, it addresses diversity issues at a greater magnitude, depth, and significance than inclusion.

So curriculum infusion disavows the following three conventions of dealing with ethnic and cultural diversity in educational planning: (1) decontextualized, isolated facts about a few exceptional individuals are adequate for a serious study of cultural and ethnic diversity; (2) the study of ethnic diversity is only for students who are members of marginalized ethnic, racial, and social groups; and (3) restricting information about cultural diversity to the periphery or margins of the curriculum is acceptable. However, the deeper structures, purposes, and characteristics of conventional curriculum are unchanged (Banks, 1993). For example, standardized achievement tests used to determine students' mastery of information and skills may be revised to incorporate cultural diversity in test items, but the appropriateness of these tests for students from different ethnic groups is not challenged.

Permeation, incorporation, integration, and *mainstreaming* are synonyms for curriculum infusion. All of them suggest that content about cultural diversity is woven into all aspects of the curriculum on a regular and routine basis. This information is to be taught to all students regardless of their ethnic, racial, and social identities in all school subjects and institutional settings. Therefore, cultural diversity, or multicultural education, is as much a part of the learning experiences designed for upper-class, European Americans attending all-White suburban schools as it is for single ethnic group students of color in inner-city settings or for poor racially mixed schools in rural communities. It is also incorporated into science, math, business education, and computer technology as readily as it is into social studies, literacy, literature, and fine arts. This permeation of cultural diversity occurs in all of the design components (rationale, goals, objectives, content, learning activities, and evaluation strategies) constituting the curriculum of these various subjects and skill areas. Curriculum infusion is an embodiment of cultural diversity and multicultural education as expansive, pervasive, comprehensive, and inclusive. In explaining this viewpoint, Nieto (1996) states that because multicultural education is "*about* all people, it is also *for* all people, regardless of their ethnicity, language, religion, gender, race, or class. . . . It permeates the physical environment in the classroom, the curriculum, and the relationships among teachers and students and community. It can be seen in every lesson, curriculum guide, unit, bulletin board, and letter that is sent home; it can be seen in the process by which books and audiovisual aids are acquired for the library, the games played during recess, and the lunch that is served" (p. 213, 215).

Another important feature that distinguishes multicultural curriculum infusion from inclusion is the magnitude and quality of the information taught about cultural diversity. The focus in infusion is more on *group* issues, experiences, and perspectives than individuals; on keeping specific issues, individuals, and events within broader historical and sociocultural contexts; and on examining present problems and future potentials in social, political, and economic areas, as well as understanding analyses among and within ethnic groups across time. This is facilitated by concentrating more on concepts, patterns, and trends than on isolated facts. For example, in an infused multicultural curriculum students might view the Civil Rights Movement as illustrating the concepts of discrimination, protest, reform, interdependence, coalition, and power and powerlessness, and as involving different phases, a multitude of multicultural actors, and a wide variety of action strategies and arenas. Attention would be given to pre- and post-1960s efforts as well as the 1960s, for example, the roles played by individuals as far reaching as Frederick Douglass, Martin Luther King, Jr., Rosa Parks, Cesar Chavez, Susan B. Anthony, Dennis Means, and Gloria Steinem; ethnicity-based national and community organizations that fight for social equality and justice; and egalitarian efforts in law, politics, economics, education, and employment. Therefore, multicultural curriculum infusion is, by nature, multiethnic, interdisciplinary, and comparative.

Multicultural curriculum infusion falls short of complete curriculum change because it does not have strong social action and transformation dimensions. Instead, its focus is on knowledge acquisition and reconstruction. The intent is to demonstrate to students that different ethnic and cultural groups have always been, and continue to be, major contributors to the making of U.S. history, life and culture, and that their contributions are evident in all areas of human endeavor and all periods of U.S. societal development. *GG* • *See also* **Curriculum Change; Curriculum Inclusion**

References

Banks, J. A. (1993). Approaches to multicultural curriculum reform. In J. A. Banks & C. A. M. Banks (Eds.), *Multicultural education: Issues and perspectives* (2nd ed.) (pp. 195-214). Boston: Allyn & Bacon.

Nieto, S. (1996). *Affirming diversity: The sociopolitical context of multicultural education* (2nd ed.). New York: Longman.

Taba, H. (1962). *Curriculum development: Theory and practice*. New York: Harcourt Brace Jovanovich.

Deconstruction

> All sentences of the type "deconstruction is X" or "deconstruction is not X," *a priori* miss the point, which is to say that they are at least false. As you know, one of the principle things at stake in what is called in my texts "deconstruction," is precisely the delimiting of ontology and above all of the third-person present indicative: S is P. (Derrida, letter to a Japanese friend, Wood & Bransconi, 1985, cited in Ayer & O'Grady, 1992, p.108.)

Deconstruction refers to a critical project of intervention in philosophical and literary studies and was promulgated in the 1960s and 1970s by the French philosopher Jacques Derrida (1967, 1982a, 1982b). As a mode of critique, deconstruction can be historically traced to the ancient Greeks through critical engagement with such diverse twentieth-century thinkers as Nietzsche, Heidegger, Saussure, and Lacan. Today, however, deconstruction is associated with postmodernist or, more specifically, poststructuralist analyses of modernism and is predominant in academic conventions of critical theory, feminism, and critical pedagogy science (Cherryholmes, 1988; Luke & Gore, 1992; Morrow & Torres, 1995; Stanley, 1992). The term is also evoked—albeit less rigorously and at times in pun— in a wide range of lay contexts including bureaucracy, journalistic media, popular culture, and counterintelligence parlance (Esch, 1992; Woodward, et al., 1981).

The radical enterprise of deconstruction is the destabilization of foundational (transcendental or universal) concepts central to the grand narratives of Western thought that privilege traditional criteria for rationality, representation, and truth. Through deconstructive scrutiny, assumptions under the rubric of *logocentrism* in spoken and written language (but also in history, culture, and technology) are deconstructed to expose their *always-already* contradictions (*aporias*). Deconstructive practice holds that each *text-context* is shadowed by its own inherent (self-) discrepancies. The existence of such difference (*différance*) constitutes a destabilizing internal force—an undermining from within—which subverts the desired unity or epistemological closure of any term, criteria, or practice of the *real* sought in language.

Critical (re-)reading against the grain (or *misreading*) of texts-contexts reveals the production and reproduction of universal ideologies. Dominant ideas achieve their status through mechanisms of repression and subordination of certain terms, knowledge, or experience within the social world. Derrida identifies this as a demarcation process involving "opposition of metaphysical concepts (for example, speech/writing, presence/absence) [that] is never the face-to-face of two terms, but a hierarchy and an order of subordination" (Derrida, 1982a, p. 329). Hierarchies of metaphysical concepts are constructed through binary oppositions or polarities, which arbitrarily privilege one pole of the opposition over the other, for example, RATIONALITY/irrationality, WHITE/Black, and MALE/female (*AAE*, 1992). Subordinate terms in this dualism thereby appear as the *unthought* (voicelessness) and thereby the *unthinkable* (invisibility). One immediate consequence of deconstructive criticism's dislocating and overturning the power-knowledge authority of dominant conceptual structures is the recognition that meaning can be framed in different ways. As a tool of critique, deconstruction thus provides a necessary point of departure for the recovery and empowerment of voice-voicings among formerly silenced *Others*, and for the recuperation of suppressed stories, forms of knowledge, and ways of being.

Deconstructive analysis can effectively be brought to bear on a range of educational-theory, practice, or policy questions. As a critical strategy, deconstruction enables educators to challenge and transform curricular or reform projects whose rhetoric obscures deeper interests and commitments to traditional conceptions of education. (See, e.g., Derrida, 1967, on Rousseau's *Emile;* Usher & Edwards, 1994, p. 129–30; and Cherryholmes, 1988, on curriculum theorists Tyler, Bloom, and Schwab.) For example, deconstruction destabilizes the existing thinking on the role of teachers. The teacher can no longer be seen as the expert who delivers truth, or a civil servant of the state who reproduces hegemonic relationships outside the classroom in the education system and the larger society. Rather, deconstruction opens the possibility of the teacher as fellow discoverer who, with students, engages in a search for meanings, not all of which are secured in any final way.

Deconstructive analysis alters the sanctity of the curriculum as a fixed entity. It shifts the emphasis of curriculum from the content to be learned to the process of learning—to questions of disciplinarity and pedagogy. In addition, deconstruction raises questions not only about the practice of evaluation—what is to be evaluated: effort, process, or product—but also about the purposes of evaluation. Acutely aware of the shifting relationship between discourse and social structure, deconstruction links the narrative of education more firmly to the world (context), whether that world is the teacher's, the students', or a shared reality of larger institutional or political matters. Deconstruction implies multiple logics of resistance as well as the transformative potential of critical engagement. *WEC & CP*

References

Academic American encyclopedia (AAE). (1992). Danbury, CT: Grolier

Cherryholmes, C. H. (1988). *Power and criticism: Poststructural investigations in education.* New York: Teachers College Press.

Derrida, J. (1967). *Of grammatology.* Translated by G. C. Spivak. Baltimore, MD: Johns Hopkins University Press.

_____. (1982a). *Margins of philosophy.* Translated by A. Bass. Chicago: University of Chicago Press.

_____. (1982b). *Positions.* Translated by A. Bass. Chicago: University of Chicago Press.

_____. (1985). Letter to a Japanese friend. In D. Wood & R. Brasconi (Eds.), *Derrida and différance* (pp. 107-27). Coventry, England: Parouvia Press. Quoted in A. J. Ayer & J. O'Grady, (Eds.), *A dictionary of philosophical quotations* (Oxford: Blackwell, 1992).

Esch, D. (1992). Deconstruction. In S. Greenblatt & G. Gunn (Eds.), *Redrawing the boundaries: The transformation of English and American literary studies* (pp. 374–91). New York: Modern Languages Association of America.

Luke, C., & Gore, J. (1992). *Feminisms and critical pedagogy.* New York: Routledge.

Morrow, R. A., & Torres, C. A. (1995). *Social theory and education: A critique of theories of social and cultural reproduction.* New York: State University of New York Press.

Stanley, W. B. (1992). *Curriculum for utopia: Social reconstructionism and critical pedagogy in the postmodern era.* New York: State University of New York Press.

Usher R., & Edwards, R. (1994). *Postmodernism and education.* London: Routledge.

Woodward, R., with Salholz, E., Kirkland, R., & Sullivan, S. (1981). A new look at lit crit. *Newsweek,* June 22, p. 80–83.

Democratic Education

Democratic education is the education of children and youth—planned cooperatively and in a principled way—by parents, professional educators, and citizens. In brief, it is democratically planned education. What makes it

democratic is the countervailing influences within and among the sometimes overlapping stakeholder roles (parents, professionals, and citizens)
combined with a morally principled approach to decision making. Principles of this approach include the value of deliberating on education in a
consensus-oriented way with those who may differ in their visions of the
good life and the value of the deliberative standard of open and critical
inquiry. Gutmann (1987) has called these principles *nondiscrimination* and
nonrepression.

Democratic education is aimed at preparing children and youth for a life
of civic self-governance; that is, it is aimed at popular sovereignty (rule by
the citizens as opposed to rule by a monarch or elites). Its aim is to create
citizens who are competent to share in the rights and obligations of ruling.
This aim must also be applied to the planning of educational experiences. In
this way, democratic education is itself one instance of popular sovereignty.

This democratic approach to planning the education of children and
youth can be contrasted with state-centered and individual choice-centered
schemes (Gutmann, 1987). The approaches advocated by Plato's *Republic*
and modern totalitarian states such as Hitler's Germany, Stalin's Soviet
Union, and Khomeini's Iran are, more or less, extreme examples of state-
centered schemes. North American and European societies lean toward the
individual choice-centered schemes. Democratic education aims at integrating and joining dialectically the two forces, relying on public delibera-
tion while educating students for it at the same time. *WCP*

References

Gutmann, A. (1987). *Democratic education*. Princeton, NJ: Princeton University Press.

Desegregation

Desegregation is a term used to denote the bringing together of students from
different racial and ethnic backgrounds who have previously attended racially or ethnically homogeneous schools or who would do so otherwise.
Desegregation in the United States was spurred by the 1954 Supreme Court
case *Brown v. Board of Education*. The *Brown* decision overturned the earlier
Plessy v. Ferguson decision, which had held that racially separate facilities
were acceptable as long as they were equal. In contrast, the Court held in the
Brown decision that separate facilities were inherently unequal, thus laying
the groundwork for school desegregation. In considering the situation
existing before desegregation, a distinction is often made between de jure
segregation, in which there were formal dual school systems as was common in southern states, and de facto segregation, in which government
action contributed to the separation of different racial or ethnic groups

without actually creating a formal dual school system. Examples of such actions might be locating new school buildings so that the racial homogeneity of the schools in a district would be maximized or drawing oddly shaped attendance boundaries for schools for the same purpose.

Little desegregation occurred in the first decade following the *Brown* decision, due primarily to White resistance, which was expressed in ways ranging from physical attacks on Black students attempting to desegregate previously all-White schools, to legal strategies aimed at delay, and to the founding of over 3,000 private schools. However, a substantial amount of desegregation occurred between 1965 and 1972. Since 1972 there has been little change in the overall proportion of Black students in schools composed predominately of students of color. Over time White public opinion has increasingly accepted desegregation in principal. However, reactions to the specific means available to achieving this end remain markedly less positive. Furthermore, the attitudes of African Americans towards various implementation strategies have actually become less positive over time, perhaps because much of the burden of desegregation has fallen on communities of color. So, for example, in the dismantling of dual school systems, teachers of color teaching in schools of color were proportionately more likely to lose their jobs than dominant group teachers. Also, children of color are more likely to have been involved in extensive *busing* than dominant group children.

A wide variety of approaches have been used to desegregate previously segregated school systems. Common among these have been the closing of some highly segregated schools, the busing of students from their neighborhoods (which are frequently racially or ethnically segregated) to schools whose student bodies are from heterogeneous backgrounds, the creation of *magnet schools*, and a strategy called *controlled choice*, which allows parents a choice in selecting their children's schools as long as certain guidelines about the racial and ethnic composition of the schools are not violated. Although much of the desegregation that has occurred has been in response to court orders, some school systems have voluntarily set up various kinds of programs designed to foster desegregation.

Conceptions of desegregation have changed as the social and demographic fabric of the United States has changed. For example, for at least two decades after the *Brown* decision, desegregation was generally seen as involving two groups—Blacks and Whites. More recently, with increasing immigration and the pronounced movement of Whites from urban to suburban areas, attention has been paid to the role of other ethnic and linguistic groups in desegregation programs. Indeed, as White enrollments in schools in many major urban centers have dropped markedly and cities have increasingly become home to a wide variety of ethnic and racial groups, it has become essentially impossible to desegregate many major urban school systems in the original meaning of the term. *JWS* • *See also* **Brown v. Board of Education; Educational Choice; Magnet Schools; Plessy v. Ferguson; Resegregation; Segregation**

References

Allport, G. W. (1954). *The nature of prejudice*. Cambridge, MA: Addison-Wesley.

Braddock, J. H., II, Crain, R. L., & McPartland, J. M. (1984). A long-term view of school desegregation: Some recent studies of graduates as adults. *Phi Delta Kappan, 66*(4), 259–64.

Gerard, H., & Miller, N. (1975). *School desegregation*. New York: Plenum.

Patchen, M. (1982). *Black-White contact in schools: Its social and academic effects*. West Lafayette, IN: Purdue University Press.

Pettigrew, T. (1969). The Negro and education: Problems and proposals. In I. Katz & P. Gurin (Eds.), *Race and the social sciences* (pp. 49–112). New York: Basic Books.

Schofield, J. W. (1982). *Black and White in school: Trust, tension, or tolerance?* New York: Praeger. A revised and updated version of this book was published by Teachers College Press in paperback, 1989.

———. (1991). School desegregation and intergroup relations: A review of the research. In G. Grant (Ed.), *Review of research in education* (Vol. 17, pp. 335–409). Washington, DC: American Educational Research Association.

Deterritorialization *See* Border Studies

Dialogic Pedagogy

Dialogic pedagogy is rooted in diverse sources from the Socratic method in the West to traditional philosophies of Africa, Asia, and the Americas and from pedagogies of liberation like Freire and critical theorists to the Russian linguist Mikhail Bahktin's work on the dialogic imagination in literature.

A challenge for students of the foundations of education is to expand the curriculum from Eurocentric to non-Western sources of knowledge. For example, in Eastern traditional philosophy one learns how to be human, not in isolation from others but in *dialogic* relationship with others. This quest to learn to be human in Confucian, Taoist, and Buddhist traditions is set not only in the midst of human relationships but also in the universe as a reflection of Chinese cosmology (Tu, 1985).

Contemporary Brazilian educator Paulo Freire has developed a dialogic pedagogy of liberation which is also rooted in the problem of "humanization" (1970). As a Marxist, for Freire the problem of dehumanization is not merely an "ontological possibility" but a "historical reality." The origin of dehumanization lies in the contradiction between the oppressors and the oppressed. It is the result of an unjust order. In the tradition of Socrates and Marx, Freire utilized the metaphor of the midwife to describe the process of learning as an act of liberation.

Freire's concept of the teacher-to-students relationship emphasizes mutual discovery and exploration. He criticizes what he calls "banking pedagogies" in which the teacher talks about reality as if it were "motionless, static, compartmentalized and predictable." In banking pedagogies the task of the teacher is to fill the students with the contents of the teacher's narration. Freire calls instead for a "problem-posing" concept of education as an instrument of liberation.

Mikhail Bahktin's work in the novel laid the theoretical foundation for dialogics, heteroglossia, and multiple voices (1981). For Bahktin there are two forces operating simultaneously in language: centripetal forces that unify and centralize and centrifugal stratifying forces of historical heteroglossia. By *heteroglossia,* Bahktin (1981) refers to the interaction that exists within any utterance between the systematic aspect of transcription and the multiple possibilities of meaning within the particular context. Bahktin's understanding of multiple meanings leads to an interpretive stance in search of meanings and a search for submerged voices—works of women and *strangers*—African Americans and immigrants—voices that have been subjugated and memories that have been silenced (Greene, 1988). His theoretical work in linguistics and literary criticism has led to the development of dialogic pedagogy in which students are encouraged to develop their own voices in responding to and writing texts (Cazden, 1992).

In developing multicultural curriculum, four features of dialogic pedagogy are an (1) emphasis on a process of inquiry and exploration, rather than a set of material to be learned (Cummins, 1986; Ward, 1994); (2) respect for cultural identities and reciprocity in teaching and learning in the teacher-student relationship (Nieto, 1992; Wong, 1993); (3) learning by doing (Mao, 1971; Shor, 1992); and (4) posing of questions of equity, justice, and social transformation or the "knowledge for whom" question (Banks, 1993; Edelsky, 1991). *SDW*

References

Bahktin, M. M. (1981). *The dialogic imagination: Four essays.* Translated by C. Emerson and edited by M. Holquist. Austin: University of Texas Press.

Banks, J. A. (1993). The canon debate, knowledge construction, and multicultural education. *Educational Researcher, 22*(5), 4–14.

Cazden, C. (1992). In *Whole language plus.* New York: Teacher College Press.

Cummins, J. (1986). Empowering minority students: A framework of intervention. *Harvard Educational Review, 56*(1), 13–36.

Edelsky, C. (1991). *With literacy and justice for all: Rethinking the social in language and education.* London: Falmer Press.

Freire, P. (1970). *Pedagogy of the oppressed*. New York: Herder and Herder.

Greene, M. (1988). *The dialectic of freedom*. New York: Teachers College Press.

Mao, Tse-tung [Mao Zedong]. (1971). *Selected readings from the works of Mao Tse-tung*. Beijing: Foreign Language Press.

Nieto, S. (1992). *Affirming diversity: The sociopolitical context of multicultural education*. White Plains, NY: Longman.

Shor, I. (1992). *Empowering education: Critical teaching for social change*. Chicago: University of Chicago Press.

Tu, W. M. (1985). *Confucian thought: Selfhood as creative transformation*. Albany: State University of New York Press.

Ward, I. (1994). *Literacy, ideology and dialogue: Towards a dialogic pedagogy*. Albany: State University of New York Press.

Wong, S. (1993). Cultural context: Exploring the nexus between medicine and ministry. In T. Boswell, R. Hoffman, & P. Tung (Eds.), *Perspectives on English for professional communication* (pp. 115–26). Hong Kong: City Polytechnic.

Difference

The term difference has various meanings in multicultural education. For instance, some multicultural educators employ the term *difference* after deconstructionist Jacques Derrida (1978) who uses the term *différance* to refer to the logic of supplementarity, the play of difference, or the deferral or postponement of meaning. Such a concept of difference is used to disrupt the logocentric desire for fixed essence or to unsettle the metaphysics of presence associated with modernist articulations of ethnic identity. The term *difference* is also used in cybernetic systems theory, social semiotics, and sociolinguistic theory to refer to the ways in which binary oppositions and distinctions privilege certain individuals and groups over others in relation to the ongoing historical struggle over signs and significations.

Usually the term *difference* is employed in multicultural education in terms of its relationship to the concepts of pluralism and diversity. In the struggle to make history and to act on the understanding of knowledges of dominant cultural fictions, critical multiculturalists foreground marginal and excluded voices. Such voices help them to understand what constitutes central cultural values. With these understandings, critical postmodern multicultural educators utilize marginal voices—such as those of Black writers, scientists, musicians, and composers, as well as indigenous people and feminist epistemologies—to create counter discourses or an ongoing deconstruction of cultural power. As teachers employ such perspectives, or as students bring them into the classroom, students come to see their own points of view as only one in a galaxy of socially constructed worldviews. Engaging with many excluded voices, students and teachers expand their epistemological vocabularies in the process, reaching new horizons of meaning and of learning to criticize and adjudicate competing discourses. Such forms of teaching are grounded on the concept of difference.

There are many benefits that can be garnered from this *pedagogy of difference*. The value of understanding ideologies and worldviews that are not Western, patriarchal, Christian, or heterosexist invites students and teachers to consider alternative and oppositional ways of seeing the world, themselves, other human beings, the purpose of education, and the nature of a democratic community. For example, scholars have long contended that the foundation of political and ethical thinking has rested on a close-knit community with a common set of precepts. An epistemology of difference challenges such a perception, asserting that heterogeneous communities with differing principles may, in some important contexts, better contribute to the cultivation of critical thinking and moral reasoning. A homogeneous community often is unable to criticize the injustice and exclusionary practices that afflict a social system. *JLK & PM2*

Reference

Derrida, J. (1978). *Writing and difference.* Translated by A. Bass London: Routledge & Kegan Paul.

Disability Studies

A society is judged by the manner in which it treats those who are different. By this criterion the American educational system has had a less-than-distinguished history regarding the educational needs of people with disabilities (Heward & Orlansky, 1988). The education of people with disabilities and the evolution of special education did not begin with the passage of the Education of All Handicapped Children Act in 1975 (PL 94-142); however, a new era in special education did begin at that time. This legislation marked a rite of passage from the social-political injustices and pathological identities that once defined and excluded people with disabilities to their inclusion into the educational mainstream as contributing and respected individuals (Ferguson, Ferguson, & Bogdan, 1987).

Disability studies is a field of study that addresses the terminology associated with people with disabilities and describes their relationship with the educational system in the United States. Diversity, its central characteristic, encompasses individuals who are different academically, developmentally, and cognitively, as well as those who are different in physical ability. The negative terminology once associated with people with disabilities focused on the nature of the condition and the physical or mental challenges they experienced. These have been transformed to positive terms that focus on the person, hence, the term *handicapped* has become *people with disabilities*.

The new focus is on the capacity and ability of the person to acquire skills commensurate with his or her potential and level of competence in performing particular tasks. Thus, placing the individual first honors their personhood, their talents, and their gifts. *Ablism* is a form of discrimination against people with disabilities that presumes *able-bodiness* as the only acceptable condition for social benefits such as employment, housing, and schooling.

Prior to World War II, many states denied educational access to children considered physically or mentally incapacitated (Heward & Orlansky, 1988). However, with the advent of compulsory education attendance laws and the passage of Public Law 94-142, the public schools began to accept responsibility for educating children who were deaf, blind, and/or mentally retarded. The schools and children with disabilities "were forced into a reluctant, yet separate mutual recognition of each other" (Hollingsworth, 1923, cited in Dunn, 1968). After the war, the field of special education became recognized as a generic approach in all areas of disability in public school systems (Dybwad, 1980). However, a philosophy of segregation prevailed with the establishment of self-contained special programs administered as separate categorical entities for students with disabilities (Dunn, 1968; Reschly, 1987).

These fundamental philosophies remained unchanged until the justice and equality of such a system were challenged by educators like Dunn and Deno in the late 1960s and 1970s. Dunn (1968) questioned the disproportionate incidence of students of color in segregated classrooms for the educable mentally retarded and raised serious civil rights issues (Chinn & Selma, 1987). Deno (1970) argued against the pathological nature of categorical programming of special education (York & Tundidor, 1995). Their arguments led to intensified debate by other critics like Alan Gartner, Dorothy Lipsky, Maynard Reynolds, Herbert Walberg, Margaret Wang, and Madeline Will regarding effective education for students with disabilities.

Because exclusionary programs and segregated placements were so unfair (Kaufman, 1993), civil rights advocates and educational leaders joined forces to apply the principles set forth in court decisions about race to special education and to guarantee the right of students with disabilities to receive their education in the least restrictive environment (Ferguson et al., 1987). The concept of "least restrictive environment," a central element of Public Law 94-142, presumes that all students should learn together. Seen in a broader perspective, Public Law 94-142 is strengthened by other legislation that benefits persons with disabilities. As an outgrowth of the Civil Rights Movement, legislation served as a catalyst for providing appropriate education to students who were formerly at the margins (Artiles & Trent, 1994; Deno, 1970; Dunn, 1968; Dybwad, 1980; Kaufman, 1993). As a result, several court decisions and legislative mandates have influenced the education of students with disabilities: *Brown v. Board of Education,* 1954; *Pennsylvania Association for Retarded Children v. The Commonwealth of Pennsylvania,* 1972; *Mills v. Board of Education of Washington, D.C.,* 1972; and Public Law 94-142. Together, these enactments support each other and are tangible expressions of new societal concerns that all students with disabilities have the legal right to have their educational needs met in the least exclusionary, least restrictive way possible (Ferguson et al., 1987; Kaufman, 1993); that integration is better than segregation; and that it is normal to be different (Shapiro, 1994). *JBT* • *See also* **Inclusive Education**

References

Artiles, A. J., & Trent, C. (1994). Overrepresentation of minority students in special education: A continuing debate. *The Journal of Special Education, 27*(4), 410–37.

Chinn, P. C., & Selma, H. (1987). Representation of minority students in special education classes. *Remedial and Special Education, 8,*41–46,

Deno, E. (1970). Special education as developmental capital. *Exceptional Children, 37,* 229–37.

Dunn, L. M. (1968). Special education for the mildly retarded: Is much of it justifiable? *Exceptional Children, 35,* 5–22.

Dybwad, G. (1980). Avoiding misconceptions of mainstreaming, the least restrictive environment, and normalization. *Exceptional Children, 47*(2), 85–111.

Ferguson, D. L., Ferguson, P. M., & Bogdan, R. C., (1987). If mainstreaming is the answer, what is the question? In V. Richardson-Koehler (Sr. Ed.), *Educators' Handbook: A research perspective* (pp. 394–419). New York: Longman.

Heward, W. L., & Orlansky, M. D. (1988). *Exceptional children: An introductory survey of special education.* Columbus, OH: Merrill.

Kaufman, J. M. (1993). How we might achieve the radical reform of special education. *Exceptional Children, 60*(1), 6–16.

Reschly, D. J. (1987). Minority mild mental retardation overrepresentation: Legal issues, research findings, and reform trends. In M. C. Wang, M. C. Reynolds, & H. J. Walberg (Eds.), *Handbook of research on special education* (Vol. 2, pp. 23–41). New York: Pergammon.

Shapiro, J. P. (1994). *No pity: People with disabilities forging a new Civil Rights Movement.* New York: Random House.

York, J., & Tundidor, M. (1995). Issues raised in the name of inclusion: Perspectives of educators, parents, and students. *Journal of Association of Severe Handicaps, 20*(1), 31–44.

Disadvantaged *See* Culturally Deprived

Diversity

Diversity refers to differences among people. Although there are many individual differences among individuals, multicultural educators are usually referring to group differences. In the United States the focus traditionally has been on racial and ethnic diversity, in part because of the great economic and political disparities that exist among these groups. Many of the current writers in the field of multicultural education describe diversity in terms of racial, ethnic, gender, and economic groups. Others have added language, religion, ability, age, and sexual orientation to the array of groups that are addressed under the auspices of multicultural education.

At the beginning of the twentieth century diversity in schools focused primarily on the assimilation of European immigrants. The intergroup education movements in the middle of the century began to recognize the racial and ethnic diversity of the country and strived to reduce the prejudice and discrimination against groups whose origins were other than western European. Unequitable conditions for racial groups were highlighted during the Civil Rights Movements of the 1960s. In the 1970s many individuals, including those from European backgrounds, began to recognize and celebrate their ethnic heritages. At the same time, speakers of languages other than English, women, elderly, and people with disabilities began to exert their influence on discussions of diversity and public policy. During the 1990s some religious groups tried to seize control of the public debate related to diversity issues such as sexual orientation and the role of women. Diversity issues currently intersect with public debates and policies about groups, for example, affirmative action, targeted funding for women's equity, bilingual education, and special education.

As the scope of diversity has expanded to include more and more groups, it has become clear that intragroup differences also exist. Not all members of the same group have the same values, cultural traditions, and behaviors. Understanding diversity has become very complex because it also includes attention to conflict among and within groups. One of the key components of diversity is the relationship of groups to the dominant society.

Diversity is at the heart of education that is multicultural. Multicultural educators understand, value, and integrate diversity throughout the educational process. Their curriculum is expected to be inclusive of diverse groups and not centered around a single group. Teachers have high academic expectations for all students and draw upon the diverse cultural backgrounds of students to ensure that they learn. The inclusion of diversity both in the formal and informal curriculum, as well as in school activities, is the norm of a multicultural school. At the same time that diversity becomes an integral part of education, students learn about similarities across groups. They also learn to be active and contributing participants in a democracy in which diverse groups work together to forge a better society. *DMG* • *See also* **Intragroup Diversity**

References

Banks, J. A., & Banks, C. A. M. (1993). *Multicultural education: Issues and perspectives* (2nd ed.). Boston: Allyn & Bacon.

Banks, J. A., & Banks, C. A. M. (Eds.). (1995). *Handbook of research on multicultural education*. New York: Macmillan.

Gollnick, D. M., & Chinn, P. C. (1994). *Multicultural education in a pluralistic society* (4th ed.). Columbus, OH: Merrill.

Perry, T., & Fraser, J. W. (Eds.). (1993). *Freedom's plow: Teaching in the multicultural classroom*. New York: Routledge.

Sleeter, C. E., & Grant, C. A. (1994). *Making choices for multicultural education: Five approaches to race, class, and gender* (2nd ed.). New York: Merrill.

Dominated Cultures

Dominated cultures are those cultural groups that are forcefully made part of a nation by enslavement, conquest, or colonization. Dominated groups in the United States include African Americans, who were forced to come to the United States as enslaved persons; Native Americans, who were conquered by European and United States governments; Mexican Americans, who were living in the southwestern part of what is now the United States at the time of the Mexican-American War; and Puerto Ricans, who were conquered by the United States government during the Spanish-American War. (See Spring, 1994, for a brief history of this latter conquest.)

The educational issues created by forced domination are different from those faced by recent and voluntary immigrants (i.e., first-generation Americans). Dominated groups often feel a level of hostility toward the institutions that subjugated them, while voluntary immigrants enter the United States with the hope that these institutions will provide them with improved living conditions. Voluntary immigrants can face the same discrimination and bigotry as experienced by dominated groups, but immigrants often see these negative experiences as part of the price for improving their conditions in the United States. In fact it can be argued that many immigrant groups, particularly people of color, encounter the same problems of racism and cultural exclusion as dominated groups.

Dominated groups often feel some antagonism towards government and public institutions, such as public schools, because these institutions have in the past been a vehicle for slavery and control. In contrast, Kevin Brown (1993) writes that for voluntary immigrants "cultural and language differences enshrined in public schools are not generally perceived as oppositional nor as threats to the identity that they wished to maintain." Indeed, if voluntary immigrants believe they are not better off in the United States, those who have the option may choose to return to their former countries.

Consequently, voluntary immigrants have different attitudes regarding public schools than do dominated cultures.

Therefore, while dominated and immigrant groups might share similar problems of prejudice and discrimination, they often differ with regard to how they see their possibilities for advancement in U.S. society. For instance, the experiences in U.S. schools of African Americans, Native Americans, Mexican Americans, and Puerto Ricans—who are from dominated cultures—have often been negative and have created a level of suspicion, and sometimes hostility, toward the institutions. These feelings of suspicion and hostility often manifest in forms of resistance to public schools. *JS* • *See also* **Resistance**

References

Brown, K. (1993). Do African American males need race and gender segregated education? An educator's perspective and a legal perspective. In C. Marshall (Ed.), *The new politics of race and gender* (p. 111). Washington, DC: Falmer Press.

Spring, J. (1994). *Deculturalization and the struggle for equality: A brief history of the education of dominated cultures in the United States*. New York: McGraw-Hill.

Dysconscious Racism *See* Racism

Ebonics *See* African American Language

Educational Choice

Educational choice means different things to different people—educators, researchers, and policy officials. A generic meaning of the term implies that families will have school choices for their children other than the geographically assigned, attendance-area schools traditionally prescribed by public school districts.

Contained within that broad definition of educational choice are numerous types of policies, programs, and individually generated mechanisms by which families seek education for their children. The most common option in our early history was *home schooling*—which today is a constitutionally protected choice of families but which was earlier most often dictated by the absence of free and universal public education. With the organization of public schools, choices were restricted by geographic attendance areas drawn around school buildings. Private schools have, of course, been an option since well before the founding of the nation. The early history of private schools, which were usually religious, was as elite schools to educate the rich. This changed in the nineteenth century when Catholic schools emerged in reaction to the Protestant orientation of the public schools and became the most prevalent form of private school. They also adopted geographic attendance areas for their elementary schools, following the boundaries of church membership.

The first consistent breaks with attendance area assignments came in the form of specialty schools in larger cities. Schools, which would probably be termed magnet or charter schools today, emerged to either emphasize specific curricula or teaching methods or to select elite students. Such schools as the Bronx School of Science or the famous University of Chicago Lab School created by John Dewey were prominent examples. Although of historic interest and producing a number of illustrious graduates, the mass effects of these early schools of choice were slight. This changed when choice emerged as a mechanism to aid racial integration beginning in the 1960s. Three forms of public school choice have emerged from efforts to integrate schools within a district and, less so, across district lines.

Magnet schools, magnet programs, and most recently schools-within-schools emerged in the 1970s, spreading to nearly every large school district in the United States in the 1980s. The initial intent was to enhance voluntary integration, which primarily meant keeping White students from leaving city districts. However, in the last decade magnet schools have been viewed as a vehicle for improving educational outcomes and increasing choice in its own right.

More recently, but still cognizant of integration patterns, some large school districts have extended choice to all students in accordance with plans labelled as *controlled choice*. These plans usually split districts into a small number of choice zones and allow families to select any school within the zone, as long as racial balances are maintained. The provision of school choices between districts, or *interdistrict choice*, also began primarily as a mechanism to enhance voluntary interdistrict integration. Thus, programs were established in cities such as St. Louis, Milwaukee, and Kansas City to allow non-White children to transfer to suburban districts, and White children to attend city schools.

As with magnet programs, such programs have expanded in the last decade to accommodate the growing feeling that choices can further educational outcomes for all children and that choice is an important value in itself. This has led many states to create *open enrollment* systems in which, in theory, students may attend any public school in the state. In practice there are often a number of constraints, the most important being that receiving districts often can limit the number of students they will take from outside their boundaries.

The most recent extension of the concept of educational choice has been to *private schools* and *charter schools*. Recent efforts to expand private school choice have been either to provide public subsidies to the general population to attend private schools (usually in the form of a government voucher to be cashed by the private school) or to create more narrow, targeted programs to help poor populations, usually in large cities. General voucher programs, which have been the subject of statewide referenda in Oregon, Colorado, and California, have all been defeated at the polls. Targeted programs have been proposed in many states, but only enacted in Milwaukee, Wisconsin and recently in Cleveland, Ohio.

Charter school legislation has been enacted in many states. Charter schools can best be thought of as hybrids, somewhere between public and private schools. They vary considerably across states, but usually provide for unique schools to be *chartered* with special provisions often exempting them from many state and school district regulations.

Educational choice incorporates a number of meanings and includes a range of programs. There can be no doubt, however, that the idea that families should have extensive choice in terms of the location and type of school their children attend has become extremely popular in recent years. What began as a movement within certain public schools, primarily to achieve voluntary racial integration, has expanded to include most public schools. Current controversies involve extending government support to private schools. *JFW* • *See also* **Magnet Schools**

Educational Equality

According to Secada (1989) much of the current debate and literature on educational equality traces its roots to the Coleman report (1967). Secada (1989) recognizes the limitations and ambiguity associated with the concept of educational equality, yet he provides a succinct definition of equality in education: "Equality in education often gets defined in terms of inequality—its opposite. Commonly, groups are defined along some demographic characteristic: social class, race, gender, ethnicity, language background. Aggregate differences among these groups are then explored using some educationally important index. Group differences are interpreted to demonstrate the existence of inequality. Equality, therefore, is defined implicitly as the absence of those differences" (p. 69).

Secada's definition of educational equality, while succinct, does not reflect the multiple interpretations of the concept in the broader literature of antidiscrimination law. The legal construction of educational equality has a long history in American jurisprudence. (See, e.g., *Roberts v. City of Boston*, 1850.) According to Crenshaw (1988), there are two distinct rhetorical visions of equality of opportunity in the body of antidiscrimination law—*expansive* and *restrictive*. The expansive view stresses equality as a *result* and looks to create real consequences for oppressed people. It interprets the goal of antidiscrimination law as the elimination of substantive conditions of subordination, and it seeks to incorporate the power of the courts to achieve the goal of eradicating the effects of oppression. Thus, educational equality built on an expansive view would stress results.

The restrictive vision, which coexists with the expansive view, treats equality of opportunity as a *process*, minimizing the importance of actual results. The goal of antidiscrimination law, according to this vision, is to prevent future injustice rather than to redress current products of past wrongdoing. Thus, educational equality built on the restrictive view would stress inputs or process, while largely ignoring results.

Because antidiscrimination law contains both the expansive and the restrictive view, educational equality can refer to either. This duality of meaning suggests that politicians and policy makers can claim to support the notion of educational equality by designing policies built on the expansive or restrictive view.

Crenshaw's (1988) constructs of expansive and restrictive visions of equality provide a framework to explore legal and policy-related development and implementation. Desegregation and the *Brown v. Board of Education* (1954) decision together are a case in point. Using Crenshaw's constructs, Tate, Ladson-Billings, and Grant (1993) analyzed the *Brown* decision, in part, to determine the vision of equality associated with the law. More specifically, they remarked on the evolution of educational equality in the courts:

> The legal construction of equality in education always began with the assumption that school inequality did not exist and that it was the plaintiff's responsibility to produce contradictory evidence. Using this method, the court constructed a model of equality by validating educational inequality. There was, and still is, a limitation with using an indirect mathematical proof to achieve equality in a social context. It is a very static process, making it nearly impossible to capture and change dynamic social realities. . . . Under our system, the courts assume that inequality does not exist, and thus the burden of providing contradictory evidence or, in essence, the construction of a new model of equality rests with the citizen who is compelled to challenge the school system's policy. The use of an indirect mathematical proof to both legally and socially construct equality was, and continues to be, a time-consuming and restrictive process. Further, the indirect method is not an expansive process that initiates the construction of equality in education or anticipates policies that promote inequalities and prevent their implementation. Nor has this method framed equality as a result. Rather, equality is viewed as a process. (p. 264)

Educational equality is a fluid concept that changes over time. That is, inputs and outcomes of importance change with new insights into the educational process. Educators, researchers, and policy makers should be mindful of this evolution and its implications for students. *WFT*

References

Brown v. Board of Education of Topeka, 347 U. S. 483 (1954).

Coleman, J. (1967). *The concept of equality of educational opportunity*. Baltimore, MD: John Hopkins University Press. ERIC Document Reproduction Service No. ED 012275.

Crenshaw, K. W. (1988). Race, reform, and retrenchment: Transformation and legitimation in anti-discrimination law. *Harvard Law Review, 101*, 1331–87.

Roberts v. City of Boston, 59 Mass. (5. Cush.) 198 (1850).

Secada, W. G. (1989). Educational equity versus equality of education: An alternative conception. In W. G. Secada (Ed.), *Equity in Education* (pp. 68–88). London: Falmer Press.

Tate, W. F., Ladson-Billings, G., Grant, C. A. (1993). The *Brown* decision revisited: Mathematizing social problems. *Educational Policy, 7*, 255–75.

Educational Equity

In its broadest definition *equity* refers to the state or quality of being equal or fair and is considered synonymous with fairness, rights, rectitude, honesty, uprightness, justness, or justice (*Webster's Collegiate Dictionary*). Equity also has several legal definitions, including an equitable claim or right, and the formal system of legal and procedural rules and doctrines according to which justice is administered (within certain legal limits of jurisdiction).

Opposites of equity include bias, prejudice, inequality or unequal treatment, and injustice. Since inequity can be defined as injustice and injustice can be defined as social disparity or lack of proper proportion or distribution, it can be argued that equity requires social parity, balanced proportion, and redistribution of power, access, rights, and opportunities.

In educational contexts, equity has been used in contrast to "equal opportunity," with opportunity being viewed as a necessary, but not sufficient, step for educational equity to occur. For example, equal opportunity might provide that all children get "in the door" of an integrated or fully inclusive classroom. Educational equity, in contrast, would not only get the children "in the door" but would also address children's cultural and individual differences in curriculum and instruction. In an equitable classroom, activities would be adapted to meet the learning challenges of children with developmental differences, and teachers would not make assumptions that all children had similar middle-class, dominant culture background experiences and would not make academic "success" dependent on these experiences. In other words, equal opportunity is the first step toward educational equity.

Historically, educational equity has often been discussed in terms of its absence or as educational inequity. From Frederick Douglass and W. E. B. Dubois' discussion of the illegal literacy activities of those teaching African Americans to read, to the protracted desegregation battles in public education, educational equity has often been discussed in terms of parity, equal access to comparable or the same educational services and opportunities, and the struggle to move away from an educational apartheid of "separate and unequal" schools in the United States.

The landmark decision of *Brown v. Board of Education* is an example of a legal ruling in support of educational equity which also points to the complexity of legal attempts to remedy this separate and unequal or inequitable school funding and access across not only color but also class and ability/disability lines. More recently, the issues of least restrictive environment, the regular education initiative, and the full inclusion movement have sought to address the educational inequities facing students with disabilities. Most recently, issues of educational equity have been reflected in legislation, such as that passed by the Commonwealth of Massachusetts, which bars school practices that discriminate against gay, lesbian, and bisexual students or their parents or guardians.

In contemporary usage, particularly in (some) multicultural or antioppression contexts, it is important to distinguish equity from "fairness," because members of the dominant culture have at times co-opted the term *fairness* in deceptive ways that are actually inequitable. For example, some argue that affirmative action and equal opportunity policies are unfair and that reverse discrimination is possible. Many working in Civil Rights and doing antioppression work would choose the word "equity" over "fairness," given the inherent inequity of the dominant power structures. Fairness is often used as a term applied to individual situations, whereas equity is more frequently used to denote the situation of status of a group (i.e., by gender, race/ethnicity, ability, age, religion, and sexual orientation).

In their book *Choosing Equality: The Case for Democratic Schooling,* Bastian, et al. (1985), discuss "elitism versus equity" and argue that in the eyes of many neo-conservatives, "the egalitarian goals of education are reduced to their narrowest definition. Uniformity and standardization are considered sufficient conditions for equality" (p. 21). This definition is highly problematic, given that it assumes that all children are similarly supported with resources for learning and other conditions that can optimize learning, and that all are equally "prepared" for success in school, an assumption which books such as Jonathan Kozol's *Savage Inequalities* (1991), Valerie Polakow's *Lives on the Edge* (1993), and other studies of societal stratification and the funding-based inequities of public education have documented.

Whether using the existential narratives of such texts or more instrumental policy arguments (e.g., statistics about the resources available or comparisons of district per-pupil expenditures), the educational and structural inequities in the U.S. are now well recognized and accepted. In fact, the most recent data indicate that the gap between rich and poor is greater in the U.S. than in any other nation.

This fundamental inequality, reflected in the dramatic social and economic stratification in the U.S., is directly related to the issue and working definition of educational equity. Sonia Nieto (1996) states that "multicultural education cannot be understood in a vacuum," and defines educational worth in terms of "raising the achievement of all students and thus providing them with an *equitable* (emphasis added) and high-quality education" and "providing . . . an apprenticeship in the opportunity to become critical and productive members of a democratic society" (p. 9).

Thus, a working definition of educational equity might be equality of access to and opportunities for meaningful, authentic learning experiences, which are inclusive of learners from diverse backgrounds, which are relevant to learners, and which benefit from comparable fiscal and physical resources and support regardless of the backgrounds (e.g., race, gender, class) of learners. Educational equity includes the right to learn in the least restrictive environment in which individual needs (and, particularly in the case of younger learners, family needs) and potential are addressed.

Educational equity also includes the right to learn in an environment in which students (and families) are not discriminated against because of their race/ethnicity, language, religion, gender, class, family makeup, living situation, physical and mental abilities or limitations, or sexual orientation (of students or their parents or guardians). This inclusive and empowering state of learning potential is a goal to which all educational settings must aspire to achieve and actively pursue through policies and practices in a timely fashion.

Finally, educational equity includes the protection of the rights of children and youth, as specified in the United Nations Convention for the Rights of the Child, a document that asserts the right of all children to be protected against abuse, neglect, child labor, violence, exploitation, and the right to have basic needs of survival, health, food, clothing, shelter, and education met.

In summary, educational equity can be defined as follows: Justice and respect for individual and group rights, which actively promotes the view that all persons are equal, personally and socially, although living within a fundamentally unequal, stratified, and biased dominant culture. Thus, the pursuit of equity in education is a dynamic process that recognizes contextual realities (e.g., institutionalized racism and sexism) and barriers to the achievement of a truly just distribution of power and opportunity, and works constantly to name, address, and dismantle systems of oppression which keep inequality in place. *BBS* • *See also* **Inclusive Education**

References

Bastian, A., Fruchter, N., Gittell, M., Greer, C., & Haskins, K. (1985). *Choosing equality: The case for democratic schooling*. Philadelphia: Temple University Press.

Kozol, J. (1991). *Savage inequalities: Children in America's schools*. New York: Crown Publishers.

Nieto, S. (1996). *Affirming diversity: The sociopolitical context of multicultural education* (2nd ed.). Chicago: University of Chicago Press.

Polakow, V. (1993). *Lives on the edge: Single mothers and their children in the other America*. Chicago: University of Chicago Press.

Education That Is Multicultural and Social Reconstructionist *See* Multicultural Education, Approaches To

Empowering School Culture *See* Multicultural Education, Dimensions Of

English as a Second Language

From a global perspective, the United States falls at one end of a global continuum of contexts in which English is learned—a continuum that ranges from settings in which English is the native language of most of its population to countries in which English is acquired as a foreign language such as Japan, Italy, Egypt, Brazil, and Venezuela. Given this spectrum of language settings, in 1976 Alatis broadly defined English as a Second Language (ESL) as "the field of teaching English to speakers of other languages" (TESOL position paper, p. 2). In the same year TESOL (Teachers of English to Speakers of Other Languages), the international organization of educators in this field, recognized that implementation of ESL instruction for language minority students in the United States requires (1) *culture* or the "incorporation of the cultural aspects of the students' backgrounds into meaningful language learning experiences," (2) *language skills and development* or the teaching of "vocabulary and structures relevant to students' learning experiences," and (3) *content-area instruction* or the "application of English as a second language techniques to content areas taught through the second language" (p. 2).

Today's vision of English as a second language for students in the United States is far reaching and all encompassing because "the ultimate goal of teaching ESL to non-English-speaking students is to give them the benefits of a challenging and comprehensive general education not simply to teach them English" (Genesee, 1994/1995, p. 3). TESOL's new standards for effective English-as-a-second-language instruction for K–12 students are consistent with the principle that the educational needs of language minority students are academic, cultural, and linguistic. Instructional goals for ESL embody participation in a variety of sociocultural environments, effective communication in English, and the use of English for academic achievement (UCLMRI, 1995).

English-as-a-second-language programs are diverse and complex. They differ with respect to features such as the allocation of time, the language(s) and culture(s) served, proficiency levels in English as well as in the primary language(s), curriculum emphases, and the program model (Tedick, et al., 1993). Scheduling and grouping at both elementary and secondary levels vary considerably. There are self-contained classrooms that serve newcomers, pull-in programs that bring support services into the regular classroom, and pull-out programs that provide a period of individual or small-group ESL instruction outside of the mainstream classroom. In English language development programs, teachers with specialized training are assigned to teach classes consisting primarily of ESL students (or those who speak a nonstandard dialect). Such programs offer a full curriculum while promoting English language and literacy development. Sheltered language, sheltered content, or language-sensitive classes provide access to content instruction that is both cognitively demanding and age appropriate, using strategies and techniques sensitive to students' limitations in language proficiency and the demands of language in the content area (Chamot & O'Malley, 1994).

In response to sociopolitical preferences, limited resources, increasingly multilingual student populations, and insufficient numbers of fully qualified bilingual teachers, many school districts implement ESL rather than bilingual programs, which provide instruction in a student's primary language (Tedick, et al., 1993). Among the issues that divide educators and policy makers with respect to ESL are the role of primary language development and the use of pull-out programs providing only limited support for language minority students. On the whole, however, educators have been able to agree that English as a second language is an essential and integral part of programs designed to promote the language proficiency and academic development of language minority students: "English as a second language is a component of virtually all bilingual education programs in the United States. Owing to the shortage of bilingual teachers, for many LEP [limited-English-proficient] children it is the only special assistance available" (Crawford, 1991, p. 177). *HH See also* **Bilingual Education; Limited English Proficiency (LEP)**

References

Chamot, A. U., & O'Malley, J. M. (1994). *The CALLA handbook*. Reading, MA: Addison-Wesley.

Crawford, J. (1991). *Bilingual education: History, politics, theory and practice* (2nd ed.). Los Angeles: Bilingual Educational Services.

Dubin, F., & Olshtain, E. (1986). *Course design: Developing programs and materials for language learning*. New York: Cambridge University Press.

Genesee, F. (1994/1995). ESL and classroom teacher collaborations: Building futures together [President's message]. *TESOL Matters, 4*(6), 3.

Peregoy, S. F., & Boyle, O. F. (1993). *Reading, writing and learning in ESL: A resource book for K–8 teachers*. White Plains, NY: Longman.

Tedick, D. J., Walker, C. L., Lange, D. L., Paige, R. M., & Jorstad, H. L. (1993). Second language education in tomorrow's schools. In G. Gunterman (Ed.), *Developing language teachers for a changing world* (pp. 43–75). Lincolnwood, IL: National Textbook Company.

Teachers of English to Speakers of Other Languages (TESOL). (1976). *Position paper on the role of English as a second language in bilingual education*. Washington, DC: Georgetown University.

University of California Linguistic Minority Research Institute (UCLMRI). (1995). TESOL developing standards for K–12. *LMRI News, 4*(5), 3.

English Only/English Plus *See* Official English (English Only) Versus English Plus

Environmental Racism *See* Racism

Equity Pedagogy *See* Multicultural Education, Dimensions Of

Ethnic Identity Theory

Ethnic identity theory refers to the process of defining for oneself the personal significance and social meaning of belonging to a particular ethnic group. The concept of ethnic identity is closely related to *racial identity* and the terms are often used synonymously, although a distinction can be made between the two. Van den Berghe (1967) defines race as "a group that is socially defined but on the basis of *physical* criteria" (i.e., skin color, facial features), whereas an ethnic group is socially defined based on *cultural* criteria (i.e., language, customs, shared history). One may identify as a member of an ethnic group (e.g., Irish, Italian) but may not think of oneself in racial terms (e.g., as White). On the other hand, one may recognize the personal significance of racial group membership (i.e., think of oneself as

Black) but may not consider ethnic identity (e.g., West Indian) to be particularly meaningful.

Both racial and ethnic categories are socially constructed, and social definitions of these categories have changed over time. For example, Alba (1990) points out that the high rates of intermarriage and the dissolution of other social boundaries among European ethnic groups in the United States have reduced the salience of ethnic identity for these groups. However, Alba argues that a new ethnic identity is emerging, that of European American. When others respond to the individual based on his or her racial categorization rather than particular ethnic group, racial identity may be more salient for that individual than ethnic identity. However, ethnic identity and racial identity may intersect. For example, dark-skinned Puerto Ricans may identify culturally as Puerto Rican and yet be racially categorized by others as Black on the basis of physical appearance. Within a pluralistic society, ethnic or racial identity is typically most salient for those individuals belonging to ethnic or racial groups that have been historically disadvantaged or marginalized within the society.

Much of the current research on ethnic identity development theory can be found in the counseling psychology literature. The *Handbook of Multicultural Counseling* (Ponterotto, et al., 1995) provides a comprehensive review of the various ethnic identity models currently in use (e.g., Asian, Hispanic, American Indian, biracial, White). Most of these models have been influenced by the Black racial identity models that were developed in the early 1970s as part of the Black consciousness movement. Most notably, Cross's (1971, revised in 1991) four-stage model of "psychological nigrescence" describes a process of moving from low racial consciousness through a period of active examination of the meaning of Blackness (often precipitated by personally significant encounters with racism), to the internalization of a positively defined, stable Black identity. Parham (1989) has extended Cross's model across the lifespan, emphasizing a spiral, rather than linear, progression through the stages. Hardiman (1982, 1994) and Helms (1990) have also used the stages construct to describe White identity development.

While most ethnic identity models describe adult attitudes and behaviors, Jean Phinney's research (1989, 1992) focuses on adolescent identity development. Using Erikson's (1968) work on adolescent ego-identity formation as her theoretical starting point, Phinney has investigated ethnic identity development among diverse groups of high school students. She describes a three-stage progression from an unexamined ethnic identity through a period of exploration to an achieved, committed ethnic identity.

Another strand of research on ethnic identity theory is derived from Tajfel's (1978) social identity theory, which considers ethnic identity as a component of an individual's self-concept. (See Phinney, 1990, or Gonzales

& Cauce, 1995, for a more in-depth discussion.) Social identity theory predicts that when one perceives his or her social identity as problematic (because of low status, for example), the individual will seek to change group affiliation, if possible, or change his or her evaluation of the group to which they belong. As with the other models, this version of ethnic identity theory highlights the active role of the individual in constructing a positive group identity. *BDT*

References

Alba, A. (1990). *Ethnic identity: The transformation of White America*. New Haven, CT: Yale University Press.

Cross, W. E., Jr. (1971). The Negro-to-black conversion experience: Toward a psychology of black liberation. *Black World, 20*(9), 13–27.

———. (1991). *Shades of black: Diversity in African-American identity*. Philadelphia: Temple University Press.

Erikson, E. (1968). *Identity: Youth and crisis*. New York: Norton.

Gonzales, N. A., & Cauce, A. M. (1995). Ethnic identity and multicultural competence: Dilemmas and challenges for minority youth. In W. D. Hawley & A. W. Jackson (Eds.), *Toward a common destiny: Improving race and ethnic relations in America*. San Francisco: Jossey-Bass.

Hardiman, R. (1982). White identity development: A process-oriented model for describing the racial consciousness of White Americans. Ph.D. diss., University of Massachusetts, Amherst.

———. (1994). White racial identity development in the United States. In E. P. Salett & D. R. Koslow (Eds.), *Race, ethnicity and self: Identity in multicultural perspective*. Washington, DC: National MultiCultural Institute.

Helms, J. E. (1990). *Black and White racial identity: Theory, research and practice*. Westport, CT: Greenwood Press.

Parham, T. A. (1989). Cycles of psychological nigrescence. *The Counseling Psychologist, 17*(2), 187–226.

Phinney, J. S. (1989). Stages of ethnic identity in minority group adolescents. *Journal of Early Adolescence, 9*, 34–39.

———. (1990). Ethnic identity in adolescents and adults: Review of research. *Psychological Bulletin, 108*(3), 499–514.

———. (1992). The multigroup ethnic identity measure: A new scale for use with diverse groups. *Journal of Adolescent Research, 7*, 156–76.

Ponterotto, J. G., Casas, J. M., Suzuki, L. A., & Alexander, C. M. (Eds.). (1995). *Handbook of multicultural counseling*. Thousand Oaks, CA: Sage.

Tajfel, H. (1978). *The social psychology of minorities*. New York: Minority Rights Group.

van den Berghe, P. L. (1967). *Race and racism*. New York: Wiley.

Ethnicity *See* Ethnic Studies

Ethnic Studies

It is virtually impossible to establish the parameters of the academic programs labeled ethnic studies in the United States without first confronting several quite disparate definitions of the concept of *ethnicity*. Significant differences concerning the definition exist among the public-at-large as well as within and between various fields of academic endeavor. Among the general population one trend has been to associate ethnicity with diverse groups who have been somehow identified as physically or culturally different from mainstream culture. In terms of everyday talk ethnicity is something to be ascribed to people of color and those who are linguistically diverse, not to members of the dominant culture. In this context the term *ethnic studies* typically refers to the study of diverse groups living in the United States, in particular, such politically significant groups as African Americans and Latinos. Ethnic and multicultural studies programs are often referred to interchangeably. The purpose of these studies is to acknowledge the cultural significance of diverse groups to American macroculture as well as to increase understanding of their history, traditions, and behavioral characteristics.

Another, but quite different, perception often found among the public-at-large in the United States associates ethnicity with diverse international populations. That is, groups that may well be the cultural majority of their respective nations are perceived to be *ethnic*. In this sense, *intercultural, global*, and *(multi)ethnic* studies are viewed as synonymous. Lasting peace through increased global understanding is a major purpose of these studies.

Regardless of the interpretations associated with ethnic studies, the development of respect and appreciation among disparate cultural groups for each other is an ever-present goal. While the nature of ethnic studies programs supported by universities remains somewhat obscure, scholars have worked throughout the twentieth century to refine their conception of ethnicity. That the members of an ethnic group share cultural norms and patterns of behavior is widely accepted. How and why that sharing occurs is a matter of considerable discussion.

Some sociologists have suggested that the conscious awareness of one's membership in an ethnic group is a necessary attribute of ethnicity (Francis, 1947; Gordon, 1964). Rotheram and Phinney (1987) have even suggested that an ethnic group may be established by any collection of people who view themselves as having common attributes and who are willing to call themselves an ethnic group. This means that being a member of a minority group is not at all a condition for being part of an ethnic group. Self-identification is sufficient. Drieger (1989) has elaborated on the meaning of ethnic identity in a somewhat different fashion by relating identification with a cultural group to using of the group's language; sharing its religious traditions, values, and historical symbols; and participating in its educational institutions. This position logically leads to an understanding of ethnic identity as a largely involuntary phenomenon. The educator James Banks (1994) has pursued the idea of ethnic identification from still another perspective by suggesting that schools "within a pluralistic democratic nation should help ethnic students develop clarified, reflective, and positive ethnic identification" (p. 55). From this perspective ethnic identity may develop in ways that are harmful to the ethnic group but that may be repaired by the cogent efforts of society's schools.

In all of the preceding instances the conception of ethnicity has been closely linked to the individual's more-or-less voluntary, more-or-less conscious identification with an ethnic group. However, it is entirely possible to perceive the development of ethnicity as a biological-cultural phenomenon in which both identification with and voluntary participation in cultural patterns and beliefs are incidental, albeit significant, by-products of ethnicity (Longstreet, 1978). That is, ethnicity is conceived to be the part of cultural development that occurs prior to the biological onset of a child's abstract intellectual power, and, therefore, prior to the child being able to evaluate or control the cultural norms and patterns being learned. Ethnic identity is involuntary and unconscious, as is most of our development in our very youngest years. Ethnicity is thus something everyone has and everyone must struggle to fully understand about themselves and their own ethnic group as well as about other ethnic groups. Without referring to the biological stages of intellectual development, anthropologist Edward T. Hall (1977) makes a considerable case for deeply embedded cultural learnings that "are relegated to that part of the consciousness over which people have little or no control" (p. 152). Hall distinguishes between individual and cultural types of identification, with the latter being more likely to be beyond the realm of awareness than the former.

Ethnic studies in U.S. academic institutions typically function as historical, sociological, cultural, and artistic studies of and about specific cultural groups. Questions about the nature of ethnicity may or may not be explored in such courses. Ethnic studies courses often supplement other course offerings such as U.S. history, English literature, art, or music, which may have a more Eurocentric focus. *WSL*

References

Banks, J. A. (1994). *Multiethnic education: Theory and practice* (3rd ed.). Boston: Allyn & Bacon.

Drieger, L. (1989). *The ethnic factor: Identity in diversity*. Toronto: McGraw-Hill Ryerson.

Francis, E. K. (1947). The nature of the ethnic group. *American Journal of Sociology, 52*(5), 393–400.

Gordon, M. M. (1964). *Assimilation in American life: The role of race, religion, and national origins.* New York: Oxford University Press.

Hall, E. T. (1977). *Beyond culture.* Garden City, New York: Anchor Books.

Longstreet, W. S. (1978). *Aspects of ethnicity: Understanding differences in pluralistic classrooms.* New York: Teachers College Press.

Rotheram, J., & Phinney, J. (Eds.) (1987). *Children's ethnic socialization: Pluralism and development.* Beverly Hills, CA: Sage Publications

Ethno-Aesthetics

The concept of ethno-aesthetics emerged in the 1920s (Clifford, 1988) when primarily Western scholars categorized the artistic values of specific ethnic or cultural groups as revealed in their literatures, arts, performances, and music. Predominantly Western anthropologists, historians, and critics have used ethno-aesthetics to describe, interpret, classify, and judge the artistic communication and aesthetic preferences of indigenous Asians, Africans, Australians, Oceanians, Arcticans, and Americans, as well as people of color in the West.

Richard Flores, an anthropologist working in performance studies, researches Los Pastores, a group that performs folk dramas in San Antonio, Texas. Their "values or judgments come from different aesthetic criteria" or "cultural sensitivities," and their ethno-aesthetics are enacted by "particular performances or actions" which have evolved over time (Flores, 1995).

Moyo Okediji, a Yoruba artist and art historian, applies Yoruba-based ethno-aesthetics to the art of African American artists Jeff Donaldson and Muneer Bahauddeen as well as to his own acrylic paintings. Although each has studied Western formalism, all have elected to refer to Yoruba aesthetics and iconographies to "uncover and recover their collective history, based on individualistic exploration of the self and the community" (Okediji, 1995, p. 3).

According to Thompson (1973) many West African and Afro-American art forms impart "an aesthetic of the cool," that is, "the primary metaphorical extension of this term in most of these cultures seems to be *control*, having the value of *composure* in the individual context, *social stability* in the context of the group. These concepts are often linked to the sacred usage of . . . substances drenched with associations of coolness and cleanliness . . . as powers which purify men and women" (p. 40).

Biodun Jeyifo (1995), a Nigerian Marxist theater critic, argues that

> Ethno-aesthetics can hardly be found in any pure form. . . . Cultures and ethnic groups, which have been subjected to cultural domination by external colonial or imperial forces, face the threat of cultural genocide

or ethnicide . . . It takes more subtle and complex forms but it hasn't stopped. I know many people in Nigeria who deliberately work within what they identify as the classical traditions of the Yoruba art forms. . . . [but] there have been massive historical and economic pressures on these traditions which have transformed them.

Amalia Mesa-Bains, et al., (1993) recommend a deep examination of Chicano cultural developments corresponding to the complex and contra-dictory experiences that individuals negotiate: nationality, sexuality, lan-guage, class, citizenship, culture, geography, personality, family, and colo-nial histories. Chicanos' resistance to exploitive Anglo values often demands inventive cultural resiliency.

Freida High (1995), an African American artist and art historian (conver-sation, 9/5/95), Moyo Okediji (1995), and Henry Drewal, an Africanist art historian, believe that *all* world art reflects ethnic biases. "Ethno-aesthetics should be applied as a term everywhere in the world since all people create their sense of ethnicity or cultural identity. Culture may be viewed as an aesthetic system writ large" (Drewal, 1995).

Kathryn Morgan (1995), a feminist philosopher, raises critical reserva-tions when the term is applied to a group as a whole so that members (e.g., women) are "denied access to multiple forms of literacy which are the preconditions of artistic production . . . or when their aesthetic work is not considered legitimate art (such as weaving)." (1995).

While the concept of *ethno-aesthetics* may be useful when groups are carefully contextualized, scholars find it problematic when researchers essentialize any group's artistic values, ignore the ramifications of historical power relationships, dismiss multiple forces acting on and within cultures, present a Eurocentric representation with ethnographic authority (Clifford, 1988, p. 24), exclude nonethnic Western art and regard ethnic art as inferior, deny members access to artistic production or legitimacy, neglect the dy-namic nature of the arts, and bypass individual artists who deviate from so-called cultural norms. *NP*

References

Clifford, J. (1988). *The predicament of culture: Twentieth-century ethnography, literature and art.* Cambridge, MA: Harvard University Press.

Drewal, H. (1995). Telephone conversation with author. September 6.

Flores, R. (1995). Telephone conversation with author. September 6.

High, F. (1995). Telephone conversation with author. September 5.

Jeyifo, B. (1995). Telephone conversation with author. September 6.

Mesa-Bains, A., Arceo-Frutos, R., & Guzman, J. (1993). *Art the other Mexico: Sources and meanings.* Chicago: Mexican Fine Arts Center Museum.

Morgan, K. (1995). Telephone conversation with author. September 16.

Okediji, M. (1995). Semioptics of amnesia: Yoruba images in the work of Jeff Donaldson, Howardena Pindell and Muneer Bahauddeen. Ph.D. diss. Madison: University of Wisconsin.

———. (1995). Telephone conversation with author. June 1.

Thompson, R. F. (1973). An aesthetic of the cool. *African Arts*, 7(1), 40–43, 64–66, 89.

Ethnocentrism

The *Random House Dictionary of the English Language* (1987) defines *ethnocentrism* as "the belief in the inherent superiority of one's own ethnic group or culture" and "the tendency to view alien groups or cultures from the perspective of one's own" (p. 665). Some scholars in the field of multicultural education and other fields have written definitions of ethnocentrism that are consistent with typical dictionary definitions. For example, Sumner (1940) defines *ethnocentrism* as a "view of things in which one's own group is the center of everything, and all others are scaled and rated with reference to it" (p. 13). Biehler and Snowman (1993) define ethnocentrism as "the belief that one's culture is superior to other cultures" (p. 240). Dictionary definitions tend not to describe ethnocentrism as a narrow-minded worldview that predisposes people to make judgments or develop negative views about other ethnic and cultural groups.

However, other scholars in the field of multicultural education have expanded these brief dictionary definitions of ethnocentrism to include four points that are important in understanding ethnocentrism as it has evolved as an academic term used in the fields of education and such behavioral sciences as sociology, psychology, and anthropology: (1) Ethnocentrism tends toward the closed-minded belief that one's own culturally learned norms, because they are believed to be valid and superior, should be the standards for other cultures; (2) ethnocentrism as a worldview encompasses the belief that other cultures or ethnic groups are inferior if they do not meet the norms of one's own cultural or ethnic group; (3) ethnocentrism is a worldview that limits one's ability to perceive other ethnic groups without bias or to relate to other cultures respectfully; and (4) ethnocentrism includes the belief that other cultures or ethnic groups, being inferior, should at best be changed by education or coercion to adopt the norms of one's own culture and at worst should be denigrated, segregated, discriminated against, and oppressed. One or more of these points form the basis of definitions written by several scholars in the field of education and in the behavioral and social sciences. For example, Stopsky and Lee (1994) define ethnocentrism as "the view that the attitudes, behaviors and way of life of one group are more valuable than those of other cultures and should be uncritically and unquestioningly accepted" (p. 429). Similarly, Baruth and Manning (1992) define ethnocentrism as "the belief that one's cultural ways are not only valid and superior to those of others, but also universally applicable in evaluating and judging human behavior" (p. 156). Tiedt and Tiedt (1990) define ethnocentrism as "the centrality of dominance of the national group identity that may limit an individual's perspective" (p. 11). Gollnick and Chinn (1994) define ethnocentrism as "the inability to view other cultures as viable alternatives for organizing reality" (p. 9). To these definitions, Nieto (1996) adds that ethnocentrism is "discriminatory beliefs and behaviors based on ethnic differences" (p. 306). Equating ethnocentrism to "cultural arrogance," Adler (1993) describes ethnocentrism as "a dangerous form of provincial naïveté" (p. 41).

The following description by Pai (1990), however, includes all four points and provides a comprehensive contemporary definition of ethnocentrism as the term has come to be used in the field of multicultural education:

> Ethnocentrism, the belief in the superiority of our own culture, leads us to judge others in terms of our own cultural norms and inclines us to conclude that those who do not conform to our norms must be stupid, depraved, irresponsible, psychopathic, inferior, or sinful to a point beyond all redemption. When the dominant group in a society adopts the posture that its own set of values constitutes the only idealized norm in the society, the ethnic practices or traits of minority cultures are likely to be seen as deficient patterns that must be corrected either through education or coercion. (p. 34)

GPS • *See also* **Eurocentrism**

References

Adler, S. (1993). *Multicultural communications skills in the classroom*. Boston: Allyn & Bacon.

Baruth, L. G., & Manning, M. L. (1992). *Multicultural education and children and adolescents*. Needham Heights, MA: Allyn & Bacon.

Biehler, R. F., & Snowman, J. (1993). *Psychology applied to teaching*. Boston: Houghton Mifflin.

Gollnick, D. M., & Chinn, P. C. (1994). *Multicultural education in a pluralistic society* (4th ed.). New York: Macmillan College.

Nieto, S. (1996). *Affirming diversity: The sociopolitical context of multicultural education* (2nd ed.). White Plains, NY: Longman.

Pai, Y. (1990). *Cultural foundations of education*. New York: Macmillan.

Random House Dictionary of the English Language (2nd ed.). (1987). New York: Random House.

Stopsky, F., & Lee, S. S. (1994). *Social studies in a global society*. Albany, NY: Delmar.

Sumner, W. G. (1940). *Folkways*. Boston: Ginn.

Tiedt, P. L., & Tiedt, I. M. (1990). *Multicultural teaching: A handbook of activities, information, and resources*. Needham Heights, MA: Allyn & Bacon.

Ethnography

For some the term *ethnography* is loosely applied to any qualitative research project whose purpose is rich description. A more precise definition, rooted in ethnography's disciplinary home of anthropology, is that it is a qualitative research process and product whose aim is cultural interpretation. The ethnographer goes beyond reporting events and details of experience and works to explain how these represent the webs of meaning in which we live.

Ethnographers generate understandings of culture through portrayal of an epic perspective, often described as the "insider's point of view." This understanding is developed through close exploration of three sources of data. The first, long-term engagement in the field setting, is called *participant observation*. This term represents the dual role of the ethnographer. To develop an understanding of what it is like to live in a setting, the researcher must become a participant in the life of the setting while also maintaining the stance of an observer, or someone who describes the experience. The second source is interviews, which provide targeted data-collection opportunities by asking specific but open-ended questions to elicit cultural knowledge. Finally, researchers collect representative artifacts that embody characteristics of the topic of interest. Using these data sources as a foundation, the ethnographer relies on a cultural frame of analysis to infer tacit meanings shared by the group.

Developed within the field of cultural anthropology, ethnography was initially employed to describe the life patterns of colonized peoples far from the ethnographer's homeland. The practice of ethnography was moved closer to home by the Chicago School of Sociology in the 1920s. Studies focused on the exploration of groups in urban settings—hobos, men on the street corner, alcoholics. Key to this early work was cultural comparison—groups were studied that were different from the predominantly White, middle-class male anthropologists who undertook the work. Ethnographers began to focus on education in the 1970s when the area of anthropology and education was formed (see, e.g., Spindler, 1982). Ethnographic work was instrumental in bringing to light new ways of looking at cultural discontinuity in education, at variation within racial and ethnic group school performance and cultural meanings for schooling, and at resistance to power structures.

Today ethnography could be seen as a family of approaches ranging from descriptive accounts of cultural groups to activist-oriented critical ethnographies whose aim is empowerment through the study of domination and potential sources of resistance. The incorporation of theoretical frameworks such as feminist and Marxist theories into the traditional anthropological notions of culture have broadened the terrain addressed by ethnography and have opened new questions and methodological concerns. Ethnographic examination of cultural practices can be a rich source of reflection on bridging the needs of diverse students and the schools in which they learn. *MEG*

Reference

Spindler, G. (Ed.). (1982). *Doing the ethnography of schooling.* New York: Holt, Rinehart & Winston.

Ethnomathematics

Ethnomathematics is the study of the mathematical practices used by specific cultural groups in the course of dealing with their daily environment and activities. For example, the manner in which professional basketball players estimate angles and distances differs greatly from the corresponding manner used by truck drivers. Both professional basketball players and truck drivers are identifiable cultural groups that use mathematics in their daily work. Similarily, African American quilters may develop and use mathematical patterns that are different from those of factory stitchers. All of these groups have their own language and specific ways of obtaining mathematical estimates; ethnomathematicians study their techniques.

The prefix *ethno-* refers to identifiable cultural groups, such as national-tribal societies, labor groups, children of a certain age bracket, and professional classes, and includes ideologies, language, daily practices, and their specific ways of reasoning and inferring. The prefix *mathema-* means to explain, understand, and manage reality, specifically by ciphering, counting, measuring, classifying, ordering, inferring, and modeling patterns arising in the environment. The suffix *-tics* means art or technique.

Thus, ethnomathematics is the study of mathematical techniques used by identifiable cultural groups to understand, explain, and manage problems and activities arising in their own environment. *GFG*

Eurocentrism

The *Random House Dictionary of the English Language* (1987) does not list the noun *Eurocentrism* but does define the adjective *Eurocentric.* Historically, scholars in the field of multicultural education and the behavioral and social sciences have tended to use the adjective *Eurocentric* (e.g., Eurocentric worldviews, Eurocentric point of view, Eurocentric curriculum) more frequently than the noun *Eurocentrism.* Eurocentric is defined as "centered on Europe and Europeans" and as related to "considering European as focal to world culture, history, economics, etc." (*Random House Dictionary,* 1987, p.

669) or "reflecting the culture and history of ethnic groups of European origin" (Ornstein & Levine, 1987, p. 431). Nieto (1996) defines *Eurocentric curriculum* as "curriculum that focuses on the values, lifestyles, accomplishments, and worldviews of Europeans and/or European Americans" (p. 391). These brief dictionary, textbook, and glossary definitions of Eurocentric are neutral and nonjudgmental and, therefore, do not imply that Eurocentrism is a biased, closed-minded worldview that leads to oppression of non-European peoples or the denigration of non-European cultures, worldviews, and contributions to world civilization.

Modern usage by scholars in the field of multicultural education in the United States indicates that the full meaning of Eurocentrism as a worldview includes several beliefs: (1) belief in the inherent superiority of all things European (i.e., European cultures, perspectives, values, behaviors); (2) belief that these various aspects of European culture are valid universal norms for judging non-European cultures; (3) belief that non-European cultures are inferior; and (4) belief that non-European cultures should be denigrated and dominated. Swartz (1992), for example, captures these points in her definition of Eurocentrism as "a hegemonic or dominant worldview that exclusively values European culture, and denigrates and subordinates the cultures of peoples from all other lands and origins" (p. 35). GPS   • *See also* **Ethnocentrism**

References

Nieto, S. (1996). *Affirming diversity: The sociopolitical context of multicultural education* (2nd ed.). White Plains, NY: Longman.

Ornstein, A. C., & Levine, D. U. (1987). *Foundations of Education* (5th ed.). Boston: Houghton Mifflin.

Random House Dictionary of the English Language (2nd ed.). (1987). New York: Random House.

Swartz, E. (1992). Multicultural education: From a compensatory to a scholarly foundation. In C. A. Grant (Ed.), *Research and multicultural education* (pp. 32–43). London: Falmer Press.

The Fantasy Heritage

The fantasy heritage, as first proposed by Carey McWilliams (1948), is a mythical and romanticized view of the sociocultural history of the Spanish-speaking people of the Southwest. This fantasy heritage, practiced since the mid-1800s, exists today and is epitomized by the Spanish Days Fiesta held in August in Santa Barbara, California, and similar events throughout the Southwest. The fiesta is a sublimated pastiche of stereotypes: Spanish costumes, flamenco, castanets, and horse-riding *caballeros* mostly impersonated by Anglo Americans. This construction originated during the transition of government under the terms of the Treaty of Guadalupe Hidalgo of 1848, when Mexico ceded a vast territory to the United States including California, Arizona, New Mexico, and Texas. Although the treaty provided specific guarantees for the property and political rights of the native population, the right to retain their language, religion, and culture, as well as the Mexican population, has been socially, culturally, and economically marginalized.

This fantasy heritage serves to subordinate the Spanish-speaking people of the Southwest. A technique used to effect this subordination has been to drive a wedge between the native-born and the foreign-born and to cultivate the former at the expense of the latter. To some extent elements of the native-born have encouraged this strategy by seeking to differentiate themselves from the immigrants. By emphasizing the Spanish part of the tradition and consciously repudiating the Mexican-Indian side, it has been possible to rob the Spanish-speaking community, as an ethnic group, of the legitimate representation of their heritage. Even today some aspects of

Anglo-Hispanic relations hinge on the dichotomy between Spanish and Mexican-Indian heritages. This dichotomy between what is Spanish and what is Mexican is a functional, not ornamental, arrangement; its function is to deprive Mexican Americans of an understanding of their history and to keep them in a subordinate position economically, socially, and politically. As McWilliams stated, the cultures of the Southwest before the Anglo American settlements were a trinity, a whole consisting of three intricately interwoven, interpenetrated, thoroughly fused elements: Native Americans, Spanish, and Mexicans. To attempt to unravel any single strand from this pattern and label it *Spanish* or *Hispanic* is to do serious injustice to the Mexicans and Indians through whom, and only through whom, Spanish cultural influences survived in the region.

Today the diversity that exists within the Spanish speaking communities in the United States is complex and multidimensional. The Mexican American population in the Southwest has increased tremendously and has gained political and cultural clout since Carey McWilliam's analysis. In spite of this, the perpetuation of fantasy heritage, enhanced through semiotic subliminal messages of commercialized technological representation, continues to maintain the history of the Mexican culture in the Southwest in negative, stereotypic images. This prevents a legitimate understanding of their existence and a recognition of the cultural fusion produced by history in all aspects of cultural and sociopolitical life in the United States. *SSG*

References

Limon, J. E. (1994). *Dancing with the devil: society and cultural poetics in Mexican-American South Texas*. Madison: University of Wisconsin Press.

McWilliams, C. (1948). *North from Mexico: The Spanish-speaking people of the United States*. New York: Greenwood Press.

Feminism

Feminism is an umbrella concept applied to the politics of the (Western) Women's Movement beginning in the 1960s. It is linked, however, to the ongoing struggle of European-American women's political activism that stretches back to the founding of the nation. *Feminism,* weakly defined, recognizes the historical plight of all or most women under patriarchy; *feminism,* strongly defined, actively attempts to change patriarchal situations and conditions. Feminism is both theory and practice. Feminist theory refers to the intellectual arm of the social movement known as feminism and is included in feminist studies, women's studies, and gender studies. This theoretical rubric is avowedly political.

The history of modern feminism in the United States is in some ways parallel to that of the history of civil rights, but between these two movements there is both solidarity and conflict. During what are known as the first and second Women's Movements there was an active participation in the abolitionist cause beginning around 1830, extending through the fight for women's suffrage around the turn of the century, and ascending to the human rights activism of the mid to late twentieth century. At different historical, social, and political moments, women of color and White women have seen their causes as connected as they engaged in "common struggles": and conversely, as disconnected when their interests have collided.

Historically, within modern capitalism, social structures create a hierarchy of power relations that produce "real" or concrete effects. For example, patriarchy creates complex power relationships between men and women that are further complicated by race, class, sexual preference, and other forms of difference. Historically, men of all racial and class groups have dominated women, but these relationships also are complex as gendered relations differ across racial and class groups—and as groups relate to each other. In the case of a poor, single-parent woman of color, one might identify those power relationships as exponentially harmful.

Also related to the everyday issues of feminist struggle is a symbolic context. This encompasses the "language of practices of women's lives." Theoretically in a patriarchal society, the conceptual categories of "man" and "woman" place women in an unequal, hierarchal dualism that attributes certain positive and powerful meanings to men while simultaneously imputing negative and powerless meanings to women. Thus, even seemingly "neutral" categories, concepts, or terms are charged with meaning about difference, power, and status. Language itself is "sexed" or "gendered" because in many languages there are masculine, feminine, and neutral designations to words. The increasing recognition of the power of language to circumscribe and create relations of power is an important component of contemporary feminist work.

Symbolic discourse practices in feminism also change over time. This change is illustrated in recent denotative and connotative images and impressions about feminism. In the 1960s there were statements such as "the personal is political," consciousness-raising events, and calls for solidarity. Activist "bra-burners" combined their efforts with those fighting for human rights, combating an unjust war, and seeking individual and collective civil rights and opportunities. This early phase of the modern feminist movement was carried out largely by middle-class, White women who "appeared to forget" that their lives were not "the same" as all others and who concentrated only on specific changes in relations with White men.

Some women of color pointed out that solidarity clearly was not inclusive and were suspicious of White women speaking for them. This speaking for all of any group is known by feminists as *essentialism*. The symbolic result of these protests has been a change in feminist discourse to emphasize *difference*. While difference has been championed in theory, in practice it may have meant some harm to the feminist movement. For example, while academic theorists debated the meanings of feminism among themselves, they appeared to lose concern for the everyday lives and issues of everyday women. They also participated in a splintering of the political left that occasioned the rise of the right.

Also part of the contemporary feminist terrain is the concern for representation and identity. Thus, race, class, and sexual preference all have become important constituent components of feminist discourses. In the case of sexuality, the symbolic and theoretical work has been to examine the coupling of *woman* and *heterosexuality* and to recognize variations of men-women relations. Once again, it is important not to view all women as "the same."

Finally, because feminism concerns itself with political work that differentially affects the lives of various women and men, it must be understood as a complex phenomenon. Unpacking this complexity while simultaneously recognizing its complexity is the "job" of feminist theory, and the work of feminist theory and practice cannot be separated. *LS2*

References

Anderson, M., & Collins, P. H. (Eds.). (1992) *Race, class, and gender: An anthology.* Belmont, CA: Wadsworth.

Belenky, M., Clinchy, B., Goldberger, N., & Tarule, J. (1986). *Women's ways of knowing: The development of self, voice, and mind.* New York: Basic Books.

bell hooks. (1984). *Feminist theory: From margin to center.* Boston: South End.

Cohen, M. (1988). The sisterhood: The inside story of the women's movement and the leaders that made it happen. New York: Fawcett Columbine.

Davis, F. (1991). Moving the mountain: The women's movement in America since 1960. New York: Simon & Schuster.

Eisenstein, H. (1983). *Contemporary feminist thought.* Boston: G. K. Hall.

Faludi, S. (1991). Backlash: The undeclared war against American women. New York: Crown.

Friedan, B. (1963). *The feminist mystique.* New York: Norton.

Friedan, B. (1986). *The second stage* (2nd ed.). New York: Summit.

Giddings, P. (1985). When and where I enter: The impact of Black women on race and sex in America. New York: Bantam.

Gilligan, C. (1982). In a different voice: Psychological theory and women's development. Cambridge: Harvard University Press.

Ilich, I. (1982). *Gender.* New York: Pantheon.

Jaggar, A. (1983). *Feminist politics and human nature.* Totowa, NJ: Roman & Allanheld.

Lerner, G. (1986). *The creation of patriarchy* (vol. 1). Oxford: Oxford University Press.

Lerner, G. (1993). The creation of feminist consciousness: From the middle ages to eighteen seventy (vol. 2). Oxford: Oxford University Press.

Mitchell, J., & Oakley, A. (Eds.). (1986). *What is feminism? A re-examination*. New York: Pantheon.

Mohanty, C. T., Russo, A., Torres, L. (Eds.). (1991). *Third world women and the politics of feminism*. Bloomington: Indiana University Press.

Morgan, R. (1970). The anatomy of freedom: An anthology of writings from the women's liberation movement. New York: Vintage.

Phelan, S. (1989). Identity politics: Lesbian feminism and the limits of community. Philadelphia: Temple University Press.

Riley, D. (1988). *"Am I that name?" Feminism and the category of women in history*. Minneapolis: University of Minnesota Press.

Rosaldo, M., & Lamphere, L. (Eds.). (1974). *Women, culture, and society*. Stanford: Stanford University Press.

Scott, J. W. (1988). *Gender and the politics of history*. New York: Columbia University Press.

Steinem, G. (1994). *Moving beyond words*. New York: Holt, Rinehart, and Winston.

Sterling, A. F. (1986). Myths about gender: Biological theories about women and men. New York: Basic Books.

Stone, L. (Ed.). (1994). *The education feminism reader*. New York: Routledge.

Weeden, C. (1987). *Feminist practice and poststructuralist theory*. Oxford: Basil Blackwell.

Wolf, N. (1993). Fire with fire: The new female power and how it will change the twenty-first century. New York: Random House.

Feminist Studies *See* Women's Studies

Feminist Theories

Feminist theories are designed with two general purposes in mind. The first is to shed light on the nature of women's oppression by focusing on those phenomena that both shape and sustain it over time. The second is to sketch the contours of a nonoppressive society in which women are either equal with men or empowered as women. Like all theories, feminist theories are both explanatory and prescriptive. Moreover, they are self-consciously practical in their efforts to locate the conditions under which women's oppression can be overcome in practice. Not surprisingly, feminist theorists disagree among themselves about both these conditions and the nature of women's oppression.

Liberal feminist theorists tend to view sexist beliefs and discriminatory laws as the source of women's oppression. However, both Marxist feminists and radical feminists reject this liberal analysis. Marxist feminists such as Margaret Benston locate the source of women's oppression in capitalism. Radical feminists such as Shulamith Firestone argue that all sorts of oppression, including those associated with private property, have their source in patriarchy, i.e., the systematic domination of women by powerful men within hierarchically ordered institutions.

While many feminist theorists focus on society, economics, and politics in their discussions of women's oppression, other feminist theorists, such as those schooled in psychoanalysis and poststructuralism, focus on the ways in which sexuality and language create and reinforce patterns of domination for women and others. Psychoanalytic feminist theorists such as Nancy Chodorow zero in on the psycho-sexual relations between mothers and their children in their analyses of male domination. Poststructuralists articulate the ways in which language shapes our view of social and political reality and reinforces the hierarchies of power and sexual politics embodied in language itself.

Since all these theorists employ the language of gender, they inevitably posit differences between women and men at some point in their analyses. But they do not all endow such differences with the same normative status. Liberal feminists downplay gender differences in the interests of securing equal rights for women. Poststructuralists place gender differences at the center of our attention in the interests of empowering women and legitimating their gendered perspectives. Both sets of arguments together constitute what has come to be known as the "difference versus equality" debate.

While this debate initially focused primarily on differences between women and men, it now focuses largely on differences among women. At the center of the debate—which has been developed in large part by multicultural feminists such as bell hooks—are a series of insights into both the domination that results from universal claims of womanhood and the necessity of constructing gender within particular historical contexts. How, multicultural feminists ask, can we understand gender, culture, and race together in the lives of particular women? Moreover, how can we embrace such particular identities without losing sight of the importance of gender itself as a category of distinction? *MS* • *See also* **Feminism**

Gay, Lesbian, and Bisexual Studies

Notable nineteenth-century gay scholarship includes Karl Heinrich Ulrichs's "Researches on the Riddle of Love Between Males" (1864–65); the Scientific-Humanitarian Committee and its journal, *Yearbook for Sexual Intergrades* (1899–1923); and the English sexologist Havelock Ellis's seminal work *Studies in the Psychology of Sex* ([1897–1928] 1942). A generation later circles of lesbians and gay men flourished: the expatriate Paris community of the 1920s including Gertrude Stein and Natalie Barney; the English Bloomsbury group that counted among its members Virginia Woolf, John Maynard Keynes, Lytton Strachey, and E. M. Forster; and the Harlem Renaissance whose enduring prominence was established by the likes of Langston Hughes, Ma Rainey, Countee Cullen, and Alain Locke. By the mid-twentieth century, notable scholarly contributions included those of Alfred Kinsey using interview and survey methodologies, the comparative research of Evelyn Hooker, and the One Institute in Los Angeles, where courses on homosexuality were first regularly offered.

It was not until the 1970s, however, with the formation of the Gay Liberation Front and the Gay Academic Union, that the field established an academic beachhead. Following the lead of persons of color and women, these student activists and scholars sought to reinvigorate the academy. While earlier gay scholarship tended to reflect the Euro-American, male bias evidenced in much of academia, an impressive volume of culturally diverse gay and lesbian scholarship has emerged. These works include detailed historical studies of the late nineteenth-century phenomenon of female "Boston marriages" (Faderman, 1981); women's college "smashes" (McKay,

1993); turn-of-the-century European immigrant experiences in New York City (Chauncey, 1994); working-class women's bars in Buffalo, New York, following World War II (Kennedy & Davis, 1993); and the experiences and oral histories of lesbians and gay men in the American South (Sears, 1991; Sears, 1997). These works also include anthologies by gay persons of color such as *In the Life* (Beam, 1986), *Borderlands/La Frontera* (Anzaldua, 1987), and *Nice Jewish Girls* (Beck, 1989).

Under the influence of European intellectuals such as Michel Foucault, Guy Hocquenghem, Judith Butler, and Jacques Derrida and feminists and persons of color, as evidenced in the intellectual contributions of Mary Daly, bell hooks, Gayle Rubin, Marilyn Frye, Eve Sedgwick, June Jordan, and Stuart Hall, *identity politics* ushered in "queer theory" or queer studies. Here the focus is on the deconstruction of binary identities such as gay/straight, male/female, the construction of multiple racial, sexual, gender, and social class positions, and their representations in culture. Examples include *Epistemology of the Closet* (Sedgwick, 1990), *A Lure of Knowledge* (Roof, 1991), *Queer Theory* (de Lauretis, 1991), and *Gender Trouble* (Butler, 1990).

By the mid-1990s there were lesbian-gay scholarship groups in every major academic organization, several hundred colleges and universities offering courses or seminars on related issues, queer studies conferences held annually, a variety of academic programs or centers, and lesbian-gay studies anthologies (e.g., Abelove, Barale, & Halperin, 1993; Garber, 1994). *JTS* • *See also* **Identity Politics**

References

Abelove, H., Barale, M., & Halperin, D. (1993). *The lesbian and gay studies reader*. New York: Routledge.

Anzaldua, G. (1987). *Borderlands/La frontera*. San Francisco: Spinsters/Aunt Lute.

Beam, J. (1986). *In the life*. Boston: Alyson.

Beck, E. (1989). *Nice Jewish girls: A lesbian anthology*. Boston: Beacon Press.

Bullough, V. (1990). *Science in the bedroom: A history of sex research*. New York: Basic Books.

Butler, J. (1990). *Gender trouble: Feminism and the subversion of identity*. New York: Routledge.

Chauncey, G. (1994). *Gay New York*. New York: Basic Books.

de Lauretis. (1991). Queer theory: Lesbian and gay sexualities. *Special issue of differences*, 2(2).

Ellis, H. ([1897–1928] 1942). *Studies in the psychology of sex*. 2 vols. New York: Random House.

Faderman, L. (1981). *Surpassing the love of men*. New York: Morrow.

Garber, L. (1994). *Tilting the tower*. New York: Routledge.

Kennedy, E., & Davis, M. (1993). *Boots of leather, slippers of gold*. New York: Routledge.

McKay, A. (1993). *Wolf girls at Vassar*. New York: Times Change Press.

Roof, J. (1991). *A lure of knowledge: Lesbian sexuality and theory*. New York: Columbia University Press.

Sears. J. (1991). *Growing up gay in the South: Race, gender, and journeys of the spirit*. New York: Haworth.

Sears, J. (1997). *From lonely hunters to lonely hearts: An oral history of lesbian and gay Southern life, 1948–1968.* New York: Harper Collins.

Sedgwick, E. (1990). *Epistemology of the closet.* Berkeley: University of California Press.

Ulrichs, K. [Num Numantius, pseud.]. (1864–65). "Researches on the riddle of love between men," nos. 1–5. Leipsiz: Matthes.

Gender Fair Education *See* Nonsexist Education

Gender Studies *See* Women's Studies

Glass Ceiling

While women and people of color have made considerable gains entering the workforce in the last few decades, there is still a noticeable lack of people of color and women at the decision-making management levels. This phenomenon is often referred to as the glass ceiling, a term coined in 1986 by two *Wall Street Journal* reporters to describe the invisible barrier that blocks women from top jobs in corporate America. This barrier is a result of institutional and psychological practices that limit the advancement and mobility opportunities of people of color and women of diverse racial and ethnic backgrounds (U.S. Department of Labor, 1991).

The Civil Rights Act of 1964 is the backbone of efforts to eliminate employment discrimination. By allowing private litigation this act made every potential victim a monitor and put enforcement potential in the hands of those with intimate knowledge of the workplace. The Supreme Court's 1971 decision in *Griggs v. Duke Power Co.* vastly expanded the reach of Title VII of the Civil Rights Act to include facially neutral practices that have an adverse impact on people of color or women. This landmark decision has led employers to reexamine every part of their employment policies and practices for evidence of potential liability in adverse impact claims, and it has opened numerous doors for people of color and women (Leonard & Walter, 1994).

The United States Department of Labor released a report in 1991, entitled *The Glass Ceiling Commission,* concerning the progress of companies the Department of Labor had monitored through pilot reviews and compliance reviews. The report cites some barriers to career advancement warranting greater attention such as recruitment practices, lack of opportunity to contribute and participate in corporate development practices, general lack of corporate ownership of equal opportunity principles, performance measures, and mobility. The report also identifies several successful approaches to removing glass ceiling barriers: tracking women and people of color with advancement potential; ensuring access and visibility; ensuring a bias-free workplace; and continuing placement of women, people of color, and people with disabilities into entry-level professional positions.

According to the report the way to eliminate the glass ceiling effect is to address it as a civil rights issue related to access to avenues of power and decision-making contexts, not separately, but in a critical combination with access to and exercise of visible power (U.S. Department of Labor, 1991).

A follow-up report by the Department of Labor, *The Glass Ceiling Initiative* (1992), discusses artificial barriers based on attitudinal or organizational bias that prevent qualified individuals from advancing upwards in their organizations (U.S. Department of Labor, 1992a). The Civil Rights Act of 1991 was designed to overcome some of the glass ceiling problems. Enforcement remains inadequate.

The glass ceiling is not unique to the corporate world; it also exists in the world of academia (Business Women's Foundation, 1992). Today it is evident that ceilings and walls exist throughout most workplaces for people of color, women, and persons with disabilities. *DE*

References

Business and Professional Women's Foundation. (1992). *You can't get there from here: Working women and the glass ceiling.* Washington, DC: Business and Professional Women's Foundation.

The Glass Ceiling Act, Section 204 of Public Law 102-166 (Part of Title II of the Civil Rights Act of 1991.)

Leonard, J., & Walter, A. (1994). *Use of enforcement techniques in eliminating the glass ceiling.* University of California, Berkeley, CA: Hass School of Business.

———. (1992a). *A report: The glass ceiling initiative.* Washington, DC.

———. (1992b). *Pipelines of progress, an update on the glass ceiling initiative. A status report.* Washington, DC.

U.S. Department of Labor. (1991). *The glass ceiling commission.* Washington, DC.

Global Education

Growing out of such fields as international relations and area studies in the 1970s, American global education has been influenced by work in international education, development education, women in development, foreign language education, and the environmental-ecological sciences. Global educators recognize that Americans need to understand the complexity of global interconnectedness and develop skills in cross-cultural interaction if they are to make effective decisions in a pluralistic, competitive, and interdependent world.

Teaching with a global perspective differs in several ways from traditional approaches to learning about ourselves, other peoples, and the planet: (1) In teaching about cultures, global educators focus as much on *cultural universals*, those things all humans have in common, as they do on *cultural differences*.

Cross-cultural experiences and understanding, open-mindedness, anticipation of complexity, resistance to stereotyping or derision of cultural differences, and *perspectives consciousness*—recognition, knowledge, and appreciation of other people's points of view—are essential in the development of a global perspective (Case, 1993; Hanvey, 1975; Kniep, 1986); (2) Global educators see the world as overlapping global systems in which technological, ecological, economic, social, health, and political issues can no longer be effectively understood or addressed by individual nations because the issues literally spill over borders and regions. The organization of curricula does not separate world cultures or regions, but brings them together through study of contact, borrowing and diffusion of ideas, antecedents to current events, and comparative themes and concepts. Persistent global issues such as land use, peace and security, and self-determination are examined across time and place (Anderson, 1990; Kniep, 1986; Merryfield & Remy, 1995); and (3) The study of local-global connections leads to recognition that each of us makes choices that affect other people around the world, and others make choices that affect us. Because of this interconnectedness, global education includes knowledge and skills in decision making and participation and long-term involvement in the local community and in the larger world beyond our borders. Students learn to find, process, and evaluate information from multiple perspectives (Alger & Harf, 1986).

Global and multicultural education approaches overlap in their goals to develop multiple perspectives and multiple loyalties, strengthen cultural consciousness and intercultural competence, respect human dignity and human rights, and combat prejudice and discrimination (Bennett, 1995). *MMM* • *See also* **Perspective Consciousness**

References

Alger, C. F., & Harf, J. E. (1986). Global education: Why? For whom? About what? In R. E. Freeman (Ed.), *Promising practices in global education: A handbook with case studies* (pp. 1–13). New York: National Council on Foreign Language and International Studies.

Anderson, L. (1990). A rationale for global education. In K. A. Tye (Ed.), *Global education from thought to action* (pp. 13–34). Alexandria, VA: Association for Curriculum and Supervision.

Bennett, C. I. (1995). *Comprehensive multicultural education*. Boston: Allyn & Bacon.

Case, R. (1993). Key elements of a global perspective. *Social Education, 57*(6), 318–25.

Harvey, R. G. (1987). Reprint. An attainable global perspective. In W. M. Kniep (Ed.), *Next steps in global education: A Handbook for curriculum development*. New York: American Forum. Original edition, New York: Center for War Peace Studies, 1975.

Kniep, W. M. (1986). Defining global education by its content. *Social Education, 50*(10), 437–66.

Merryfield, M. M., & Remy, R. C. (1995). *Teaching about international conflict and peace*. Albany, NY: State University of New York Press.

Handicap *See* Disability Studies

Hate Group

A hate group is characterized as any organized body that denigrates select groups of people based on their ethnicity, race, or sexual orientation or that advocates the use of violence against such groups or their members for purposes of scapegoating. *Hate group* is a somewhat foggy concept and should not be regarded as a precise or technical term. Rather, it must be understood within its limited context.

In the United States the term is usually applied to White supremacist groups or movements. These include the Ku Klux Klan, the Church of the Creator (COTC), the skinheads, the White Aryan Resistance (WAR), and the Church of Jesus Christ Christian/Aryan Nations. Leaders of some White supremacist groups often admit being racist but shun the label of hate monger or hate group—arguing instead that they hate no one and merely love their own race. While White hate groups tend to focus hostility toward those ethnic or racial minorities most prominent in their area, all of the known groups are definitely anti-Black and anti-Semitic.

The number of White supremacist groups in the United States fluctuates between 250 and 400. Estimates of membership in such groups vary from 20,000 to 200,000. Some of these groups limit their activities to the production and dissemination of hate literature. Others are known to have committed overt acts of violence including vandalism, intimidation, assault, and murder.

Of course not all hate groups are White. Furthermore, a group's leadership often determines whether or not it is viewed as a hate group. For example, under its current leadership, the Nation of Islam, a Black Muslim separatist group, is regarded by some people as a hate group. Its main targets are considered to be Whites and Jews, but the hatred expressed has been limited to antilocution and printed material. Unlike many White supremacist groups, the Nation of Islam has not engaged in violence against target groups. *MK*

References

Definitions of a Hate Group. (1994). *CSERV Bulletin: Journal of the Center for the Study of Ethnic and Racial Violence, 3*(1), 64.

Kleg, M. (1993). *Hate, prejudice, and racism.* Albany: State University of New York Press.

————. (in press). *Encyclopedia of hate, racism, and ethnic violence in America.* Santa Barbara: ABC-CLIO.

————. (1997). Technology and the darkside: Hate on line. In P. H. Martorella (Ed.), *Interactive technologies and the social studies: Emerging issues and applications.* Albany: State University of New York Press.

Hegemony

Hegemony refers to a process in which dominant groups in society come together to form a bloc to sustain leadership and control over subordinate groups. One of the most important implications of this concept is that it implies that a power bloc does not necessarily have to rely on coercion to control. Rather, it relies on winning consent to the prevailing order by forming an ideological umbrella under which different groups who might not ordinarily totally agree with each other can stand. The key is to offer a compromise so less powerful groups believe that their concerns are being listened to but dominant groups do not have to give up their control of general social tendencies in the economy, schools, and government.

Hegemony, then, concerns the process by which a socially accepted commonsense is created, one that is sponsored and led by the most powerful groups in society. For example, dominant groups often seek to win acceptance and institutionalize their limited ideas about democracy in education and the economy at the expense of broader ideas that may be held by oppressed populations.

It is crucial to note that in any given historical situation, hegemonic control is usually found only as a partial exercise of leadership by the dominant alliance. It may be more successful in some spheres of society than in others. Thus, the most powerful forces in our society will not be equally successful in controlling commonsense in the economy, law, mass media, families, or education. In fact, there is no guarantee that those forces will be successful. There will always be *counter-hegemonic* activity in which less powerful groups struggle against dominant social policies, practices, and ideologies. Furthermore, there are multiple hegemonic relations involving race, class, gender, and sexuality. All of these involve complicated power relations, compromises, and continuing conflicts among dominant groups and between dominant groups and oppressed groups. *MWA*

References

Apple, M. W. (1990). *Ideology and curriculum* (2nd ed.). New York: Routledge.
————. (1995). *Education and power* (2nd ed.). New York: Routledge.
Connell, R. W. (1982). *Making the difference*. Boston: Allen and Unwin.

Heterosexism *See* Homophobia/Heterosexism

Hidden Curriculum

Students learn more in schools than algebra, history, and how to read and write. They learn how to act to stay out of trouble, what counts as work and what counts as play, and who has the right to decide what is to be learned. These are examples of the hidden curriculum.

The term *hidden curriculum* originated in a description of classroom life by Philip Jackson (1968). Jackson categorized schools as complex, highly stylized social environments. In them students learn to take on social roles that lead to their class-determined place in the adult world.

The hidden curriculum in U.S. schools evolved as a late nineteenth-century response to massive immigration. Schools were seen as a mechanism of social control by which new immigrants would become citizens who shared common values and were prepared for lives of productive work. However, once this social control agenda had become established, references to it faded (Vallence, 1973–74). Its continued existence is evident in schooling practices in which normative values (e.g., punctuality, neatness, compliance) are combined with the teaching of technological-bureaucratic skills (e.g., rule following). In such schooling, information is often taught out of context and external "experts" continually evaluate and compare students' learning (Gatto, 1992).

Multicultural educators question whose values and what social order are supported in this hidden curriculum. If only the values of the dominant social and economic class have cultural capital, that is form the normative expectations for behavior and learning (Apple & King, 1983), then students may learn that competition is more valued than cooperation or that students earn what they deserve—in spite of initial inequities. Critical theorists see the hidden curriculum as hegemonic, that is contributing with or without conscious intent to the oppression of non-White, nonmiddle-class students. The everyday pattern of school interactions, they claim, leads to cultural and economic reproduction of the existing dominant class and perpetuates the existing unequal and stratified social order (Giroux, 1983).

The hidden curriculum operates simultaneously with an official curriculum, which is formally approved by school authorities. The choice of content in the official curriculum (e.g., the "discovery" of America by Columbus) may likewise glorify the events that validate the power of the dominant group. Learning objectives may employ racial, ethnic, social, or sex stereotypes, contributing to the maintenance of power relationships. To teach multiculturally may require systemwide changes in the official and hidden curriculum (Posner, 1995). *EK*

References

Apple, M. W., & King, N. (1983). In H. Giroux & D. Purpel (Eds.), *The hidden curriculum and moral education*. Berkeley, CA: McCutchan.

Gatto, J. T. (1992). *Dumbing us down: The hidden curriculum of compulsory schooling*. Philadelphia: New Society.

Giroux, H. (1983). In H. Giroux & D. Purpel (Eds.), *The hidden curriculum and moral education*. Berkeley, CA: McCutchan.

Jackson, P. (1968). *Life in classrooms*. New York: Holt, Rinehart & Winston.

Posner, G. J. (1995). *Analyzing the curriculum*. New York: McGraw-Hill.

Vallance, E. (1973–74). Hiding the hidden curriculum. *Curriculum theory network, 4*(1), 5–12.

Homophobia/Heterosexism

Thomas Weinberg (1972) first popularized the concept of homophobia, defining it as "the dread of being in close quarters with homosexuals . . . the revulsion toward homosexuals and often the desire to inflict punishment as retribution" (pp. 4, 129). In recent decades the term has evolved to have a less clinical meaning, referring to overt violence such as physical assault and verbal harassment, psychological battering resulting in fear of self-disclosure or the absence of same-gender intimacy, and social and political offensiveness ranging from state referenda to legislative initiatives which have fostered and reinforced antigay sentiments and behaviors.

A related concept, *internalized homophobia*, has come to mean the conscious or subconscious adoption and acceptance of negative feelings and attitudes about homosexuals or homosexuality by gay men and lesbians. The manifestation of these negative feelings is evidenced in fear of discovery, denial or discomfort with being homosexual, and aggression against other lesbians and gay men, as well as exaggerated gay pride or rejection of all heterosexuals. Other concepts such as *biphobia* (Hutchins & Kaahumanu, 1991, p. 6) and *transphobia* (Denny, 1994) are useful extensions in directing our thinking toward other areas of sexual prejudice.

There is also the less overt, more subtle manifestation of uneasiness with persons whose sexual identity is nonheterosexual. Herek (1990, p. 319) distinguishes between two manifestations of heterosexism. *Cultural heterosexism* is evidenced in the stigmatization, denial, or denigration of nonheterosexuality in cultural institutions ranging from the church to the courthouse. *Psychological heterosexism* is a person's internalization of this worldview which erupts into antigay prejudice. Thus, heterosexism is a belief in the superiority of heterosexuals or heterosexuality evidenced in the exclusion, by omission or design, of nonheterosexual persons (including bisexuals and transgendered individuals) from policies, procedures, events, or activities.

There has been substantial research into the measurement of homophobia and personality-demographic characteristics that are often associated with homophobes (Herek, 1990), the relationship of homophobia to other forms of prejudice (e.g., Pharr, 1988), and some documentation of effective educational interventions that reduce homophobia (Sears, 1996a). However, there has been considerably less work exploring the relationship between U.S. ethnic and cultural groups vis-à-vis homophobia. While some evidence suggests differences in attitudes among various groups such as Native Americans (Williams, 1986) and African Americans (Clarke, 1983; Rhue & Rhue, 1996), and although some educators have documented effective strategies targeted at particular groups (e.g., Blumenfeld, 1996; Mager & Sulek, 1996), for multicultural educators this area of research and pedagogy is in its infancy (Sears, 1996b). *JTS*

References

Blumenfeld, W. (1996). Homophobia and anti-Semitism. In J. Sears & W. Williams (Eds.), *Combating heterosexism and homophobia*. New York: Columbia University Press.

Clarke, C. (1983). The failure to transform: Homophobia in the Black community. In B. Smith (Ed.), *Home girls: A Black feminist anthology* (pp. 197–208). New York: Kitchen Table/Women of Color Press.

Denny, D. (1994). You're strange and we're wonderful: The gay and lesbian transgender communities. In J. Sears (Ed.), *Bound by diversity* (pp. 47–53). Columbia, SC: Sebastian Press.

Herek, G. (1990). Homophobia. In W. Dynes (Ed.), *Encyclopedia of homosexuality* (pp. 552–55). New York: Garland.

Hutchins, L., & Kaahumanu, L. (Eds.). (1991). *Bi any other name*. Boston: Alyson.

Mager, D., & Sulek, R. (1996). Teaching about homophobia at a historically Black university. In J. Sears & W. Williams (Eds.), *Combating heterosexism and homophobia*. New York: Columbia University Press.

Pharr, S. (1988). *Homophobia: A weapon of sexism*. Little Rock, AR: Chardon.

Rhue, S., & Rhue, T. (1996). Reducing homophobia in African American communities. In J. Sears & W. Williams (Eds.), *Combating heterosexism and homophobia*. New York: Columbia University Press.

Sears, J. (1996a). Thinking critically/intervening effectively about homophobia and heterosexism: A twenty-five year retrospective. In J. Sears & W. Williams (Eds.), *Combating heterosexism and homophobia*. NY: Columbia University Press.

————. (1996b). Beyond zero tolerance: Four approaches to integrating lesbian/gay issues into multicultural education. In G. Smith & C. Grant (Eds.), *Sociocultural contexts of human growth and psychological development in non-mainstream ethnic and racial cultures*. Washington, DC: American Association of Colleges of Teacher Education.

Weinberg, G. (1972). *Society and the healthy homosexual*. New York: St. Martin's Press.

Williams, W. (1986). *The spirit and the flesh*. Boston: Beacon Press.

Human Relations *See* Multicultural Education, Approaches To

Hyphenated Americans

Hyphenated American was the catchphrase used during World War I to hint at disloyalty among foreign-born citizens in the United States. The term was not restricted to immigrants but was freely applied to any group for which evidence of ethnic loyalty could suggest anything less than total commitment to the United States. The more-or-less steady presence of nativism after 1890 provided the emotional framework within which the concept of hyphenism could flourish, and the outbreak of the war itself brought forth the greatest surge of nativism the country had ever witnessed (Moquin, 1971, p. 107).

Before and during World War I, German-Americans were the first and main targets of the antihyphenate campaign (Higham, 1988; Moquin, 1971). However, by the early 1920s "anything that seemed alien, or radical, or even merely different, was the target of charges of disloyalty" (Moquin, 1971, p. 107). For example, the use of non-English languages in press, schools, and religious services was suspected and attacked.

Theodore Roosevelt and Woodrow Wilson both played a major role in this antihyphenate campaign. Roosevelt's "America for Americans" slogan bolstered the Americanization Movement and suspicion of disloyalty on the part of German-Americans who identified as such. While Wilson did not mention any specific national group by name, he fully exploited the issue of disloyalty and hyphenism (Higham, 1988; Moquin, 1971).

Although the hyphenated theme may not have arose again in the manner such as with the German-Americans during World War I, it is important to note that such invalid suspicions of disloyalty towards U.S. citizens have reoccurred in U.S. history. An example would be the internment of Japanese Americans during World War II.

Currently the use of hyphens rarely carries the same negative meanings that existed in the World War I era and during the antihyphenated campaign. In the current social context, issues of hyphenism have re-emerged within discussions about identity labels and identity politics. Many people of color have identified themselves as hyphenated Americans, that is African-American, Asian-American, or Mexican-American, to acknowledge their ancestral origins. This practice, however, has not been taken up by most of the White American community (except by some members of the Jewish-American community), which raises concerns as to whether White Americans are represented as just *Americans* while people of color are relegated to a marginalized American status. While most people refer to White Americans as *White*, others have begun to use *European-American* to note ancestral origins just as with people of color. Still when there is a reference to hyphenated Americans, it is usually in reference to a person or group of color.

Although many printing presses, publishing houses, and public documents currently use hyphens to note a person or group's ethnic background, a significant number of people choose to leave out the hyphen, for example, Japanese American, or Haitian American. By leaving out the hyphen, the ethnicity—in the above examples, Japanese and Haitian—serves as an adjective, referring to ancestral background, "rather than implying a half-half status; i.e., that one's loyalties/identities might be half Japanese and half American. Rather . . . the accent is on the 'American'." (Kondo, 1990, p. 309). For those who *choose* to identify with a panethnic label or for those who leave out the hyphen, the choice is usually political in nature. *JLL* • *See also* **Identity Politics; Naming; Panethnicity**

References

Higham, J. (1988). *Strangers in the land: Patterns of American nativism, 1860–1925*. New Brunswick, NJ: Rutgers University Press.

Kondo, D. K. (1990). *Crafting selves: Power, gender, and discourses of identity in a Japanese workplace*. Chicago: University of Chicago Press.

Moquin, W. (Ed.). (1971). *Makers of America—Hyphenated Americans, 1914–1924*. Vol. 7. Chicago: Encyclopaedia Britannica.

Identity Politics

The term *identity politics* has been the focus of much bitter argument: it is employed far more regularly, in fact, as an epithet than as an avowal of one's own practices. This discord is compounded by significant variation in what different speakers mean by identity politics. However, for all it refers to the idea—in one sense or another—that one's politics grow out of who one is.

The first explicit use of the term is often attributed to a statement made in 1977 by the Combahee River Collective (Eisenstein, 1979), a Boston-based Black feminist group. The collective chose to focus on their own oppression: "We believe that the most profound and potentially the most radical politics come directly out of our own identity" (p. 365). The Combahee statement reflects one root of identity politics: the new social movements of the 1960s and 70s (Civil Rights, Black Power, Women's Liberation, and Gay Liberation) staked claims based on the oppression experienced by one or another identifiable sector of society, rather than on an appeal to (purportedly) universal ideals. Moreover, as certain participants in these largely separate movements recognized their own marginal status *within* each liberation movement (e.g., women working in the Black Power Movement, persons of color and lesbians working in the Women's Movement) and encountered resistance upon trying to address the blind spots in each movement's analyses, they began to organize independently on the basis of the insights afforded by their own particular social locations.

Meanwhile, an intellectual tide within the academy formed a second foundation for identity politics. Across the disciplines insurgent thinkers such as people of color, women, and non-Westerners strove to circumvent tacit presumptions about who-can-do theory and to infuse the academy with both themselves and their oppositional knowledge. They adopted diverse strategies in challenging traditional canon, ranging from critiques of false universalism and grand narratives to advocacy of standpoint epistemologies and situated knowledge.

Despite their varied strategies, many share the tenet that what counts as knowledge depends on who's doing the counting. Arguing that different experiences lead to different knowledge appeals, in effect, to identity for validation of oppositional knowledge (in close accord with concurrent thinking in activist circles). Whether those experiences are seen as simple irreducible fact becomes a significant question.

Criticisms of identity politics (e.g., Bourne, 1987; Dyson, 1995; Gitlin, 1995) accuse it of *essentialism* (i.e., attributing to social groups a transhistorical, invariant essence), exclusive concern with the personal, and abandonment of real political struggle for ephemeral debates over language. Such criticism is an apt response to simplistic versions of identity politics, but it is less clear how well it applies to more nuanced approaches. Among scholars who advocate treating identity as a basis for political understandings, a number see identity crucially as an intermediate rather than foundational term; that is, while identity underpins politics, identity is itself a fluid entity, unstable and continually reconstructed. Rather than attributing political understandings directly to people's experiences—unmediated by social construction— these thinkers, as members of oppressed groups, are very concerned, while referring to those experiences, with the indeterminate interpretation of experience, with the way people assign meaning to their experiences, and hence with identity as a continual accomplishment rather than a given fact.

One feature of this approach is an appreciation of the multiplicity of identity. It is not just a matter of one's race or gender but of numerous interlocking dynamics. Thus, individuals and groups are both internally complex and far more heterogeneous than is captured by such labels as *woman, Chicano,* or *gay.* These theorists are concerned with the personal, but not exclusively so; they wish to link the personal to the political, connecting individual experience with social structure. (See Bromley, 1989, for a discussion of how this framework would apply to the practices of feminist pedagogy.)

Among those active in this area, to whose work the term *identity politics* has been applied (some claiming it for themselves and some not), are Teresa de Lauretis, Diana Fuss, Stuart Hall, June Jordan, María Lugones, Biddy Martin and Chandra Mohanty, Minnie Bruce Pratt, and Bernice Johnson Reagon. (See Tessman, 1995, for an informative current discussion of the various threads in this body of work, ranging from the Combahee statement to the present.)

[I would like to thank Hester Eisenstein, Rinaldo Walcott, and Matthew Weinstein for some very helpful conversations.] *HB*

References

Bourne, J. (1987). Homelands of the mind: Jewish feminism and identity politics. *Race & Class, 29*(1), 1–24.

Bromley, H. (1989). Identity politics and critical pedagogy. *Educational Theory, 39*(3), 207–23.

de Lauretis, T. (1986). Feminist studies/critical studies: Issues, terms, and contexts. In T. de Lauretis (Ed.), *Feminist studies/critical studies* (pp. 1–19). Bloomington: Indiana University Press.

———. (1990). Upping the anti[sic] in feminist theory. In M. Hirsch & E. F. Keller (Eds.), *Conflicts in feminism* (pp. 255–70). New York: Routledge.

Dyson, M. (1995). Contesting racial amnesia: From identity politics toward post-multiculturalism. In M. Bérubé & C. Nelson (Eds.), *Higher education under fire: Politics, economics, and the crisis of the humanities* (pp. 336-44). New York: Routledge.

Eisenstein, Z. R. (Ed.). (1979). *Capitalist patriarchy and the case for socialist feminism.* New York: Monthly Review Press.

Fuss, D. (1989). *Essentially speaking: Feminism, nature, and difference.* New York: Routledge.

Gitlin, T. (1995). The rise of "identity politics": An examination and a critique. In M. Bérubé & C. Nelson (Eds.), *Higher education under fire: Politics, economics, and the crisis of the humanities* (pp. 308–19). New York: Routledge.

Hall, S. (1989). Cultural identity and cinematic representation. *Framework, 36* (special issue entitled "Third scenario: Theory and the politics of location"), 68–81.

Jordan, J. (1985). Report from the Bahamas. In *On call: Political essays* (pp. 39–49). Boston: South End Press.

Lugones, M. (1994). Purity, impurity, and separation. *Signs, 19*(2), 458–79.

Martin, B., & Mohanty, C. T. (1986). Feminist politics: What's home got to do with it? In T. de Lauretis (Ed.), *Feminist studies/critical studies* (pp. 191–212). Bloomington: Indiana University Press.

Pratt, M. B. (1984). Identity: Skin blood heart. In E. Bulkin, et al. (Eds.), *Yours in struggle* (pp. 11–63). New York: Long Haul Press.

Reagon, B. J. (1983). Coalition politics: Turning the century. In B. Smith (Ed.), *Home girls: A Black feminist anthology* (pp. 356–68). New York: Kitchen Table Women of Color Press.

Tessman, L. (1995). Beyond communitarian unity in the politics of identity. *Socialist Review, 94*(1–2), 55–83.

Ideology

Ideology usually refers to a system of ideas, beliefs, fundamental commitments, and values about social reality. Historically, its role has been seen in two ways: (1) as a system of meanings that justifies the vested interests of existing or contending groups in society; or (2) as a set of knowledge and beliefs that provides meaning and enables people in their everyday lives to make sense out of the complexity of society. Both senses of ideology are necessary.

In education, ideological influences are visible in the selective tradition of the curriculum. Out of the vast universe of possible knowledge, only some groups' knowledge, history, and values are selected to become official knowledge taught to everyone. Particular beliefs and assumptions about what is important to know and to do now and in the future—usually those of the most powerful segments of society—provide the filter through which decisions about curriculum, teaching, and evaluation are made. Therefore, ideologies can be invisible in that they are embodied in the daily events and commonsense activities that organize the social relations and educational events—and even the very architecture—of classrooms and the relations between schools and communities.

Ideologies are not necessarily uniform. They may contain elements that challenge dominant beliefs. There may be elements of both *good* and *bad* sense in them. Thus, the ideologies of oppressed race, gender, and class groups can include conscious and unconscious beliefs that both support the power of dominant forces and act against it at the same time. Because of this, it is important to think about ideologies as having contradictions. They can allow for insight into differential power relations in education and the larger society and also limit one's understanding of the root causes of inequalities. *MWA*

References

Apple, M. W. (1990). *Ideology and curriculum* (2nd ed.). New York: Routledge.
———. (1993). *Official knowledge*. New York: Routledge.
Willis, P. (1981). *Learning to labor*. New York: Columbia University Press.

Immigrants

Immigrants, those who have migrated voluntarily to the United States, have figured importantly in U.S. education. Pre-Civil War "common schools" were designed to be "culture factories" (Schultz, 1973) that homogenized polyglot populations while inculcating personal morality and civic virtue. Turn-of-the-century urban school systems joined in the crusade to culturally and ideologically Americanize immigrants. Today, guided by assumptions somewhat more tolerant of diversity, U.S. schools still seek to provide immigrant students with the linguistic, social, and academic capital required for participation in the mainstream.

Immigrants' responses to U.S. schools have been complex. Immigrants have welcomed opportunities for inclusion and advancement offered by the schools, while at the same time they have often resisted, sometimes vociferously, cultural and religious denigration. For example, throughout the nineteenth century Catholics protested the Protestant hue of the public schools and subsequently constructed a school system of their own.

Immigrants have been an important impetus to accommodate diversity, albeit the effort is often controversial and always constrained within a fundamentally assimilationist framework. Nineteenth-century rural midwestern schools often were taught in German and other non-English languages. Several midwestern cities sustained German bilingual schools during the last quarter of the nineteenth century. Even during the period of the Americanization movement, special classes using immigrants' languages appeared. In part in response to the second-generation problem of immigrant youth, schools in the late 1930s undertook *intercultural education*, a direct precursor to contemporary multicultural education. And it was the demands on behalf of Chinese-speaking students that resulted in the 1974 Supreme Court decision in *Lau v. Nichols* that put the federal government on the side of bilingual education.

Immigrants have also been an important impetus to broaden educational reform. The necessity of coping with large immigrant populations in the early twentieth century spurred the creation of bureaucratized education systems, curriculum tracking, and pedagogical innovations such as kindergartens. The desire to make *good Americans* out of immigrants significantly advanced the teaching of civics in the 1920s. Communities of second-generation immigrants were instrumental in broadening foreign-language study.

The success of immigrants in school has been a prominent part of U.S. American mythology, extolling the virtues of individualistic hard work, self-advancement, and assimilation. The myth of the *model minority*, depicting Asian Americans as frequent honor roll students, class valedictorians, and scholarship winners, is the contemporary version of this longstanding theme.

In truth the academic success of immigrant students has been historically variable, with sometimes pronounced differences among groups arising in relation to historical circumstances and cultural orientation. Of particular interest is the fact that, contrary to popular belief, it is those immigrant students who retain fluency in their native languages and affirm strong ethnic identities whose achievement is the highest in contemporary U.S. schools.

Mythology also extols the role of schools in providing the occasion for immigrants to meet, mix with, and ultimately blend with their U.S. American peers. The encounter between immigrants and the schools, however, has been, and continues to be, less smooth than our mythology supposes. Mutual misperceptions, cultural discontinuities, and nativist prejudice all can exacerbate social distance and the marginality of immigrant students.

The reluctance, for example, of some immigrants to engage in publicly competitive and individualistic displays of academic prowess, behavior presupposed by the pedagogic regimes of many U.S. classrooms (Delgado-Gaitan & Trueba, 1991; Gibson, 1988), can isolate immigrant students from their teachers, fellow students, and classroom activities. Overt racial hostility and anti-immigrant resentment can intensify boundaries (Gibson, 1988).

Paradoxically, special programs intended to respond to students' distinctive needs, such as transitional bilingual education and soccer teams categorized as clubs but not intervarsity sports, can, in certain circumstances, consign the immigrant to a school's periphery (Goldstein, 1985; Grey, 1990), thus illustrating a dilemma endemic to multicultural education. *MRO* • *See also* **Intergroup Education; Lau v. Nichols; Mainstream; Model Minority**

References

Delgado-Gaitan, C., & Trueba, H. (1991). *Crossing cultural borders: Education for immigrant families in America*. London: Falmer Press.

Gibson, M. (1988). *Accommodation without assimilation: Sikh immigrants in an American high school*. Ithaca, NY: Cornell University Press.

Goldstein, B. L. (1985). *Schooling for cultural transitions: Hmong girls and boys in American high schools*. Ph.D. diss., Department of Educational Policy Studies, University of Wisconsin-Madison.

Grey, M. A. (1990). Immigrant students in the heartland: Ethnic relations in a Garden City, Kansas, high school. *Urban Anthropology, 19*, 409–27.

Schultz, S. K. (1973). *The culture factory: Boston public schools 1789–1860*. New York: Oxford University Press.

Inclusive Education

Inclusive education is a value-based practice that attempts to bring all students, including those with disabilities, into full membership within their local school community. The philosophy underlying inclusive education promotes each child, regardless of the type or intensity of his or her perceived educational, physical, or psychological challenges, as valued and capable of participation (Udvari-Solner & Thousand, 1995). The substantive difference in service delivery and programming for students with disabilities is that they are educated alongside their nondisabled peers in general education classrooms (Stainback & Stainback, 1992).

With an inclusive approach—as opposed to separate, pull-out, or resource room models of special education—specialized services are brought to the child and delivered by support personnel (e.g., teachers, instructional assistants, therapists) in the context of general education classes. Supplementary aids and services in the form of curricular and instructional adaptations are engineered collaboratively by general educators, special educators, related service personnel, and families to facilitate social and academic success.

The tenets of inclusive education mesh cohesively with the ideology of reconstructivist thought, the ethics of social justice, and the principles that frame multicultural education (Udvari-Solner & Thousand, 1996). Specifically, inclusive education propels a critique of contemporary school culture and thus encourages practitioners to reinvent what can and should be reinvented to realize more humane, just, and democratic learning communities. Inequities in treatment and educational opportunity are brought to the forefront, thereby fostering attention to human rights, respect for difference, and the value of diversity.

There are basic standards of practice in inclusive schools. Although not an exhaustive listing, the following characteristics could be considered fundamental quality guidelines for implementation:

- Students are members of chronological age appropriate classrooms in the school they would attend if they were not disabled. In other words, the child attends his or her neighborhood school, a magnet school, or a school of choice when these options are available to students without disabilities (Brown, et al., 1989a; Sailor, 1991).
- The principle of *zero reject* is upheld, that is, the severity or type of disability does not prevent participation in general education settings (Sailor, et al., 1989).
- *Natural proportions* are observed, that is, the number of students with disabilities in any one school or classroom represents the proportion found in the general population. Consequently, students are not to be clustered in number or by type of disability in particular schools or classrooms (Brown, et al., 1989b).
- Separate or special classes of homogeneous groups of students do not exist. If individualized assistance outside of the regular classroom is deemed necessary for a student with disabilities, the same learning environments available to nondisabled students are utilized (e.g., a learning center, library, computer lab).
- Special and general educators collaborate to provide adaptation of the curriculum and materials to facilitate participation and acquisition of individual educational objectives. Flexible learning goals and outcomes, cooperative learning, peer-mediated approaches, heterogeneous grouping, thematic instruction, and activity-based, community-referenced, and experiential learning are considered essential strategies (Giangreco & Putnam, 1991; Heron & Jorgensen, 1995; Thousand, Villa, & Nevin, 1994; Udvari-Solner, 1992).

- Special education and related services (e.g., communication, mobility, vision) are provided when necessary in the context of inclusive classroom and community environments. School personnel may practice collaborative consultation, co-teaching, team teaching, itinerant, and cross-categorical support models to provide assistance to students with diverse learning needs (Friend, Reising, & Cook, 1993; Thousand & Villa, 1992; York, Giangreco, Vandercook, & MacDonald, 1992).

Inclusive education has emerged as a critical force in the larger reform movement to reconceptualize mainstream educational practice so that it is responsive to the needs of all learners. Proponents of inclusive education anticipate that the term itself will soon be obsolete and unnecessary as more and more school districts begin to reorganize their current practices and demonstrate ways to make all children integral members of the school community. *AUS*

References

Brown, L., Long, E., Udvari-Solner, A., Davis, L., VanDeventer, P., Ahlgren, C., Johnson, F., Gruenewald, L., & Jorgensen, J. (1989a). The home school: Why students with severe disabilities must attend the schools of their brothers, sisters, friends and neighbors. *The Journal of the Association for Persons with Severe Handicaps*, 14(1), 1–7.

Brown, L., Long, E., Udvari-Solner, A., Schwarz, P., VanDeventer, P., Ahlgren, C., Johnson, F., Gruenewald, L., & Jorgensen, J. (1989b). Should students with severe intellectual disabilities be based in regular or special education classrooms in their home schools? *Journal of the Association for Persons with Severe Handicaps*, 14(1), 8–12.

Friend, M., Reising, M., Cook, L. (1993, Summer). Co-teaching: An overview of the past, a glimpse at the present, and considerations for the future. *Preventing School Failure*, 6–10.

Giangreco, M., & Putnam, J. (1991). Supporting the education of students with severe disabilities in regular education environments. In L. Meyer, C. Peck, & L. Brown (Eds.), *Critical issues in the lives of people with severe disabilities* (pp. 245–70). Baltimore, MD: Paul Brookes.

Heron, E., & Jorgensen, C. (1995). Addressing learning differences right from the start. *Educational Leadership*, 52(4), 56–59.

Sailor, W. (1991). Special education in a restructured school. *Remedial and Special Education*, 12(6).

Sailor, W., Anderson, J., Halvorsen, A., Doering, K., Filler, J., & Goetz, L. (1989). *The comprehensive local school: Regular education for all students with disabilities*. Baltimore, MD: Paul Brookes.

Stainback, W., & Stainback, S. (1992). *Curriculum considerations in inclusive classrooms: Facilitating learning for all students*. Baltimore, MD: Paul Brookes.

Thousand, J., & Villa, R. (1992). Collaborative teams: A powerful tool in restructuring. In R. Villa, J. Thousand, W. Stainback, & S. Stainback (Eds.), *Restructuring for a caring and effective education: An administrative guide* (pp. 73–108). Baltimore, MD: Paul Brookes.

Thousand, J., Villa, R., & Nevin, A. (1994). *Creativity and collaborative teaching: A practical guide to empowering students and teachers.* Baltimore, MD: Paul Brookes.

Udvari-Solner, A. (1992). *Curricular adaptations: Accommodating the instructional needs of diverse learners in the context of general education.* Kansas State Board of Education, Services for Children and Youth with Deaf-Blindness Project.

Udvari-Solner, A., & Thousand, J. (1995). Effective organizational, instructional, and curricular practices in inclusive schools and classrooms. In C. Clark, A. Dyson, & A. Millward (Eds.), *Towards inclusive schools?* (pp. 147–63). London: David Fulton.

Udvari-Solner, A., & Thousand, J. (1996). Creating a responsive curriculum for inclusive schools. *Remedial and Special Education, 17(3),* 182–92.

York, J., Giangreco, M., Vandercook, T., & MacDonald, C. (1992). Integrating support personnel in the inclusive classroom. In S. Stainback & W. Stainback (Eds.), *Curriculum considerations in inclusive classrooms: Facilitating learning for all students* (pp. 101–16). Baltimore, MD: Paul Brookes.

Infusion

Infusion is that part of the multicultural education process that, among other things, addresses the deliberate exclusion of various perspectives, concepts, and themes from the textbook and curricula. It attempts to balance distorted information reinforced through a Eurocentric knowledge base with more accurate historical representations and a broader literary selection so that all students see themselves mirrored in curricula.

For example, students in U.S. schools typically study what is called "American History" and "American Literature." Heretofore, this historical-literary canon has primarily included the works and deeds of European American men. Infusion requires that this canon be reexamined and be made inclusive of other perspectives. In the classroom, for example, a study of World War II would encompass not only military and political history, that is, great battles and great generals, but also history and literature from other perspectives. Stories of the Japanese internment, the participation of segregated African American and Japanese American troops, and the pivotal role of women and the Navajo *code-talkers* would represent a fuller and more accurate telling of this period of history. It would also include perspectives that extend beyond U.S. borders, such as Mexico, whose citizens' participated in the *bracero* program, and North Africa, which served as a staging ground for some battles.

Infusion requires that teachers have a broader knowledge base in order to make relevant historical-literary connections. It may also require a transformation of current curriculum structure. *PLB* • *See also* **Curriculum Infusion**

Institutional Racism

Institutional racism is the support of racism through various social institutions that tend to favor one race over others. Institutional racism is different from individual racism. According to Parsons (1966) and Banks and Banks (1993), an institution is an action system or agency of interrelated systems of social roles and norms organized to satisfy basic social and human needs. Feagin and Feagin (1978) point out that *institution* is a word that is used in several different senses. According to these authors, "[o]ne common usage is in regard to specific organizations such as a business, a corporation, a union, a school, a hospital and so on. These are formally, legally constituted organizations, with written and unwritten rules governing the conduct of those who fill positions therein, such as supervisor or teacher" (p. 12). The authors go on to describe another usage as "for larger sets of combinations of organizations such as 'the economy' or 'the family'" (p. 12). Other examples of institutions within our society include courts for handling law and order, systems of banks for finances, and the military as an action system that looks after defense.

Institutional racism occurs when one race has the power and desire to design roles, norms, and social expectations for our social institutions to favor members of its own group and to disfavor or oppress members of other racial groups. Historical examples of institutional racism in our society are the United States Constitution's definition of a slave as three-fifths of a person and the denial of African American men's right to vote until 1865. The Supreme Court ruled in *Plessy v. Ferguson* (1896) that separate but equal facilities for African Americans and Whites were constitutional. Segregation continued to be legal in public facilities until 1954, when the ruling was reversed in *Brown v. Board of Education*, which decided that separated facilities were inherently unequal.

The existence of institutional racism in education is evident historically by the development in this country of inequitable and segregated schooling. As Jonathan Kozol points out in *Savage Inequalities: Children in America's Schools* (1991), our schools are more segregated and more unequal than they were in 1954. His analysis of our primary funding approach for public schools—with its obvious inequities—uncovers an implicit support for institutional racism in our schools. The concept of multicultural education emerged partly because of the political necessity to openly combat educational institutional racism. *HPB*

References

Banks, J. A., & Banks, C. A. M. (Eds.). (1993). *Multicultural education: Issues and perspectives*. New York: Macmillan.

Bennett, C. (1986). *Comprehensive multicultural education: Theory and practice.* Boston: Allyn & Bacon.

Feagin, J. R., & Feagin, C. B. (1978). *Discrimination American style: Institutional racism and sexism.* Englewood Cliffs, NJ: Prentice Hall, Inc.

Kozol, J. (1991). *Savage inequalities: Children in America's schools.* New York: Crown.

Parsons, T. (1966). *Societies: Evolutionary and comparative perspectives.* New York: Prentice Hall.

Integration

The term *integration* usually conjures up the idea of people, things, or objects coming together to form a common, singular unit that is indistinguishable from the original parts. Within this context, integration represents a coming together for a common cause on an equal basis. Integration is not easily accomplished, and those who oppose the idea can usually find ways to avoid the process. It has been demonstrated that attempts to integrate evolve through various stages such as avoidance techniques and that as solutions are found at one level, other modes of segregation quickly emerge. We have seen shifts from physical or external segregation to in-school segregation and to differential academic outcome measure in our attempts to integrate schools. The process of school integration has been like hitting a moving target.

Integration in schools means putting into action the foundation upon which our democratic society stands; that is, given that all people are created equal, each of us has the potential to achieve and the right to equal educational opportunities. Integration ultimately means the positive interaction of individuals of equal power, authority, status, and involvement in schools and society regardless of innate individual attributes. Integration requires that classrooms reflect the rich fabric of our nation's diversity—which includes male and female students of different races, cultures, linguistic backgrounds, and ethnicity—in quality educational programs. It requires equal access to all programs and activities, equal opportunity for academic achievement, fair treatment in policy and practice, and equitable rewards and outcomes.

By creating environments that promote academic excellence, integration ultimately benefits society as students interact constructively with one another in ways that work toward prejudice reduction. Integration at the school level leads to integration at the societal level.

Unfortunately, the history of public education quickly reveals a system that has not always valued integration. In fact, it has only been during the twentieth century that any significant action has been taken to address equal educational opportunities for all. While the process has begun in earnest, integration of public education has not yet been fully achieved.

Brown v. Board of Education (1954), as the impetus for school integration, essentially marks the first phase of the yet incomplete integration of public education in this country through pupil reassignment, that is, the physical movement of students (and sometimes staff) of different races from one school building to another.

Ten years after the *Brown* decision, the passing of Title VII of the 1964 Civil Rights Act, in an attempt to address the problems that remained after student reassignment, marked a new era of integration in public schools. Issues such as unequal access to classes, teaching bias, and ability grouping surfaced and were recognized as critical to the integration process. *Lau v. Nichols* (1974) paved the way to address issues of equal access and equitable treatment for language-diverse students. Title IX of the 1972 Education Amendment recognized that equal access and equal educational opportunity were being denied to some students because of their gender.

In spite of the fact that at least two generations of children have attended public school in the United States since the *Brown* decision and at least one generation since Title IX and *Lau*, problems in achieving full integration persist. There has been a resegregation of Black students in many states, the desegregation of Hispanic students essentially never happened, and there is an increase in incidents of racial, ethnic, and gender bias and harassment in schools.

Complicating the prospects for achieving full integration in public education are issues of increased ethnic and linguistic diversity, increased poverty, family structures undergoing change, and the demands of a fast-changing workforce requiring full participation of all citizens at their optimal levels. Even some of the more recent attempts to achieve full integration—such as magnet schools—have yet to be proven successful. Thus, until integration is fully achieved, we will continue to deal with some very persistent barriers to equity and the attainment of equal education outcome for all students. *PB & MA* • *See also* **Brown v. Board of Education; Desegregation; Lau v. Nichols; Resegregation; Segregation**

Intercultural Communication

To define intercultural communication, it is helpful to first examine its component terms. Broadly defined, the term *culture* refers to "all that humans learn, in contrast to that which is genetically endowed" (Keesing & Keesing, 1971). Things that are learned include social organization, family structure, religious practices and beliefs, ways of knowing, and ways of communicating. The concept of *communication* is multidimensional, encompassing not just oral and written language but nonverbal elements (e.g., personal space, turn-taking styles, body language, touch) and orientations to time, space, and body positions (Longstreet, 1978, p. 12). Clothing, jewelry, hairstyles, and other aspects of physical appearance also contribute to any act of communication. Furthermore, communication takes place in social contexts that shape the form and quality of verbal and nonverbal communicative acts.

Members of a culture share unspoken and often unconscious knowledge about these and other aspects of communication. For example, few mainstream Americans would consider showing up 30 minutes late for a job interview, wearing soiled clothing, and then aggressively questioning the interviewer about his or her qualifications. It is a taken-for-granted aspect of communication in mainstream American culture that one arrives on time for interviews, dresses neatly, and answers rather than asks questions. For the most part, such unspoken rules of communication help societies function smoothly and efficiently.

Problems in communication often arise, however, when members of different cultures attempt to communicate. Cultural differences exist not just between nations (e.g., the United States and Japan) but within them (e.g., Navajo and White mainstream culture). Effective intercultural communication requires an understanding of cultural and social norms, that operate in any communicative situation. This is particularly true in schools, where the predominant style of communication is that of White mainstream culture. For example, in schools where European American English is the preferred dialect, students who speak country, Black vernacular, or any other nonstandard dialect may be labeled as illiterate or less intelligent (Bennett, 1990, p. 58). In White mainstream school culture students generally raise their hands to signal that they wish to speak in the class discussion. This can be frustrating, even damaging, for students from cultures where spontaneous voicing of opinions is valued or where individuals speak only after careful reflection. Teachers may describe these students as "shouting out of turn" or "never speaking up in class."

Teachers must be aware of cultural differences in communication styles so that they can create learning environments that give each student the maximum opportunity to learn and succeed. A student who is trying to figure out whether it's her turn to speak or who hesitates to speak because she might say "ain't" is not concentrating on the subject at hand.

Furthermore, students themselves need to be aware of cultural differences in communication styles so that they can communicate effectively with one another and with other people who may not share their home culture.

Intercultural initiatives surfaced in the 1940s during the intergroup education movement and were sometimes called cultural consciousness, intercultural competence, and cultural awareness programs. Many were targeted for school personnel such as teachers, principals, and counselors, but with recent advancements in technology, programs have been targeted to individuals who interact in what is commonly called the global community. *ES* • *See also* **Culture; Mainstream**

References
Baruth, L. G., & Manning, M. L. (1992). *Multicultural education for children and adolescents.* Needham Heights, MA: Allyn & Bacon.
Bennett, C. I. (1990). *Comprehensive multicultural education.* Boston, MA: Allyn & Bacon.
Jacob, E. (1987). Qualitative research traditions: A review. *Review of Educational Research,* 57(1), 1–50.
Keesing, R., & Keesing, R. (1971). *New perspectives in cultural anthropology.* New York: Holt, Rinehart and Winston.
Longstreet, W. (1978). *Aspects of ethnicity: Understanding differences in pluralistic classrooms.* New York: Teachers College Press.
Marshall, P. (1994). Four misconceptions about multicultural education that impede understanding. *Action in Teacher Education, 16*(3), 19–27.
O'Hair, M. J., & Odell, S. J. (Eds.). (1993). *Diversity and teaching: Teacher education yearbook I.* New York: Harcourt Brace Jovanovich.
Sleeter, C. E., & Grant, C. A. (1988). *Making choices for multicultural education.* Columbus, OH: Merrill.

Intergroup Education

Nestled between the periods when writers were identifying and creating curricular material on the African American experience in the early decades of the twentieth century and the ethnic studies movement of the 1960s was the intergroup education movement. Its major objective was to reduce prejudice and discrimination among U.S. Americans. Many of the programs that surfaced out of this movement were focused on the schools (Garcia, 1984).

The movement surfaced in the 1940s when a world war and a war economy enticed African and Mexican Americans and poor Whites to move beyond their historical confines to shore up a depleted labor force. During the war the movement gained in intensity as these newcomers and an established White labor force competed for jobs and housing. Invariably racial incidents occurred as established U.S. Americans accused the newcomers of taking White men's jobs and moving into White neighborhoods. The newcomers accused established U.S. Americans of restricting job opportunities, maintaining a ceiling on wages, and limiting social opportunities. Increasingly these clashes spilled over into neighborhoods and schools (Banks, 1979).

U.S. Americans became concerned as these incidents increased and drew national attention. They became an international embarrassment as the

United States led the effort to rid the world of totalitarian forms of government. Moreover, the realization after the war that Nazi Germany had exterminated six million Jews underlined the seriousness of the problem (Kane, 1970).

U.S. American education organizations (e.g., National Council for the Social Studies, American Council on Education) took the initiative and developed programs aimed at combating prejudice and discrimination against African and Mexican Americans and, to a lesser extent, poor Whites. One of the more popular approaches was the development of curricular materials (e.g., lessons, units, curriculum guides) aimed at providing teachers and students with an understanding of the historical experiences of the targeted groups with special attention given to incidents of prejudice and discrimination. Projects were also developed that reflected the latest theoretical findings in intergroup interactions.

In its efforts to develop curriculum aimed at addressing interracial tensions, the intergroup education movement gained substantial support from a number of nationally known educators, social scientists, and philosophers. Individuals contributed to the movement such as Louis Wirth, a University of Chicago sociologist; Gordon W. Allport, a Harvard social psychologist; Alain Locke, an African American philosopher at Howard University; and Allison Davis, a noted African American anthropologist at the University of Chicago (Banks, 1995).

Several important studies in the area of race relations were also undertaken during this time. The American Jewish Committee and Anti-Defamation League of B'nai B'rith sponsored studies in the area of race relations and examination of curriculum materials—particularly textbooks—for their treatment of minorities, Jews, and other groups (Kane, 1970). In 1954 Allport's major study *The Nature of Prejudice* was published detailing "influential principles about ways to create effective intergroup interactions" (Banks, 1995, p. 8).

Educators, social scientists, and philosophers who were part of the intergroup education movement believed that public education was the vehicle by which the country could reduce its ethnic and racial tensions. Teachers who were informed about racial and ethnic groups and encouraged contact among isolated groups with mainstream U.S. Americans could help students develop more democratic racial attitudes and values. The success of many of the projects and studies conducted during this period suggests that they were correct. *JG*

References

Allport, G. (1954). *The nature of prejudice*. Cambridge, MA: Addison-Wesley.

Banks, J. A. (1979). *Teaching strategies for ethnic studies* (2nd ed.). Boston: Allyn & Bacon.

———. (1995). Multicultural education: Historical development, dimensions, and practices. In J. A. Banks & C. A. M. Banks (Eds.), *Handbook of research on multicultural education* (pp. 3–24). New York: Macmillan.

Garcia, J. (1984). Multiethnic education: Past, present, and future. *Texas Tech Journal of Education, 11*(1), 13–29.

Garcia, R. (1991). *Teaching in a pluralistic society.* New York: HarperCollins.

Grant, C. A. (1994). Best practices in teacher preparation for urban schools: Lessons from the multicultural teacher education literature. *Action in Teacher Education, 16*(3), 1–18.

Kane, M. B. (1970). *Minorities in tradebooks: A study of their treatment in social studies texts.* Chicago: Quadrangle Books for Anti-Defamation League of B'nai B'rith.

Kushner, K., et al. (1995). *Human diversity in education: An integrative approach.* New York: McGraw-Hill.

Intragroup Diversity

Consciously and unconsciously people are placed into categories. These categories may be based upon assumptions due to language, ethnicity, culture, sexual orientation, socioeconomic status, political beliefs, and race. However large the categories may be, they mask important within-group, or *intragroup*, differences.

For example, all Asian Pacific Americans are not the same. They may differ in a variety of ways (Pang, 1995; Young & Pang, 1995). First, Asian Pacific Americans are made up of many distinctive ethnic groups including Bangladeshi, Bhutanese, Bornean, Burmese, Cambodian, Celbesian, Cernan, Chamorro, Chinese, East Indian, Filipino, Hawaiian, Hmong, Indonesian, Korean, Japanese, Samoan, and Vietnamese communities. Secondly, Asian Pacific Americans may differ by place of birth, generation in the United States, age, level of income, educational achievement, and numerous other aspects. Similarly, all women are not the same. Women share a history of fighting for civil rights in the United States as well as biological attributes and characteristics. However, women are also different. Some are older and others are younger. Some choose to marry and have children, and others choose to remain single. Yet, no matter who they are as individuals, they are members of the collective group called women who represent vast within-group differences.

Robert S. McNamara, who was the secretary of defense during the Kennedy administration, provides a thoughtful example of the results when the leaders of our nation do not consider intragroup diversity. In his book *In Retrospect: The Tragedy and Lessons of Vietnam* (1995) McNamara writes,

> Like most Americans, I saw Communism as monolithic. I believed the Soviets and Communists were cooperating in trying to extend their hegemony. In hindsight, of course, it is clear that they had no unified strategy after the late 1950s. It seemed obvious that the Communist

movement in Vietnam was closely related to guerrilla insurgencies in Burma, Indonesia, Malaya, and Philippines during the 1950s. We viewed these conflicts not as nationalistic movements—as they largely appear in hindsight—but as signs of a unified Communist drive for hegemony in Asia. (p. 30–31)

The perception of Communism as a powerful unified movement, in part, led to the long and misguided involvement of the United States in Vietnam and other countries in Southeast Asia.

Members of cultural, political, religious, racial, ethnic, and other communities may display general trends; however, subgroups and individuals within large categories will demonstrate a wide range of differences because each person and community are unique combinations of an infinite number of factors. *VOP*

References

McNamara, R. S. (1995). *In retrospect: The tragedy and lessons of Vietnam.* New York: Random House.

Pang, V. O. (1995). Asian Pacific American students: A diverse and complex population. In J. A. Banks & C. A. M. Banks (Eds.), *Handbook of research on multicultural education* (pp. 412–24). New York: Macmillan.

Young, R. L., & Pang, V. O. (1995). Asian Pacific American students: A rainbow of dreams. *Multicultural Education, 3*(2), 4–7.

Knowledge Construction *See* Multicultural Education, Dimensions of

Language

Language is the means by which humans communicate. It is what makes our behavior human (Gollnick & Chinn, 1998). Language has many different functions. It can be used to inspire, incite, arouse feelings of fear and intimidation, and elicit feelings of affection. Language serves as a bond between individuals. Those who share a common language, share a bond of cultural identity.

There are literally thousands of different languages in the world, with some estimates reaching ten thousand (Crystal, 1997). In addition, each language may have several different dialects. For example, the English language has dialects that are peculiar to the United States such as a Brooklyn dialect, a Texas drawl, or Black vernacular English. In addition there are several different dialects found in the British Isles, and different English dialects are found in countries such as Australia and New Zealand.

With the many different languages and dialects in the world, there are inevitable attempts to designate one language as superior to another. All languages have been developed to express the needs of their users. In that sense all languages are equal. Consequently the complexity of languages differ. Since there is nothing limiting, demeaning, or handicapping about the different languages, it can be argued that all languages are equal (Crystal, 1997).

One of the characteristics of language is that it is adaptable. As with other aspects of culture, language adapts to the needs of the situation or its users. For example, immigrants who come to the United States often find new items that did not exist in their homeland. New words or adaptations of the English word have to be created for the object to be incorporated into their language. Another characteristic of language is that it is dynamic. Language is constantly changing. Expressions change with generations and the terms and colloquialisms used by the youth of today are likely to be significantly different 50 years from now.

In the United States there are many different regional or social dialects. Dialects differ from one another in different ways. Regional dialects tend to differ primarily in the use of vowels. Social dialects tend to have differences in the use of consonants. It should be noted, however, that it is often difficult to separate the use of social class and regional dialects, as the dialects of many individuals are a blend of both.

Black English or Black vernacular English (Ebonics) is one of the most recognizable and controversial dialects spoken in the United States today. It is the dialect used by most working-class African Americans in their own communities. It is estimated that as many as 80 percent of African Americans use Black English consistently, while 19 percent use speech that, with the exception of minor differences in pronunciation or vocal quality, is indistinguishable from Standard English. Although ethnically based, Black English is also rooted in class origins. Black English is often attacked by educators as are Appalachian English and Hawaiian Pidgin English, since individuals whose spoken English is limited to these dialects are sometimes at an educational, social, and occupational disadvantage.

Black English and Appalachian English have rule systems of their own. Therefore, most linguists consider these dialects to be legitimate systems of communication and not substandard, deviant, or improper forms of English. Hawaiian Pidgin has a lexicon that is predominantly English but is influenced by Chinese, Hawaiian, Portuguese, and Ilocano. Consequently it is viewed by some as an English dialect, a pidgin, or a creole by others. Like Black vernacular English, the Hawaiian Pidgin or Creole— spoken by many working-class Hawaiians—is stigmatized and attacked by educational policy makers (Ovando, 1993).

In addition to written and spoken language, there is also nonverbal communication. The total meaning of communication goes beyond the *surface message* as it is stated. The undercurrent message includes the emotions or feelings associated with the content or surface message. Meaning is often sent nonverbally through body language. Nonverbal communication is explored in *proxemics,* the study of social space. One's proxemics is often related to one's cultural background. Arabs, Latin Americans, and southern Europeans tend to be from *contact* cultures. Asians, Indians, Pakistanis, and northern Europeans tend to be from *noncontact* cultures. Touching among individuals from these groups is less frequent and conversational distances tend to be greater. *Kinesics* is the study of body language: facial expressions, posture, gestures, and other body movements, which often carry messages.

Some nonverbal communication is vocal. *Paralanguage* is communicated through the sounds that are vocal but not verbal. Paralanguage may be characterized by *vocalizations* or by *vocal qualities*. Vocalizations are sounds and noises that are not words (e.g., a laugh or sigh). Vocal qualities include resonance, tempo, articulation control, and rhythm control. Vocal qualities can be utilized to express anger, sadness, or other emotions (Gollnick & Chinn, 1998).

Manual communication is used primarily by individuals who are deaf. There are two components of manual communication: *fingerspelling* and *signs*. Fingerspelling spells out words letter-by-letter using a manual alphabet. Signing involves symbolic representations of words made with the hands. In the United States, American Sign Language (ASL) is considered by many deaf adults to be their native language. While the grammatical structure of ASL differs from English, it does use the same lexicon, or vocabulary (Hunt & Marshall, 1994). ASL is considered a legitimate language by linguists. However, because it does not correspond directly to English, and because there is no widely practiced method of writing ASL, it is not generally used as a primary language of instruction with children. Sign language systems such as Signed English and Signing Exact English are the most commonly utilized sign language systems for education. These English-order systems seek to sign every word and inflection. Verb tense markers such as *-ed* and *-ing* are signed (Hunt & Marshall, 1994).

Total communication is currently the most commonly utilized system of communication for students who are deaf. This approach uses oral speech and manual communication together. Total communication encourages children to speak but also allows them more options for receiving and sending messages. This approach advocates using whatever channels are available to learn and comprehend messages (e.g., ASL, speech, speech reading, fingerspelling) (Smith & Luckasson, 1995). *PCC*

References

Crystal, D. (1997) *The Cambridge encyclopedia of language,* 2nd ed. Cambridge: Cambridge University Press.

Gollnick, D. M., & Chinn, P. C. (1998) *Multicultural education in a pluralistic society* (5th ed.). Columbus, OH: Prentice Hall.

Hunt, N., & Marshall, K. (1994). *Exceptional children and youth.* Boston: Houghton Mifflin.

Ovando, C. J. (1993). Language diversity and education. In J. A. Banks & C. A. M. Banks (Eds.), *Multicultural education: Issues and perspectives* (2nd ed.). Boston: Allyn & Bacon.

Smith, D.D., & Luckasson, R. (1995). *Introduction to special education* (2nd ed.). Boston: Allyn & Bacon.

Latino Studies

Latino studies refers to a recent interdisciplinary area of research dedicated to the study of Latinos and Latinas in the United States. Generally, scholars focus on key critical issues in discussing Latino cultures in the United States. Lynn Heyck (1994) identifies those issues as demographics, diversity among Latinos, an extended presence (predating that of Anglos), a history of discrimination and victimization, and cultural richness. Other key issues are language maintenance, self-identification, political representation, positioning in society, and efforts to redefine the United States as a nation. These concerns dominate current U.S. Latino literature and art.

Latinos are the largest and fastest-growing diverse group in the country. Scholars estimate that there are 30 million Latinos in the United States, including those who are undocumented, of whom 90 percent speak Spanish. (According to the 1990 U.S. Census there were 24 million Latinos in the nation, representing 9 percent of the country's total population of 255 million. This source also estimated that there will be 49 million Latinos by the year 2020 and 81 million by 2050, representing 40 percent of the entire U.S. population.) In a few years California will be a Latino state—the majority of the population will be Latino or Latina.

The term *Latinos* refers to all people living in the United States whose origin is Latin American, including the Spanish speakers from the Caribbean. There are three main groups of Latinos in the United States: Mexicans, Puerto Ricans, and Cubans. But there are also large communities of Salvadoreans, Colombians, Dominicans, Peruvians, Guatemalans, Chileans, and other peoples from Latin America. Thus, Latinos represent diverse racial and national combinations, and many identify themselves as Native American, African, European, Asian, Arabic, or *mestizo* (racially and culturally mixed heritage).

Most people prefer the term *Latino* over *Hispanic*. The term Hispanic, which is used by the U.S. State Department, mainstream politicians, and marketing experts, tends to erase the cultural diversity of Latinos, suggesting a direct origin from Spain. The term Latino, instead, acknowledges differences and diverse national origins among Latinos (short for *Latinoamericanos*) as well as an indigenous cultural heritage.

Each Latino group has a distinct history and length of residence in what is now the United States. Although the Spanish presence in the Southwest and Florida dates back to 1513 and the first Spanish settlement was established in 1565, some Latino groups are in the U.S. due to expansionism and intervention in Latin America. Like Native Americans, Chicanos (Mexican origin people in the U.S.) are a *conquest people*, displaced and dispossessed of their land and political power in the Southwest by Anglos during the nineteenth century; some Puerto Ricans are in the U.S. due to colonialism; many Cubans entered the U.S. as political refugees; and many other Latin Americans are economic immigrants.

Recognizing differences and commonalities, Latino studies programs have merged Chicano and Puerto Rican studies in some areas of the country (Chicano-Boricua studies). Due to the increased demand from students, scholars, and community members to develop interdisciplinary programs and curricula that reflect their own historical and cultural experience, Latino studies promises to grow. The substantial number of studies on Latinos and Latinas published in recent years points in that direction, whether conducted under the name Latino studies, Chicano-Boricua studies, or within an ethnic studies setting. *RM*

References

Flores, J. (1993). *Divide borders: Essays on Puerto Rican identity*. Houston: Arte Publico Press.

Heyck, D. L. (1994). *Barrios and borderlands: Cultures of Latinos and Latinas in the United States*. New York: Routledge.

Martínez, R. (1993). *The other side: Notes from new LA, Mexico City, and beyond*. New York: Vintage.

Masud-Piloto, F. (1995). Nuestra realidad: Historical roots of our Latino identity. In J. Solís & S. Jackson (Eds.), *Beyond comfort zones in multiculturalism: Confronting the politics of privilege as educators*. Westport, CT: Bergin & Garvey.

Oboler, S. (1995). *Ethnic labels, Latino lives: Identity and the politics of (re)presentation in the United States*. Minneapolis: University of Minnesota Press.

Pérez Firmat, G. (1994). *Life on the hyphen: The Cuban-American way*. Austin: University of Texas Press.

Vigil, J. D. (1984). *From Indians to Chicanos*. Prospect Heights, IL: Waveland Press.

Lau v. Nichols

In 1974 the Supreme Court ruled in *Lau v. Nichols* that public schools must take positive and demonstrative steps to ensure that children with a lack of or limited English skills are provided with an equal educational opportunity. This case was inspired by Chinese students and parents in the San Francisco public school system who had become increasingly dissatisfied with the quality of education they were receiving and the absence of bilingual programs in their classrooms.

The *Lau* decision stemmed from the realization that equality of educational treatment did not occur simply by providing all students with the same physical opportunities. Offering students access to the same buildings, books, teachers, and curriculum does not compensate for other cultural differences such as language, and it leaves space for the creation of barriers that preclude meaningful education. As early as the 1960s the activist group

La Raza Unida Party boycotted the Crystal City, Texas, schools, won the electoral majority on the school board, and began bilingual programs at the elementary level. Although the actions of the party were viewed as extremist by the majority of Hispanic Americans (the largest group of bilingual education students in America), mainstream Hispanic educators also argued for bilingual education as a means of transition between the two languages and as a chance to maintain the native language. Hearings on the Bilingual Education Act of 1968 (which appropriated funds for the development of educational programs designed to meet the needs of children with limited English-speaking abilities) named societal, individual, and psychological aspects among the benefits of preserving these non-English-speaking students' native tongues.

With the *Lau* decision firmly in place during the mid-1970s, governmental support aided in the creation of the *Lau remedies*. These guidelines initially required schools to commit to a greater bilingual education effort than had been demonstrated in the past. It outlined specific ways in which schools could address bilingual education goals such as using the students' native languages, transitional learning toward English proficiency, bilingual-bicultural learning that offers dual fluency, and methods that encourage a dense multicultural curriculum and fluency in several languages. These remedies came under attack in 1980 when even stricter guidelines regarding implementation were proposed. The conservative influences of the 1980s generated support to eliminate the native language component of bilingual programs, which was believed to be more in line with an Americanization concept. This move toward total English proficiency resulted in a 47 percent spending cut for Bilingual Education Act programs between 1980 and 1988.

Still a topic of heavy debate, the issue of bilingual education is as much a struggle about power as it is about language. Undoubtedly, denying students the opportunity to begin their educational journeys from a place of familiarity and to move forward—maintaining a vital link with their native cultures—is not providing an equal or progressive education. Furthermore, the "present overdose of monolingualism and Anglocentrism that dominates the current educational debate not only contributes to a type of mind-tied America, but also is incapable of producing educators and leaders who can rethink what it means to prepare students to enter the ever-changing, multilingual, and multicultural world of the 21st century" (Macedo, 1995, p. 249). *WCF & RBJ*

References

Macedo, D. (1995). English only: The tongue-tying of America. In J. W. Noll (Ed.), *Taking sides: Clashing views on controversial educational issues* (8th ed.) (pp. 249–58). Guilford, CT: Dushki.

Limited English Proficiency (LEP)

Limited English proficiency (LEP) is a term used to classify students whose lack of facility in the English language may have negative consequences for their academic achievement in monolingual English classrooms (Nieto, 1992). The growth in the number of LEP students is due to a trend of increased immigration, particularly from Asia and Latin America. According to the 1990 census, one of eight families speaks a language other than English at home. The 1968 Title VII Bilingual Education Act and the U.S. Supreme Court decision *Lau v. Nichols* have provided the legal basis for equitable treatment of LEP students in the U.S. schools (Ovando, 1993). However, only 15 percent of students who need bilingual services are in federally funded programs, and only about one-third receive any language assistance at all (Nieto, 1992).

The term *LEP* has been criticized as having a deficit orientation towards language-diverse students because it emphasizes what they cannot do—they have *limited proficiency* in English—rather than what they can do—they may be *highly proficient* in the language(s) they do know (Freeman & Freeman, 1994). By negatively valuing or ignoring students' primary languages, teachers may inadvertently view language-diverse students as *handicapped* or *deficient*. A disproportionate number of second language learners are identified as having learning disabilities. Labeling children as *limited* may also result in lower expectations, lower achievement, and lower self-esteem.

An unfortunate consequence of a deficit orientation towards language-diverse students may be that it discourages them from speaking or writing in their home language and from expressing their own ethnic or community identities. Rather than seeing the first language as an asset and the bilingual person as being linguistically gifted, educators with a deficit orientation penalize students for using their first language. Related to the deficit linguistic orientation is an assimilationist cultural orientation that views the goal of education to be the assimilation of students into American mainstream culture. Educators with assimilationist views may marginalize language-diverse students by viewing them as foreign or as refusing to be American. In addition, language-diverse groups may face accent discrimination.

Terms such as *English language learners* or *second language learners* have been suggested to replace the designation of limited English proficient. Some teachers have replaced the negative label with positive labels such as PEP (*potentially English proficient*) or LG (*linguistically gifted*) (Freeman & Freeman, 1994). The deficit orientation of the term *LEP* reflects unequal power relations between dominant and subordinate linguistic groups in society (Phillipson, 1992), institutional racism, and systematic inequities between the education of rich and poor children (Kozol, 1991). Addressing inequities in power requires strategies of empowerment—which include educational terminology—such as categorization, naming and self-definition, involvement of communities, honoring home languages and cultures, classroom pedagogies of empowerment, and assessment that advocates the empowerment of language-diverse students (Cummins, 1994). *SDW*

References

Cummins, J. (1994). The socioacademic achievement model. In R. A. De Villar, C. J. Faltis, & J. P. Cummins (Eds.), *Cultural diversity in schools: From rhetoric to practice* (pp. 363–90). Albany: State University of New York Press.

Freeman, D. E., & Freeman, Y. S. (1994). *Between worlds: Access to second language acquisition.* Portsmouth, NY: Heinemann.

Kozol, J. (1991). *Savage inequalities.* New York: Harper.

Nieto, S. (1992). *Affirming diversity: The sociopolitical context of multicultural education.* White Plains, NY: Longman.

Ovando, C. J. (1993). Language diversity and education. In J. A. Banks & C. A. M. Banks (Eds.), *Multicultural education* (2nd ed.) (pp. 215–38). Needham Heights, MA: Allyn & Bacon.

Phillipson, R. (1992). *Linguistic imperialism.* Oxford: Oxford University Press.

Magnet Schools

Magnet schools are public schools defined by three characteristics. First, they are formally desegregated schools where seats are allocated according to formulas that take official account of race and seek racial balance. Second, they are innovative schools that differ in a formal way from regular public schools—in mode of instruction, curricular emphasis, or a program of career preparation. Third, they enroll students on a voluntary basis and from beyond the borders of regular attendance areas, hence their *magnetic* character.

These schools were initially developed in the 1970s as part of voluntary or court-ordered desegregation plans. They were encouraged starting in 1976 through federal funding under the Emergency School Aid Act and later under a federal magnet school grants program.

Some magnet schools have academic entrance criteria or advanced curricula, making them accessible only to specially skilled students. Such schools are inaccessible to most students, and they reportedly cream the best students out of other schools in a school district. However, the best data available (Blank, 1990) suggest that the majority of magnet schools have no formal selection criteria. Moore and Davenport (1990) point out that even without entrance requirements, parents' perceptions and differential access to information often leads to self-selection that favors high achievers. Some plans, for example, the controlled-choice plans where all schools become magnets promoted by Alves and Willie (1990), attempt to deal with this problem with aggressive and culturally sensitive programs to provide parent information.

Metz (1986) argues that the most important differentiating quality of magnet schools lies in their symbolic difference from regular public schools and thus in the indirect implication that they are formally superior to regular schools. This problem is exacerbated where there are more applicants than seats and students must be turned away, forcing them to attend second-choice schools. Metz argues that magnet schools' practical contributions to equity should be measured not against ideal schools with egalitarian student bodies but against the reality of neighborhood schools based on discriminatory housing patterns, which are far more differentiated in social class and achievement than most magnet schools. Such schools, unlike magnet schools, are also usually segregated by race. Ironically, the differentiation in class, academic skills, and race between city and suburban schools (or even between suburbs) is starker than that between magnet and regular schools in city systems. Yet they are less often subject to attack for inequity since the Supreme Court's *Milliken* decision. The *Milliken* decision advocated local control and stated that a school district should not be forced to participate in a school desegregation remedy unless the communities could be found guilty of intentional segregation or unless it could be shown that state action created the pattern of all-White suburbs and a predominantly Black urban distinct.

Magnet schools' formal license for educational difference offers some real chances for educational innovation and for the matching of students' interests or styles with that of the school. However, these differences can make it difficult to use standard accountability measures. Both recruitment of appropriate teachers and daily school practices often conflict with union rules. Magnet schools' relationship with centralized and standardized systems is likely to generate conflict on both sides.

Though much more research is needed, there is some suggestive evidence that magnet schools further desegregation (Rossell, 1990), improve academic achievement (Blank, 1990), provide opportunities and models for innovation or restructuring (Metz, 1986), and—when appropriately designed and conducted—improve relations among students of different races (Metz, 1986; Schofield, 1989). *MHM*

References

Alves, M. J., & Willie, C. V. (1990). Choice, decentralization and desegregation: The Boston "controlled choice" plan. In W. H. Clune & J. F. Witte (Eds.), *Choice and control in American education volume 2: The practice of choice, decentralization, and school restructuring* (pp. 17–75). New York: Falmer Press.

Blank, R. K. (1990). Educational effects of magnet high schools. In W. H. Clune & J. F. Witte (Eds.), *Choice and control in American education volume 2: The practice of choice, decentralization, and school restructuring* (pp. 77–110). New York: Falmer Press.

Metz, M. H. (1986). *Different by design: The context and character of three magnet schools*. New York: Routledge.

Moore, D. R., & Davenport, S. (1990). School choice: The new improved sorting machine. In W. L. Boyd & H. J. Walberg (Eds.), *Choice in education: Potential and problems* (pp. 187–223). Berkeley, CA: McCutchan.

Rossell, C. H. (1990). *The carrot or the stick for school desegregation policy: Magnet schools or forced busing*. Philadelphia: Temple University Press.

Schofield, J. W. (1989). *Black and White in school: Trust, tension, or tolerance?* New York: Teachers College Press.

Mainstream

Though the term *mainstream* has been used for years—as though we know what it means—its meaning is by no means clear. In *The American Cultural Dialogue and Its Transmission* the concept is discussed at length. For most of its usage, the term has been a loose reference to a demographic majority, that is, the European American majority (about 75 percent of the total population), which presumably shares a common culture. Class differences within this demographic majority have been considered, or not considered, depending upon the persuasion of the analyst. This demographic definition of mainstream will no longer suffice since there are people of every racial and ethnic identity who exhibit cultural features in common with persons of White ancestry. While the demographic dimension of mainstream has shrunk in proportion to the population in the United States as a whole, it has increased in number due to the inclusion of persons of other-than-European-American ancestry who exhibit common cultural features. Therefore, mainstream is now a cultural statement, not a demographic one.

What is the culture of the mainstream? There are those who would deny that there is a mainstream culture. Instead, they would argue that there is only one U.S. American culture that is historically derived from northern European, Anglo Saxon traditions—which have long comprised U.S. American mainstream culture—but that have been substantially added to by African American, American Indian (Native American), Asian American, and many other cultural traditions. This model includes special attention to the individual and his or her rights, belief in hard work as the legitimate means to success, value of success as exemplified in material display, belief that "all men are created equal," optimism about the future, a strong value placed upon freedom, and emphasis on absolute morality. These core orientations are combined with other orientations that are explicated into an American *cultural dialogue*. That is, we talk about them, argue about them, act upon them, write about them, and erect government programs upon the ideology they furnish. In short, we engage in a continuous dialogue about them. Although there are other components of mainstream culture, such as styles of dress, demeanor, speech, and food preferences that vary by region and class, this broad cultural definition of mainstream includes a wide variety of such customs.

This broad definition of mainstream is the most appropriate for the U.S. American culture of today; that is, those persons who in their habits of thought and action are engaged in the U.S. American cultural dialogue. *GS2 & LS1* • *See also* **Minority**

Reference

Spindler, G., & Spindler, L. (1990). *The American cultural dialogue and its transmission.* London and Bristol, PA: Falmer Press.

Majority *See* Mainstream

Marginalization

When people speak of being marginalized or being on the margins, they are referring to their position on the periphery of social, political, cultural, economic, and educational life. Persons who see themselves as living on the boundaries of U.S. society may include persons of color; persons living in poverty; people with disabilities; persons who are gay, lesbian, and bisexual; persons who are from language backgrounds other than English; and women. It is important to recognize that there are multiple ways in which people can be positioned or position themselves in relation to the margins and the mainstream. Often people are placed or pushed to the margins by others. Some people choose boundaries as desirable places to be. Living on the margins does not necessarily imply that those who live and work there are passive victims of others and of their status. Rather, many who are boundary dwellers deploy their resources as a means of altering the status quo. *MLG* • *See also* **Mainstream**

Melting Pot

The first recorded reference to the United States as a melting pot can be found in J. Hector St. John de Crevecoeur's *Letters from an American Farmer* (1782). De Crevecoeur, himself an immigrant, wrote a collection of letters to his former friends in France glorifying the U.S. countryside and the unique U.S. American character. His best-remembered letter—"What is an

American?"—describes how "individuals of all nations are melted into a new race of men."

The idea that immigrants to America would leave behind their previous customs, manners, and prejudices and would carve out a *new race* that was an amalgam of the many races that had emigrated to the new land was an idea close to the heart of the American self-image. But as the century passed and the number of individuals and nations involved grew, their confidence that they could become one waned, and so too did the belief that it would be possible for all Americans to melt into one.

In 1882 the Chinese were excluded from immigration and the first of many immigration laws was enacted. By the time the National Origins Act of 1924 was passed, the nation had formally adopted a policy that used immigration to reinforce, rather than further dilute the racial stock of the early America that de Crevecoeur had known.

Considering the hostility toward immigrants during this time period, it is difficult to understand the success of Israel Zangwill's 1909 play *The Melting Pot*. The play has as its central theme the ideal that people of many backgrounds could come to America and merge into one new race. Zangwill's main character, David Quixano, a Russian Jewish immigrant who was a pogrom orphan, says of his new country, "America is God's Crucible, the great Melting Pot where all the races of Europe are melting and re-forming!" (Zangwill, 1909, pp. 37–38). Zangwill's character was referring especially to the immigrants of Eastern Europe who were the major characters in his play, and in particular he was referring to Jews and Gentiles living together as one.

However, a single U.S. American nationality never emerged. The resulting blend always included ethnic groups that continued to maintain some of their original characteristics but at the same time were modified by their interactions with others. In time Zangwill himself retreated from his earlier position on racial and religious mixture. Only eight years after the opening of *The Melting Pot* he was writing that "It was vain . . . to declare that there should be neither Jew nor Greek. Nature will return even if driven out with a pitchfork, still more if driven out with a dogma" (Leftwich, 1957, p. 255).

Not only did the melting pot not amalgamate, it never came close to absorbing Americans from Africa, Asia, Central and South America, or Native Americans. Therefore, over the past 25 years writers have used metaphors that more closely describe a situation in which different racial, ethnic, religious, and other cultural groups come together in one place. The salad bowl, mosaic, symphony, rainbow, and kaleidoscope metaphors all take into account the reality that groups both maintain some of their characteristics and are modified by their interactions with others. *DAB*

References

de Crevecoeur, J. H. S. J. (1782). *Letters from an American farmer*. London: Thomas Davies.
Leftwich, J. (1957). *Israel Zangwill*. New York: Thomas Yoseloff.
Zangwill, I. (1909). *The melting pot*. New York: Macmillan.

Mestizaje *See* Border Studies

Mexican American Studies

The goal of Mexican American studies (MAS) programs and courses is to increase students' understanding of the history, culture, socioeconomic status, and political behavior of Mexican Americans in the Southwest and elsewhere in the United States. The MAS curriculum provides specialized knowledge about Mexican Americans, who comprise the second largest diverse ethnic group in the United States. The proximity of the Mexican border to the Southwest provides a continuous revitalization of cultural traditions and the Spanish language, which insures a continuous means of self-expression and communication for Mexican Americans and provides opportunity for study. The impact of this group is studied in terms of cultural change, acculturation, racial mixture, assimilation, language, emancipation, and development, as well as its effects on sociocultural views.

The struggle of the Mexican American groups in the 1950s and 1960s for political and economic justice form the core for Chicano studies. The term Chicano is used by Mexican Americans to emphasize a political identity. Born out of the racial and ethnic strife of people of color, Chicano studies began by describing the Mexican American community as more "homogenous and unified than it really was" (Winkler, 1990). Soon feminists began to challenge this universal definition in scholarship forcing Chicano studies to change by exploring the way race, gender, sexual orientation, and geographic location alter identity and cultural awareness (Klora de Alva, 1990).

Today, Mexican American studies programs have taken the knowledge learned over the last years in Chicano scholarship and have redefined these programs. Students develop the ability to critically analyze the importance of ethnicity, race, gender, religion, and socioeconomic factors to Mexican Americans and to the country as a whole. MAS programs will increase students' understandings of ethnic identities and of multicultural societies.

ERC • *See also* **Chicano and Chicana Studies; Latino Studies**

References

Klora de Alva, J. J. (1990). Chicana history and historical significance: Some theoretical considerations. In A. R. Del Castillo (Ed.), *Between borders: Essays on Mexicana/Chicana history*. Encino, CA: Foricanto Press.

Winkler, K. J. (1990). Scholars say issues of diversity have "revolutionized" field of Chicano Studies. *Chronicle of Higher Education, 37*, A4–A8.

Migrant Education

Migrant education is a term used to describe the variety of services designed to help the children of migratory workers succeed in school. The term derives its meaning from the national program that the United States Congress established in 1966 under the authority of the Title I Elementary and Secondary Education Act. The political impetus for this program was powered in part by Edward R. Murrow's documentary *Harvest of Shame*, which aired on Thanksgiving Day in 1960 in households across the United States. The film focused on the plight of United States workers and their families who move from town to town and from state to state to plant and harvest our nation's crops.

Migrant children were being systematically denied the educational opportunities offered to other children because they were poor and because they were disenfranchised from the communities in which their parents toiled. Frequently, families would not live long enough in a single community to establish residency to be able to vote or to exercise the rights of their children to receive adequate schooling.

The rationale provided by the U.S. Congress for establishing this program was as true in 1966 as it is today:

> The children of migratory agricultural workers present a unique problem for educators. Migratory workers travel from community to community in order to work. They often settle in a single community for two months or less. Consequently, their children are seldom in school long enough to participate in school activities; some spend only two to six weeks in any one school district during the harvest season. Well over half of all migrant children are not achieving at their grade level, a substantial number of them are two years or more behind in their schooling. . . .

> The amendment offered by the Committee will permit the Commissioner to make special grants to state educational agencies for the purpose of establishing special education programs for these children. It is expected that the state educational agencies will be imaginative in designing these special programs and that they will cooperate among themselves whenever it is appropriate. (U.S. House, 1966, p. 10)

Taken individually, migrant children differ one from another. As a group, however, they have common characteristics that impede their growth and success in school. Migrant children are poor, they move from one school district to another, they have little access to adequate health care, they live in substandard housing, and they toil at hard labor beginning from a very young age. Ninety percent of migrant children today are children of color, many of whom do not speak English well.

Migrant education distinguishes itself from other educational programs in several ways. First, program funds can be spent on a constellation of services—including the purchase of clothing and eye glasses or the provision of dental and health care—so that migrant children may enter the classroom without the distractions caused by such basic deterrents as untreated health problems. Second, programs are designed to provide educational continuity for students enrolling in different school systems and, frequently, in different states. Since the United States does not have a national curriculum, nor is there a procedure for uniformly agreeing on the acceptance of high school credits from one school district to the next, migrant educators design and promote individual compacts among state and local educational agencies to help migrant students overcome the educational disadvantage they face from frequent dislocations. More generally, migrant education frequently provides a host of basic education-related services that simply may not exist in their communities, such as summer school, preschool, and English language assistance. *KG*

References

Chavez, L. (1992). *Invisible children: A portrait of migrant education in the United States.* Washington, DC: National Commission on Migrant Education.

Cox, J. L., et al. (1992). *Descriptive study of the Chapter I Migrant Education Program.* Research Triangle Park, NC: Research Triangle Institute.

Ford, W. D. (1987). *Migrant education: A consolidated view.* Denver, CO: Education Commission of the States.

Glover, R. E., Lugo, T., & Friend, R. E. (1992). *Rethinking migrant education.* Baton Rouge, LA: National Association of State Directors of Migrant Education.

U.S. House. (1966). House of Representatives report no. 1814 to accompany H.R. 13161. 89th Congress, 2nd sess.

Martin, P. L., & Martin, D. A. (1994). *The endless quest—Helping America's farm workers.* Boulder, CO: Westover Press.

Newman, J. (1977). *Promises to keep: The continuing crisis in the education of migrant children.* New York: National Child Labor Committee.

Prewitt-Diaz, J. O., Trotter, R. T., & Rivera, V. A. (1988). *The effects of migration on children: An ethnographic study.* Harrisburg, PA: Department of Education.

Minority

A minority is any group that devitates from established cultural norms. This deviation may or may not follow racial categories. For instance, there are many African Americans, Native Americans, Latinos, and Asian Americans who participate as fully in the *American cultural dialogue* (see *Mainstream*) as any European American.

If one defines the *mainstream* group most narrowly as White, Anglo Saxon, and Protestant, it might include as little as 20 percent of the total U.S. population. Given this definition of mainstream, approximately 80 percent of the American population would be termed minority. Within this large group there would, of course, be a number of culturally distinctive groups such as continental Europeans, Catholic Americans, Native Americans, Chinese Americans, African Americans, and Mexican Americans. If one defines *mainstream* more broadly, including all persons of European descent, irrespective of religious affiliation, the mainstream group would constitute an actual demographic minority.

Whatever definition is used for *mainstream*, the power relations between the groups remains clear. About 80 percent of all positions of power, such as U.S. Senator, university president, and corporate board member, have been held by the ethnic class we identify as middle class, White Anglo Saxon Protestant. The power of the mainstream has begun to erode of late but still exhibits tenacity. This exercise of power has often not corresponded to the cultural and social needs of the people served, as in schools where the student poulation is composed of ethnic minorities but the enterprise is organized to transmit Euro-American values and customs.

The United States is a dynamic, changing place unparalleled elsewhere, but it has its special problems. One of its strengths is that *mainstream* is not a narrow concept. In its broadest definition it can include most of the U.S. population. Minority, then, is a temporary position in the United States.
GS2 & LS1 • *See also* **Mainstream**

Model Minority

Asian American students are commonly depicted as model minorities who excel in school. Images of the Asian American valedictorian and Asian American computer genius have been promoted by the popular press. The stereotype implies that Asian Americans have overcome discrimination and are *out-Whiting* Whites in their success. Although the model minority stereotype may appear to be a positive one, it denies the experiences of many Asian Americans who have not experienced success, and it denies the fact that Asian Americans do face racism.

The model minority stereotype emerged in the 1960s in the midst of the Civil Rights Era. Asian American scholars have argued that the dominant group began to stereotype Asian Americans as model minorities in order to silence other groups of color (Osajima, 1988; Suzuki, 1977; Takaki, 1989). One of the earliest examples of the model minority representation was published in a 1966 *US News and World Report* article entitled "Success Story of One Minority Group in the U.S." The author wrote, "At a time when it is being proposed that hundreds of billions be spent to uplift Negroes and other minorities, the nation's 300,000 Chinese Americans are moving ahead on their own—with no help from anyone." According to the article Chinese Americans were a group of color who managed to earn success through hard work without depending on the government. Furthermore, the article suggested that African Americans should model their behavior after Chinese Americans. The implicit argument was that equal opportunity existed, and that failure is the fate of those who do not adhere to the value of hard work. This model minority stereotype has continued to be used since that time to delegitimize claims of inequality made by people of color, and, thus, the use of the model minority stereotype against other groups of color has contributed to interracial tension between Asian Americans and other groups of color (Cho, 1993).

Despite the model minority image, not all Asian Americans excel in school. Asian American students from homes where English is not spoken may face language and cultural barriers to educational success. In the Seattle School District, 39 percent of the Asian Pacific American high school students scored below the fiftieth percentile on the reading section of the California Achievement Test in the 1986–1987 school year (Pang, 1995). By lumping all Asian ethnic groups together, the model minority stereotype conceals the differences among Asian American groups. For example, in Seattle, while only 5.1 percent of Japanese American students dropped out of school, 34.6 percent of Samoan American students dropped out of school. Using data from the National Education Longitudinal Study of 1988 (NELS), Kao (1995) found that Pacific Islanders have lower grades, lower test scores, and lower educational aspirations compared to Whites and other Asian ethnic groups. High-achieving Asian American students may feel a great deal of pressure to live up to the standards of the model minority stereotype. Failure to live up to the image can lead to low self-esteem (Lee, 1994; Pang, 1995). Furthermore, the stereotype has also contributed to the image of Asian Americans as one-dimensional nerds.

In summary, the description of Asian Americans as model minorities hides the diverse and complex experiences of Asian Americans. The stereotype paints Asian Americans as a homogenous group, thereby erasing ethnic, social-class, gender, language, sexuality, generational, and academic differences. It contributes to anti-Asian sentiment, and it silences the fact that Asian Americans do face obstacles to success. *SJL*

References

Cho, S. K. (1993). Korean Americans vs. African Americans: Conflict and construction. In R. Gooding-Williams (Ed.), *Reading Rodney King, reading urban uprising* (pp. 196–211). New York: Routledge.

Kao, G. (1995). Asian Americans as model minorities? A look at their academic performance. *American Journal of Education, 103*(2), 121–59.

Lee, S. (1994). Behind the model minority stereotype: Voices of high and low achieving Asian American students. *Anthropology and Education Quarterly, 25*(4), 413–29.

Osajima, K. H. (1988). Asian Americans as the model minority: An analysis of the popular press image in the 1960s and 1980s. In G. Y. Okihiro, S. Hune, A. A. Hansen, & J. M. Liu (Eds.), *Reflections on shattered windows: Promises and prospects for Asian American students* (pp. 165–74). Pullman, WA: Washington State University Press.

Pang, V. O. (1995). Asian American children: A diverse population. In D. T. Nakanishi & T. Nishida (Eds.), *The Asian American educational experience: A source book for teachers and students* (pp. 167–79). New York: Routledge.

Success story of one minority group in the U.S. (1966). *U.S. News and World Report*, 73–78. December 26.

Suzuki, R. H. (1977). Education and the socialization of Asian Americans: A revisionist analysis of the "model minority" thesis. *Amerasia Journal, 4*(2), 23–52.

Takaki, R. (1989). *Strangers from a different shore: A history of Asian Americans.* New York: Penguin.

United States Commission on Civil Rights. (1992). *Civil rights issues facing Asian Americans in the 1990s.* Washington, DC: U.S. Government Printing Office.

Multicultural Education

Multicultural education is a philosophical concept and an educational process. It is a concept built upon the philosophical ideals of freedom, justice, equality, equity, and human dignity contained in the U.S. Constitution and Declaration of Independence. It recognizes, however, that equality and equity are not the same thing; that is, equal access does not necessarily guarantee fairness. Multicultural education is a process that takes place in schools and other educational institutions, and informs all subject areas and other aspects of the curriculum. It prepares all students to work actively toward structural equality in the organizations and institutions of the United States. Like all good educational strategies, it helps students to develop positive self-concepts and to discover who they are, particularly in terms of their multiple group memberships. Multicultural education does this by providing knowledge about the history, culture, and contributions of the diverse groups that have shaped the history, politics, and culture of the United States.

Multicultural education acknowledges that the strength and riches of the United States are the results of its human diversity. It demands college and school staffs that are multiracial and multiculturally literate, including K–8 staff members who are capable of teaching students who are not native

English speakers. It demands a curriculum that organizes concepts and content around the contributions, perspectives, and experiences of the groups of people that are U.S. citizens. It confronts social issues involving race, ethnicity, socioeconomic class, gender, sexual orientation, and disability. Multicultural education provides instruction in familiar contexts that are built upon students' diverse ways of thinking. It encourages students to investigate world and national events, as well as how these events affect their lives. It teaches critical thinking skills, as well as democratic decision making, social action, and empowerment skills. Finally, multicultural education is a total process that cannot be truncated: all components of its definition must be in place for multicultural education to be genuine and viable (Grant, 1994, p. 31).

The ethnic studies movement, which grew out of the Civil Rights Movement of the 1960s and 1970s, is also central to the development of multicultural education. During this movement, African Americans and many other groups of color demanded equity and equality in the policies and practices of schooling. At numerous schools ethnic study courses became a part of the curriculum, and at a number of universities ethnic studies departments or programs were established. It was also during the Civil Rights Movement that several other groups (women, people with disabilities, the poor, and gays, lesbians, and bisexuals) began to increase their efforts to make schooling equal and equitable for members of their groups. It was during the 1970s that the multicultural education movement began to hit its stride. For the past 20 years multicultural education has become the educational vision and idea advocated by some and objected to by others. *CAG* • See also **Multicultural Education, Approaches To; Multicultural Education, Dimensions Of**

References

Grant, C. A. (1994). Toward a common definition of multicultural education. In *Insights on diversity*. (p. 31), A Kappa Delta Publication, West Lafayette, IN: Kappa Delta Pi.

Ladson-Billings, G. (1996). Lifting as we climb: The womanist tradition in multicultural education. In J. A. Banks (Ed.), *African American foundations of multicultural education*. New York: Teachers College Press.

Sleeter, C. E., & Grant, C. A. (1994). Making choices for multicultural education: Five approaches to race, class, and gender (2nd ed.). New York: Merrill.

Multicultural Education, Approaches To

Multicultural education is conceptually defined in several different ways, and educational practices described as multicultural are implemented based upon several different frameworks. A number of educators have attempted to deal with the different meanings by developing typologies or approaches to multicultural education (e.g., Banks, 1994; Gibson, 1976; Pratte, 1983). Grant and Sleeter (1985), after a review of the educational literature and observing K–college teachers' practices, argue that when multicultural education is generally put into practice, one of five approaches to instruction is used: teaching the exceptional and culturally different; human relations; single group studies; multicultural education; and education that is multicultural and social reconstructionist. (*See also*: Grant, Sleeter, & Anderson, 1986; Sleeter & Grant, 1987, 1994.) Grant and Sleeter also observed that although the concept and purpose of each approach differ somewhat, there is some overlap between these approaches.

The goal of *teaching the exceptional and culturally different* is to affirm the existing assimilationist ideology in the United States. In schools the purpose is to prepare students to acquire the habits and learn the academic basics in order to fit into mainstream society. This approach accommodates students who are considered exceptional or culturally different through the use of teaching strategies or culturally relevant materials that otherwise might be used in pull-out programs for students with special needs. For example, for students with limited English proficiency, school practices would be based on English immersion programs.

Proponents argue that students of color, low-income students, and non-native-English-speaking students need instructional help in the basics and that teachers are encouraged to build bridges between the students' background and the curriculum. While this approach may help students achieve the necessary academic performance to remain in the regular classroom, problems of cultural discontinuity and the lack of analysis of sites of oppression are left unchallenged. The theoretical foundation for this approach is based on theories of assimilation, human capital, and compensatory education.

The goals of the *human relations* approach are to promote unity, tolerance, and acceptance within the existing social structure. In school the focus is to foster positive relationships among students of diverse backgrounds and personal characteristics so that each student develops a strong self-concept. The curriculum includes lessons about stereotyping and individual differences and similarities. This approach encourages instruction that promotes cross-cultural communication, collaboration, and cooperative learning among students.

The growing recognition of people with different lifestyles and growing student diversity increases the need for the human relations approach. The human relations approach is grounded in the theories of general and social psychology. The work of Gordon Allport (1979) in *The Nature of Prejudice* played a major role in helping to understand why people develop prejudice and how to eliminate it.

A shortcoming of this approach is that actual conflicts between individuals and groups may be glossed over in support of an "I'm okay, you're okay" ideology. Also, the human relations approach does not deal with poverty and political powerlessness. For the most part it teaches that such problems will be resolved if people communicate better and appreciate each other more.

The goals of the *single group studies* approach to multicultural education are to increase students' knowledge about the history and culture of their own group(s) (e.g., Japanese Americans, females); to empower the group, raise their social status, and have them achieve equality throughout society; and to make teaching culturally responsive. The single group studies approach argues that since knowledge is socially constructed and not neutral, it should be understood that portrayals of groups (e.g., Native Americans, people with physical disabilities) in text materials are based upon the authors' interpretation and construction of knowledge. Thus, the portrayal may be accurate or inaccurate, and/or may disagree with how the identified group would present itself.

The single group studies approach accepts the socialization purpose of schools but argues that this socialization is mainly based upon a White, middle-class, male-centric model. Therefore, those who are different are required, by and large, to fit into society, even when it undermines their self-concept.

Some advocates argue that school practices should be designed around Freire's (1970) idea of "critical consciousness." Freire believes that when students learn about their cultural heritage and contributions to society, they participate in a process of self-discovery and growth in social consciousness. This leads students to the realization that their actions can be part of a transforming process and can positively influence their lives. Also, teaching about their history and heritage can promote positive relations with other groups.

Other proponents of the single group studies approach argue that educational practice should be centered upon the student group being taught (e.g., African Americans). Asante (1995) explains that "each centered person becomes an owner, not a renter, of knowledge" (p. 1). Afrocentricity, according to Asante, is "the process of viewing African people as subjects in history rather than as victims who operate on the fringes of society" (p. 462). In this approach the curriculum includes units and/or courses about a specific group written from the group's perspective. In addition, information and materials about the group are integrated throughout the remainder of the school curriculum. Several successful schools are based upon the principles of single group studies (e.g., the freedom schools; women's colleges such as Wellesley College, Agnes Scott College, Mount St. Mary College, and Simmons). Ethnic studies and women's studies majors are examples of programs based upon the theoretical underpinnings of the single group studies approach. A shortcoming of this approach is that it may not address other characteristics of the identified group (e.g., gender, class) and that it may not encourage the group to learn about and work with other marginalized groups.

The goals of the *multicultural education (MCE)* approach are social equality and cultural pluralism. This approach supports several ideas important to the human relations approach, i.e., developing a positive self-concept, learning how to work in groups, and learning how to respect and get along with others. It also supports some of the ideas of the single group studies approach, i.e., equality in social structure and the study of multiple perspectives. In this approach curriculum concepts are organized around the perspectives of people of different ethnic, gender, socioeconomic, and ability groups, and curriculum is culturally responsive to the culture, language, and learning styles of the students. MCE teaches disciplines like science and math as subject matters, where the knowledge, once acquired, becomes power for students as both consumers and leaders. MCE teaches and applies critical thinking skills to all subject areas. Also, issues of equity, power, and privilege are studied. This approach argues that all parents should be actively involved in schools, especially those who have been previously marginalized, and the teaching staff should be diverse and nontraditional, for example, science and shop teachers who are female and home economic teachers who are male. The multicultural education approach is guided by theories of cultural pluralism, social learning theories, and the cultural transmission theory. The shortcoming of the multicultural approach is that it does not assertively address issues dealing with poverty and unemployment, nor does it necessarily help build the political skills and group solidarity that some ethnic groups need.

The goal of *education that is multicultural and social reconstructionist (EMC-SR)* is social structure equality and cultural pluralism. This approach supports most of the ideas of the multicultural education approach, including some of the ideas of the human relations approach (i.e., developing a positive self-concept, cooperative learning, and getting along with others) and the ideology of social structure equality from the single group studies approach. Social reconstruction as a concept was born in the writings of Theodore Brameld (1950) and others who argue that philosophies including those in education are culturally based and evolve from cultural patterns that are shaped by living in a particular place at a given time. Social reconstructionists argue that culture is a dynamic process which is ever growing and changing. Human beings who live in these cultures often refashion their culture to promote more optimum possibilities for human development and fulfillment. Education, according to social reconstructionists, is a powerful vehicle for radical social transformation (Stone, 1994). Brameld describes social reconstruction as a utopian philosophy. By this he means it is a construction of the imagination that extends beyond the here and now to become a far-reaching idealization of human, especially cultural, potentialities. Utopia for Brameld and other reconstructionists is a realizable vision of what can be and should be attained in order that men and women may be happier, more rationale, and more humane than they have ever been.

The uniting of education that is multicultural and social reconstructionist is to have a philosophical concept that explicitly articulates educational transformation in a society that addresses issues of race, class, gender, disability, and sexual orientation. EMC-SR believes that in a world society that is undergoing constant technological and social change, along with dealing with new and old issues of social justice and diversity, education is vital for continual renewal and revitalization of society. This approach argues that all schooling (e.g., staffing patterns, curriculum, instruction, evaluation, counseling) should be multicultural. Curriculum concepts should take into account multiple perspectives and social issues involving race, class, gender, disability, and sexual orientation; instruction should put democratic principles to use in classrooms; and students should be taught to use the tools of democracy, e.g., debating, becoming informed on issues, being fair, analyzing circumstances that shape one's life, and taking action to bring about change. These tools will give students greater control over their lives and will help them become more productive citizens.

The existence of several different approaches to multicultural education can lead to conceptual confusion. This confusion suggests to some that multicultural education is inconsistent, making it the subject of criticism. Critics argue that the teaching the exceptional and culturally different and human relations approaches ignore inequality and oppression and that the single group studies approach deals too much with the concerns of a particular group. Other critics argue that the multicultural education approach undercuts the Western tradition and that the education that is multicultural and social reconstructionist is too radical. As scholars continue to study multicultural education and try to define it to meet the context of this ever-changing society, the meanings that characterize the different approaches will change, and/or some of the approaches will give way to make room for new ideas and meanings. This is as it should be, because if multicultural education is to be accepted and affirmed, scholars and practitioners must understand its meanings and continue to refine its definition so that multicultural education is appropriate for the time and social context. *CAG*

References

Allport, G. W. (1979). *The nature of prejudice* (25th anniversary ed.). Reading, MA: Addison-Wesley.

Asante, M. K. (1995). *African American history: A journey of liberation.* Maywood, NJ: The Peoples Publishing Group.

Banks, J. A. (1994). *An introduction to multicultural education.* Boston: Allyn & Bacon.

Brameld, T. (1950) *Patterns of educational philosophy.* New York: World Book, Yonker on Hudson.

Freire, P. (1970). *Pedagogy of the oppressed.* Translated by Myra Bergman Ramos. New York: Seabury Press.

Gibson, M. A. (1976). Approaches to multicultural education in the United States: Some concepts and assumptions. *American Journal of Education, 95,* 96–121.

Grant, C. A., & Sleeter, C. E. (1985). The literature on multicultural education: Review and analysis. *Educational Review, 37,* 97–118.

Grant, C. A., Sleeter, C. E., & Anderson, J. (1986). The literature on multicultural education: Review and analysis. Part II. *Educational Studies, 12,* 47–71.

Pratte, R. (1983). Multicultural education: Four normative arguments. *Educational Theory, 33,* 21–32.

Sleeter, C. E., & Grant, C. A. (1987). An analysis of multicultural education in the United States. *Harvard Educational Review, 57*(4), 421-44.

———. (1988). *Making choices for multicultural education.* Columbus, OH: Merrill.

———. (1994). *Making choices for multicultural education: Five approaches to race, class, and gender* (2nd ed.). New York: Macmillan.

Stone, F. A. (1994). Educational reconstruction and today's teacher education. *Teacher Education Quarterly, 21*(4), 9–21.

Multicultural Education, Dimensions Of

Many people think that multicultural education consists only or primarily of content related to ethnic, racial, cultural, and gender groups. Conceptualizing multicultural education exclusively as content related to various groups is problematic for several reasons. Teachers who cannot easily see how their content is related to cultural and normative issues may dismiss multicultural education with the argument that it is not relevant to their disciplines. This "irrelevant of content" argument could become a legitimized form of resistance to multicultural education if it is conceptualized primarily or exclusively as content. Teachers of mathematics and science often perceive multicultural education as an endeavor for social studies and language arts teachers but not for themselves. Multicultural education needs to be broadly defined and conceptualized so that teachers from a wide range of disciplines and subject areas can respond to it appropriately and resistance to it can be minimized. When multicultural education is conceptualized only or primarily as content integration, it is essentialized, and its other important components, such as knowledge construction and prejudice reduction, are ignored.

Narrow and misleading conceptions of multicultural education are often presented in popularized accounts (e.g., D'Souza, 1991; Schlesinger, 1991).

Banks (1994a, 1995) conceptualizes multicultural education as a broad interdisciplinary field with five interrelated dimensions. When trying to determine the extent to which they are implementing multicultural education and how effectively, educators can use the dimensions as benchmarks. The dimensions are (1) content integration, (2) the knowledge construction process, (3) prejudice reduction, (4) an equity pedagogy, and (5) an empowering school culture and social structure.

Content integration deals with the extent to which teachers use examples and content from a variety of cultures and groups to illustrate key concepts, principles, generalizations, and theories in their subject area or discipline (Banks, 1991). The infusion of ethnic and cultural content into the content area or subject should be logical and not contrived. More obvious opportunities exist for the integration of ethnic and cultural content into some subject areas than into others. In social studies, language arts, and art, there are frequent and ample opportunities for teachers to use ethnic and cultural content to illustrate concepts, themes, and principles. There are also opportunities to integrate multicultural content into mathematics and science (Atwater, 1994; Secada, 1992); however, they are often more difficult for practitioners to conceptualize and implement. A conceptual and theoretical literature is developing that describes how educators can think creatively about integrating cultural content and topics into mathematics and science courses and activities (Atwater, 1994; Secada, 1992; Secada, Fennema & Adajian, 1995).

The *knowledge construction process* describes the extent to which teachers help students understand, investigate, and determine how implicit cultural assumptions, frames of reference, perspectives, and biases within a discipline influence the ways in which knowledge is constructed within it. Feminist scholars use *positionality* to describe factors such as race, gender, and class, which influence the construction of knowledge (Tetreault, 1993). An important assumption within ethnic studies and multicultural education is that knowledge reflects the position and lived reality of knowledge constructors (Banks, 1996). Another important assumption is that knowledge is related to action and that an important goal of knowledge is to improve society to make it more democratic and just (Banks, 1996). These postmodern assumptions are inconsistent with those of the Western empirical tradition, which has dominated social science research in the United States since the turn of the century. This tradition contends that knowledge is unrelated to human interests and that the purpose of science is to build theory (Greer, 1969).

Students can analyze the knowledge construction process in science by examining how racism has been perpetuated by scientists who embraced genetic theories of intelligence, Darwinism, and eugenics. In *The Mismeasure of Man*, Gould (1981) describes how scientific racism developed and was influential in the nineteenth and twentieth centuries. Scientific racism has had a significant influence on the interpretations of mental ability tests in the United States. The publication and popularity of *The Bell Curve* (Herrnstein & Murray, 1994) indicates the extent to which race still influences the construction of knowledge in the United States. Students can examine the arguments in *The Bell Curve* and the reactions it evoked when studying knowledge construction (Jacoby & Glauberman, 1995).

Students should also examine the ways in which science has contributed to the development of liberatory knowledge. This knowledge has helped groups on the margins of society to contest the knowledge that supports hegemonic social and political structures. Social science research by African American scholars such as DuBois ([1935] 1963) and Woodson ([1919] 1991)—and by Jewish American scholars such as Boas (1928) and Herskovits (1941)—constructed theories and paradigms that challenged racist views, which had been institutionalized within popular and academic cultures.

Students can examine the knowledge construction process in social studies when they study such units and topics as "The European Discovery of America" and "The Westward Movement" (Banks, 1994b). Teachers can ask students to consider the latent meanings of concepts such as "The European Discovery of America" and "The New World." Students can discuss what these concepts imply or suggest about the Native American cultures that had existed in the Americas approximately 40,000 years before the Europeans arrived (Weatherford, 1991). When studying "The Westward Movement" teachers can ask students: "Whose point of view or perspective does this concept reflect, the European Americans or the Lakota Sioux?" "Who was moving West?" "How might a Lakota Sioux historian describe this period in United States history?" and "What are other ways of thinking about and describing the Westward Movement?"

The *prejudice reduction* dimension of multicultural education describes the characteristics of children's racial attitudes and strategies that can be used to help students to develop more democratic attitudes and values. Researchers have been investigating the characteristics of children's racial attitudes since the 1920s (Lasker, 1929). Since the Intergroup Education Movement of the 1940s and 1950s (Trager & Yarrow, 1952), a number of investigators have designed interventions to help students develop more positive racial attitudes and values.

Research indicates that children develop racial preferences as early as ages three and four, and that most children—of all racial groups—tend to have a

White racial preference at an early age (Cross, 1991; Spencer, 1984). However, research on interventions indicate that deliberate and effective instruction can help students, especially at an early age, to develop more positive racial attitudes and more out-group racial preferences (Williams & Morland, 1976). Because of the racial crisis in our nation, teachers in all subject areas and disciplines and at every level of education should initiate interventions to help students develop the attitudes and skills needed to function effectively in diverse racial and ethnic settings.

Teachers in each subject area can analyze their teaching procedures and styles to determine the extent to which they reflect multicultural issues and concerns. An *equity pedagogy* exists when teachers modify their teaching in ways that facilitate the academic achievement of students from diverse racial, cultural, gender, and social-class groups. Successfully implementing an equity pedagogy requires a variety of teaching styles and approaches consistent with the wide range of learning and cultural characteristics of these groups (Delpit, 1995; Ladson-Billings, 1994), e.g., being demanding but highly personalized when working with students such as Native American and Alaskan students (Kleinfeld, 1975), and using cooperative learning techniques in mathematics and science instruction in order to enhance the academic achievement of students of color (Slavin, 1995). When equity pedagogy is successfully implemented in the classroom, teachers use culturally sensitive instruction and activities that enable students from diverse racial, ethnic, and cultural groups to experience academic success (Au, 1980; Ladson-Billings, 1994; Shade & New, 1993).

Another important dimension of multicultural education is an *empowering school culture and school structure*. To implement this dimension, the culture and organization of the school must be examined by all members of the school staff. The entire staff must also participate in restructuring the school. Grouping and labeling practices (Oakes & Guiton, 1995), sports participation, disproportionality in achievement, disproportionality in enrollment in gifted and special education programs (Sapon-Shevin, 1994), and the interaction of staff with students across ethnic and racial lines (Cohen & Lotan, 1995) are important variables that must be examined in order to create a school culture that empowers students from diverse racial, ethnic, and gender groups. Effective implementation of the dimensions of multicultural education in a highly interrelated and thoughtful way will increase the possibility of creating schools in which all students can experience academic, social, and cultural success. *JAB*

References

Atwater, M. M. (1994). Research on cultural diversity in the classroom. In D. L. Gabel (Ed.), *Handbook of research on science teaching and learning* (pp. 558–76). New York: Macmillan.

Au, K. H. (1980). Participation structures in a reading lesson with Hawaiian children: Analysis of a culturally appropriate instructional event. *Anthropology and Education Quarterly, 11*(2), 91–115.

Banks, J. A. (1991). *Teaching strategies for ethnic studies* (5th ed.). Boston: Allyn & Bacon.

———. (1994a). *Multiethnic education: Theory and practice* (3rd ed.). Boston: Allyn & Bacon.

———. (1994b). *An introduction to multicultural education*. Boston: Allyn & Bacon.

———. (1995). Multicultural education: Historical development, dimensions, and practice. In J. A. Banks & C. A. M. Banks (Eds.), *Handbook of research on multicultural education* (pp. 3–24). New York: Macmillan.

Banks, J. A. (Ed.). (1996). *Multicultural education, transformative knowledge, and action: Historical and contemporary perspectives*. New York: Teachers College Press.

Boas, F. (1928). *Anthropology and modern life*. New York: Norton.

Cohen, E. G., & Lotan, R. A. (1995). Producing equal-status interaction in the heterogeneous classroom. *American Educational Research Journal, 32*(1), 99–120.

Cross, W. E., Jr. (1991). *Shades of Black: Diversity in African American identity*. Philadelphia: Temple University Press.

Delpit, L. (1995). *Other people's children: Cultural conflicts in the classroom*. New York: New Press.

D'Souza, D. (1991). *Illiberal education: The politics of race and sex on campus*. New York: Free Press.

Du Bois, W. E. B. ([1935] 1963). *Black reconstruction*. Millwood, NY: Kraus-Thomson.

Gould, S. J. (1981). *The mismeasure of man*. New York: Norton.

Greer, S. (1969). *The logic of social inquiry*. Chicago: Aldine.

Herrnstein, R. J., & Murray, C. (1994). *The bell curve: Intelligence and class structure in American life*. New York: Free Press.

Herskovits, M. J. (1941). *The myth of the Negro past*. Boston: Beacon Press.

Jacoby, R., & Glauberman, N. (Eds.). (1995). *The bell curve debate: History, documents, opinions*. New York: Times Books.

Kleinfeld, J. (1975). Effective teachers of Eskimo and Indian students. *School Review, 83*(2), 301–44.

Ladson-Billings, G. (1994). *The dreamkeepers: Successful teachers of African American children*. San Francisco: Jossey-Bass.

Lasker, B. (1929). *Race attitudes in children*. New York: Holt, Rhinehart & Winston.

Oakes, J., & Guiton, G. (1995). Matchmaking: The dynamics of high school tracking decisions. *American Educational Research Journal, 32*(1), 3–33.

Sapon-Shevin, M. (1994). *Playing favorites: Gifted education and the disruption of community*. Albany: State University of New York Press.

Secada, W. G. (1992). Race, ethnicity, social class, language, and achievement in mathematics. In D. Grouws (Ed.), *Handbook of research on mathematics teaching and learning* (pp. 623–60). New York: Macmillan.

Secada, W. G., Fennema, E., & Adajian, L. B. (Eds.). (1995). *New directions for equity in mathematics education*. Cambridge: Cambridge University Press.

Schlesinger, A. M., Jr. (1991). *The disuniting of America: Reflections on a multicultural society*. Knoxville, TN: Whittle Direct Books.

Shade, B. J., & New, C. A. (1993). Cultural influences on learning: Teaching implications. In J. A. Banks & C. A. M. Banks (Eds.), *Multicultural education: Issues and perspectives* (pp. 317–31). Boston: Allyn & Bacon.

Slavin, R. E. (1995). Cooperative learning and intergroup relations. In J. A. Banks & C. A. M. Banks (Eds.), *Handbook of research on multicultural education* (pp. 628–34). New York: Macmillan.

Spencer, M. B. (1984). Personal and group identity of Black children: An alternative synthesis. *Genetic Psychology Monographs, 106,* 59–84.

Tetreault, M. K. T. (1993). Classrooms for diversity: Rethinking curriculum and pedagogy. In J. A. Banks & C. A. M. Banks (Eds.), *Multicultural education: Issues and perspectives* (pp. 129–48). Boston: Allyn & Bacon.

Trager, H. G., & Yarrow, M. R. (1952). *They learn what they live: Prejudice in young children.* New York: Harper & Brothers.

Weatherford, J. (1991). *Native roots: How the Indians enriched America.* New York: Fawcett Columbine.

Williams, J. E., & Morland, J. K. (1976). *Race, color, and the young child.* Chapel Hill: University of North Carolina Press.

Woodson, C. G. ([1919] 1991). *The education of the Negro prior to 1861.* Salem, NH: Ayer.

Multiculturalism

Multiculturalism is a philosophical position and movement that assumes that the gender, ethnic, racial, and cultural diversity of a pluralistic society should be reflected in all of its institutionalized structures but especially in educational institutions, including the staff, norms and values, curriculum, and student body (Banks & Banks, 1993).

In the United States it is sometimes thought that the roots of cultural pluralism can be traced to the democratic pluralism envisioned by the framers of the Constitution. However, their concern was to build and maintain one dominant culture from the political and economic factions represented in the original 13 states. Although diversity existed, the cultural stock of America in the final quarter of the eighteenth century remained predominantly British. Only very perceptive individuals could have envisioned the mass immigration that was to follow. Thus, as originally conceived, multiculturalism in the United States was concerned with liberty and equality and not with promoting the historic identities of non-English subcultures. Although the legal framework was established with the adoption of the first 10 amendments to the Constitution, multiculturalism as an ideal to protect ethnic and cultural diversity evolved much later.

Today the United States is an ethnically, culturally, and linguistically diverse society. According to the *Harvard Encyclopedia of American Ethnic Groups* (Thernstrom, 1980), the U.S. is composed of at least 276 different ethnic groups, including 170 different Native American groups. The U.S. Department of Education, Office of Bilingual Education and Minority Languages Affairs, has identified at least 220 languages spoken in the United States. However, to define multiculturalism by these categories alone would be misleading because it suggests that only issues of race and ethnicity are of concern. Instead, cultural identity is based on traits and values learned as part of our ethnic origin, religion, gender, age, socioeconomic level, primary language, geographical region, place of residence (e.g., rural or urban), and disabilities or exceptional conditions. Each of these groups has distinguishable cultural patterns shared with others who identify themselves as members of that particular group.

These subsocieties within the United States share cultural elements, institutions, and patterns not common to the larger U.S. society. Traditionally these groups have been called subsocieties or subcultures by sociologists and anthropologists because they exist within the context of a larger society and share political and social institutions as well as some of the traits and values of the *macroculture*. These cultural groups are also called *microcultures* to indicate that they have distinctive cultural patterns while sharing some cultural patterns with members of the U.S. macroculture. People who belong to the same microcultures share traits and values that bind them together as a group. Although numerous microcultures exist within most nations, the United States is exceptionally rich in the many distinct cultural groups that make up its population.

Goodenough (1987) defines multiculturalism as the normal human experience. Since all Americans participate in more than one culture group or microculture, most persons have already become proficient in multiple systems of perceiving, evaluating, believing, and acting according to the patterns of the various microcultures in which they participate. Individuals with competencies in several microcultures develop a fuller appreciation of the range of cultural competencies available to all individuals. Individuals who have competencies in and can operate successfully in two or more different cultures are bicultural or multicultural and are often multilingual as well. One's identity is more flexible, autonomous, and stable to the degree that one recognizes one's self as a member of various different subcommunities simultaneously. *HC*

References

Abercrombie, N., Hill, S., & Turner, B. S. (1984). *Dictionary of sociology*. New York: Penguin.

Banks, J. A., & Banks, C. A. M. (Eds.). (1993). *Multicultural education: Issues and perspectives*. Boston: Allyn & Bacon.

———. (Eds.). (1995). *Handbook of research on multicultural education*. New York: Macmillan.

Gollnick, D. M., & Chinn, P. C. (1994). *Multicultural education in a pluralistic society*. New York: Macmillan.

Goodenough, W. (1987). Multiculturalism as the normal human experience. In E. M. Eddy & W. L. Partridge (Eds.), *Applied anthropology in America* (2nd ed.). New York: Columbia University Press.

Thernstrom, S. (Ed.). (1980). *Harvard encyclopedia of American ethnic groups*. Cambridge: Harvard University Press.

Multicultural Literacy

A definition of *multicultural literacy* must begin with a definition of *cultural literacy* since the two are so often presented as polar opposites. The National Society for the Study of Education (NSSE, 1988) defines cultural literacy in their *Eighty-seventh Yearbook* as "language learning" requiring three major functions of the language curriculum in the schools: (1) enabling individuals to communicate with others in the culture, (2) promoting cultural loyalty through an acceptance and valuing of norms and routines of the culture, and (3) developing individuality ("Once one has learned to communicate within the culture and developed a loyalty to it, then one is able to become independent of it. Before then, independence of those norms and values is seen as naive, illiterate, or childish" [p. 3]). The *Yearbook* editors further charge that those advocating cultural literacy through a definition of "culture primarily in belle-literalistic terms" (p. 4) are guilty of promoting an education inappropriate for contemporary American culture. The NSSE *Yearbook* editors refute the shallowness of the academic application for a number of reasons, charging it is *too Western, too masculine, ignorant of technological information,* and *neglectful of the specialization required by many fields of study.* In America, multicultural literacy has largely been a response to these calls for "cultural literacy," a counter to the entrenched Western canon.

The teaching of literature, as Henry Louis Gates (1992) rightly recognized, is the teaching of values. The high canon of Western tradition teaches the values of slavery, sexism, racism, subjugation, and gold/silver/bronze people—it creates voiceless, misrepresented and unrepresented people. A multicultural canon includes "distinct literary voices and artistic eyes that are unique, yet embody universal themes and values" (Harris in Harris, Yokota, Johnson, & de Cortes, 1993, p. 215).

In Harris's historical analysis of the literacy movement for African Americans, she identifies the characteristics of cultural literacy education to effect essential political, cultural, social, and economic change through literacy that apprises individuals of and prepares them for the dominating culture's institutions, counteracting the "pernicious and venal images of African Americans prevalent in popular culture and engendering group solidarity and commitment to uplift" (Harris, 1992, p. 276).

Reformation of the canon forces us to rethink our relationship to each other in this country. But this transformation has made traditional canon advocates uneasy, as well it should since, as James Baldwin so eloquently stated in "A Talk to Teachers": "Because if I am not what I've been told I am, then it means that you're not what you thought you were either!" (Simonson & Walker, 1988, p. 8). Multicultural literacy demands a new definition of the canon that includes all of America's stories, all of America's voices. *TH*

References

Gates, H. L. Jr. (1992). *Loose canons: Notes on the culture wars.* New York: Oxford University Press.

Harris, V. J. (1992). African-American conceptions of literacy: A historical perspective. *Theory Into Practice. 31*(4), 276–86.

Harris, V. J., Yokota, J., Johnson, G., & de Cortes, O. G. (1993) Bookalogues: Multicultural literature. *Language Arts, 70* (March), pp. 215–24.

National Society for the Study of Education. (1988). *Cultural literacy and the idea of general education,* Eighty-seventh Yearbook. National Society for the Study of Education.

Simonson, R., & Walker, S. (Eds.). (1988). *The Graywolf Annual Five: Multicultural literacy.* Saint Paul, MN: Graywolf Press.

Multicultural Literature Selection

Multicultural literature is a category of literature that reflects the diverse life experiences, traditions, histories, values, worldviews, and perspectives of the diverse cultural groups that make up a society. It includes fiction and nonfiction—novels, stories, essays, biographies, personal narratives, children's literature, oral traditions, and poetry—as well as new and hybrid literary genres. In the United States multicultural literature revises traditional Eurocentric beliefs about history and challenges monocultural social models.

Multicultural literature can be used effectively in classrooms at all levels to give students a frame of reference for discussing cultural diversity and cultural pluralism because it offers both broad historical patterns and individual experiences within the context of history. It also gives students a framework for addressing social justice issues and for recognizing multiple perspectives, and it has great potential as a tool for breaking down stereotypes and broadening cognitive sophistication. In addition, multicultural literature offers valuable insights about sources of intergroup conflict and responses to conflict. It often includes stories of struggle against discrimination and oppression within the dominant culture, as well as stories of overcoming oppression and ideas for building harmony in multicultural communities. The best works provide readers with new opportunities to see themselves portrayed in literature and to help them develop positive personal and communal identities.

Those who select multicultural books need to take into account the authenticity of characterizations, plot, themes, and setting, as well as the author's or illustrator's background and qualifications. Currentness, accuracy, and balance are primary concerns in the evaluation of materials, along with the clarity and interest of the writing. The quality and appropriateness of illustrations, as well as their relationship to the text, are principal issues in evaluating books and other visual materials. Selectors of multicultural literature should also be sensitive to the overall impact that these materials may have on a reader's self-image.

Educators should look to librarians for advice in selecting books. The library is a vital source for collecting and providing relevant literature to all groups in a community. Librarians are being asked to work more closely with classroom teachers to provide books and collections that support a broader and more culturally diverse curriculum. Librarians, teachers, and others who are working to make their environments more multicultural strive to provide a balanced book collection in various languages and about various cultures. *LM & AS*

References

Council on Interracial Books for Children. (1984). *Guidelines for selecting bias-free textbooks and storybooks*. New York: Council on Interracial Books for Children.

Harris, V. J. (Ed.). (1992). *Teaching multicultural literature in grades K–8*. Norwood, MA: Christopher-Gordan.

Lindgren, M. V. (Ed.). (1991). *The multicolored mirror: Cultural substance in literature for children and young adults*. Cooperative Children's Book Center. Fort Atkinson, WI: Highsmith Press.

Miller-Lachmann, L. (1992). *Our family, our friends, our world: An annotated guide to significant multicultural books for children and teenagers*. New Providence, NJ: R. R. Bowker.

Slapin, B., & Seale, D. (1992). *Through Indian eyes: The Native experience in books for children* (3rd ed.). Philadelphia, PA: New Society.

Multicultural Schools

Multicultural schools are schools whose mission, policies, curricula, and practices "prepare future citizens to reconstruct society so that it better serves the interests of all groups of people" (Sleeter & Grant, 1994). A multicultural school does not necessarily enroll a racially or ethnically diverse student body. While student diversity is desirable, it is possible for a school with a monocultural student population to provide an education that promotes social structural equality, affirms societal diversity, achieves academic excellence for all students, and prepares students to become active members of a democratic society.

The faculty, staff, and administration of a multicultural school are committed to and knowledgeable about the link between schools and social structural inequality in the United States. There is a constant effort to evaluate and revise, when necessary, individual and collective work to reflect an emphasis on equity and academic excellence and, as Nieto (1995) states, "cause students to challenge a country with democratic ideals to put them into practice" (p. 207).

In a multicultural school, the traditional curriculum is transformed so that all students receive a solid academic background that is student-centered, antiracist and antisexist, and grounded in the "authentic and realistic" incorporation of the experiences, "cultures, lifestyles, and histories of formerly excluded groups" (Nieto, 1995, p. 211). Curriculum transformation applies to all subject areas, not just to those traditionally designated as appropriate for multicultural education (e.g., social studies).

Instruction in a multicultural school is varied because teachers recognize that students enter school with different knowledge bases, skill levels, and experiences and that they learn best through multiple modes of instruction. Teachers emphasize the development of skills needed for critical thinking, democratic participation, and the ability to work cooperatively and collaboratively with others.

The environment of a multicultural school affirms the diversity of the United States regardless of the schools' student population. Parents and students are partners with teachers and administrators in designing, implementing, and constantly monitoring curricula, policies, and practices to ensure equitable participation and educational outcomes for all students. Students' work is displayed throughout the building, and students share responsibility for designing and maintaining the school environment with faculty and staff. Art, music, drama, and cultural artifacts that represent the depth of culture in various groups are infused into the curriculum and the environment. Staffing patterns in a multicultural school are equitable and represent the diversity in our society. Library and media materials, cafeteria menus, computer facilities, and extracurricular activities are inclusive.

The school serves as a resource for the community. Community involvement in all aspects of the school is encouraged. The importance of senior citizens as community elders is evident by their involvement in all aspects of the school. A multicultural school is connected to the community it serves and draws heavily on community resources to enrich the educational environment. *MG*

References

Nieto, S. (1995). From Brown heroes and holidays to assimilationist agendas: Reconsidering the critiques of multicultural education. In C. A. Sleeter, & P. McLaren, (Eds.), *Multicultural education, critical pedagogy, and the politics of difference.* Albany: State University of New York.

Sleeter, C. E., & Grant, C. A. (1994). *Making choices for multicultural education: Five approaches to race, class, and gender* (2nd ed.). New York: Merrill.

Multicultural Studies

The most common interpretation of the term *multicultural studies* is as a broad-field academic focus on the history, perspectives, culture, and current concerns of groups that have been historically left out or underrepresented in traditional courses of study (e.g., people of color, women, gay and lesbian people, persons with disabilities). Presently, multicultural studies does not exist, for the most part, as a distinct department. In practice, university students who major or minor in multicultural studies often take a smorgasbord of courses from several areas representing facets of multicultural education. For example, students might take courses in such ethnic studies departments as African American studies, Puerto Rican studies, and Asian American studies. In secondary schools specific courses may be offered that focus on the perspectives of one or more groups.

The terms *multicultural studies* and *ethnic studies* are sometimes used interchangeably. This is problematic for two reasons. Equating multicultural studies with ethnic studies masks the commitment by proponents of multicultural education to all groups that have been left out of traditional courses of study (e.g., women, people with disabilities, gay and lesbian people). Using these terms synonymously masks the complexity and interrelated nature of multicultural concepts such as race, class, and gender.

Additionally, while individual courses and departments serve an important purpose, multicultural studies can have a broader transformative agenda. Banks (1994) describes the transformative approach to multicultural studies as fundamentally different from separate courses. He states that from a transformative perspective, a multicultural curriculum "changes the canon, paradigms, and basic assumptions of the [traditional] curriculum and enables students to view concepts, issues, themes, and problems from different perspectives and points of view" (p. 26). He adds that the "major goals of a transformative curriculum that fosters multicultural literacy should be to help students *to know, to care,* and *to act* in ways that will develop and foster a democratic and just society in which all groups experience cultural democracy and cultural empowerment" (p. 27). *MG*

Reference

Banks, J. A. (1994). *An introduction to multicultural education.* Boston, MA: Allyn & Bacon.

Multiethnic Education

Multiethnic education refers to educational practices that incorporate a comparative study of U.S. ethnic and racial groups such as African Americans, American Indians, Asian Americans, European Americans, and Latinos (Banks, 1981). It provides students with the skills and knowledge necessary to live and work in a multiethnic society, serves as a foundation for the development of new curriculum initiatives, addresses the total school as the unit of change, and embraces the idea that racially and ethnically diverse groups have cultures that are different from, but not inferior to, mainstream

Anglo culture (Banks, 1994). Multiethnic education is based on the assumption that ethnic and racial groups have similarities as well as differences. By using a comparative approach, multiethnic educators can identify and examine important concepts, generalizations, and theories about the nature of race and ethnicity in the United States. This comparative approach also provides a means for schools and colleges to include a wide range of ethnic and racial groups in their curricula without having to offer separate courses on each group.

Multiethnic education is part of a long tradition of transformative scholarship in education. Some of its transformative characteristics are that it embraces the idea of curriculum transformation, gives voice to people of color, works to improve intergroup relations, challenges the dominance of Eurocentric curriculum, and incorporates social action into the curriculum (Banks, 1977; Garcia, 1978). It is also interdisciplinary; multiethnic education draws concepts, generalizations, and theories from history and social science disciplines such as sociology and psychology (Banks, 1994).

It is difficult to understand multiethnic education without considering its relationship to ethnic studies and multicultural education. Multiethnic education grew out of the ethnic studies movement and was a precursor to multicultural education (Banks, 1994; Garcia, 1984). It developed during the late 1960s and 1970s (Gay, 1983) and was constructed from knowledge and perspectives that were generated by scholars in areas such as African American studies and curriculum and instruction. Unlike multicultural education, which is broad and addresses educational issues related to race, class, gender, social class, exceptionality, language, and their interaction (Banks & Banks, 1995; Grant & Sleeter, 1985), multiethnic education focuses on race and ethnicity (Banks, 1994; Gay, 1983). The goals of multicultural education are also somewhat broader than those in multiethnic education. Two important goals of multiethnic education are to provide students with information on the heritage and contributions of ethnic and racial groups in U.S. society (King, 1990) and to help students function within their ethnic or racial group, the mainstream culture, and across other racial and ethnic cultures (Banks, 1994). Whereas multiethnic education primarily focuses on content integration, multicultural education also includes knowledge construction, prejudice reduction, an empowering school culture, and social action (Banks, 1995).

While the term *multiethnic education* has not been widely used by educators to describe their work, it represents an important distinction among the many transformational educational initiatives being implemented in public schools and universities (Banks, 1995). Multiethnic education provides the terminology for educators to clearly identify and distinguish a comparative educational approach that centers on race and ethnicity from other transfornational initiatives such as multicultural education and ethnic studies. The use of multiethnic education terminology allows for more effective communication among educators, establishes a knowledge base for clearly defining an important educational initiative, and provides a departure point for more focused inservice training. Without the use of more precise terminology to describe educational programs, perspectives, and courses, there will continue to be conceptual confusion about the meaning and focus of various transformational initiatives, dysfunctional conflict based on misunderstanding, and communication barriers limiting and distorting discourse about the proper role of educators in acknowledging and responding to diversity in U.S. society. *CAMB*

References

Banks, J. A. (1977). *Multiethnic education: practices and promises*. Bloomington, IN: Phi Delta Kappa Education Foundation.

———. (1981). *Education in the 80s: Multiethnic education*. Washington, DC: National Education Association.

———. (1993). Multicultural education: Characteristics and goals. In J. A. Banks & C. A. M. Banks (Eds.), *Multicultural education: Issues and perspectives* (2nd ed.) (pp. 3–28). Boston: Allyn & Bacon.

———. (1994). *Multiethnic education: Theory and practice* (3rd ed.). Boston: Allyn & Bacon.

———. (1995). Multicultural education: Historical development, dimensions, and practice. In J. A. Banks & C. A. M. Banks (Eds.), *Handbook of research on multicultural education* (pp. 3–24). New York: Macmillan.

Banks, J. A., & Banks, C. A. M. (Eds.). (1995). *Handbook of research on multicultural education*. New York: Macmillan.

Garcia, J. (1984). Multiethnic education: past, present, and future. *Texas Tech Journal of Education, 11*(1), 13–29.

Garcia, R. L. (1978). *Fostering a pluralistic society through multi-ethnic education*. Bloomington, IN: Phi Delta Kappa Education Foundation.

Gay, G. (1983). Multiethnic education: Historical developments and future prospects. *Phi Delta Kappan, 64*(8), 560–63.

Grant, C. A. (Ed.). (1992). *Research and multicultural education: From the margins to the mainstream*. Washington, DC: Falmer Press.

Grant, C. A., & Sleeter, C. E. (1985). The literature on multicultural education: Review and analysis. *Educational Review, 37*(2), 97–118.

———. (1988). *Making choices for multicultural education: Five approaches to race, class, and gender*. Columbus, OH: Merrill.

Hu-DeHart, E. (1995). Ethnic studies in U.S. higher education: History, development, and goals. In J. A. Banks & C. A. M. Banks (Eds.), *Handbook of research on multicultural education* (pp. 696–707). New York: Macmillan.

King, E. W. (1990). *Teaching ethnic and gender awareness: Methods and materials for the elementary school*. Dubuque, IA: Kendall/Hunt.

Naming

Often people are confused about how to refer to groups they do not belong to—particularly racial and ethnic groups. Multiple names are often available and heated debate surrounds such terminology. Usually this confusion is accompanied by a lack of understanding of the historic and political context of naming. Names carry baggage. Baggage accumulates through use and from the context of the name's origin. Names that have become contested, such as *Negro* versus *Black* versus *African American* or *Hispanic* versus *Latino*, are situated in social relations of oppression. It matters who creates a name and whether its use has been associated with oppression or liberation. Often members of dominant groups are oblivious to such relationships but members of oppressed groups are not.

For example, many Latino people dislike the term *Hispanic* because it was thought to have been created by the Bureau of the Census and because it emphasizes the Spanish but not the Indian part of their heritage. Conversely, many do not see one as preferable to the other, and some prefer to be identified as Spanish. The term *Chicano* originated in the Civil Rights Movement as Mexican American activists sought to empower their communities politically. Mexican Americans today who identify with that struggle prefer to call themselves Chicanos or Chicanas, rather than Mexican Americans.

The name *Euro-American* or *European American* draws attention to the location of ancestry and roots of one's family culture. The name *White* draws attention to a group's location in a racist social structure. Both names refer to the same category of people, but they draw attention to different dimensions of that group's experience and identity. Anglo-Saxons are a subset of European Americans, and technically a fairly small subset (historically both the Anglos and the Saxons were Germanic tribes who invaded Britain and colonized the people already there); although some people apply the terms interchangeably, the term *Anglo-Saxon* actually excludes many European ethnic groups such as the French, Poles, or Swedes.

Historically Western culture placed everyone within its own narrative of human history, explaining differences among people in relation to a social Darwinist belief that cultures evolve through a hierarchy from primitive to modern. Because that conception ordered civilizations hierarchically and explained differences in terms of genetic potential, names originating within it purported to refer to the *natural order* of things. This conception helped give legitimacy to Europe's colonization of major parts of the world. Group names created and used within this conception, such as *Negro* and *Oriental*, still carry colonial baggage (Mudimbe, 1988; Rosaldo, 1989; Said, 1978).

Conversely, names that oppressed groups choose for themselves serve the purpose of galvanizing politically resilient identities and modes of action aimed toward collective liberation. We might define such *renaming* as a process of dismantling demeaning identities that parade as the natural order of things and of reconstructing politically strategic identities. Dismantling naturalized categories that are popularly presumed to have a biological basis is part of this process. The concept *race*, for example, has been constructed differently in different locations and historical contexts (Davis, 1991). Both *White* and *Negro* are categories that Euro-Americans created in the process of consolidating slavery (Omi & Winant, 1986). To dismantle racism, the notion of race as a biological construct must be dismantled, as well as group names that have come to be associated with White supremacy. Gender and sexuality, too, are popularly conceived as being rooted primarily in biology rather than social relationships. Thus, names associated with the Women's Movement or the Gay Liberation Movement are important (Rubin, 1993).

The same holds true for disability: does the name suggest a problem within the individual, or a challenge to social arrangements? The name *handicapped* locates disability within individuals and focuses on a medical basis. Alternative names challenge social arrangements that benefit socially constructed ideas of normalcy, such as the names *physically challenged, differently abled,* or *person with a disability.* Questioning disability as a medical phenomenon and rejecting names associated with it, which the Disability Rights Movement does, supports interrogation of what and who counts as normal and how such definitions of normalcy are upheld politically (Oliver, 1986). Many people within the Disability Rights Movement prefer to be called *people with disabilities* because that name associates them with a social movement aimed toward improving their lives, without minimizing the difficulties of living with a disability.

The task of creating emancipatory identities through renaming is the other side of the process of dismantling and reconstructing identities. For example, Carol Padden and Tom Humphries (1988) differentiate between *Deaf* with a capital "D" to designate affiliation with the Deaf community and *deaf* with a lower-case "d" to designate a physical condition of the individual: "Ways of living proposed for Deaf people that ignore their past, that attempt to remove, either directly or indirectly, their historically created solutions, are not possible lives. . . . When deaf children are denied connections with Deaf people . . . they lose access to a history of solutions created for them by other people like themselves" (p. 120).

Identities are emancipatory when they inscribe power and strength on people and point toward social arrangements that are free of subjugation. The reconstruction of names, imagery, and identity is an ongoing process: names and identities shift as the social context shifts. As Cornel West (1993) argues,

> The main aim now is not simply access to representation in order to produce positive images of homogenous communities—although broader access remains a practical and political problem. Nor is the primary goal here that of contesting stereotypes—although contestation remains a significant albeit limited venture. . . . Black cultural workers must constitute and sustain discursive and institutional networks that deconstruct earlier modern Black strategies for identity formation, demystify power relations that incorporate class, patriarchal, and homophobic biases, and construct more multivalent and multidimensional responses that articulate the complexity and diversity of Black practices in the modern and postmodern world. (p. 19)

In so doing, terms, labels, and names are reworked to connect with more sophisticated liberation strategies.

Thus, the array of names proliferates, as do discussions about baggage associated with them. Because of the importance of renaming, conflicts and differences of perspective within groups sometimes result in a lack of consensus about the most preferred name. For example, women who endorsed the Women's Movement of the 1970s proudly carry the label *feminist*, while many of their juniors—who share their same broad goals but not their generation's history—abhor that name.

Another point of confusion is understanding which of various levels of names may be appropriate. Ethnic groups such as Hmong and Vietnamese, for example, also refer to themselves as Asian American. Native people (Native American or American Indian?) are members of particular nations, such as Mohawk or Menomonee.

Umbrella names, such as Latino or American Indian, have been created by groups that differ culturally but share common concerns which can be addressed by forming an alliance. Felix Padilla (1985), for example, studied the formation of ethnic consciousness in Chicago. He argues that a collective Latino identity had to be constructed before Latinos—who identified themselves mainly as either Chicano or Puerto Rican—could exercise political power effectively. He found that it was necessary for Puerto Rican and Mexican community leaders to convince members of their communities that they share common interests, to provide settings in which members of different Latino ethnic groups can mix, and to mobilize cultural symbols (particularly language) that bind groups together. In the process individuals came to see themselves as both Mexican and Latino, or as both Puerto Rican and Latino.

Members of the dominant culture often become frustrated with the politics of names and labels. A different response is to view names as an interesting reference point for exploring history, politics, and social dynamics. Instead of struggling to determine what to name a person outside of your cultural or ethnic group, you should simply ask him or her. Most people prefer to name their own identity, and will tell you who they are, if asked.
CES

References

Davis, F. J. (1991). *Who is Black?* University Park, PA: Pennsylvania State University Press.

Mudimbe, V. Y. (1988). *The invention of Africa: Gnosis, philosophy, and the order of knowledge.* Bloomington: Indiana University Press.

Oliver, M. (1986). Social policy and disability: Some theoretical issues. *Disability, Handicap, & Society, 1*(1), 5–18.

Omi, M., & Winant, H. (1986). *Racial formation in the United States.* New York: Routledge & Kegan Paul.

Padden, C., & Humphries, T. (1988). *Deaf in America: Voices from a culture.* Cambridge: Harvard University Press.

Padilla, F. M. (1985). *Latino ethnic consciousness.* Notre Dame, IN: University of Notre Dame Press.

Rosaldo, R. (1989). *Culture and truth: The remaking of social analysis.* Boston: Beacon Press.

Rubin, G. S. (1993). Thinking sex: Notes for a radical theory of the politics of sexuality. In H. Abelove, M. A. Barale, & D. M. Halperin (Eds.), *The lesbian and gay studies reader* (pp. 3–44). New York: Routledge.

Said, E. (1978). *Orientalism.* New York: Pantheon.

West, C. (1993). The new cultural politics of difference. In C. McCarthy & W. Crichlow (Eds.), *Race, identity, and representation in education* (pp. 11–23). New York: Routledge.

Narrative Inquiry

Narrative inquiry is a methodological approach of understanding people's representations of the world, and their actions in it, through the stories they tell. The roots of narrative inquiry lie in various disciplines, including literary criticism, philosophy, and psychology. Today researchers working in many fields and drawing on differing theoretical models (e.g., reader response or reception theory, critical theory, feminist theories) utilize narrative inquiry as a method for their work. What these scholars hold in common is a view that the narratives or stories that people tell are frameworks through which they impose order on and make sense of their own and others' experiences.

Researchers using a narrative inquiry approach gather the stories people tell and examine their various dimensions. Analyses of narratives are primarily conducted on the content of stories—the actors and actions portrayed and the places and times in which actions are located—or on their discourses—the words, voices, and forms people use when telling them. A researcher might examine the content of tales told in one place and time by several people in an affiliated group. For instance, one could study the stories of different members of a multigenerational family regarding the ways each thinks about their changing rural community and members' evolving roles in it. Analyses could be conducted on the different images family members draw upon when considering the past and their contemporary lives. Or one could study how a teenager talks about her moral code over time and across many occasions—with a teacher at school, with friends on her soccer team, and with her family. A researcher might attempt to understand how she negotiates differing beliefs about what is moral via analyses of her choices of when to speak and with what words when interacting with those whom she is most closely affiliated.

Whether we study one person's stories or those of a group of people, narrative researchers aim to understand why people think and act as they do in the situated contexts in which they live and labor. Recently scholars in education have begun to use narrative inquiry as a way to comprehend how and why teachers, students, and families think about and act towards one another as they do. In particular, researchers are trying to understand the lenses through which teachers view learners traditionally marginalized in U.S. schools—including students of color, children from low-income families, and gay and lesbian students—and to understand how these students and their families see their schooling experiences. (See, for example, the work of Anne Haas Dyson and David Schaafsma.) From this work, researchers hope to develop experiences for teachers, students, and families that enhance, interrupt, or challenge their current relations and improve schooling for all. Other investigators are using storytelling to help prospective and practicing teachers understand how our perspectives—our fundamental attitudes, values, and belief systems—are cultural constructs. Teachers come to understand how these constructs create frames through which they see themselves, their teaching, their students, and their students' learning. (See, for example, the work of Ardra Cole, Gary Knowles, and Mary Louise Gomez and colleagues.) Again, the goal is to challenge teachers' thinking and practices so that they will provide an excellent and equitable education for all of our students. *MLG*

References

Dyson, A. H. (1993). *Social worlds of children learning to write in an urban primary school.* New York: Teachers College Press.

Gomez, M. L. (in press). Learning to speak and teach in a new genre. In C. A. Grant, G. P. Smith, & M. Dilworth (Eds.), *Parameters of the knowledge base for a culturally responsible pedagogy for teacher education.* Washington, DC: American Association of Colleges for Teacher Education.

———. (1996). Telling stories of our teaching, reflecting on our practices. *Action in Teacher Education 18*(3), 1–12.

Gomez, M. L., & Abt-Perkins, D. (1995). Sharing teaching stories for practice, analysis, and critique. *Education Research and Perspectives, 22*(1), 39–52.

Gomez, M. L., & Tabachnick, B. R. (1992). Telling teaching stories. *Teaching Education, 4*(2), 129–38.

Knowles, J. G., Coles, A. L., with Presswood, C. S. (1994). *Through preservice teachers' eyes: Exploring field experiences through narrative and inquiry.* New York: Merrill.

Schaafsma, D. (1993). *Eating on the street: Teaching literacy in a multicultural society.* Pittsburgh, PA: University of Pittsburgh Press.

Native American Studies *See* American Indian Studies

Neo-Marxism

In 1914 Lenin wrote that "Marxism is the system of the views and teaching of Marx. Marx was the genius who continued and completed the three main ideological currents of the nineteenth century, belonging to the three most advanced countries of mankind: classical German philosophy, classical English political economy, and French Socialism together with French revolutionary doctrines in general" (p. 13). Marxism draws from German philosophy two key elements, the notion of dialectics and historical materialism, and hence the dialectical materialist conception of history. Key notions are the ideas that historical development implies a seemingly endless evolution (the negation of negation), development occurs by leaps, revolutions, and catastrophes rather than in a straight linear manner, and quantity is transformed into quality based on the notion of contradiction and conflict among several social forces in society.

The materialist conception of history is well defined by Marx when he argues that: "In the social production which men carry on they enter into definitive relations that are indispensable and independent of their will; these relations of production correspond to a definite stage of development of their material forces of production" (Marx, 1935, p. 356).

From classical English political economy came the notion of human labor value (distinguishing between use value and exchange value) as the basic concept needed to understand the production of commodities in capitalism. Surplus value is the key to understanding the process of capital accumulation as expropriation of the immediate producers given the private ownership of the means of production and the ensuing exploitation of labor as a factor of production by capital.

From French Socialism came the notion of socialism as an outcome of the socialization of production which is "bound to lead to the conversion of the means of production into the property of society, to the 'expropriation of the expropriators'" (Lenin, p. 34). Socialism is a political strategy and ultimately a mode of production that will replace capitalism in the transitional stages towards a communist society and mode of production "by leading to the abolition of classes, [which] will thereby lead to the abolition of the state." (Lenin, p. 36).

In contrast, neo-Marxist theories

> represent the most well-known type of conflict theory, one for which the contradictions in the capitalist mode of production, especially those between labor and capital, are taken to be decisive. Further, it is argued that as contradictions, such deep conflict cannot be resolved within the framework of capitalism. . . . Neo-Marxist theory differs from that of Marx and Engels primarily because it has attempted to take into account subsequent changes in capitalism, especially the increased importance of massive cultural institutions (such as education and the mass media), as well as the strategic role of the liberal democratic state. (Morrow & Torres, 1995, p. 21)

As a theoretical and political approach, neo-Marxism critiques the earlier philosophical, economic, and political conceptions tied to the contributions of Marx, Engels, Lenin, Mao Tse-tung, Trotsky, and many other revolutionaries. Neo-Marxism emerges as a product of the institutionalization of Marxism in the West (Anderson, 1984), particularly due to its inception in universities as a legitimate theoretical and philosophical current. While it will be impossible to trace the development of neo-Marxism in a few sentences, it includes major contributions by the Italian thinker and revolutionary Antonio Gramsci, by the French philosopher Louis Althusser, and by developments in social science exemplified in the analysis of the Frankfurt School of Critical Theory—itself a tributary of Marxist analysis—including contributions by Herbert Marcuse, Walter Benjamin, Theodor Adorno, Max Horkheimer, and the more contemporary Jürguen Habermas.

For neo-Marxism there is the important role of culture in the constitution of the political order and in the process of social transformation of reality. Gramsci's theses on hegemony and the role of ideology, intellectuals, and moral-ethical principles in contemporary politics point in that direction and directly challenge what many have termed "Marxist economism" (Gramsci, 1975). Similarly, while class continues to play a pivotal role in neo-Marxist analysis, Michael Apple has highlighted the difficulties of classical Marxism in the treatment of class, race, and gender (Apple, 1993). He argues that

> any attempt at understanding our social formation that does not combine *in an unreductive way* analyses of class and gender together is only half a theory at best. . . . The same, of course, needs to be said of race as well. The rejection of major aspects of the received orthodox Marxist tradition and the emerging sensitivity to the truly constitutive nature of gender and race demonstrate not a weakness but the continued growth and vitality of a tradition of critical analysis that is attempting to deal honestly and openly with the complexity of life under present conditions of domination and exploitation. (Apple, 1986, pp. 320–21, emphasis added)

Hence, Apple argues that class itself is—and always was—increasingly becoming gendered and raced. Thus, "we cannot marginalize race and gender as constitutive categories in any cultural analysis. If there is indeed basic cultural forms and orientations that are specifically gendered and raced, and have their own partly autonomous histories, then we need to integrate theories of patriarchal and racial forms into the very core of our attempt to comprehend what is being reproduced and changed. At the very least, a theory that allows for the contradictions within and among these dynamics would be essential" (Apple, 1992, p. 143).

Despite this theoretical insight, changes in the labor process cannot be overlooked. For neo-Marxism, recent changes from a mode of production—defined as the transformation of Fordism into a post-Fordist model—have important implications for the process of capitalist globalization of science, technology, communications, and labor and capital. (Torres, 1995). This in turn has implications for the process of skilling and de-skilling of the labor force, and implications for the logic of technical control in curriculum (Apple, 1982).

Another important contribution of neo-Marxism particularly relevant for education is the theoretical reconstruction of the role of the state in cultural reproduction and schooling (Carnoy, 1984; Morrow & Torres, 1995). Neo-

Marxism views the state as a site of multiple conflicts based on class conflict, gender, race, and ethnicity struggles (Arnove, 1994; Carnoy & Samoff, 1990; Torres, in press; Whitty, 1985). Apple argues that "the history of the state, in concert with capital and a largely male academic body of consultants and developers, intervenes at the level of practice into the work of a largely female workforce" (Apple, 1988, pp. 36–37).

The notion of dialectics and contradictions in educational policy formation continues to be central for neo-Marxism, particularly in light of privatization and market-oriented policies, "especially if they have been articulated through the State, are the results of conflicts, compromises, and accords within various levels of the State, and between the State, and a wide array of social movements and forces in the wider society" (Apple, 1988, pp. 36–37). The call is for a more subtle analysis of the state, which should include the advances made in the political economy study of gender and race. This is certainly an analysis that complements discussions of the central place of democratic conflicts in the State itself facing politics of privatization, centralization, vocationalization, and differentiation (Ball, 1993; Dale, 1989).

Social contradictions, dialectics, exploitation, and domination based on class are made analytically compatible with discrimination and exploitation based on other key dimensions of human life, most prominently race and gender relationships. Culture plays a central role in the production of hegemony and in common sense interpretations of everyday life. The state appears as a site for contradictions and contested terrain and therefore, changes in the political alliances controlling the states are central to neo-Marxist analysis (Bowles & Gintis, 1986). However, the role of socialism and the importance of the proletariat as the class that will eliminate all classes has been drastically tempered if not simply abandoned as a political program (Laclau & Mouffe, 1985; Laclau, 1990). Finally, while not a monolithic approach, neo-Marxist analysis includes a call for democratic renewal, highlighting the importance of emancipatory social movements for democracy in contemporary capitalist societies. *CAT*

References

Anderson, P. (1984). *In the tracks of historical materialism*. London: Verso.

Apple, M. W. (1982). Curricular form and the logic of technical control: Building the possessive individual. In M. W. Apple (Ed.), *Culture and economic reproduction in education: Essays on class, ideology, and the state* (pp. 247–74). London and Boston: Henley, Routledge & Kegan Paul.

———. (1986). Curriculum, capitalism, and democracy: A response to Whitty's critics. *British Journal of Sociology of Education, 7*(3).

———. (1988). *Teachers and texts: A political economy of class and gender relations in education*. New York: Routledge.

———. (1992). Education, culture and class power: Basil Bernstein and the Neo-Marxist sociology of education. *Educational Theory, 42*(2).

————. (1993). *Official knowledge: Democratic education in a conservative age.* New York: Routledge.

Arnove, R. (1994). *Education as contested terrain.* Boulder, CO: Westview.

Ball, S. J. (1993). Educational markets, choice and social class: The market as a class strategy. *British Journal of Sociology of Education, 14*(1), 3–19.

Bowles, S., & Gintis, H. (1986). *Democracy and capitalism: Property, community, and the contradictions of modern thought.* New York: Basic Books.

Carnoy, M. (1984). *The state and political theory.* Princeton, NJ: Princeton University Press.

Carnoy, M., & Samoff, J. (Eds.). (1990). *Education and social transition in the Third World.* Princeton, NJ: Princeton University Press.

Dale, R. (1989). *The state and educational policy.* Philadelphia: Open University Press.

Gouldner, A. W. (1980). *The two Marxisms.* New York and Toronto: Oxford University Press.

Gramsci, A. (1975). *Quaderni del carcere* (4 vols.), ed. Valentino Gerratana. Turin: Einaudi Editore.

Laclau, E. (1990). *New reflections on the revolution of our time.* London and New York: Verso.

Laclau, E., & Mouffe, C. (1985). Hegemony and socialist strategy: *Towards a radical democratic politics.* Translated by W. Moore & P. Cammack. London: Verso.

Lenin, V. I. (n.d.). *V. I. Lenin: Selected works. Volume 11: The theoretical principles of Marxism.* New York: International Publishers.

Marx, K. (1935). *Selected works. Vol. 1.* Engels editor. New York: International Publishers.

Morrow, R. A., & Torres, C. A. (1995). *Social theory and education: A critique of theories of social and cultural revolution.* New York: State University of New York Press.

Torres, C. A. (1995). State and education revisited. Or why educational researchers should think politically about education. *Review of Research in Education 21,* 255–331.

Whitty, G. (1985). *Sociology and school knowledge: Curriculum and theory, research, and politics.* London: Methuen.

Niuyorican *See* Puerto Rican Studies

Nonsexist Education

Nonsexist education refers to the goals, processes, and outcomes of an education that promotes equal or comparable educational opportunities for girls and boys, and men and women. Nonsexist perspectives, policies, and practices function to identify, challenge, and remediate sexism in schools generally and in curricula, programs, policies, and practices specifically. Some of the concerns that nonsexist education has attempted to address and remediate are classroom practices that inappropriately segregate girls and boys; textbooks and media that discriminate in language, pictures, and content; personnel practices that create or sustain job segregation; career counseling that contributes to depressed aspirations; and beliefs about gender that contribute to lower or different expectations for girls and women—at all levels of formal education systems—while promoting boys and men's opportunities for scholarship and leadership.

While gender differentiation has been part of the fabric of public and private education since the advent of publicly funded schools in the United States in the early nineteenth century, the term *nonsexist education* is a more recent phenomenon. The use of the term can be traced to the late 1960s and the birth of women's liberation in the wake of the Civil Rights Movement. Education, both formal and informal, was identified as a major source of inequality between males and females. Remediation was sought through national legislation. Subsequently, the United States Congress passed the Title IX Education Amendment of 1972 to address key ares of discrimination and to guarantee students' rights to access and equitable treatment in programs, courses, funding, and educational outcomes.

Title IX resulted in some changes in school programs, procedures, and funding. For example, the disparate amounts of resources devoted to male and female athletic programs were remediated. Girls and women are now afforded more opportunities to train for competitive sports, and female sports teams are supported with coaching, uniforms, and opportunities for achievement. The fact that more young women now go on to higher education institutions on athletic scholarships is a direct benefit of Title IX.

Ensuring equal opportunities in career education, encouraging and recruiting girls and women in mathematics and science, disseminating the burgeoning new knowledge in social sciences, and supporting women reentering the workforce were landmarks of the nonsexist educational landscape of the 1970s. Increased numbers and percentages of women entering law, medicine, science, and trades were outcomes of Title IX efforts in the 1970s and 1980s. Some of this success can also be attributed to support generated through federal funding from the Women's Educational Equity Act, passed in 1974.

The nonsexist educational movement lost momentum in the 1980s during the Reagan and Bush administrations. Attacks by Washington conservatives on government funding resulted in skeleton budgets for Women's Education and Equity Act projects and Title IX enforcement. Moreover, popular writing on the crisis in education seemed to ignore sex and gender as a variable.

At the same time, however, the definition and scope of nonsexist education shifted from equity and access to include concerns about specific populations. While gender equity and access remained centerpieces, burgeoning gender-feminist research identified the different experiences, expectations, and participation levels of girls and boys, and men and women from different class, race, religious, and ethnic groups in multiple educational contexts. The needs of specific populations raised questions about the utility of blanket policies without sensitivity to gender, race, ethnic, religious, and sexual identity.

Gender, the term used in the platform developed at the Fourth World Conference on Women in Beijing, China, in 1995, is a lens and a condition of life. Hence, *gender fair education* means paying attention to gender issues whenever and wherever they arise and in any combination with other aspects of identity in educational contexts.

Researching and gathering data on gender effects in schooling at all levels—early childhood, elementary, secondary, post secondary, and higher education—are the cornerstones of gender fair education. Continual evaluation and revision of scope and sequence framework, syllabi, curricular materials, practices, and policies for currency and salience are the other cornerstones of gender fair education. Finally, gender fair education acknowledges that gender fairness can be achieved through specific remediations in education but that it is an ongoing process, shaped by the dynamics of shifting school populations, changing communities, research, and political-economic circumstances within a global context. *JBP*

References

Biklen, S. K., & Pollard, D. (Eds.). (1993). *Gender and education.* Chicago: University of Chicago Press.

Klein, S. (Ed.). (1985). *Handbook for achieving sex equity through education.* Baltimore, MD: John Hopkins University Press.

Official English (English Only) Versus English Plus

Since 1981, when Senator S. I. Hayakawa introduced a constitutional amendment to make English the official language of the United States, a national debate has ensued. The Official English/English Only movement is led primarily by two organizations, U.S. English and English First, who claim that English is under attack as a result of federally funded programs like bilingual education and bilingual ballots, and because today's immigrants, unlike those in the past, are not motivated to learn English. Official English proponents believe that legislating English as the official language is necessary to preserve unity and the national culture. Although efforts have failed at passing congressional legislation making English the official language, to date 22 states have passed such laws. (Arizona's Official English law was struck down by federal courts as unconstitutional and violative of the First Amendment right to free speech.)

Opposition to the Official English/English Only Movement comes principally from civil rights and educational organizations, some of whom promote the alternative concept of "English Plus," which holds that the national interest is best served when all members of society have the opportunity to acquire English proficiency *plus* mastery of a second or multiple languages. Opponents of Official English/English Only maintain (1) that the movement is motivated by ethnic intolerance and even racist sentiments; (2) that immigrant groups well understand the value of learning English (when California's Official English measure was passed in 1986, for instance, there were 40,000 prospective ESL students on waiting lists in Los

Angeles County alone), and that, indeed, immigrants are shifting to English within one or two generations anyway, a much faster rate than for previous immigrant groups; and (3) that legislating English as the official language will help no one learn it. (None of the proposed bills allocate fiscal or other resources for this purpose.) Furthermore, opponents of Official English/English Only criticize U.S. English for its funding ties to immigration restrictionist and eugenics organizations, and for accepting donations from questionable sources. *PJA & MCC*

References

Crawford, J. (Ed.). (1992). *Language loyalties: A source book on the official English controversy.* Chicago, IL: University of Chicago Press.

English Plus Information Clearinghouse (1987). *Statement of Purpose.* Washington, DC: Author.

U.S. Senate Judiciary Subcommittee (1984). *English Language Amendment: Hearings on S. J. Resolution 167,* 18th congress, 2nd Session. Washington, DC: U.S. Government Printing Office.

Oppression

The relevance of multicultural education lies in its drive to challenge oppression. Oppression limits spiritual and mental growth and is exercised by an authority that is unjust or insensitive. It is perpetrated by elements of power and influence in society which serve to perpetuate inequalities and discrimination—sometimes overtly but more often concealed behind seemingly natural systems of stratification which define the worthiness of knowledge and how that knowledge is to be distributed.

Traditional educational practices perpetuate the disempowerment of oppressed groups by continually reinstating systems of stratification by defining school knowledge as different from cultural knowledge, by placing students without school knowledge into lower tracks designed to help them fit in with the mainstream, or by depicting education in a society as an equal opportunity venture that can be mastered with a little hard work. While seemingly benevolent, educational techniques such as these actually disable members of oppressed groups by inculcating the dominant assumptions of the best ways to behave and the best things to learn in school. (See Sleeter, 1991, pp. 4–5.) The histories of discrimination as well as the cultural knowledge and personal identities that students from oppressed groups bring with them to school are ignored in traditional education, and the disempowerment of oppressed groups continues.

While inequalities and oppressive social relationships may often appear to be a thing of the past, Henry Giroux (1989) points out the strong links between culture and power by saying that "social relations are structured within class, sexual, and age formations that produce forms of dependency and oppression" (p. 125). One look at, in Sleeter's (1989) words, "the persistence of poverty and discrimination among historically disenfranchised groups" (p. 61) shows that there is still a dominant culture and that social relationships are still oppressive.

However, Sleeter (1989) also points out that "[m]ulticultural education can be viewed as a form of resistance to oppressive social relationships" (p. 59). This requires an education of empowerment in the face of oppression. Multicultural education is more than an attempt to assuage the inequalities brought about by oppression and is more than an effort to acquaint students with other ways of being within the same oppressive social and economic contexts. The issues surrounding social inequalities need to be addressed directly in education with an eye toward social change. As Christine Sleeter (1991) reminds us, "empowerment for social change is an inextricable component of multicultural education" (pp. 1–2). *DH*

References

Giroux, H. A. (1989). Schooling as a form of cultural politics: Toward a pedagogy of and for difference. In H. Giroux & P. McLaren (Eds.) *Critical pedagogy, the state, and cultural struggle* (pp. 125–51). New York: State University of New York Press.

Sleeter, C. E. (1989). Multicultural education as a form of resistance to oppression. *Journal of Education, 171*(3), 51–71.

———. (1991). *Empowerment through multicultural education.* Albany: State University of New York Press.

Oral History

What oral history is and means differs considerably depending on one's relationship to oral history. For some it consists of verbal forms of expression that are essential to the survival and identity of a culture. For others it is an interviewing method to obtain and preserve significant memories for future use in archival form (Morrisey, 1996).

Throughout history people worldwide have passed on important information to future generations by word of mouth. The spoken word was used as a tool to ensure a culture's continued existence by consistently reminding people of their relationship to their ancestors and to the land. These traditions may have taken the form of song, chant, speech, storytelling, or life story. They were the major source of a culture's knowledge and way of life where people depended on one another to remember and pass on information contained in the traditions.

Traditional historians would argue that these verbal forms of expression might be better categorized as myths, tales, or folklore since they have been viewed as forms of entertainment without any historical significance. Others still make a distinction between oral history and oral tradition, in which oral history deals primarily with the recent past. However, those who practice oral histories contend that they contribute significantly to the survival and identity of a community.

The first books to help establish oral history in academia as a valid and legitimate method of research were Jan Vansina's *Oral Tradition As History* (1985) and Paul Thompson's *The Voice of the Past* (1978). In 1948 Allan Nevins established the Columbia University Project, a project in which he interviewed *great men* before they passed on. As a result of these publications and the Columbia Project, oral history has taken on a different form and meaning. What originally qualified as oral history was reduced to carefully structured interviews, asking precise and specific questions of individuals about recent events in the past or about their life histories. Literature produced by anthropologists, sociologists, and historians discussed oral history in terms of collecting evidence, which transformed both the content and purpose of history, shifted the focus of history, and opened new areas of inquiry.

With the upheaval of the Civil Rights, Women's, and American Indian movements, scholars and historians began to question their methods of writing and researching history. They asked themselves the questions: Whose history? In whose voice(s)? From whose perspective? This sparked an increased interest in obtaining information from families, women, communities, and groups who otherwise would go unnoticed. It also helped oral history find a place in popular culture. Studs Terkel interviewed *common folk* for his radio show in Chicago, and his books became popular across the country. Eliot Wiggington, known for the Foxfire Project, brought oral history into the high school classroom.

There are still considerable differences among those who use oral history as a research method and those who practice it for cultural survival. The former concern themselves with the amount of time passed, for example, generations passed or recent passed, while those who practice it are concerned with the *way* in which information is passed (Wilson, forthcoming). *JL*

References

Brown, C. S. (1988). *Like it was: A complete guide to writing oral history*. New York: Teachers and Writers Collaborative.

Cajete, G. (1994). *Look to the mountain: An ecology of Indigenous education*. Durango, CO: Kivaki Press.

Davis, C., Back, K., & MacLean, K. (1977). *Oral history from tape to type*. Chicago: American Library Association.

Deloria, V., Jr. (1991). *Indian education in America*. Boulder, CO: American Indian Science and Engineering Society.

Grele, R. J. (1991). *Envelopes of sound: The art of oral history* (2nd ed.). New York: Praeger.

Henige, D. (1982). *Oral historiography*. New York: Longman.

Montejo, V. (1994). Ancient words: Oral tradition and the Indigenous People of the Americas. *Akwe:kon Journal, 11*(3&4), 139–45.

Morrisey, C. (1996). Telephone conversation with the author. Houston, TX, January.

Sitton, T., Mehaffy, G. L., & Davis, O. L., Jr. (1983). *Oral history: A guide for teachers (and others)*. Austin, Texas: University of Texas Press.

Terkel, S. (1974). *Working: People talk about what they do all day and how they feel about what they do*. New York: Pantheon Books.

Terkel, S. (1970). *Hard times: An oral history of the great depression*. New York: Pantheon.

Thompson, P. (1978). *The voice of the past: Oral history*. Oxford: Oxford University Press.

Vansina, J. (1985). *Oral tradition as history*. Madison: University of Wisconsin Press.

Wiggington, E. (1985). *Sometimes a shining moment: The foxfire experience*. Garden City, NY: Anchor Doubleday.

Wilson, A. C. (forthcoming). Power of the spoken word: Native oral traditions in American Indian history. In D. Fixico (Ed.), *Rethinking American Indian History*. Albuquerque: University of New Mexico Press.

The Other

The definition of the Other is based on difference: that which is not the same or that which is something *other than*. Therefore, the only way to think about, and thus define, a term like *the Other* is in context. There can be no Other outside of a context of relations and no Other outside of a comparison to that which is *the same*. In multicultural terms, that which is not the same, that which is the Other, is that which is not part of the dominant culture.

One role of multicultural education is to unmask the dominant ideologies that keep the Other at bay. These dominant ideologies embody the power and influence of Western culture through traditional educational practices in a daily way. Not only is the content of education derived from a history of dominance in determining what knowledge is of most worth, but the techniques of education—such as scope and sequence or stages of cognitive development—also play a part in regulating and defining students in comparison to a perceived norm. In its reproduction of dominant ideologies, education effectively closes the door to other forms of knowledge and to other ways of learning, thinking, and being. When education is not excluding the Other in terms of content, it is attempting to help those seen as Other into the mold of a student who is able to learn that very same prescribed, unquestioned, and oppressive content. Particular attitudes toward race, class, gender, homelessness, ability levels, or sexual orientation make forms of Otherness into objects to be scrutinized and described. These dominant ideologies in education minimize, marginalize, and label those who do not fit into the norm.

In discussions of multicultural education and Otherness it is important to keep in mind the fact that all identities are formed and described in terms of the dominant norm. Stuart Hall (1992) explains how the Other is necessary "to our own sense of identity; how even the dominant, colonizing, imperializing power only knows who and what it is and can only experience the pleasure of its own power of domination in and through the construction of the Other" (p. 16). Once again, Otherness could not be *other than* if it were not distinct from a predefined standard. Yet this distinction does not depict a mere difference between two equal parties since the predefined standard is always already dominant. The Other is not only a construction that is different from the norm, but it is also unequal to the norm in terms of history and cultural capital. When distinctions are constructed and used, such as naming who is different or who is Other, there is always the risk that the Other remains an object in relation to the dominant subject.

Multicultural education at its best, however, creates a space for nondominant voices to speak as subjects in history—subjects of an unequal world, subjects defined by boundaries, and subjects of oppression. In Paul Julian Smith's (1992) words "[t]he quest to demystify the dominant white mythology must also be the attempt to disentangle the differing historical positions of subaltern groups hitherto forced to play the role of Other" (p. 3). Since the Other is always defined in relation to the dominant power, there is a danger in homogenizing all forms of Otherness, as if there is only one particular and unified type of the Other to consider. In (re)reading and (re)writing the positions of the Other, it is most helpful if diversity, or Otherness, is historically placed in its numerous contexts. *DH* • *See also* **Difference**

References

Hall, S. (1992). Race, culture and communications: Looking backward and forward at cultural studies. *Rethinking Marxism, 5*(1), 10–18.

Smith, P. J. (1992). *Representing the Other: 'Race', text, and gender in Spanish and Spanish American Narrative*. Oxford: Clarendon Press.

Panethnicity

Panethnicity is the generalization of solidarity among ethnic subgroups. In the United States examples of newly forged panethnic groups include Native Americans, Latino Americans, and Asian Americans. These groups enclose diverse peoples who are nevertheless seen as homogeneous by outsiders: the Native American label unites people of linguistically and culturally distinct tribes; the Latino American category combines colonized Mexicans, Puerto Ricans, and Cuban refugees, as well as documented and undocumented immigrants; and the Asian American unit comprises groups of different national origins that continue to be divided along class, linguistic, and generational lines. Despite their distinctive histories and separate identities, these ethnic groups have united to protect and promote their collective interests. They may not always do so, but for certain purposes panethnic organization takes precedence over tribal or national affiliations.

Panethnic activism was prompted by the social struggles that swept across the United States in the 1960s. These movements—Civil Rights, Anti-War, Women's, Students', and People of Color—fought against racism, poverty, war, and exploitation. These social struggles led groups of color to recognize that their interests could be advanced only by forming coalitions. Whatever the balance of sentiment, most of the subethnic groups within each racial group concur that political alliances at the panethnic level are important, even essential, for protection and advancement. In these new or previously marginalized populations, political power is heavily dependent on the ability of the subgroups to speak with one voice. This is true not only because there is strength in numbers but also because outsiders are rarely willing to listen to myriad voices representing numerous subethnic groups.

The phenomenon of panethnicity calls attention to the imposed nature of ethnicity. While ethnicity may be an exercise of personal choice for Euro-Americans, it is not so for groups of color in the United States. For these *visible* groups ethnicity is not always voluntary but may be coercively imposed. An imposed category ignores subgroup boundaries, lumping diverse peoples together into a single, expanded ethnic framework. Individuals so categorized may have nothing in common except that which the categorizer uses to distinguish them. Although it originated in the minds of outsiders, today the panethnic concept is a political resource for insiders, a basis on which to mobilize diverse peoples and force others to be more responsive to their grievances and agendas. *YLE*

References

Cornell, S. (1988). *The return of the native: American Indian political resurgence.* London: Oxford University Press.

Padilla, F. (1985). *Latino ethnic consciousness: The case of Mexican Americans and Puerto Ricans in Chicago.* Notre Dame, IN: University of Notre Dame Press.

Espiritu, Y. L. (1992). *Asian American panethnicity: Bridging institutions and identities.* Philadelphia: Temple University Press.

Parental and Community Involvement

Historically, parents and community members have chosen to participate in the process of schooling. However, a variety of factors—economic, social, political—have prevented people of color and poor families from having access to this level of participation. Parental and community involvement is also often used interchangeably with *participation*. Sarason (1994), for example, argues that the call for increased parental involvement can be traced to the 1954 Supreme Court desegregation decision which mandated that there be a designated external force influencing and monitoring educational decision making, previously the sole responsibility of professional educators. The 1954 decision was used for many challenges to power relations within and beyond schools, especially in urban areas. During the social movements of the 1960s, activists called for more just power relations in both society at large and within specific social institutions, including schools (Banks, 1988). Parents, community representatives, and youth demanded more control over schools and other social institutions, arguing that traditional educational structures and processes were not serving the needs of their communities. Demands ranged from calls for community-controlled schools to curricula on racial and ethnic histories and cultures (McCarthy & Apple, 1988). These activists and activist organizations can be considered the early advocates of multicultural education (Gay, 1983). The subsequent decline of such social movements has led to a decrease in parent-community activism in urban areas.

Barriers for low-income parents and parents of color to actively involve themselves in their children's schooling are numerous: poverty, discrimination, the intimidation of parents by school professionals, cultural differences in parental assumptions regarding schooling, and few institutional mechanisms for genuine participation of parents or community representatives over key aspects of a school's operations (Densmore, 1995; Lareau, 1987; McLaughlin & Shields, 1987). Current site-based management schemes that include parents as stakeholders represent attempts to involve more constituencies in school governance (e.g., Bastian, et al., 1985).

Research demonstrates that while students generally benefit from parent or caregiver involvement in education, students of color, including language-diverse students and students from low-income backgrounds, have gained the most in terms of academic achievement (Chavkin, 1993; Henderson, 1981, 1987; Scarcella, 1990). Contrary to popularly held beliefs that low-income parents and parents of color are disinterested in their children's schooling, Schneider and Coleman (1993) found that African American and Hispanic parents exhibit higher rates of parental involvement when compared to White parents of the same social class. Levels and kinds of parental involvement vary enormously from school to school (Epstein, 1987, 1994), depending in large part upon a school's policies and structures and the resources caregivers have at their disposal (Schneider & Coleman, 1993). While earlier studies focused more on the effects of family background on school achievement (Coleman, 1966; Jencks, 1972), more recent research looks at the processes within families and on parents' interactions with schools (Coleman, 1987; Comer, 1980; Heath, 1983; Lightfoot, 1978; Scott-Jones, 1984; Walberg, 1984). The value of participation for parents themselves has received some, although little, attention (e.g., Delgado-Gaitan, 1990). Increased research in this area may be promising in that it may develop our understanding of the potential of community involvement as individual caregivers experience and develop their civic responsibility. *KD*

References

Banks, J. (1988). *Multiethnic education: Theory and practice* (2nd ed.). Boston: Allyn & Bacon.

Bastian, A., Fruchter, N., Gittell, M., Greer, C., & Haskins, K. (1985). *Choosing equality: The case for democratic schooling*. Philadelphia: Temple University Press.

Chavkin, N. F. (Ed.). (1993). *Families and schools in a pluralistic society*. Albany: State University of New York Press.

Coleman, J. S. (1966). *Equality of educational opportunity*. Washington, DC: U.S. Government Printing Office.

———. (1987). Families and schools. *Educational Researcher, 16*, 32–38.

Comer, J. P. (1980). *School power*. New York: Macmillan.

Delgado-Gaitan, C. (1990). *Literacy for empowerment: The role of parents in children's education*. New York: Falmer Press.

Densmore, K. (1995). An interpretation of multicultural education and its implications for school-community relationships. In C. A. Grant (Ed.), *Educating for diversity* (pp. 405–18). Boston: Allyn & Bacon.

Epstein, J. (1987). What principals should know about parent involvement. *Principal, 66*(3), 6–9.

———. (1994). Theory to practice: School and family partnerships lead to school improvement and student success. In C. L. Fagnano & B. Z. Weber (Eds.), *School, family, and community interaction: A view from the firing lines* (pp. 39–52). Boulder, CO: Westview Press.

Gay, G. (1983). Multiethnic education historical developments and future prospects. *Phi Delta Kappan, 64*, 560–63.

Heath, S. B. (1983). *Ways with words.* Cambridge: Cambridge University Press.

Henderson, A. (1987). *The evidence continues to grow: Parent involvement improves student achievement.* Columbia, MD: National Coalition of Citizens in Education.

———. (Ed.). (1981). *Parent participation-student achievement: The evidence grows.* Columbia, MD: National Committee for Citizens in Education.

Jencks, C. (1972). *Inequality.* New York: Basic Books.

Lareau, A. (1987). Social class difference in family-school relationships: The importance of cultural capital. *Sociology of Education, 60*(2), 73–85.

Lightfoot, S. (1978). *Worlds apart: The relationship between families and schools.* New York: Basic Books.

McCarthy, C., & Apple, M. W. (1988). Race, class, and gender in American educational research: Toward a non-synchronous parallelist position. In L. Weis (Ed.), *Class, race, and gender in American education.* Albany: State University of New York Press.

McLaughlin, M. W., & Shields, P. M. (1987). Involving low-income parents in the schools: A role for policy? *Phi Delta Kappan, 69*(2), 156–60.

Sarason, S. (1994). *Parental involvement and the political principle.* San Francisco: Jossey-Bass.

Scarcella, R. (1990). *Teaching language minority students in the multicultural classroom.* Englewood Cliffs, NJ: Prentice Hall.

Schneider, B., & Coleman, J. S. (1993). *Parents, their children, and schools.* Boulder, CO: Westview Press.

Scott-Jones, D. (1984). Family influences on cognitive development and school achievement. In E. W. Gordon (Ed.), *Review of research in education.* Washington, DC: American Educational Research Association.

Walberg, H. J. (1984). Families as partners in educational productivity. *Phi Delta Kappan, 65*(6), 397–400.

People of Color

People of color generally refers to populations that are not part of the White population and are often part of underrepresented groups.

Carl Grant used this term at a Midwest Holmes Group meeting in the mid-1980s. When Dr. Grant was asked what he knew about the history of the term and if it had originated with him, he reported not having heard the term before, but he felt that it was a term whose time had come and that it might have originated simultaneously from several sources.

It turns out that the term *people of color* had been used occasionally in the past (1960s) and generally referred to African Americans. The contemporary definition (non-White populations) gained acceptance in the late 1980s and began to appear frequently in scholarly literature as well as in newspapers and news magazines.

Currently, *people of color* is often used in place of the term *minority,* as a growing number of people find the latter problematic. Minority is not just a quantitative term denoting the size of a population; it also has political connotations referring to the status of groups. The term *people of color* represents a respectful alternative which is neither quantitative nor judgmental.

Those who find the term *people of color* problematic believe that it implies that Whites are somehow colorless or that all people of color share a common experience. However, many who express these concerns still find people of color the most acceptable description of non-White populations.

There has been much discussion and controversy about changes in language dealing with diversity (i.e., political correctness), and the motives for these changes are often misunderstood. For example, changes in language are not a sinister political agenda as some may suggest; instead they simply reflect the fact that society is changing faster than our ability to describe it. In short, people of color is simply a term that meets a contemporary semantic need—and does so well. *MLF* • *See also* **Minority; Naming**

Perspective Consciousness

Perspective consciousness is the recognition or awareness on the part of an individual that he or she has a view of the world that is not universally shared, that this view of the world has been and continues to be shaped by influences that often escape conscious detection, and that others have views of the world that are profoundly different from one's own. *RGH*

Reference

Hanvey, R. (1975). *An attainable global perspective.* New York: Center for War/Peace Studies.

Plessy v. Ferguson

Plessy v. Ferguson is the 1896 Supreme Court case whose decision contended that "separate but equal" public railroad facilities for diverse groups did not obstruct their rights to equal protection of the laws, which are guaranteed by the Fourteenth Amendment of the United States Constitution. Eight of nine justices ruled against Homer Adolph Plessy, a mulatto arrested for his refusal to move from a "Whites only" rail car after the conductor had asked him to move. The court used this case as a precedent in a school conflict in 1927 to support its ruling in favor of segregation. Although challenged, the Court's decision was not reversed until the *Brown v. Board of Education* case of 1954. Then it was argued that segregation had a detrimental effect on colored children even though the facilities were purported to be equal. By reversing the *Plessy v. Ferguson* decision, the Court helped to further open the way for desegregation and showed that separate public school facilities are "inherently unequal." *JT* • *See also* **Brown v. Board of Education**

References

Brown v. Board of Education, 347 U.S. 483 (1954).
Plessy v. Ferguson, 163 U.S. 537 (1896).

Political Correctness

Political correctness is a term of murky origin, generally believed to have emerged in the late 1970s or early 1980s and commonly shortened to the initials P.C. It is often used erroneously (and sometimes disingenuously) as a virtual synonym for multiculturalism, although political correctness and multiculturalism have only a tangential and sometimes conflicting relationship. Despite its recent origin the term *political correctness* has evolved rapidly, accumulating at least six different meanings and types of usage.

Usage One: Excesses of the authoritarian, dogmatic, and hypersensitive left. The most widely disseminated hypothesis concerning the origin of political correctness is that it began as a campus-level joke among college and university liberals. They used the label politically correct to express friendly derision for those left-leaning colleagues and fellow students whom they considered to be too self-righteously authoritarian (e.g., supporters of restrictive campus speech codes), dogmatic (e.g., developers of rigid lists of forbidden group terms), or hypersensitive (e.g., those who made an avocation of looking for statements, labels, or illustrations that might somehow be construed as offensive).

Usage Two: Educational initiatives or actions on behalf of such groups as people of color and women. Some opponents of certain prodiversity efforts soon arrogated the label, expanding its application well beyond the original authoritarian, dogmatic, or hypersensitive meaning. Instead it was used to vilify a much wider range of college-level or K–12 prodiversity initiatives or activities, such as multicultural education, affirmative action, ethnic and women's studies, bilingual education, and the inclusion of people of color and women in such courses as U.S. history or literature.

Usage Three: Any actions or expressions on behalf of people of color; women; groups such as gays, lesbians, or people with disabilities; or certain beliefs such as environmentalism. As the meaning of political correctness expanded beyond the criticism of diversity-related educational efforts, the term became a label for smearing an increasingly varied collection of targets, including environmentalism, gay and lesbian rights, sensitivity to the disabled, opposition to hate speech, museum exhibits that challenged traditional interpretations of U.S. history, or motion pictures or television programs that cast people of color or women in a positive light. Political correctness became a convenient all-purpose slur, often used in knee-jerk fashion as a simplistic rhetorical substitute for serious analysis or argumentation concerning a specific issue or action. Concurrently, some politicians, pundits, and college denizens appointed themselves to be icons of courage standing up against the supposed forces of political correctness, even when such forces hardly existed.

Conversely, the best way to escape being branded politically correct was to proclaim oneself to be *anti-P.C.* and to avoid saying anything positive about or taking action in favor of the ever-growing list of positions or groups labeled P.C.

Usage Four: Multiple meanings and applications. With wider usage P.C. accumulated not only more numerous but sometimes even conflicting interpretations, sometimes far removed from its early usage. For example, in his book *Culture of Complaint: The Fraying of America*, Robert Hughes provides an interesting perspective on this process by arguing that there are really two P.C.'s: the politically correct and the *patriotically correct*. The latter usage embraces those people who commonly accuse others of being politically correct and at the same time assert and defend their own kind of self-righteous authoritarianism, dogmatism, and hypersensitivity. According to Thomas C. Holt (1995), former president of the American Historical Association, "under the guise of freedom, it [this patriotically correct kind of P.C.] seeks to re-exclude those only recently accepted as worthy of inclusion" (p. 20).

Usage Five: As a source of humor and satire. Political correctness has now become part of the public domain. In particular, it has become a widespread source of jocularity, with myriad books and articles having fun with the idea of political correctness (e.g., *Politically Correct Bedtime Stories* by James Finn Garner). Some humorists now label their show routines as *politically incorrect* (e.g., Bill Maher on television and Jackie Mason in his stand-up comedy show). Yet the targets of this humor now range so far beyond those included in the formative stages of P.C. that, in this comedic sense, P.C. can now be found in nearly limitless contexts and with nearly limitless applications.

Usage Six: As a journalistic cliché. As the uses of political correctness continue to multiply, the label has steadily and inevitably suffered an erosion of precision. Thus, this ultra-broad, multifaceted P.C. has now attained the status of a public cliché, often used lazily by journalists and other public pundits. Because of its varied meanings, the contemporary reader or listener is faced with the following dilemma: When different people say or write

"P.C.," it is difficult to know which correctness they oppose and which correctness they support. *CEC*

References

Garner, J. F. (1994). *Politically correct bedtime stories.* New York: Macmillan.

Holt, T. C. (1995). Marking: Race, race-making, and the writing of history. *American Historical Review, 100*(1), 1–20.

Hughes, R. (1993). *Culture of complaint: The fraying of America.* New York: Oxford University Press.

Positionality

Positionality, and its related term *social location,* mean the shifting ways individuals are located within broader societal structures of political, cultural, and economic domination, and of equality. Thus, gender, race, culture, sexual orientation, and social class, for example, are historically based, representing evolving sets of relational dynamics rather than fixed identities. The meanings of these dynamics change in different contexts. Although one is often uncomfortable as an outsider, settings with a majority of people of color position a single White observer differently than predominantly White settings position a person of color. Both societal structures and the varieties of specific contexts are always at play. Positionality marks identity as both sturdy and fluid and as always reflective of societal power arrangements.

In a study of college teaching two researchers found that participants' involvement in the power relations of various oppressions resulted in widely different positions from which to construct knowledge (Maher & Tetreault, 1994). By drawing upon multiple viewpoints teachers and students were able to engage in more fluid appraisals and complex analyses of their experiences and social locations. When multicultural educators explored these factors, not as essentialized differences but as historically grounded and socially constructed relationships, they began, as one of the students in their research study said, to "make connections that made education education."

Classroom discussions sometimes spawned heated arguments about whether to define *woman* in terms of gender or class. These debates demonstrated both the impossibility of determining primary oppositions and the limitations of social analysis that is based only on abstract concepts. The study of peoples' lives in terms of any one category, such as ethnicity, ignores other important dimensions of their experience and location (Sleeter & Grant, 1987). In societies like ours, which are organized into multiple dimensions of power and inequality, focusing on one category of oppression leads to blindness about differences and conflicts within categories as well as the similarities between them. And yet as additional categories of identity are stipulated and added on to solve this problem, the more marked people's differences and isolation from each other become.

The challenges mounted by multiculturalists, feminists, and others in regard to the assumptions and terminologies of identity and identity politics led to the articulation of positionality as a way out of these dangers. The term was first proposed by postmodern feminist theorists such as Julia Kristeva in France and Linda Alcoff in the United States. Alcoff sought to describe woman relative to a network of relations that involve "other people, economic conditions, cultural and political institutions and ideologies" (Alcoff, 1988, p. 433).

Multicultural education is weakened by the simplistic goal of pluralism, or the joining up of supposedly equal cultural groups in celebration of their differences and commonalities. The historical, political and economic inequalities that underlie racial classification are underplayed by an emphasis on ethnicity (Sanjek, 1994). Unless we position cultural groups in relation to each other or around multiple dimensions of social class and gender as well as race, we will not be able to challenge inequalities and thereby create a truly multicultural society. *MKTT & FAM* • *See also* **Identity Politics**

References

Alcoff, L. (1988, Spring). Cultural feminism versus post-structuralism: the identity crisis in feminist theory. *Signs, 13*(3), 405–36.

Maher, F. A., & Tetreault, M. K. T. (1994). *The feminist classroom: An inside look at how professors and students are transforming higher education for a diverse society*. New York: Basic Books.

Maher, F. A., Tetreault, M. K. T., & Sanjek, R. (1994). The enduring inequalities of race. In S. Gregory & R. Sanjek (Eds.), *Race* (pp. 1–17). New Brunswick, NJ: Rutgers University Press.

Moi, T. (1985). *Sexual/textual politics: Feminist literacy theory*. London and New York: Methuen.

Sanjek, R. (1994). The enduring inequalities of race. In S. Gregory & R. Sanjek (Eds.), *Race* (pp. 1–17). New Brunswick, NJ: Rutgers University Press.

Sleeter, C. E., & Grant, C. A. (1987). An analysis of multicultural education in the United States. *Harvard Educational Review, 57*(4), 421–44.

Positivism

In recent years the most common use of the term *positivism* by educational researchers has been as an epithet with which to disparage research considered to be *scientistic* (i.e., placing exaggerated trust in the application of methods of physical and biological science to social and psychological inquiry). Persons who use positivism as an epithet sometimes freight it with connotations and features that would be unrecognizable to an actual proponent of positivism. An effort is made here instead to acquaint the reader with the problems that some self-possessed positivists are attempting to solve.

The term *positive philosophy* was coined by Auguste Comte (1798–1857) in his six-volume work *Cours de Philosophie Positive* (published between 1830 and 1842). (Comte is considered by some to have founded the field of sociology, which is another term that he coined in the same work.) In proposing his positive philosophy Comte was seeking a better term than the two then-prevalent alternatives, which he found disagreeable: *theology* and *metaphysics*. In sympathy with earlier criticism that Voltaire (1694–1778) had made of religious bigotry in France, Comte distrusted religious domination. He claimed that attempts to explain observable phenomena by attributing them to supernatural beings represented the least advanced stage of human thinking (which he termed the *theological stage*). Comte found metaphysical explanations, which replace supernatural beings with equally elusive abstract forces, to be little better. Lacking any factual basis for resolving disagreements, debates over competing metaphysical explanations were equally dogmatic, endlessly speculative, and dangerously heated. Comte proposed his positive philosophy as a constructive alternative to theology and metaphysics. In it, disagreements could be resolved by referring to observable facts.

In 1924 Moritz Schlick brought together a group of philosophers, scientists, and mathematicians who came to be known as the Vienna Circle. Among the group were Rudolf Carnap and Kurt Gödel. Members of the Vienna Circle considered themselves to be heavily influenced by the writings of Gottlob Frege (mathematician and logician, 1848–1925), Ernst Mach (physicist, 1838–1916), George Edward Moore (philosopher, 1873–1958), Bertrand Russell (philosopher and mathematician, 1872–1970), and Ludwig Wittgenstein (philosopher, 1889–1951). Calling themselves logical positivists and logical empiricists, the group combined Comte's critique of metaphysics with a twentieth-century interest in the analysis of language use. The group set up criteria by which one could judge the meaningfulness of a proposition (Ayer, [1936] 1952, 1959). Some illustrative criteria of meaningfulness are the following: propositions verifiable from experience (i.e., judged through experience to be probable) are *meaningful;* the laws of logic and mathematics, while not themselves verifiable through experience, are tautologously true, hence meaningful; propositions that can be derived from other meaningful propositions in accord with the laws of logic and mathematics are also considered meaningful; and assertions are *meaningless* if they can neither be verified in experience nor be validly inferred from meaningful propositions.

There are various grounds for criticism of positivism. Realists (who are sometimes mistakenly confused with positivists) criticize positivism on the grounds that some things existing in reality are, at least with our present capabilities, unobservable. Therefore, positivism might inappropriately classify true claims about things that really exist as meaningless. Postpositivists challenge the implicit assumption of positivism that the evaluation of observations can be isolated from theoretical preconceptions and purposes of the observer—a criticism also voiced by Friedrich Nietzsche (1844–1900) who called it the dogma of "immaculate perception." Relativists and solipsists argue that one person's experiences and meanings for words and propositions can never be fully matched with those of another person. It is, consequently, futile to expect that experiences and verbalized descriptions of them will lead to intersubjective agreement. Also present among the critics of positivism are apologists for the positions originally attacked by Comte: proponents of theological explanations, who make reference to the supernatural, and proponents of metaphysical explanations, who draw unspecific connections to abstract forces. *GGP*

References

Ayer, A. J. ([1936] 1952). *Language, truth, and logic*. New York: Dover.
———. (1959). *Logical positivism*. Glencoe, IL: Free Press.
Nietzsche, F. ([1891] 1954). *Thus spake Zarathustra*. Translated by W. Kaufman. New York: Viking Penguin.
Voltaire. ([1741](1994) *Letters concerning the English nation*. New York: Oxford University Press.

Postmodernism

The concept of postmodernism appeared first in the art world during the 1950s as the confluence of several movements: (1) cultural critiques of modern art; (2) poststructural French philosophy and literary theory; and (3) sociopolitical histories of contemporary society. Postmodern studies question the relations of knowledge and power, the construction of identities (or subjectivities), and the systems of reasoning themselves. For the purposes of this discussion we will use the term *modern* to refer to most contemporary analyses that fall within liberal and Marxist traditions. Although few analyses can be characterized as purely modern or postmodern, they do make assumptions and exhibit understandings about social categories, power, and history that distinguish them.

Regarding the use of categories, both modern and postmodern studies recognize that social distinctions exist. However, they make different assumptions about how these distinctions are made. Most modern analyses tend to assume that race, class, and gender categories are based in nature, culture, science, or social structures. That is, a modern analysis may assume that gender differences can be attributed to biology or that racial differences can be attributed to culture. This type of attribution is often called *essentialism* because there is an essential (or necessary) foundation for the category.

Postmodern analyses, on the other hand, tend to study the categories that construct identities—such as race, class, and gender—as problematic. For example, postmodern analyses assume that race, class, and gender differences are products of history. Postmodern studies, however, explore socially constructed categories in a special way that relates knowledge to power. That is, a postmodern theory assumes that not only gender but any biological characteristic of individuality was itself made up (constructed) as a product of power relations. Hypothetically speaking, for example, people could be categorized according to their respective talents: crafts, music, athletics, and communicative abilities. Historically speaking, however, people have been divided by reproductive capacity. Even though division by reproductive capacity is no more natural or reasonable than division by talent, it has become commonsense to think of people as having an essential biological identity, and this socially constructed biological identity now effectively serves as a logical basis for classifying and discriminating among people.

A characteristic postmodern question is "How did a made-up system like biology become so fundamental as a means for differentiating and categorizing people?" Postmodern studies, for example, treat the way we reason (about childhood, pedagogy, family, and religion) as not descriptive of events but as generative of principles of action that are, in fact, not the same for everyone. In other words, in a postmodern analysis categories are only real in that they have the social effect of differentiation, but categories have no essential, natural, or necessary foundation; rather, categories were historically constructed and can therefore be deconstructed.

In regard to power both modern and postmodern theories recognize inequalities, and both struggle against injustice. However, power is understood differently. For example, the existence of oppressive power in the world is patently obvious in many cases; however, most modern analyses proceed as if oppressive power was always obvious and readily recognizable. In terms of multicultural education modern analyses assume power lies in the dominant structures that marginalize the voices of oppressed people. Moreover, modern analyses usually assume that people have an autonomous capacity for resistance, voice, and experience and, furthermore, that autonomy and voice are recognizable and good. Modern empowerment, then, is generally the condition in which people have overcome an oppressive power.

Postmodern analyses, on the other hand, tend to be more skeptical of power, believing instead that the techniques of oppression and liberation may not always be so immediately obvious. For example, many postmodern studies have examined the ways many liberatory discourses actually reinscribe the very relations of power they seek to challenge. Postmodern analyses focus not only on the structural level of power (such as who participates in institutional practices) but also at intimate and personal levels at which the very identities of people—both the oppressed and oppressors—have been shaped (subjected) by conditions of power. Therefore, postmodern theories examine power as exercised in many subtle ways, not only as oppressive but also as productive of people's personal identities, tastes, values, and beliefs.

In regard to history, both modern and postmodern theories recognize change and differences over time. On the one hand, modern analyses of history tend to explain history in terms of generalizable or universal principles that emphasize time dimensions (e.g., processes of change). That is, modern histories seek a single overall pattern by which to explain causality and predict outcomes. Examples of such universalizing principles to explain history are science, progress, and dialectics. Moreover, modern historical principles tend to rationalize time; that is, they tend to appeal to an orderly movement of people and events over time (rather than to mystical forces) as the reason for the way things happen, thus producing a stable notion of context or space.

Postmodern theories of history, on the other hand, posit that (1) history is not predictable, (2) no occurrence in history was inevitable, and (3) occurrences in history cannot be attributed to a single original cause. Further, postmodern theories focus upon dimensions of differential concepts of space-in-time to understand a complex nexus of social circumstances. Where modern thought fixes the concept of space in order to consider time, postmodern theories problematize the notion of space. Space is not only a concept of physical dimensions but also of social and discursive dimensions. For example, in its focus on subjectivity (i.e., how individuality is constructed) postmodern theory assumes that people occupy multiple social spaces such as woman, child, worker, and author. Moreover, a postmodern approach assumes that each of these differentiations normalizes and naturalizes a specific set of tastes and dispositions. These tastes and dispositions then form particular identities (subjectivities), which then provide the basis for judging others as (un)reasonable, (ab)normal, or (un)truthful.

This notion of space is potentially important to the concept of multiculturalism. Social spaces entail norms of inclusion and exclusion. Placing a child in a system of reasoning about childhood, for example, involves unspoken norms about growth, adolescence, and cognition, which now seem natural. These norms effectively privilege some ways and erase other ways of being in the world. In response to such normalization postmodern theory allows a researcher to challenge the very systems of reasoning that label a child as *gifted*, *at risk*, or *inner-city youth*. In this way postmodern research critiques the systems of reasoning that created categories of people.

A postmodern multicultural educator, then, begins with an attitude of skeptical critique that is always questioning what kind of power is embedded in assertions, categories, and questions used to construct the reasoning of teaching and school reform. A postmodern multicultural education would ask the questions such as What happened—politically, legally, culturally, institutionally, artistically, or intellectually—that resulted in categorizations that differentiate people and norms that construct relative values? What dividing and differentiating practices operate through concrete pedagogical discourses by constructing raced, classed, and gendered identities? and What categories of analysis—such as voice, experience, and empowering—do we take for granted?

Postmodern theories enable us to consider the concrete pedagogical knowledge of schooling as a material practice that may enable or disable children. It asks the questions, How is our reasoning about problems constrained by our social and historical circumstances? In what ways are our subjective identities already being produced in historical discourse? and Whose voice is speaking through whom? It also asks, What new social spaces could be created if analyses could break away from same/different dichotomies and begin thinking in terms of hybridity, multiplicity, and multidimensional diversity?

The political implication of a postmodern intellectual move is to foreclose the possibility of determinism. By questioning and interrogating assumptions, categories, and systems of reasoning the old and entrenched patterns of power become visible, fragile, and potentially subject to change. *TSP, LF, & JEB*

Prejudice

Prejudice is a complex and multifaceted way of thinking and feeling about people that attributes particular characteristics to people and groups as more or less desirable than others. Thus, individuals and groups having such ascribed traits are viewed more or less favorably than others. Often, persons feeling or holding prejudice place themselves and others with similar attributes above those who have different attributes. However, it is also possible for people to view the ascribed traits of others as positive and more valuable than those credited to themselves. Prejudice is personal in that individuals can feel and act in ways that diminish and demean other individuals. Prejudice is public and institutionalized in that it affects the relations of people in the public sphere in schooling, employment, government, and the legal system. Prejudice is, as Columbia University Law Professor Patricia J. Williams (1991) has recently pointed out, persistent. It is difficult to disrupt. Prejudice is tenacious, long-lasting, and everywhere around us. Prejudice is an often-unrecognized and -unexamined part of the daily life of the people in this country and is the basis for racism, sexism, and homophobia.

For example, consider the terrible pain and consequences of prejudice in one family. Mary L. Gomez is the granddaughter of Josefa Lavin and Joaquin Gomez and of James Thomas Butler and Mildred May Mullally. One set of grandparents immigrated to the United States at the turn of the century, seeking social and economic prosperity in Vermont. The other set had already lived in New England for several generations by the early 1900s. Neither they nor their sons were pleased or welcoming to Gomez's father when he courted her mother. Her father's cultural background and socioeconomic circumstances were markedly different from their own middle-class ones. As a first-generation English speaker, his nouns and verbs frequently failed to match in tense and number; his manners lacked polish; and in his thirties, he still lived at home with his widowed mother while working as a bartender to support her. The traits ascribed to her father, Manuel Gomez, were ignorance, rudeness, and lack of initiative.

Regardless of her mother's family's feelings, Gomez's parents married. Her father died in 1993, shortly before her parents' forty-fourth wedding anniversary. By then, his nouns and verbs almost always matched, his economic circumstances were much improved, and he had developed an expanded repertoire of social skills. He had raised two daughters: one a university professor and one a lawyer. He had become a union leader, the president of an organization devoted to senior rights, and the chairman of the local housing authority, which built and oversaw low-income housing for older and disabled citizens in his community. Yet, with all of these accomplishments Gomez's father still keenly felt—in his 70s—the sting of prejudice. And the difficult, complex relations between the different sides of their family, begun in the 1940s, persist to this day. *MLG*

Reference

Williams, P. J. (1991). *The alchemy of race and rights.* Cambridge: Harvard University Press.

Prejudice Reduction *See* Multicultural Education, Dimensions Of

Privilege

According to the 1996 edition of the *American Heritage Dictionary, privilege* is "a special advantage, immunity, permission, right, or benefit granted to or enjoyed by an individual, class, or caste. Such a right or advantage, the editors state, is "held as a prerogative of status or rank, and exercised to the exclusion and detriment of others."

During the 1970s and 1980s attention increased toward equity issues. Terry, Wellman, and McIntosh, among others, further analyzed and illuminated structures of society to recognize not only structures of discrimination, but also concomitant structures of privilege. By 1995 most scholars of multiculturalism in the United States were aware of the concept of privilege as an unearned benefit, rarely recognized by the beneficiary, that has an important bearing on life outcomes. Multiple meanings developed by McIntosh (1988) include (1) unearned overadvantage for some, linked to unearned disadvantage for others; (2) superiority or dominance imputed to, or projected onto, persons of a given race, sex, ethnicity, religion, region, sexual orientation, nation, occupation, body type, physical ability, age, or other circumstance, whether or not evidence supports such imputation or projection; (3) unconscious enjoyment of the rewards of imputed superiority, including money, fame, knowledge, approval, advancement, or authority; (4) exemption or protection from violence, fear, anger, worry, anxiety, or deprivation, which may be experienced by some as a result of having greater inferiority imputed to or projected onto them; (5) empowerment not asked for, and not necessarily sought, but that is granted as a concomitant of high status in hierarchical systems of power inherited from the past; (6) a habit of seeing oneself as both normal and ideal and of seeing others as defective variants of oneself or one's kind; (7) a system of hierarchical ranking that arbitrarily entitles some to benefits that others cannot enjoy, but whose arbitrariness is not acknowledged by those who benefit; (8) denial by those who have power that some of their circumstances may be a result of imputed superiority rather than deservedness; (9) societal permission for some to dominate, control, or colonize conferred on them implicitly at birth or by later connections to power; and (10) nonrecognition by powerful people or institutions of the benefits they have gained through deservedness being arbitrarily imputed to the behaviors, attributes, and conventions of their group, kind, or institution.

In the 1980s and 1990s the new recognition of privilege as a force in making and maintaining social structures has led to an expanded understanding of discrimination. That is, racism consists not only of racially based discrimination for some, but also of racially based privilege for others. Sexism involves not only gender-based discrimination for some, but also gender-based privilege for others. Heterosexism brings about both discrimination against gays and unearned benefits for heterosexuals.

At the same time, however, the word *privilege* has come to be loosely and problematically used in the media and by activist groups, often in the phrase "power and privilege." These two concepts are not the same, and the workings of invisible, formerly unacknowledged systems of unearned advantage are still scarcely known to the people of the United States. In fact, skin-color privilege, gender privilege, and heterosexual privilege, as defined above, remain taboo subjects in general thought, as do class privilege, colonial privilege, and Protestant privilege. The reason for this is that the phenomenon of privilege cannot be recognized within the American ideology of meritocracy, democracy, and the individual as the unit of society.

Those who benefit most from privilege systems as described above by McIntosh are kept most blinded to the existence of privilege systems.

Students of multiculturalism should not assume that citizens or colleagues are aware of the ways in which systemic overadvantaging has been kept from their sight and out of the awareness of the powerful. Nor should they assume that privilege systems, having been seen, can be easily dismantled. They are inherited systems with long traditions. They are not cause for blame or guilt: people do not choose the circumstances of their birth into systems they did not invent. McIntosh raises the question, however, of how those who realize they have unearned power can use it to share power or "use unearned advantage to weaken or end systems of unearned advantage." *PM1*

References

bell hooks. (1990). *Yearning: Race, gender, and cultural politics.* Boston: South End Press.

Frankenberg, R. (1993). *The social construction of Whiteness: White women/race matters.* Minneapolis: University of Minnesota Press.

Kivel, P. (1996). *Uprooting racism: How White people can work for racial justice.* Philadelphia: New Society.

McIntosh, P. (1992). White privilege and male privilege: A personal account of coming to see correspondence through work in Women's studies. In M. Anderson & P. H. Collins (Eds.), *Race, class, and gender.* Belmont, CA: Wadsworth. Originally published as working paper #189 (Wellesley, MA: Wellesley College Center for Research on Women, 1988).

Morris, W. (Ed.). (1996). *The American heritage dictionary of the English language.* New York: Houghton Mifflin.

Morrison, T. (1992). *Playing in the dark: Whiteness and the literary imagination.* Cambridge: Harvard University Press.

Smith, L. (1949). *Killers of the dream.* New York: W. W. Norton.

Terry, R. W. (1970). *For Whites only.* Grand Rapids, MI: Eerdmans.

Wellman, D. (Ed.). (1977). *Portraits of White racism.* New York: Cambridge University Press.

Puerto Rican Studies

Puerto Rican studies is an academic field that focuses on the history, culture, and society of the Puerto Rican people, whether in Puerto Rico, the United States, or elsewhere. Begun in the 1960s, Puerto Rican studies was part of the national trend in which ethnic diversity was recognized as worthy of serious study and scholarship in its own right. Although there were at the time almost two million Puerto Ricans living in the United States (and the current number is approaching two and a half million), little reference had been made to Puerto Rico or Puerto Ricans in traditional history, social science, or arts and humanities courses, in spite of the colonial relationship of Puerto Rico to the United States since 1898. As a result of vigorous student activism and active community support, Puerto Rican studies departments were started at a number of colleges and universities, primarily in New York City, which has historically had the largest Puerto Rican community in the United States. The departments were meant to serve primarily New York–born or –raised Puerto Ricans, who are sometimes referred to as *Niuyoricans*, although this term is not universally accepted in the Puerto Rican community because some perceive it to have negative connotations.

Given the unique experiences of Puerto Ricans born and raised in the United States, Puerto Rican studies, as it has developed in this country, tends to focus on both island-based history and culture and on U.S.-based realities and challenges, including history, the arts, and other cultural manifestations. In addition, Puerto Rican studies courses and programs generally reflect the ongoing economic and social struggles of Puerto Ricans, the working-class status of the majority of the community, and the colonial relationship of Puerto Rico to the United States.

Puerto Rican studies departments have made four major contributions. They have (1) forged new interdisciplinary fields of study; (2) represented the perspectives and interests of a hitherto largely invisible group in the academy; (3) encouraged traditional departments to incorporate some of the new scholarship concerning Puerto Ricans in their curriculum; and (4) developed strong links with communities outside the academy in ways not tried before. Puerto Rican studies departments tend to focus their scholarship and service in Puerto Rican communities themselves rather than isolating themselves in the academy. Many departments have struggled for autonomy within systems that seek to delegitimize them, and some have consciously sought alliances with other departments and institutions in order to strengthen their base. *SN*

Reference

Sanchez, M. E., & Stevens-Arroyo, A. M. (Eds.). (1987). *Toward a renaissance of Puerto Rican studies: Ethnic and area studies in university education.* Highland Lakes, NJ: Social Science Monographs.

Queer Studies *See* Gay, Lesbian, and Bisexual Studies

Race

At its most basic level *race* can be defined as a concept that signifies and symbolizes sociopolitical conflicts and interests in reference to different types of human bodies. Although the concept of race refers to biologically based human characteristics (so-called phenotypes), selection of these particular human features for purposes of racial signification is always and necessarily a social and historical process. Race is understood in common sense terms as a matter of biological variation among humans, but there is actually as much differentiation within particular racially defined groups as there is across groups (Cavalli-Sforza & Cavalli-Sforza, 1995). Thus the traits that supposedly differentiate among these groups are revealed, upon serious examination, to be at best imprecise and at worst completely arbitrary. This recognition has led to the idea of race as a social construct and the theory of *racial formation* (Omi & Winant, 1994), which explains the creation, transformation, and destruction of racial categories in respect to their changing historical contexts.

The origins of the concept of race are extremely diverse. Some type of group identity seems universal and primordial. The group's idea of itself may take many forms—tribal, spatial, linguistic, or perhaps religious—all serving to distinguish between members and outsiders. Some form of ethnocentrism probably characterizes all human societies. The articulation of this concept in phenotypic terms is also found in early texts. It is a big jump, however, from this tendency to modern notions of race. Only in the last few centuries, under the tutelage of a hegemonic Europe, have the world's peoples been classified relatively systematically along racial lines. Religion, science, and politics are all implicated in the gestation of racial logic. Probably the most significant examples of this classification—the fierce anti-Jewish and anti-Islamic campaigns of the Crusades and the Inquisition—drew their inspiration from religious sources. The Enlightenment contributed to the process: Blumenbach applied the principles of Linnaean taxonomy to humans at the end of the eighteenth century (Gould, 1981), and the great philosophers and statesmen of the period, from Kant and Hume to Jefferson and Napoleon, all endorsed the hierarchical division of humanity into superior and inferior races. The immense historical rupture represented by the rise of Europe, the onset of African enslavement, the conquista, and the subjugation of much of Asia ratified these beliefs and, ultimately, forged not only the colonial world but the postcolonial world as well.

It is paradoxical that a concept whose truth-value is so negligible has developed, over the centuries, rather comprehensive significance in the political, economic, social, and cultural systems which structure human existence. Indeed, many now urge the abolition of outmoded race-thinking, arguing that all racial classification is inherently invidious. The problem with this, though, is that race is not only a concept, but a social fact. Its elimination is, therefore, no more likely than that of other social constructs such as gender and class, which also have significant worldwide historical consequences.

To the multitude of racially defined minorities the world over whose ceaseless resistance to their subordination has often been articulated in racial terms, the reality of the "race-concept" (Du Bois, cited in Lewis, 1995) is hardly in doubt. Their challenges to this concept have grown more effective in recent decades and will increasingly render the meaning of race more variegated and problematic. For this reason alone the idea of race can be expected to retain its salience, even though the original logics that gave rise to it have been surpassed: it continues to serve as a relevant measure both of inequality and injustice and of the desire to overcome them. *HW* • *See also* **Racism**

References

Cavalli-Sforza, L. L., & Cavalli-Sforza, F. (1995). *The great human diasporas: The history of diversity and human evolution.* Reading, MA: Addison-Wesley.

Gould, S. J. (1981). *The mismeasure of man.* New York: W.W. Norton.

Lewis, D. L. (Ed.). (1995). *W. E. B. Du Bois: A reader.* New York: Henry Holt.

Omi, M., & Winant, H. (1994). *Racial formation in the United States: From the 1960s to the 1990s* (2nd ed.). New York: Routledge.

Race, Gender, and Class

The emergence of the synthesized concept of race, gender, and class is directly linked to Black Women's studies, which began to surface as an academic area in the United States in the latter part of the 1970s. At the center of this theorizing about race, class, and gender in the United States is a group of Black feminist intellectuals. They are academics, independent scholars, and activists who are writing and rethinking social theory from their own experiences of multiple oppressions (Brewer, 1993).

As Higginbotham (1994) writes, "Traditionally, we have used these concepts, but *only* employ them when looking specifically at the groups which are disadvantaged with regard to these issues. Race *only* comes up when we talk about African American and other people of color, gender *only* comes up when we talk about women, and class *only* comes up when we talk about the poor and working class" (p. 14).

As King (1988) defines it, "[M]ultiple jeopardy refers not only to several simultaneous oppressions but to the multiplicative relationships among them as well." She goes on to state that "the equivalent formulation is racism multiplied by sexism multiplied by classism." By placing Black women's experiences at the center of analysis, Afrocentric feminists developed the theorizing and conceptualization of race, gender, and class as simultaneous forces (Collins, 1991). From the insights of feminist women of color into the complex interconnections between race, class, and gender, we see how "race, class, and gender are not independent variables that can be tacked onto each other or separated at will: they are concrete social relations [that] . . . are enmeshed in each other and the particular intersections involved produce specific effects. . . . [E]ach element exists in the context of the others and [thus] any concrete analysis has to take this into account" (Anthias & Yuval-Davis, 1983, pp. 63–65).

The concept of the simultaneity of the race-gender-and-class intersection in people's lives is one of the greatest gifts of Black feminism to social theory as a whole and will help produce an integrative understanding of racism, sexism, and classism. As Smith (1983) stated: "If we have to wait for racism to be obliterated *before* we can begin to address sexism, we will be waiting for a long time. Denying that sexual oppression exists or requiring that we wait to bring it up until racism, or in some cases, capitalism, is toppled, is a bankrupt position" (p. xxviii).

An integrative race-gender-and-class perspective has no use for the ranking of social inequality, but instead demonstrates the simultaneity of inequalities as they affect women's and men's lives across cultures. Just as African American feminists have done, Asian American, Native American, Hispanic American, and European American feminists have adopted this theoretical perspective, which examines the consequences of racism, sexism, and classism in the daily lives of people.

The lessons to be learned are that first—to the extent that everyone belongs to a race, a gender, and a class—each of us can identify herself or himself with this approach; second, the premise basic for antiracism discourses should be race, gender for antisexism, and class for anticlassism (but the centrality of race, or gender, or class is only a *point of entry* through which the varied forms of social inequality can and must be understood); and third, the importance of any one factor in explaining a specific social inequality varies depending on the particular issue analyzed. A race-gender-and-class analysis shows the complex relationships between race, gender, and class.

In using this three-way analysis, we can see evidence of the importance of the multiple interactions between race, gender, and class. In the integrative and interactive analysis the relative significance of each factor in determining social inequality is neither fixed nor absolute but rather, is dependent on the sociohistorical and cultural context under analysis. *JTB*

References

Anthias, F., & Yuval-Davis, N. (1983). Contextualizing feminism: Ethnic, gender, and class divisions. *Feminist Review, 15* (Nov.) p. 62–75.

Belkhir, J. (1995). The roots of the race, gender, and class section. *American Sociological Association Section Race, Gender and Class Newsletter, 1*(2), 3–4.

Belkhir, J., with Vanfossen, B., Charlemaine, C., & Berry, K. (1996). *The intersection of race, gender, and class: An interdisciplinary bibliography*. Towson, MD: Institute for Teaching and Research on Women, Towson State University.

Brewer, R. M. (1993). Theorizing race, class and gender: The new scholarship of Black feminist intellectuals and Black women's labor. In S. James & A. Busia (Eds.), *Theorizing Black feminisms: The visionary pragmatism of Black women* (pp. 13–30). New York: Routledge.

Calliste, A., Sefa Dei, G., & Belkhir, J. (1995). Canadian perspective on anti-racism and race, gender, and class. *Race, Gender & Class, 2*(3), 5, 10.

Collins, P. H. (1991). *Black feminist thought: Knowledge, consciousness, and the politics of empowerment*. New York: Routledge.

Higginbotham, E. (1994). Sociology and the multicultural curriculum: The challenges of the 1990s and beyond. *Race, Gender & Class, 1*(1), 13–24.

King, D. (1988). Multiple jeopardy, multiple consciousness: The context of a Black feminist ideology. *Signs, 14*(1), 42.

Smith, B. (Ed.). (1983). *Home girls: A Black feminist anthology*. New York: Kitchen Table Press/Women of Color.

Racial Identity Theory *See* Ethnic Identity Theory

Racism

A simple definition of *racism* is a set of beliefs about the superiority or inferiority of a group of people based on race. This set of beliefs accepts a notion that human groups can be ranked on the basis of inherited biological traits that produce unequal mental, personality, and cultural characteristics. However, because of the shifting and multiple meanings of race, and its embeddedness in the power relations of society, no simple definition of racism is sufficient. Wellman (1993) argues that racism is not merely prejudice nor bigotry and should not be confused with ethnic hostilities, but, rather, it is "the culturally sanctioned beliefs which, regardless of the intentions involved, defend the advantages Whites have because of the subordinated positions of racial minorities" (p. 4). Omi and Winant (1994) define racism "as a fundamental characteristic of social projects which create or reproduce structures of domination based on essentialist categories of race" (p. 162).

Katz (1978) contends that racism is a White problem with a 400-year history and that "the foundations of racism and the present-day racist system were established in western European and especially English ideology and language" (p. 8). However, the meaning of racism has shifted over time. At the end of the modern Civil Rights Movement racism generally was thought of as a combination of the relationships of prejudice, discrimination, and institutional inequality (Omi & Winant, 1994). By the 1970s neo-conservatives attempted to return its meaning to that of injustices and injuries sustained by individuals rather than groups. Because the category or term *race* is not a fixed notion, racism can take on an expanded or restricted meaning in relation to shifting notions of race.

Racism occurs on multiple levels—individual, institutional, scientific, and cultural. *Individual racism* is the belief that one's own racial group is superior and that acts of discrimination against those races perceived to be inferior should be defended. Thus, a person who acts in discriminatory ways toward others based solely on their race is practicing individual racism. *Institutional racism* refers to systematic practices that deny and exclude people of color from access to social resources and that perpetuate their subordination in political, economic, and social life. *Scientific racism* promotes and defends White supremacy through the use of ostensibly objective social scientific data, for example, the heritability of intelligence or craniology. *Cultural racism* elevates White, Anglo-Saxon, Protestant cultural heritage to a position of superiority over the cultural experiences of other ethnic groups and often involves elements of both individual and institutional racism.

More recently scholars interested in the relationship between and among science, technology, and society have identified *environmental racism* as the systematic devaluing of people of color by allowing toxic wastes and other hazardous materials to be dumped in poor and people of color's neighbor-hoods and communities. Additionally, King (1991) introduced the concept of *dysconscious racism* which she defines as "an uncritical habit of mind . . . that justifies inequity and exploitation by accepting the existing order of things as given . . . [and] tacitly accepts White norms and privileges" (p. 135). King further points out that dysconscious racism "is not the *absence* of conscious-ness (that is, not unconsciousness) but an *impaired* consciousness or dis-torted way of thinking about race, as compared to, for example, critical consciousness" (p. 135). *GLB* • *See also* **Race**

References

Katz, J. (1978). *White awareness: Handbook for anti-racism training.* Norman: University of Oklahoma Press.

King, J. (1991). Dysconscious racism: Ideology, identity, and the miseducation of teach-ers. *The Journal of Negro Education, 60*(2), 133–46.

Omi, M., & Winant, H. (1994). *Racial formation in the United States* (2nd ed.). New York: Routledge.

Wellman, D. (1993). *Portraits of White racism* (2nd ed.). Cambridge: Cambridge University Press.

Representation

The process of representation is a discursive system that codes and encodes individuals or groups in ways that construct, reflect, and reproduce the hegemonic political, social, cultural, and economic order. Through this process of sense making, social subjects (individuals and groups) are situated or positioned in relation to each other and to the world. Representation, then, is the system of the production and circulation of signs and images par excellence. The production and arrangement of these signs operates through a rhizomatic structure, which creates, produces, molds, reproduces, and controls images. These images constitute texts, which are then decoded, reconstructed, and re-articulated in schools, electronic media, popular cul-ture, and workplaces.

Within the blurred realm defined as the public/private sphere, the orches-tration of encoded texts is further inflected by the decoding of signs and markers by a mass audience stratified by race, class, gender, and so forth. In this process representation is never a one-to-one correspondence in which cultural forms imitate life. Instead, the representational process is a hybrid of associations and intertextual meanings and connections that link producers to their readers and audiences in a network or circuit (Bhabha, 1994; Hall, 1980; Said, 1978). Individuals, events, and groups cannot be transmitted in the original, but can only be signified or positioned within a circuit of meanings and associations. This positioning within discourse is always a question of power. The results are mediated images that claim "to speak for whole groups, further draining social life of its history . . . and naturalizing dominant/subordinate relations in the process" (McCarthy, 1993, p. 295).

For example, Edward Said (1978) examines *Orientalism* as a discourse that manages, regulates, reinscribes, and represents the people of Asia as the *Other* in the West in a hegemonic system driven by Eurocentric values. The Orient is constructed and controlled through the rearticulation and re-presentation of *itself* within a discursive system which is reproductive and "is a presence to the reader by virtue of its having excluded, displaced, made supererogatory any such real thing as 'the Orient'" (Said, 1978, p. 21). The Orient is a created discourse rather than an entity that naturally exists and is waiting to be described. The Orient never speaks for itself; it is spoken for and reinscribed through the hegemonic discourse that reflects everything the Occident is not. The representation of the Orient orchestrates cultural forms and speaks for groups who are silenced. These groups are consequently severed from their historical, political, economic, cultural, and social contexts. They are naturalized as if standing before a great universal mirror. Hence, the images of Africans or Latin Americans that we see in textbooks and television programs persuade us that this is the way these people *are*. We are, in effect, denied access to the processes of selection and editing of images that make the world so readily and seductively available to us.

Homi Bhabha (1994) further problematizes the notion of representation as simply a process of encoding and decoding. Indeed, he points us toward the inherent instability of the representation of the real, equating this representation with a photographic negative waiting to be converted into an image: there is no real, only an image, which is manipulated, distorted, and always a hybrid. Thus, the image is "neither the original"—by virtue of the act of repetition that constructs it—nor "identical" by virtue of the difference that defines it (p. 107). Poststructural theorists such as Jean Baudrillard (1983) challenge contemporary mainstream notions that suggest that representation is a copy of the real. For Baudrillard there is no representation as there is no original and no real, only simulcra, which "collapse the distinction between original and copy" (Cummings, cited in Lather, 1993, p. 677) and create a hyper-real, which simultaneously erases and doubles the real. Reality is always being reconstructed; it is never static. It is always being re-presented. *ND, EB, & CM* • *See also* **The Other**

References

Baudrillard, J. (1983). *Simulations*. New York: Semiotext(e).
Bhabha, H. (1994). *The location of culture*. London: Routledge.

Hall, S. (1980). Encoding/decoding. In S. Hall, D. Hobson, A. Lowe, & P. Willis (Eds.), *Culture, media, language* (pp. 128–39). London: Routledge.

Lather, P. (1993). Fertile obsession: Validity after post-structuralism. *The Sociological Quarterly, 34*(4), 673–93.

McCarthy, C. (1993). After the canon: Knowledge and ideological representation in the multicultural discourse on curriculum reform. In C. McCarthy & W. Crichlow (Eds.), *Race, identity, and representation in education* (pp. 289–305). New York: Routledge.

Said, E. (1978). *Orientalism.* New York: Vintage Books.

Resegregation

Resegregation is a regrouping of individuals, usually on the basis of race or ethnicity, after preexisting segregation, then desegregation, based on the same criterion, have occurred. The term is commonly used to refer to a process that occurs in schools. Researchers generally see resegregation as problematic because it undermines many of the possible positive consequences of school desegregation. However, the argument can be made that in an otherwise desegregated context, some resegregation results from communality of interest and shared culture among members of particular groups and that such resegregation is not necessarily deleterious. Resegregation is often referred to as a "second generation problem" since it cannot occur before some kind of desegregation has been accomplished.

Resegregation can occur as a result of both formal school policies, often those designed to meet some other valued goal, and from informal sources. It can occur within classrooms as well as between classrooms. The school policy most frequently associated with resegregation is the division of students into academically homogeneous groups (Epstein, 1985). (One alternative to homogeneous grouping and the accompanying resegregation is the use of heterogeneous groups. [See Slavin, 1995.]) School policies often lead to resegregation in schools with students for whom English is not their first language. Providing students with instruction in their native tongue often resegregates them from others for whom English is a first language, thus posing special challenges for the desegregation of Hispanic, Asian, and other children whose first language may not be English. Another policy that contributes to resegregation is the failure to provide transportation home for students who participate in after-school activities, since those relying on transportation provided by school to get to desegregated schools are disproportionately people of color.

Even if schools do not directly foster resegregation through their policies or practices, it frequently arises as a result of students' choices about whom to associate with in either classroom or informal situations, or about which classes or extra-curricular activities to participate in. This tendency for students to resegregate themselves is somewhat stronger in informal situations than within classrooms. In fact, close to complete resegregation can sometimes be observed in school lunchrooms. This is unfortunate since there is reason to expect that the kind of fairly close personal contact one often encounters in informal peer-group situations is conducive to breaking down stereotypes and fostering positive attitudes. Stephan and Stephan's (1985) work suggests that intergroup anxiety may be one cause of the tendency to avoid out-group members and hence to resegregate. Pettigrew (1969) has outlined many possible negative consequences of separation between racial and ethnic groups. However, it is also clear that contact between members of different groups, in and of itself, is not necessarily conducive to improving intergroup relations. Allport (1954), Hewstone and Brown (1986), Schofield (1993), and others have argued that carefully structuring the nature of intergroup contact is crucial, emphasizing the importance of factors such as minimizing competition, encouraging cooperation toward mutually valued goals, and providing equal status for members of all groups without the contact situation. *JWS* • *See also* **Desegregation**

References

Allport, G. W. (1954). *The nature of prejudice*. Cambridge, MA: Addison-Wesley.

Epstein, J. L. (1985). After the bus arrives: Resegregation in desegregated schools. *Journal of Social Issues, 41*(3), 23–43.

Hewstone, M., & Brown, R. (1986). Contact is not enough: An intergroup perspective on the "contact hypothesis." In M. Hewstone & R. Brown (Eds.), *Contact and conflict in intergroup encounters* (pp. 1–44). Oxford: Basil Blackwell.

Pettigrew, T. (1969). Racially separate or together. *Journal of Social Issues, 25*(1), 43–69.

Schofield, J. W. (1993). Promoting positive peer relations in desegregated schools. *Educational Policy, 7*(3), 297–317.

Slavin, R. E. (1995). Cooperative learning and intergroup relations. In J. A. Banks & C. A. M. Banks (Eds.), *Handbook of research on multicultural education* (pp. 628–34). New York: Simon & Schuster Macmillan.

Stephan, W. G., & Stephan, C. W. (1985). Intergroup anxiety. *Journal of Social Issues, 41*(3), 157–75.

Resistance

Resistance is an attitude toward public schools that is sometimes manifested by students from dominated cultures. The concept of resistance was originally developed by anthropologist John Ogbu to explain the clash between the culture of students from dominated groups and the White, Anglo-Saxon, Protestant culture embedded in U. S. public schools. This clash, he found, often results in the creation of a *culture of resistance* among students from dominated cultures. This culture of resistance manifests itself in actions that are antischool such as tardiness, absenteeism, failure to do homework, vandalism to school property, and disruption of classrooms.

Afrocentric educator Jawanza Kunjufu argues that many African American students believe that school achievement depends on *acting White*. Consequently, according to Kunjufu many African American students reject the culture of schools and accept failure in their studies. Although African American culture contains strong values regarding the importance of education, African Americans maintain a level of distrust of White people and dominant institutions. For Native Americans, Puerto Ricans, and Mexican Americans schooling represents an ongoing battle over preservation of cultures and languages. Consequently, many dominated groups have developed attitudes toward public schools that are a combination of hope, anger, frustration, and a sense of futility about the schools ever serving their needs.

Ogbu found these contradictory attitudes among African American students while doing research in the Stockton, California, school system. Black students verbalized a strong desire for education and believed that schooling was an important means of escaping poverty. Despite these attitudes about the value of education, Ogbu found these African American students behaving in ways that guaranteed their failure in school. They tended to lack a serious attitude about schoolwork, they were frequently tardy or absent, and they did not attempt to achieve in school (Ogbu, 1978, 1979).

Referring to the work of Lois Weis (1985) and the historical development of African American culture, Ogbu argues that "Blacks developed high educational aspirations and initiated a long history of collective struggle for equal education *as a form of opposition* against White people who denied them access to education and equality of educational opportunity" (Ogbu, 1988, p. 171). African Americans discovered, however, that educational achievement did not result in the same economic opportunities for them as it did for Whites. Therefore, according to Ogbu there is no contradiction between the fact that Black students verbally support the importance of education but reject a process of schooling that guarantees inequality.

In tracing the historical origins of the culture of resistance, Ogbu identifies two important causes: one is that Black youth observed their parents and other adult Blacks struggling for economic advancement through education and mainstream jobs; and second, because of racial barriers to employment, Ogbu (1988) argues that African Americans "have evolved a folk theory or folk theories of making it which do not necessarily emphasize strong academic pursuit" (p. 173).

Combined with the contemporary and historical experience that education will not, in fact, provide a road to economic opportunities is the historical distrust of Whites and their institutions. Students from dominated cultures often develop a disparaging attitude toward educational achievement especially if they are attending schools with little financial support, if they are being relegated to slow learning groups and nonacademic tracks, and if they are witnessing a world where family members and friends have not advanced despite educational achievements. Why bother? is the attitude among these students that leads to a culture of resistance against the efforts of public schools. *JS* • *See also* **Dominated Cultures**

References

Ogbu, J. (1978). *Minority education and caste: The American in cross-cultural perspective*. New York: Academic Press.

———. (1979). *Racial stratification and education: The case of Stockton, California*. IRDC Bulletin, *12*(3), 1–26.

———. (1988). Class stratification, racial stratification, and schooling. In L. Weis (Ed.), *Class, culture, and gender in American education* (p. 171, 173). Albany: State University of New York Press.

Weis, L. (1985). *Between two worlds: Black students in an urban community college*. Boston: Routledge & Kegan Paul.

Reverse Discrimination

Reverse discrimination is a curious semantic construction used to describe what occurs when members of a dominant group lose benefits and privileges as a result of measures and policies such as affirmative action and diversity initiatives. In effect, these policies are designed to redress past discrimination and to "level the playing field" so that people of color, women, and the disabled are afforded the opportunity to compete for work and college and university admission on an equal basis with privileged groups.

In order to level the playing field, employment policies and college admission criteria may be applied differentially to previously excluded groups. For example, the passing scores needed by subordinate groups on performance tests for police and fire departments may be lower than those for White males. Or acceptable mathematics scores on the SAT or ACT for women may be lower than those for males. These differential scores are meant to redress historical and social inequities experienced by subordinate groups. While critics of affirmative action and diversity policies have argued that these measures are unfair, these critics fail to recognize that historically many tests have been constructed to exclude particular groups and advantage others. (See, for example, Kamin, 1974.) Thus, many tests are not accurate assessments of the skills and abilities needed for success in a particular job or educational setting.

In instances where Whites have not been hired or admitted when subordinated group members have, some Whites have claimed to be victims of reverse discrimination. This suggests that the rules put in place to provide equal opportunity and diversity have resulted in discrimination against the former beneficiaries or perpetuators of discrimination. This term represents a curious semantic construction because reverse discrimination or "the reverse of discrimination" means the eradication of discrimination or simply, nondiscrimination. Rather than claiming themselves to be victims of discrimination, members of the dominant group should use the term *reverse discrimination* or *reverse racism* to signify their *privilege*; that is they cannot be discriminated against, and what does occur is different from what subordinated or marginalized groups experience. *GLB*

References

Kamin, L. (1974). *The science and politics of I.Q.* Potomac, MD: Erlbaum.

Scapegoat

The word *scapegoat* can be traced to the Book of Leviticus (16:20–22) where the Hebrew Day of Atonement is described. On this day a live goat was sent out into the wilderness carrying the sins of the people of Israel. With this symbolic transference of sin, the people felt purged of their guilt and misfortune. Using a goat as a way to transfer disease and misfortune was also common in much of Scotland, Wales, Ireland, and England during the eighteenth century. Goats were hung on the masts of boats, allowed to sleep with cattle and sheep to keep disease away, and kept by the back door of the farmhouse to keep illness and misfortune from entering (Opie & Tatem, 1989).

Today the term scapegoating is associated with the displacement of guilt and aggression to a weaker, more vulnerable individual or group by an individual or group with more power and influence. According to Gordon W. Allport (*ABC's*, 1985) scapegoating is the most aggressive stage in the continuum of social relationships among groups.

Blaming others for our fear, rage, and misfortune can be psychologically appealing. We find a group that we perceive as different or as causing the problem, and we place the blame at their feet. This creates the illusion of a clear cause of our circumstances, alleviates our own guilt, and provides an outlet for our anger and frustration.

History is replete with examples of individuals and groups who have been scapegoated—from the persecution of the Christians in Roman times to the hanging of innocent women and men during the Salem witch trials, the acts of violence against the Chinese in the nineteenth century, and the decimation of the Jews, as well as other groups, during the Nazi Holocaust. These individuals or groups were blamed for myriad social and economic cataclysms with no evidence to support the claims made against them. The common thread through these examples is that these targets were already the victims of stereotyping, prejudice, and often discrimination, which allowed them to be treated with open disdain, contempt, or even violence. Scapegoating is often practiced by racists—those who believe that the people against whom they are behaving aggressively are inferior and can and should be dominated.

Scapegoating does not address the real source of any problem. It does not alleviate an economic depression, for example. Scapegoating does, however, cause psychological and often physical harm to its victims. *DAB*

References

Anti-Defamation League. *ABC's of scapegoating*. (1985). New York: Anti-Defamation League.

Opie, I., & Tatem, M. (Eds.). (1989). *A dictionary of superstitions*. New York: Oxford University Press.

Segregation

While the dictionary definition of the verb to *segregate* means "to set apart from others; to isolate," (Flexner, 1987), within the context of multicultural education segregation involves broader interpretations and carries emotional meanings. Segregation within the context of education has long referred to the legal establishment of different schools for students of different races. Beyond separation based on race, contemporary debates within schools also relate to the separation of different groups of students based on such characteristics as English language proficiency, academic achievement, cognitive abilities, physical abilities, and socioeconomic class.

During the days of post-Reconstruction, public facilities in the South were separated according to Jim Crow laws into two categories: *White Only* and *Colored Only*. The laws that governed such facilities—considered separate and equal—were found to be constitutionally legal in the 1891 case *Plessy v. Ferguson*. Through this case both de jure and de facto segregation in U.S. society were legally sanctioned by the Supreme Court. It was not until 1954 that the Court ruled in *Brown v. Board of Education* that desegregated schools were inherently unequal because they conveyed a sense of Black unworthiness and inferiority. Despite whether or not the material and tangible characteristics of separate schools were the same, the psychological effects of separating the children were deemed to be damaging and harmful. In 1955 *Brown II* stated that the public schools should integrate "with all deliberate speed." This effectively allowed White communities to control the rate of desegregation. Racial integration of schools was often resisted by

Whites through *White flight*—the practice of White families transferring their children to private schools or moving into suburban school districts where students of color were either minimally represented or nonexistent. (See Harris, 1993, for a complete analysis of the ways in which the interests of Whites were protected throughout the legal history of the United States.)

The legal debates concerning racial desegregation have continued into the present. Among others, the 1974 *Milliken v. Bradley* case, set in Detroit, determined that integration across district lines could not be court mandated. In other words, predominantly White suburban schools could not be forced to integrate with predominantly Black urban schools. More recently, school districts have been going to court in hopes of proving that they have done what they can to eliminate the vestiges of segregation.

Attitudes towards racial segregation and desegregation are complex and ever changing. While proponents of racial desegregation believe that desegregated schools will teach children from different races to coexist and live desegregated adult lives (Braddock, et al., 1984), other educators are more critical of the reasoning behind desegregation. For example, as Carter (1980) explains, during the era of the *Brown* decision many people of all races thought that segregation was a disease that blocked equal educational opportunity. According to Carter the disease was, and continues to be, the belief system of White supremacy. Afrocentric educators such as Asante (1991) believe that the White hegemony inherent in the concept of desegregation forces students of color to assimilate into White institutions, losing their own sense of cultural, ethnic, and racial identity. In a move that traditional integrationists might find ironic, some Black educators (Murrell, 1993) are calling for what may be considered the ultimate in racial segregation: separate schools for African American males. These schools are far from being a form of segregated education that conveys a sense of inferiority, according to educators who believe that the unique emotional, social, and educational needs of Black students are best met through a school established with their needs—not the needs of White students and families—as the first priority.

In addition to race, segregation in the U.S. educational system is also based on English proficiency, academic achievement, physical or cognitive abilities, and more subtly, socioeconomic class. While some groupings and separations are more a result of consciously deliberate decisions by teachers than others, all ultimately raise questions of power differentials. *CMB* • *See also* **Afrocentrism; Brown v. Board of Education; Desegregation; Plessy v. Ferguson; Resegregation**

References

Asante, M. K. (1991). The Afrocentric idea in education. *Journal of Negro Education, 60*(2), 170–80.

Braddock, J. H., Crain, R. L., & McPartland, J. M., (1984). A long-term view of school desegregation: Some recent studies of graduates as adults. *Phi Delta Kappan, 66*(4), 259–64.

Carter, R. R. (1980). A reassessment of *Brown v. Board*. In D. Bell (Ed.), *Shades of Brown: New perspectives on school desegregation* (pp. 21–28). New York: Teachers College Press.

Flexner, S. B. (Ed.). (1987). *Random house unabridged dictionary* (2nd ed.). New York: Random House.

Harris, C. I. (1993). Whiteness as property. *Harvard Law Review, 106*(8), 1707–91.

Murrell, P. (1993). Afrocentric immersion: Academic and personal development of African American males in public schools. In T. Perry & J. W. Fraser (Eds.), *Freedom's plow: Teaching in the multicultural classroom* (pp. 231–59). New York: Routledge.

Separate but Equal *See* Plessy v. Ferguson

Sexism

Merriam-Webster's Collegiate Dictionary (1993) defines *sexism* as "prejudice or discrimination based on sex; especially discrimination against women." *Sexism*, the term, came into popular usage in the 1960s when the need for language to identify the phenomena of widespread discrimination against women in the United States became apparent. "Consciousness-raising" about the history, incidence, and forms of sexism in art, politics, economics, religion, education, and other dimensions of public and private life became part of popular culture's landscape and lexicon in the 1970s. Although the issues and the concerns were not new, the development of the term *sexism* opened the door to scholarship, activism, and awareness of deep cultural assumptions that were heretofore taken for granted. Scholars and researchers chronicled a mounting body of evidence of the pervasiveness of discrimination on the basis of gender. Differential treatment and access to resources for women and men in multiple societal institutions were documented by researchers, politicians, social scientists, and journalists, to name a few. While the use of the term sexism gave way to gender discrimination in the early 1980s in the United States, the evidence of discrimination has remained constant. For example, the American Association of University Women's study of gender discrimination in schooling (1992) documents the many ways that girls and women, from various ethnic, linguistic, racial, and social class backgrounds, are shortchanged in schools and education. *JBP*

References

Merriam-Webster's collegiate dictionary (10th ed.). (1993). Springfield, MA: Merriam-Webster.

The Wellesley College Center for Research on Women. (1992). *The AAUW report, how schools shortchange girls: A study of major findings on girls and education*. Washington, DC: AAUW Educational Foundation and National Education Association.

Single Group Studies *See* Multicultural Education, Approaches To

Social Contact Theory

Social contact theory originates with the work of Gordon Allport, author of *The Nature of Prejudice* (1954), which focuses on interracial contact situations such as desegregated schools, housing, and workplaces where ethnically encapsulated groups are brought together for the first time. It provides a framework to distinguish integrated schools (schools characterized by positive interracial relations and high standards of academic performance for *all* students) from desegregated schools (schools where formerly segregated groups of students attend school under business-as-usual conditions that typically favor White students).

Applied to schools, social contact theory argues that positive racial attitudes and more equitable learning environments develop out of positive interracial contact experiences. Four primary conditions must be present if students' interracial contact experiences are to be positive: (1) an equal-status environment for people of color and Whites, especially in classrooms and cocurricular activities; (2) a social climate that supports interracial associations, especially as modeled by authority figures such as teachers, principals, superintendents, and parents; (3) contact among students of color and White students that leads to an in-depth knowledge and understanding of each other's similarities and differences; and (4) opportunities for students of color and White students to work together cooperatively to achieve common goals. These four conditions provide a framework for creating school and classroom climates of acceptance and equitable academic achievement.

Most schools that serve diverse student populations will find the first condition, an equal status environment, the most challenging to achieve. When students arrive with different skills it is difficult to create a genuinely equitable classroom. Cooperative team learning is one example of an effective strategy that can help create an equal-status environment in desegregated schools. (See, for example, Cohen, 1995; Slavin, 1985.)

Educators who wish to attain or maintain an integrated school, as distinguished from a desegregated school, must take a proactive stance to implement the conditions of positive intergroup contact. Research indicates that critical areas of concern include equitable teacher expectations, interracial friendships among students, equitable school discipline policies and practices, equitable cocurricular activities, support for intragroup activities, and affirmation of the inherent value of knowing and understanding the cultural diversity of the school community. *CIB* • *See also* **Cooperative Learning**

References

Allport, G. (1954). *The nature of prejudice*. Cambridge, MA: Addison-Wesley.

Cohen, E. (1995). *Designing groupwork* (3rd ed.). New York: Teachers College Press.

Slavin, R. (1985). Cooperative learning: Applying contact theory in desegregated schools. *Journal of Social Issues, 43*(3), 46–62.

Social Context

The immense importance of social context in understanding human actions, especially intellectual performance, is widely recognized. Definitions of social context, however, and how to incorporate the concept of context into theory, methods, or practices vary widely. There are two prominent definitions or views of context in the social sciences, both treating context as a social phenomenon (Cole, 1995).

One definition treats context as background, as the broader environment or setting relevant to particular events or actions. This notion of context is often represented as a set of concentric or embedded circles or boundaries, with the individual (e.g., the teacher or student) or dyad (e.g., teacher-student interactions) in the center, surrounded by various proximal and increasingly distal levels of contexts: the classroom, the school, the district, the community, the city, and so forth. It is assumed that the center circle or primary unit (e.g., the student) is influenced or shaped by the characteristics of the surrounding units of context. The methodological and analytic task is to clarify or specify just how these social connections function and the consequences for students and teachers. Recent research (McLaughlin, Talbert, & Bascia, 1990) shows, for example, how the secondary school setting—conceptualized as multiple embedded contexts that define the teacher workplace—influences the actions and work of teachers. This work is particularly valuable in understanding how interactions shape participants' lives in complex urban schools characterized by a multicultural student body or community, various social classes, and disparate levels of student achievement.

However, Cole (1995) points out that while this notion of embedded contexts provides a valuable conceptual tool to analyze how events at one *level of context* are shaped by events at neighboring levels, it also treats context as if it were simply a unidirectional stimulus that produces a particular effect. This dangerous linear causality might lead one to posit that a particular social class or cultural background causes or produces school failure or success, thus failing to capture the dynamic and complex relationships among levels of social context.

A second definition of social context deals with context less discretely, establishing the inseparability or interdependence of individuals and their environments. Rather than search for cause or effect at particular levels of context, this view attempts to understand the interdependent social relations they constitute (Erickson & Shultz, 1992). Social actors, such as students and teachers, are seen not as passive recipients of a broader and determining social order but as active meaning makers, choosing among alternatives and creating contexts in what are often difficult and contradictory circumstances (Mehan, 1989).

This view of human beings as active social agents, although often responding to circumstances not of their choosing, has particular relevance for multicultural education. One consequence is that it challenges the normative view of culture as a well-integrated, harmonious, and cohesive entity whose values are shared by all members of a particular group. Although the tendency in the past has been to present culture as stable and generalizable traits or (often-stereotyped) attributes of particular groups—independent of social contexts—this definition sees culture in the variability of human activities or practices as they create and manage the multiple contexts that constitute their social worlds (Moll & González, in press).

Different conceptions of social contexts may also lead to different views of how people think and learn. Stated briefly, thinking is traditionally thought to take place solely within the mind of the individual, what some psychologists refer to as solo or in-the-head cognition. Accepting this notion, schools test students to determine their individual ability or intelligence which is considered to be a fixed attribute of the individual, again, independent of his or her social context. An alternative view would consider thinking and learning as mediated and distributed among persons, artifacts, activities, and settings that make up the social contexts of one's life (Lave & Wenger, 1991; Salomon, 1993). This view has led to the study of how people think and learn in conjunction with the activities and artifacts of their cultures (Moll, et al., 1992), including, in particular, interactions with other human beings. *LCM*

References

Cole, M. (1995). The supra-individual envelope of development: Activity and practice, situation and context. In J. Goodnow, P. Miller, & F. Kessel (Eds.), *Cultural practices as contexts for development*, 67 (Spring) San Francisco: Jossey-Bass.

Erickson, F., & Shultz, J. (1992). Students' experience of the curriculum. In P. W. Jackson (Ed.), *Handbook of research on curriculum.* New York: MacMillan.

Lave, J., & Wenger, E. (1991). *Situated learning: Legitimate peripheral participation.* Cambridge: Cambridge University Press.

McLaughlin, M., Talbert, J., & Bascia, N. (1990). *The contexts of teaching in secondary schools: Teachers' realities.* New York: Teachers College Press.

Mehan, H. (1989, August). Understanding inequality in schools: The contribution of interpretive studies. Invited address at the Annual Meeting of the American Sociological Association.

Moll, L. C., Amanti, C., Neff, D., & González, N. (1992). Funds of knowledge for teaching: Using a qualitative approach to connect homes and classrooms. *Theory into Practice, 31*(2), 132–41.

Moll, L. C., & González, N. (in press). Teachers as social scientists: Learning about culture from household research. In P. M. Hall (Ed.), *Race, ethnicity and multiculturalism.* (Vol. 1.) New York: Garland.

Salomon, G. (Ed.). (1993). *Distributed cognitions: Psychological and educational considerations.* Cambridge: Cambridge University Press.

Social Isolation

Neoconservative commentators have had a tendency to explain the growth of social dislocations among low-income, inner-city residents—such as chronic unemployment, crime, and patterns of single-parent-family formation—as the result of aberrant values transmitted through a self-perpetuating culture of poverty. On the other hand, in explicit opposition to this perspective, a number of sociologists, most prominently William Julius Wilson at the University of Chicago, have advanced the concept of social isolation as a key theoretical construct within the underclass debate. These researchers have emphasized that social behaviors and cultural values are influenced tremendously by changing opportunity structures and constraints in the broader society. Moreover, they have noted that the transformation of national and urban economies since the 1960s along with a mounting concentration of poverty in central cities has had differential and often devastating consequences for groups of color, which have historically been the victims of racial subjugation and discrimination.

In his influential work *The Truly Disadvantaged: The Inner City, the Underclass, and Public Policy* Wilson (1987) defines *social isolation* as "the lack of contact or of sustained interaction with individuals and institutions that represent mainstream society" (p. 60). He argues that demographic trends indicate not only a sharp rise in the number of people in the United States living in poverty (due to macrolevel changes in the national economy), but also that an increasing number of central city neighborhoods that have been adversely affected by the combined processes of an out-migration of middle-class and working-class families and an in-migration of individuals and groups whose attachments to the labor force have been marginal. The disappearance of middle- and working-class families, or *social buffers* as Wilson and others have labeled them, in conjunction with the concentrated effects of living in areas of extreme poverty (defined in the research as census tracts where over 40 percent of the residents are living below federal poverty guidelines) has intensified the social isolation of these communities and their residents. Thus, Wilson explains the development and growth of the urban underclass in terms of the declining ability of certain central city neighborhoods to maintain a sufficient level of institutional infrastructure and social organization, which can sustain residents through hard times. Social dislocations and non-normative subcultural behaviors and values have developed not because of inherently deviant beliefs among low-income, inner-city people of color but rather because changes in the national and urban economy have had a differential impact upon certain communities and groups. Poverty has become concentrated within particular neighborhoods, socially isolating residents and destroying those ecological niches that enhance access to suitable employment, quality schooling, and exposure to positive role models. From a public policy perspective, then, programs to alleviate poverty must focus on changing social and economic conditions and alleviating the concentration effects of social isolation. *MF*

Reference

Wilson, W. J. (1987). *The truly disadvantaged: The inner city, the underclass, and public policy.* Chicago: University of Chicago Press.

Social Justice

Social justice and social responsibility can be treated as synonymous concepts. These terms, to a great extent, concern institutionalized patterns of mutual action and interdependence that are necessary to bring about the realization of distributive justice. Citizens have a personal obligation, mediated through political obligations, to help create a society in which the concerns for concrete needs of all persons and the creation of reciprocal interdependence are fundamental.

Social responsibility requires that human needs take priority over claims that derive from a stratified system of role distribution in society. Justice demands equality and fairness in all private transactions, wages, and property ownership, as well as equal opportunity for all to participate in the public benefits generated by society as a whole, such as social security, health care, and education. In this view of justice all persons share in material well-being at least to a level that meets all basic human needs. Agency for change through social justice requires courageous action and strength of will in the pursuit of justice. It involves passion or anger, assertiveness, and endurance. Examples of persons who have displayed this courage and strength in action for social justice are César Chavez, Fannie Lou Hamer, John F. Kennedy, and Martin Luther King, Jr. The effective agent of social justice needs to feel and taste the reality of injustice. Courage for action towards change depends on *knowledgeability* or practical wisdom, which is the quality of mind needed to develop the ability to discern the possibilities for greater justice as they exist in concrete situations.

Education for justice is education for collaboration, cooperation, and community. More than ever in our time, in a multicultural education paradigm, justice has to be seen as plural. Justices must be understood as contextually specific in relation to the many different spheres of society and in their incommensurability. In a multicultural and just society we need to cultivate within ourselves the virtues of tolerance and acceptance, which teach us to live with that which is different. Thus, difference, diversity, and Otherness become central to the definition of the ethical perspective that underlies social justice: "aiming at the good life with and for others in just institutions" (Ricoeur, 1992, p. 172). *SSG*

References

Hollenbach, D. (1988). *Justice, peace, and human rights: American Catholic social ethics in a pluralistic context*. New York: Crossroad.

McLaren, P. (1995). *Critical pedagogy and predatory culture: Oppositional politics in a postmodern era*. New York: Routledge.

Ricoeur, P. (1992). *Oneself as another*. Translated by Kathleen Blamey. Chicago: University of Chicago Press.

Social Reconstruction *See* Multicultural Education

Social Responsibility *See* Social Justice

Socioeconomic Status

The U.S. Bureau of the Census measures the economic condition of individuals with a criterion called socioeconomic status (SES). It serves as a composite of the economic status of a family or unrelated individuals based on occupation, educational attainment, and income. Related to these three factors used by the Census Bureau are wealth and power, which also help determine an individual's socioeconomic status but are more difficult to measure through census data.

These five determinants of socioeconomic status are interrelated. Although there are many forms of inequality, these factors are probably the most salient for the individual because they affect how one lives (Rothman, 1978). A family's socioeconomic status is observable—the size of their house, the schools they attend, their neighborhood, and their club memberships. Many educators place their students at specific socioeconomic status levels based on similar observations (Gollnick and Chinn, p. 41–43). *DMG & PCC*

References

Gollnick, D. M., & Chinn, P. C. (1990). *Multicultural education in a pluralistic society* (3rd ed.). Columbus, OH: Merrill. This definition of socioeconomic status originally appeared in this book. Used by permission of Merrill.

Rothman, R. A. (1978). *Inequality and stratification in the United States.* Englewood Cliffs, NJ: Prentice-Hall.

Stereotypes

A stereotype is a belief about the personal attributes of a group, based on exaggerated and inaccurate generalizations used to describe all members of the group, without acknowledging individual differences. The term *stereotype* and the act of *stereotyping*, have been socially constructed. U.S. American journalist Walter Lippman introduced the term in 1922 to refer to "the picture in our heads" of various groups (Leyens, Yzerbyt, & Schadron, 1994). A stereotype implies undesirable rigidity, a sense of permanence, and a lack of flexibility from one group to the next and even within a group. Stereotypes about those outside a group are generally less positive than about those within a group. Stereotypes create and help preserve perceived group differences by other groups, and they help create group ideologies that might be used to justify attitudes and actions against other groups. The aim of multicultural education is to eliminate stereotypes and to take a stand against them, whether used negatively or positively. For example, stereotypes about Asian American students' school performance may create difficult peer relations and produce unreasonable teacher demands. Rather than recognizing the strengths and weaknesses of individual students, a teacher may apply stereotypes about students' groups to individual students. Eliminating stereotypical language in the curriculum will allow children to accept the social world as it exists and to think of our differences as natural phenomena. *MT*

References

Leyens, J. P., Yzerbyt, V., & Schadron, G. (1994). *Stereotypes and social cognition.* Thousand Oaks, CA: Sage.

Structural Assimilation *See* Assimilation

Teaching the Exceptional and Culturally Different
See Multicultural Education, Approaches To

U.S. v. Fordice

In 1975 a group of African Americans led by Jake Ayers filed suit against the State of Mississippi in federal court with the intent of creating a more equitable system of higher education. Specifically, they were requesting increased funding for the state's three historically Black colleges. Twelve years later the case went to trial (*Ayers v. Allain*, 1987). The court found many problems in the state's college system such as discriminatory admissions requirements, program duplication, and funding inequalities. However, the court concluded that a state's legal duty to desegregate did not include most of these issues. Rather, the intent of the law is to ensure that policies are race neutral, are created and implemented in good faith, and do not contribute significantly to the racial *identifiability* of individual schools (SEF, 1995). The district court found that, under this standard, the State of Mississippi was not in violation of federal law. The United States Court of Appeals for the Fifth Circuit concurred with the lower court's decision.

This set the stage for an appeal to the Supreme Court. The Supreme Court agreed to review the lower courts' decisions in *Ayers*. The federal government joined the plaintiffs, and the case was referred to as *U.S. v. Fordice*. The Court found that the lower courts had not applied the correct legal standard to Mississippi's higher education system. In the majority opinion written by Justice White, it was held that (1) the adoption and implementation of race-neutral policies do not alone indicate the state has met its duty—under the equal protection clause and under Title VI—to eliminate aspects of a dual system; (2) thus, even after the state has created a racially neutral admissions policy not designed for discriminatory purposes, if policies linked to the prior dual system are still in place and have discriminatory outcomes, those policies must be changed to reflect sound educational practices; (3) if the court of appeals had employed the proper legal standard, it would have been clear from the factual findings of the district court that several aspects of Mississippi's dual system continued to exist and had to be justified or eliminated, including admission standards, program duplication, institutional mission assignments, and continued operation of all eight universities; and (4) while the Supreme Court would not mandate Mississippi to enhance its three historically Black universities solely, creating publicly supported, exclusively Black institutions, the question whether such increased fiscal support was required to achieve full dismantlement of the dual system under the Supreme Court's standards was a different question that had to be dealt with on remand.

The Supreme Court discussed in detail the analysis to be used in determining whether a state retains a legal duty to desegregate. However, it did not directly address the question of what policies and practices would be appropriate to address vestiges of segregation (SEF, 1995). The question, "What policies will best support equitable education in Mississippi higher education and other southern states?" continues to be subject to considerable debate. *WFT*

References

Ayers v. Allain, 674 F. Supp. 1523, 1551 (N.D. Miss., 1987).

Southern Education Fund. (1995). *Redeeming the American promise*. Atlanta, GA: Southern Educational Fund (SEF).

U.S. v. Fordice, 505 US 717 (1992).

Voice

Voice is a basic entitlement with implied rights and authoritative boundaries. Individuals have the right to speak and represent themselves in all aspects, including disclosure, identification, description, causality, interpretation, and resolution. Events are grounded by the ethnic, racial, cultural, linguistic, and sociopolitical orientations of the participants. This indicates that the different experiential knowledge bases and the eventual perceptions and interpretations of the event are multidimensional. Each individual present is entitled to record his or her account of the event. They each have power to transmit, validate, own the experience, and speak on their own behalf by telling their own story.

In schools, students are often denied voice due to the uneven distribution of power inherent in their roles and status and by the compulsory competition with concerns and issues of the dominant voice. At times student accuracy is questioned, and their perceptual reality is minimized. Their entitlement to report and define experiences is denied. These limitations establish a spirit of inequality and an abuse of power, when the basic human entitlement to voice is silenced, manipulated, and controlled by either giving or denying the opportunity to be heard.

Multiculturalists believe that all students have the right to speak and provide differential cultural knowledge. To deny students voice limits equity of outcome, impedes access to equality of educational opportunity, and hampers the development of the skills needed to become active, critical, and productive change agents in society. It is not enough to *let* students speak, but rather the conditions of power and powerlessness need to be considered to protect students' *entitlement* to speak. *RS*

Vouchers *See* Educational Choice

Whiteness

The term *Whiteness* and its definitions are related to and complicated by understandings of class (Roediger, 1991), gender (Frye, 1992; Frankenberg, 1993), Jewish identity (Kay/Kantrowitz, 1992), and sexuality. Further, because understandings of the term *Whiteness* are recent and contested, there are multiple definitions. Whiteness appears to be an often-overlooked identity position for many Whites, therefore the discussion and contestation that follow are exploratory and partial.

Notions of representation shape our understandings and performances of race. The construction of race consciousness and of Whiteness may be formed by continual visual representations of difference. This possibility motivates Dyer (1988) in his article "White" to discuss representations of Whiteness in movies. He defines Whiteness as a culturally constructed category that is represented in Hollywood films as the norm, the natural, inevitable, ordinary way of being human. For Dyer, representations of Whiteness for White people are "invisible, everything and nothing" (p. 49). And if Whiteness is recognized by Whites in and through films, it is only in relation to an Other—Black people. Filmic representations of Whiteness are only noticeable in relation to difference.

Representations of Whiteness in literature are also relational. In her book *Playing in the Dark,* Morrison (1992) analyzes the way that White literary writers construct race. Race is constructed in these texts through relationships between White characters and African American characters. Her analysis shows that in literature written by Whites, representations of Blackness are variable. However, "[w]hiteness, alone, is mute, meaningless, unfathomable, pointless, frozen, veiled, curtained, dreaded, senseless, implacable" (p. 59). Literature portrays Whiteness, but only in relation to the variability of Blackness, and this portrayal is often invisible to Whites.

On the other hand, Whiteness is not invisible to people of color, according to bell hooks (1992) in *Representations of Whiteness in the Black Imagination*. Black people's understandings of Whiteness emerge as a response to the traumatic pain and anguish of being Black, which is a consequence of White racist domination and a psychic state that informs and shapes the way Black folks *see* Whiteness (p. 169). How Black folks see Whiteness is in direct contrast to notions of Whiteness as normative. Hooks is actually dealing with the material effects of racist domination and White supremacy on bodies, Black bodies. "In White supremacist society, White people can 'safely' imagine that they are invisible to Black people since the power they have historically asserted, and even now collectively assert over Black people, accorded them the right to control the Black gaze" (p. 168). It is obvious that many White people do not see Whiteness in a similar way. For hooks, White people's "[a]bsence of recognition [of their own race] is a strategy that facilitates making a group the Other" (p. 167).

As Dyer, Morrison, and hooks suggest, definitions of Whiteness are complicated by context, identity positions, and point of view. These definitions cannot be complete or truly meaningful removed from understandings and contestation of Whiteness in actual people's lives. *LF* • *See also* **Difference; The Other; Positionality; Representation**

References

bell hooks. (1992). Representations of Whiteness in the Black imagination. *Black looks: Race and representation*. Boston: South End Press.

Dyer, R. (1988). White. *Screen, 29*(4).

Frankenberg, R. (1993). *The social construction of Whiteness: White women, race matters*. Minneapolis: University of Minnesota Press.

Frye, M. (1992). White woman feminist: 1983–1992. *Willful virgin: Essays in feminism*. Freedom, CA: Crossing Press.

Kay/Kantrowitz, M. (1992). *The issue is power: Essays on women, Jews, and violence*. San Francisco: Aunt Lute.

Morrison, T. (1992). *Playing in the dark: Whiteness and the literary imagination*. Cambridge: Harvard University Press.

Roediger, D. (1991). *The wages of Whiteness: Race and the making of the American working class*. London: Verso.

Womanist/Womanism

Womanist is a culturally specific term coined by Alice Walker in the late 1970s; derived from *womanish*, it is a reworking of the term *feminist* in ways that takes into account the experiences of Black women. Walker uses *womanist* to denote a Black feminist or a feminist of color. The term can also denote "outrageous, audacious, courageous behavior." It characterizes a deep, spiritual love. In fact, Walker (1983) uses the word "love" 11 times in her definition. A womanist signifies a woman who loves women (sexually or nonsexually), a woman who "appreciates . . . women's culture, women . . . and women's strength." A womanist encompasses the spirit and the spiritual. She "loves music . . . dance . . . the moon." A womanist, "*loves* the Spirit. Loves love and food and roundness. Loves struggle. Loves the Folk. Loves herself. *Regardless.*" She is "committed to the survival of the race, both male and female" (pp. ix–x).

Throughout the African Diaspora the term womanist has been employed by Black women scholars espousing diverse philosophical orientations across disciplines (e.g., philosophy, theology, literary criticism, and sociology). Its usage varies from celebrating the lives and strengths of Black women to more critical and problematic interrogations of Black women's lives in a world of racism, classism, sexism, heterosexism, and ageism. Generally, the usage denotes engaged scholarship, self-definition, the search for theoretical paradigms starting from the political, social, and cultural practices of Black women, and the struggle for societal transformation. Just as there are many interpretations of feminism, the meanings of womanism have been reshaped, reworked, and popularized in the Black community into terms such as *Black womanism*, *Africana womanism*, and *Afrikana womanism*.

Indeed, womanists and feminists may espouse converging and intersecting political agendas. It is not a question of Black versus White but rather a question of self-definition—"naming our own experience after our own fashion (as well as rejecting whatever does not seem to suit)" (Walker, 1983, p. 82). Walker explains that "Womanist is to feminist as purple is to lavender" (p. x). *AH*

References

Walker, A. (1983). *In search of our mother's gardens*. San Diego and New York: Harcourt Brace Jovanovich.

Women's Movement

Women's work for their own rights formed the basis of the Women's Movement. After having been involved in a variety of social reform movements—antislavery, temperance, prison conditions—women used these experiences of struggle to fight for their own rights and issues. One of the capstone events of the early Women's Movement in the United States was the battle for women's suffrage. This movement produced important women leaders such as Elizabeth Cady Stanton, the Grimke sisters, Sojourner

Truth, and Susan B. Anthony. However, achieving the right to vote was just a beginning step in the fight for women's rights.

Women played an important role in the modern Civil Rights Movement of the 1960s. Although their primary roles were not in the movement's limelight, their contributions provided an important infrastructure for the many victories in social and legal arenas. Septima Clark, Ella Baker, Rosa Parks, Fannie Lou Hamer, and Viola Liuzzo, all are exemplars of the vital leadership needed to advance the rights of African Americans and other people of color who had been disenfranchised and marginalized by society.

At about the same time many working-class and African American women were fighting on behalf of people of color, White, middle-class women were beginning to find voices with which to express their growing awareness of the oppression visited upon all women due to sex role stereotyping and unequal access to social benefits. Betty Friedan's *The Feminine Mystique* influenced the thinking of many of these women. A middle-class home-maker, Friedan suggested that many women were unable to name the problem that plagued them; however, she acknowledged that the image of women as mother-and-wife, who lived through the dreams and aspirations of men and children, meant women were required to give up their own dreams.

In 1966, 30 women, including Betty Friedan, founded the National Organization for Women (NOW) "to take action to bring American women into full participation in the mainstream of American society." NOW focused on reproductive freedom issues, political representation, equal job opportunities, and childcare as well as other issues of importance to women. One of the major battles fought and won by women was the Supreme Court decision *Roe v. Wade,* which legalized abortion. One of the Women's Movement's major defeats was the failure of the passage of the Equal Rights Amendment (ERA).

In the 1970s women activists were picketing and demonstrating for equal job opportunities and equal access to all-male clubs, restaurants, and schools. Simultaneously, women were involved in civil rights and antiwar protests. Women's activism opened up some "small spaces" of opportunity that allowed some women to begin to reap the economic and social benefits of society. Thus, high-paying, high-prestige jobs in banking, law, engineering, medicine, and other traditionally male-dominated fields were opening up to middle-income (and mostly, White) women. This privileging of White, middle-class, heterosexual women caused the Women's Movement to experience race and class conflict with poor women and women of color, as well as with lesbians and bisexual women.

In addition to grappling with race, class, and sexual orientation differences, the Women's Movement also began to show signs of political splintering. Liberal feminists traditionally positioned themselves as advocating for equal status with men in the society. Radical feminists argued for a total restructuring of the patriarchal society, which they saw as incapable of serving the cause of justice. At the same time there were women on the right, symbolized by Phyllis Schlafly, who urged a return to the traditional roles of wife and mother because of what they saw as essentialized differences between men and women.

Just as the modern Civil Rights Movement had done, the Women's Movement provided just enough access for some to cause the movement to lose some of its energy, power, and appeal. By the 1990s feminist author Susan Faludi was documenting *feminist backlash*—growing numbers of women, although having benefitted materially from the work of feminists and the Women's Movement, were disavowing feminism. More pointed critique emerged from scholars such as Elizabeth Fox Genovese, who decried radical feminism in favor of a more liberal equal opportunity position, and Camille Paglia, who became a media sensation as a result of her open antagonism toward feminism.

Despite some setbacks for the Women's Movement, particular social events have rallied women, in general, to support women's issues. One such incident was the Supreme Court confirmation hearings of Clarence Thomas, who was accused of sexually harassing legal colleague Anita Hill. The outrage expressed by women at Hill's treatment by the Senate Judiciary Committee, along with the obvious ignorance of many men about what constituted sexual harassment, was galvanized into a powerful political force in the 1992 national election.

A second issue that once again gathered women together was the sensational O. J. Simpson trial. A central issue of this trial was that of domestic violence and the vulnerability of women in abusive domestic relationships. While the case itself was a complex interweaving of race, class, and gender issues, the domestic violence aspect of it provided another opportunity for women to speak to the ways in which they continue to be marginalized by the dominant society.

Today debate continues on the history and impact of the modern Women's Movement. Historian Linda Gordon and some colleagues are in the process of writing and editing a documentary history of the Women's Movement that traces the various tributaries of the movement to a variety of small, informal gatherings of women throughout the nation, who came together to share experiences and work on issues impacting women and families. *GLB* • *See also* **Civil Rights Movement; Feminism; Women's Studies**

References

Friedan, B. (1963). *The feminine mystique*. New York: W.W. Norton.
Zinn, H. (1980). *A people's history of the United States*. New York: HarperCollins.

Women's Studies

Women's studies, also known as feminist studies or gender studies, began to develop in the United States in the late 1960s as the educational arm of the Women's Movement. With a reawakened feminist movement as its life-blood, women's studies grew out of the progressive political activism of the 1960s, much influenced by the Civil Rights Movement, the Anti-War Movement, the student movements for educational reform in higher educa-tion, and the formation of Afro-American studies and ethnic studies. In response to the widespread discrimination against women in the academy and the absence of women and gender issues from the curriculum, women's studies began as a compensatory field whose objectives included establish-ing the study of women and gender as legitimate areas of academic inquiry, serving the unmet needs of women students, increasing the number of women faculty and administrators, and contributing to the general transfor-mation of an inequitable social order.

By the late 1970s women's studies had established a relatively strong foothold within U.S. institutions of higher education. Quickly becoming more than a corrective measure, women's studies had demonstrated its staying power as a vibrant new field producing a seemingly endless array of new research, new curricula, and innovative pedagogy that has had a perva-sive influence on higher education well beyond women's studies programs and classrooms. Initially its strongest base was in the humanities, but since its inception women's studies has substantially increased its presence in the social sciences and even developed important inroads in the sciences. As a field, women's studies exists both as a separate interdisciplinary or multidisciplinary entity and as a strongly transformative presence within traditional disciplines. Most faculty members have joint appointments or are based in a home department.

Although seldom well-funded and secure, women's studies programs exist, as of 1995, at 612 four-year college and university campuses in the United States. They offer some 224 undergraduate majors, 463 undergradu-ate minors or concentrations, 51 postgraduate certificates or concentrations, 36 master of arts degrees, 24 doctoral minors or concentrations, and 10 doctor of philosophy degrees. Interdisciplinary scholarly journals such as *Signs: Journal of Women in Culture and Society*, *Feminist Studies*, *Women's Studies*, *Genders*, *Women's Studies International Forum*, and *Women's Studies Quarterly* flourish, along with discipline-based journals such as *Tulsa Studies in Women's Literature*, *Psychology of Women Quarterly*, *Women and Politics*, *Women and Health*, *Journal of Women's History*, and *Hypatia*. Mainstream university and trade presses carry extensive lines in women's studies, while feminist presses (e.g., The Feminist Press, Kitchen Table/Women of Color Press, The

Crossing Press, and Spinsters, Ink) publish long-forgotten and new works by women. Vulnerable to attack and budget cutbacks, however, women's studies programs may develop contradictory and uneasy relationships with their home institutions, often maintaining themselves or growing as the result of political struggle, coalitions, hard work, and sometimes the support of administrators.

The theory underlying women's studies as a field has been evolving and is constantly subjected to contestation, which reflects the plurality of feminisms and changing historical conditions. Early formulations of women's studies revolved around several points of consensus: (1) all knowledge is produced from some kind of perspective or standpoint, so no knowledge is objective and value free; (2) traditional disciplines and fields have ignored, distorted, or trivialized the subject of women and gender; (3) women's studies should make women and gender the central issues of study; (4) women's studies is not just the study of women but also the study of women and gender from a feminist perspective; (5) women's studies potentially transforms traditional knowledge and disciplines by inclusion of what has been left out or interpreted androcentrically; (6) women's studies must be interdisciplinary, crossing traditional disciplinary boundaries; and (7) women's studies should work to empower women students and enhance the understanding of men students. Influenced by Thomas Kuhn's (1962) *The Structure of Scientific Revolutions*, much early theorizing emphasized that women's studies involved more than the addition of women to a course or book; rather, it involved a paradigm shift that fundamentally altered basic concepts within traditional forms of knowledge. Other much-debated issues, around which there was no easy consensus, include whether women's studies is a field or a discipline; whether it should be separate, mainstreamed, or both; whether or not feminist research requires a partially or entirely different methodology; whether or not feminist teaching requires a separate, nonhierarchical pedagogy; and, finally, the nature of the relationship between academic women's studies and community activism.

The early theoretical consensus about women's studies broke down over the meaning of the categories of women and gender upon which women's studies was founded. The initially small but increasingly widespread protests led mainly by women of color, lesbians, Jewish women, and non-Western women insisted that the exclusive focus on women and gender ignored, distorted, or trivialized the experiences of women whose lives were deeply affected by other systems of stratification like race, class, sexuality, religion, and national origin. In particular, some women charged that women's studies was mainly about White, heterosexual, middle-class, Western, and Christian women and was unable to confront its own racism, homophobia, and ethnocentrism. This led to the formation of such separate movements as Black women's studies and lesbian women's studies.

By the 1980s the emphasis on women's differences from men changed into discussion of the differences among women, not only within the United States but also worldwide. Debates in classrooms, conferences, publications, and organizations oscillated between anger and bridge-building. By the 1990s a new consensus has developed—but not without continued debate and struggle—around the need for a broadly multicultural women's studies that examines not only gender but also gender's interaction with race, ethnicity, class, sexuality, religion, national origin, ableness, and other systems of stratification worldwide.

Women's studies takes place outside academic institutions of higher education in the United States as well. The National Women's Studies Association's umbrella definition of women's studies incorporates feminist education wherever it takes place, including especially work done by K–12 teachers, community activists, and librarians. Women's studies has increasingly become an international phenomenon, producing kinds of educational feminism suited to particular histories and cultures, especially in places such as Europe, India, China, Australia, and Japan.

Women's studies is the most common name for the field, but other terms such as *gender studies* and *feminist studies* also exist, often selected to emphasize inclusiveness in the case of gender studies and advocacy in feminist studies. Some African American women in Black women's studies prefer the term *womanism* to *feminism*, to indicate their advocacy for Black men as well as women and their ties to the Black community in the African diaspora. Feminist women of color and Jewish women often work within or in close alliance with ethnic studies programs, while lesbian feminists are often allied with gay and lesbian studies. *SSF* • *See also* **Feminism; Feminist Theories; Womanism**

References

Bowles, G., & Klein, R. D. (1983). *Theories of Women's Studies*. London: Routledge and Kegan Paul.

Boxer, M. J. (1982). For and about women: The theory and practice of Women's Studies in the United States. *Signs*, 7(3), 661–95.

Culley, M., & Portuges, C. (Eds.). (1985). *Gendered subjects: The dynamics of feminist teaching*. London: Routledge and Kegan Paul.

Farnham, C. (Ed.). (1987). *The impact of feminist research in the academy*. Bloomington: Indiana University Press.

Feminist collections: A quarterly of women's studies resources. Madison: University of Wisconsin System Women's Studies Librarian.

Feminist periodicals: A current listing of contents. Madison: University of Wisconsin System Women's Studies Librarian.

Hull, G. T., Scott, P. B., & Smith, B. (Eds.). (1982). *All the men are black, all the women are white, and some of us are brave: Black women's studies*. Old Westbury, NY: Feminist Press.

Hunter College Women's Collective. (1983). *Women's realities, women's choices: An introduction to women's studies*. New York: Oxford University Press.

Kuhn, T. S. (1962). *The structure of scientific revolutions*. Chicago: University of Chicago Press.

Loeb, C. R., Searing, S. E., & Stinemen, E. (1987). *Women's studies: A recommended core bibliography, 1980–1985*. Littleton: Libraries Unlimited.

Mohanty, C. T., Russo, A., & Torres, L. (Eds.). (1991). *Third world women and the politics of feminism*. Bloomington: Indiana University Press.

Reinharz, S. (1992). *Feminist methods in social research*. New York: Oxford University Press.

Ruth, S. (1980). *Issues in feminism: A first course in women's studies*. Boston: Houghton Mifflin.

Sapiro, V. (1994). *Women in American society: An introduction to women's studies* (3rd ed.). Mountain View, CA: Mayfield.

Shult, L., Searing, S. E., & Lester-Massman, E. (Eds.). (1991). *Women, race, and ethnicity: A bibliography*. Madison: University of Wisconsin System Women's Studies Librarian.

Stanton, D. C., & Stewart, A. (Eds.). (1995). *Feminisms in the academy*. Ann Arbor: University of Michigan Press.

Wolfe, S. J., & Penelope, J. (Eds.). (1993). *Sexual practice, textual theory: Lesbian cultural criticism*. Oxford: Blackwell.

Xenophobia

Xenophobia is the fear and loathing of other nations and national cultures as well as hostility toward individuals and groups from those nations. It is expressed both toward peoples who live elsewhere and toward immigrants with different languages, traditions, religions, and complexions. It bears on the field of education because it is a source of opposition to internationalism and multiculturalism in general and to multicultural policies in particular. By no means unique to the United States, it has been a recurrent feature of U.S. political culture. It is a virulent expression of *nativism*, which in the United States is the term for political and cultural movements framed by a defense of the United States from purportedly threatening aliens.

Xenophobia is at the extreme end of the continuum of nationalist sentiment. Whereas some people merely recognize the distinct qualities of their national culture, xenophobes view their national culture as superior, yet are ever fearful it is being undermined by other, inferior cultures. Analytically distinct from racism, xenophobia is often cast in racialized terms in practice, with definitions and meanings of race and racism changing across time. In the nineteenth century anti-Catholicism, especially as expressed toward Irish immigrants, and anti-Semitism were racialized forms of xenophobia.

Three aspects of xenophobia bear on education, although opposition to multicultural educational philosophies and policies is not solely motivated by xenophobia. First, xenophobia strengthens parochialism toward the rest of the world, and to the extent that non-U.S., non-Western topics are taught, it opposes cultural relativism. Second, it is a form of identity politics in which difference is cast vertically not horizontally. Xenophobes believe that *we* do not merely have a distinct culture but a superior one to which others should aspire. Whereas many students of U.S. history believe that the process of Americanization is enriched by immigrants who contribute to as well as adopt the dominant culture, xenophobes worry that immigrants lower standards, introduce alien values, and pollute a homogenous culture. Thus bilingual education, respect for cultural diversity, and attention to different styles of learning are all opposed as threats to *our* national identity. Third, xenophobes share the view that *our* national culture and values express universal values, especially as they assert that Christianity and Western civilization are not only distinct but superior. It thus follows that the robust defense of *our* political culture and opposition to multiculturalism are not only best for us but for everyone, including those who mistakenly defend their own cultures through multicultural educational policies.

Xenophobia is the hard edge of hostility toward multicultural education and identity politics in general. Animated by hostility toward multiculturalism, xenophobia is itself a form of identity politics in which its adherents believe their own cultural values are only respected and realized by denying the values of others. Xenophobia thus reveals the inviability of an educational philosophy framed solely by a multiculturalist emphasis on respect for *difference*. While an accurate account of xenophobia can be included within a multicultural curriculum, it cannot generate educational policies that provide the context for multiculturalism. *AH*

APPENDIX A

• • • • • • • • •

A Sampler of Multicultural Education Resources

This sampler includes a selection of resources in three areas:

1. Organizations
2. Electronic Multicultural Contacts (Web sites)
3. Federally Funded Assistance Centers

While not inclusive of all the groups in each of these categories, the resources provide a sample of what is available and will lead the reader to numerous other resources.

1. ORGANIZATIONS

American Council on Education (ACE)
Office of Minorities in Higher Education
Office of Women in Higher Education
One Dupont Circle - Suite 800
Washington, DC 20036
Phone: (202) 939-9300
Fax: (202) 833-4760
E-mail: varies by department
Web site: www.ACENET.edu

Founded in 1918, ACE is an umbrella organization for higher education. It represents higher and adult education before Congress, federal agencies, the Supreme Court and federal courts. It helps shape educational policy and research at the national and international levels. ACE's Office of Minorities in Higher Education and Office of Women in Higher Education have particular focus on issues and programs for educational equity and multicultural education.

American Federation of Teachers (AFT/AFL•CIO)
555 New Jersey Avenue, NW
Washington, DC 20001-2079
Phone: (202) 879-4400
Fax: (202) 879-4537 (Ed. Issues)
E-mail: varies by department
Web site: www.aft.org

This national teachers union advocates and develops materials in all areas of education. It has divisions which focus on educational equity and multicultural education.

American Folklife Center
Library of Congress
10 1st Street, SE
Washington, DC 20540-8100
Phone: (202) 707-6590
Fax: (202) 707-2076

Founded in 1976, the American Folklife Center houses one of the largest collections of ethnographic materials in the world. Its purpose is to preserve and disseminate diverse American folklife, both historical and contemporary, through educational programs, research, exhibitions, archival materials and reference services, publications, performances and training workshops.

Anti-Defamation League of B'nai B'rith
823 United Nations Plaza
New York, NY 10017
Phone: (212) 490-2525
Fax: (212) 867-0779
E-mail: New York@adl.org
Web site: www.adl.org

Provides audiovisual, background information, curricular, and human relations materials, and prejudice reduction programs such as "A World of Difference" for school and community use.

ASPIRA
1444 I Street NW- Suite 800
Washington, DC 20005
Phone: (202) 835-3600
Fax: (202) 835-3613
E-mail: aspira1@aol.com
Web site: www.incacorp.com/aspira

ASPIRA is a national nonprofit educational organization that works with Latino youth. It offers leadership development programs, career access and higher education access programs. ASPIRA also publishes and disseminates materials related to issues and programs for Latino youth and education. Since 1961, ASPIRA has pursued its mission of empowering the Latino community through the development of its youth.

Association for the Study of Afro-American Life and History (ASALH)
Carter G. Woodson Center and Library
1407 14th Street, NW
Washington, DC 20011
Phone: (202) 667-2822
Fax: (202) 387-9802

Created by Dr. Carter G. Woodson in the early 1900s, ASALH was developed to promote appreciation and knowledge of the life, history and contributions of Black Americans. ASALH decides the theme and develops materials for the observance of African American History Month each February. Its focus is to educate about the history of African Americans and to create an understanding of present conditions in order to enrich future opportunities and achievements.

California Tomorrow
Fort Mason Center
Building B - Suite 345
San Francisco, CA 94123
Phone: (415) 441-7631
Fax: (415) 441-7635
E-mail: 6549633@mcimail.com

This advocacy organization publishes curricular and other materials focusing on issues of diversity. While focusing on California, these materials are highly applicable to other states and regions.

Center for Applied Linguistics (CAL)
1118 22nd Street, NW
Washington, DC 20037
Phone: (202) 429-9292
Fax: (202) 659-5641
E-mail: varies by clearinghouse, index on Web site
Web site: www.cal.org

The Center for Applied Linguistics houses the National Clearinghouse for Bilingual Education. CAL provides information and resources on curriculum materials, methodologies, and research on the education of persons with different languages of origin and with limited English proficiency.

Center for Multicultural Education
University of Washington
122 Miller Hall - DQ12
Seattle, WA 98195
Phone: (206) 543-3386
Fax: (206) 543-8439
E-mail: jbanks@u.washington.edu
Web site: www.educ.washington.edu

The Center for Multicultural Education focuses on research projects and activities designed to improve practice related to equity issues, intergroup relations, and the achievement of students of color. The center also engages in services and teaching related to its research mission.

Center for Research on Education, Diversity & Excellence (CREDE)
University of California, Santa Cruz
1156 High Street
Santa Cruz, CA 95064
Phone: (408) 469-3500
Fax: (408) 459-3502
E-mail: crede@cats.ucsc.edu
Web site: www.cal.org/crede

Housed at the University of California, Santa Cruz, CREDE has research sites across the United States. Funded by the U.S. Department of Education, it operates 30 research projects within the strands of language learning and academic achievement, professional development, the influence and interaction of family, peers, and community on the education of linguistically and culturally diverse students, instruction in context, integrated school reform, and assessment.

Center for Research on Women
University of Memphis
Campus Box 526105
Memphis, TN 38152-6105
Phone: (901) 678-2770
Fax: (901) 678-3652
E-mail: bsmith2@cc.kmemphis.edu

This center conducts research and issues research reports and a newsletter devoted to issues of gender and society, with particular emphasis on integrating issues of gender with race, national origin and social class.

Center for Women Policy Studies
1211 Connecticut Avenue, NW - Suite 312
Washington, DC 20036
Phone: (202) 872-1770
Fax: (202) 296-8962
E-mail: hn4066@handsnet.org

An active source of information about policies that relate to women and girls, the Center for Women Policy Studies conducts studies and programs to educate the public and policymakers about diverse areas related to gender. Among areas of in-depth analysis are bias in testing and assessment, sexual harassment and girls and violence.

Children's Defense Fund (CDF)
25 E Street, NW
Washington, DC 20001
Phone: (202) 628-8787
Fax: (202) 662-3510
E-mail: cdfinfo@childrensdefense.org
Web site: www.childrensdefense.org

A national advocacy organization for children and youth, with particular emphasis on children in need of equal opportunities and resources, CDF conducts numerous studies and issues information and policy publications on areas related to all areas of the lives of children and their families, ranging from education to health. CDF also runs ongoing programs such as "Stand For Children."

Clearinghouse for Immigrant Education (CHIME)
National Coalition of Advocates for Students
100 Boylston Street - Suite 737
Boston, MA 02116
Phone: (800) 441-7192

This organization is a clearinghouse and resource center for print, nonprint, organizational and human resources related to the positive treatment and effective education of immigrant students of diverse origins and backgrounds.

The Common Destiny Alliance (CODA)
4114 Benjamin Building, College of Education
University of Maryland
College Park, MD 20742
Phone: (301) 405-2341
Fax: (301) 314-9890
Web site: asdb-99.umd.edu/coda/

A consortium of organizations and scholars committed to improving race and ethnic relations and educational equity, CODA partner organizations and scholars represent a wide range of perspectives and utilize advocacy, program development and research to identify effective educational practices to facilitate individual and organizational change.

Council of Chief State School Officers (CCSSO)
Resource Center on Educational Equity
One Massachusetts Avenue, NW - Suite 700
Washington, DC 20001-1431
Phone: (202) 336-7007
Fax: (202) 408-8072
E-mail: individual, by staff member. director - cindyb@ccsso.org
Web site: www.ccsso.org

This council is the national association for the Chief State School Officer (usually the state superintendent of schools) for all states. The Resource Center on Educational Equity analyzes and disseminates information about all areas of educational equity.

Council for Exceptional Children (CEC)
Office of Ethnic and Multicultural Concerns
1920 Association Drive
Reston, VA 22091
Phone: (703) 620-3660
Fax: (703) 264-9494
E-mail: cec@cec.sped.org
Web site: www.education.miami.edu

A membership organization for those involved with special education and issues related to students with disabilities, CEC has a division that focuses on multicultural issues within special education, among various disability groups, and within education and society in general. CEC publishes extensive informational materials.

Council for Exceptional Children/Division for Culturally and Linguistically Diverse Exceptional Learners (CEC/DDEL)
University of Miami
School of Education
222 Merrick Building
Coral Gables, FL 33124
Phone: (305) 284-6501
Fax: (305) 284-3003 c/o David Tipmore
E-mail: dtipmore@umiami.ir.miami.edu
Web site: www.education.miami.edu

This division of the Council for Exceptional Children focuses on issues of culture and language among children and youth with disabilities, their schools, and their families/communities.

Educational Equity Concepts
114 East 32nd Street - Suite 306
New York, NY 10016
Phone: (212) 725-1803 (this is also a TTY number)
Fax: (212) 725-0947
E-mail: 75507.1306@compuserve
Web site: in process

Provides multicultural early childhood and science educational equity materials, curricula and training programs, with emphasis on gender equity, race/ethnicity and disability. EEC also offers programs and materials for both teachers and parents to create bias-free learning environments for children.

Educators for Social Responsibility (ESR)
23 Garden Street
Cambridge, MA 02138
Phone: (617) 492-1764
Fax: (617) 864-5164
E-mail: ESRMAIN@igc.apc.org
Web site: www.benjerry.com

ESR promotes the ethical and social development of children through leadership in conflict resolution, violence prevention, intergroup relation, and character education. ESR offers curricula and professional development for teachers and others concerned about diversity, mediation, and peace education.

Facing History and Ourselves National Foundation (FHAO)
25 Kennard Road
Brookline, MA 02146
Phone: (617) 232-1595
Fax: (617) 232-0281
E-mail: info_boston@facing.org
Web site: www.facing.org

Provides prejudice reduction curricular and training program that focuses on the World War II Holocaust as a vehicle to explore historical and current issues such as racism, anti-Semitism, social responsibility, violence, prejudice, and scapegoating.

Joint Center for Political and Economic Studies
1090 Vermont Avenue - Suite 1100
Washington, DC 20005
Phone: (202) 789-3500
Fax: (202) 789-6390

A nonpartisan, nonprofit institution, the center uses research and information dissemination to improve the socioeconomic status of Black Americans; increase their influence in the political and public policy arenas; and facilitate the building of coalitions across racial lines. The center provides information to elected and appointed officials, the media, and various agencies and organizations.

National Alliance of Black School Educators (NABSE)
2816 Georgia Avenue, NW
Washington, DC 20001
Phone: (202) 483-1549
Fax: (202) 483-8323

Since its founding in 1970 as the National Alliance of Black School Superintendents, NABSE has evolved to include African American educators in all positions, working to increase Black leadership within education and to impact and develop educational policy.

National Association for Asian and Pacific American Education (NAAPAE)
c/o ARC Associates
1212 Broadway, Suite 400
Oakland, CA 94612
Phone: (510) 834-9455
Fax: (510) 763-1490

Since 1977, NAAPAE has promoted the inclusion of Asian and Pacific American history and culture in school curriculum at all levels of education. Offers public awareness programs, a network of educators and community members, and assists in the development of legislation, policies and research by and about Asian and Pacific Americans.

National Association for Bilingual Education (NABE)
1220 L Street, NW - Suite 605
Washington, DC 20005
Phone: (202) 898-1829
Fax: (202) 789-2866
E-mail: www@nabe.org

A national organization, with state affiliates, NABE was founded in 1975. It is a professional organization for those who address the educational needs of language minority students and bilingualism. NABE sponsors national conferences, publishes a journal, magazine and other informational materials, and works on legislation and public policy.

National Association for the Education of Young Children (NAEYC)
1509 16th Street, NW
Washington, DC 20036-1426
Phone: (800) 424-2460
Fax: (202) 328-1846
E-mail: varies by staff member
Web site: www.naeyc.org/naeyc

This professional membership association for educators in early childhood education serves as an advocate for high quality early childhood education, the professional development of teachers and other caregivers, and for addressing bias in education and the responsive education of diverse students. NAEYC publishes books, posters and videos.

National Association for Multicultural Education (NAME)
1511 K Street, NW - Suite 430
Washington, DC 20005
Phone: (202) NAT-NAME (202-628-6263)
Fax: (202) 628-6264
E-mail: name@nicom.com
Web site: www.inform.umd:edu.8080/NAME

NAME is the primary national, and increasingly international, organization that fully focuses on education which is multicultural, both in schools and in the larger society. NAME is dedicated to respecting and appreciating cultural diversity; promoting the development of culturally responsible and responsive policy, curricula, and practices; eliminating racism and other forms of discrimination in society; and achieving social, political, economic and educational equity. NAME brings together for education and action, educators from preschool through university levels, community members, policymakers, business leaders, parents and students.

National Black Child Development Institute (NBCDI)
1023 15th Street, NW - Suite 600
Washington, DC 20005
Phone: (202) 387-1281 or 1-800-556-2234
Fax: (202) 234-1738
E-mail: moreinfo@nbcdi.org
Web site: www.nbcdi.org

Since 1970, this organization has been a national voice for the improvement and protection of the quality of life of African American children and families. National office and affiliate chapters conduct public awareness projects and provide leadership training in the areas of early care and education, elementary and secondary education, child welfare, and health.

National Coalition for Sex Equity in Education (NCSEE)
One Redwood Drive
Clinton, NJ 08809
Phone: (908) 735-5045
Fax: (908) 735-9674

NCSEE is a membership organization whose purpose is to provide leadership in the identification and infusion of sex equity in all education programs and processes and within parallel equity concerns, including, but not limited to, age, disability, national origin, race, religion and sexual orientation. Focal areas range from Title IX and Sexual Harassment to Male Issues and Students as Equity Advocates.

National Coalition for Women and Girls in Education (NCWGE)

c/o National Women's Law Center
11 Dupont Circle, NW - Suite 800
Washington, DC 20036
Phone: (202) 588-5180
Fax: (202) 588-5185

This coalition of nearly 50 national, nongovernmental organizations works together on a broad range of issues affecting the rights and opportunities of women and girls in elementary, secondary, postsecondary, professional and vocational education. The coalition represents the interests of women and girls on issues regarding Title IX of the Education Amendments of 1972, monitors federal agencies and student programs, and publishes resource materials on educational equity. NCWGE was founded in 1975.

National Coalition of Advocates for Students (NCAS)

100 Boylston Street - Suite 737
Boston, MA 02116
Phone: (617) 357-8507
Fax: (617) 357-9549
E-mail: ncasmse@aol.com

Provides informative publications and media programs advocating equal access to quality public education programs for students at risk of school failure. This parent organization to the National Center for Immigrant Students (NCIS) provides research, teaching materials, and human resources data pertaining to immigrant education.

National Coalition of Education Activists (NCEA)

P.O. Box 679
Rhinebeck, NY 12572
Phone: (914) 876-4580
Fax: (914) 876-4580 (same as phone)
E-mail: rfbs@aol.com

NCEA is an activist organization of teachers, parents, and others interested in transforming educational policies and practices that create biased or differential treatment and opportunities for diverse students and communities. The coalition focuses on areas such as curriculum, assessment, and student placement/tracking. NCEA maintains a resource bank of speakers and activists involved in school reform and schools with innovative practices.

The National Conference (TNC)

71 Fifth Avenue
New York, NY 10003
Phone: (212) 206-0006
Fax: (212) 255-6177

Founded in 1927 as The National Conference of Christians and Jews (NCCJ), The National Conference is a human relations organization dedicated to fighting bias, bigotry and racism in America. The National Conference promotes understanding and respect among all races, religions and cultures through advocacy, conflict resolution and education. TNC promotes dialogue and prejudice reduction within schools and in communities. It offers materials, diversity training, and programs for youth, organizations, agencies and communities.

The National Council of LaRaza (NCLR)
1111 19th Street, NW - Suite 1000
Washington, DC 20036
Phone: (202) 785-1670
Fax: (202) 776-1792
Web site: www.nclr.org

This national organization develops and disseminates policy analyses, research papers, newsletter dedicated to advocacy for Hispanic issues. A strong advocacy group for legal rights and social justice to improve the life opportunies for Americans of Hispanic descent, NCLR serves as an umbrella organization for more than a hundred affiliates.

National Council for Accreditation of Teacher Education (NCATE)
2010 Massachusetts Avenue, NW
Washington, DC 20036
Phone: (202) 466-7496
Fax: (202) 296-6620
E-mail: ncate@ncate.org
Web site: in process

For more than 30 years, NCATE has been the umbrella organization for the development of standards and certification for quality teacher education. NCATE includes issues of multicultural education in areas ranging from staffing to curriculum in its evaluation of teacher education programs.

National Council for the Social Studies (NCSS)
3501 Newark Street
Washington, DC 20016-3167
Phone: (202) 966-7840
Fax: (202) 966-2061
E-mail: Online - webmaster@ncss.org
Info Services - information@ncss.org
Web site: www.ncss.org

A national organization for educators and others interested in social studies, NCSS serves as an information clearinghouse on policy and effective social studies education, including multicultural curriculum development and teaching standards.

National Education Association (NEA)
Human and Civil Rights
1201 16th Street, NW
Washington, DC

Phone: (202) 833-4000
Fax: (202) 822-7578
E-mail: varies by staff member
Web site: www.nea.org

This national organization for teachers advocates for teachers' rights and educational reform. Office of Human and Civil Rights, in particular, focuses on areas related to education that is multicultural with programs, resources and publications on areas ranging from race and national origin to gender and sexual orientation.

National Institute for Dispute Resolution (NIDR)
1726 M Street, NW - Suite 500
Washington, DC 20036-4502
Phone: (202) 466-4764
Fax: (202) 466-4769

NIDR's mission is to advocate for and demonstrate effective uses of conflict resolution skills, processes, and systems to create a more civil society. NIDR is the home of The Conflict Resolution Education Network, formerly the National Association for Mediation in Education (NAME). This network is the primary national and international clearinghouse for information, resources, and technical assistance in the field of conflict resolution education.

National Multicultural Institute (NMCI)
3000 Connecticut Avenue, NW - Suite 438
Washington, DC 20008-2556
Phone (202) 483-0700
Fax: (202) 483-5233
E-mail: nmci@nmci.org
Web site: www.nmci.org/nmci/

Founded in 1983 to improve understanding and respect among people of different racial, ethnic and cultural backgrounds, NMCI offers conferences, diversity training, educational resource materials and development assistance.

National Women's History Project
7738 Bell Road
Windsor, CA 95492
Phone: (707) 838-6000
Fax: (707) 838-0478
E-mail: nwhp@aol.com
Web site: www.nwhp.org

The National Women's History Project offers training workshops about women's history and an extensive catalog of educational resource materials about the history and contributions of widely diverse women and girls. This project preserves and transmits women's history and supports the implementation of public and educational policies that fully include the contributions of women.

Network of Educators on the Americas (NECA)
P.O. Box 73038
Washington, DC 20056-3038
Phone: (202) 429-0137 or (202) 238-2379
Fax: (202) 238-2378
E-mail: necadc@aol.com
Web site: www.cldc.howard.edu/~neca

NECA promotes peace, justice and human rights through critical, antiracist, multicultural education. NECA produces and distributes educational and community resources, and offers speakers, seminars and staff development workshops.

Organization of Chinese Americans (OCA)
10001 Connecticut Avenue, NW - Suite 707
Washington, DC 20036
Phone: (202) 223-5500
Fax: (202) 296-0540

An organization dedicated to creating accurate public and educational awareness about Chinese Americans, OCA brings Chinese Americans together to preserve their cultural heritage, work toward equal rights and opportunities, and support community involvement of Americans of Chinese ancestry.

Quality Education for Minorities (QEM) Network
1818 N Street, NW - Suite 350
Washington, DC 20036
Phone: (202) 659-1818
Fax: (202) 659-5408
E-mail: qemnetwork@qem.org
Web site: qemnetwork.qem.org

The QEM Network was created to increase the opportunities for and participation of minorities in mathematics, science and technology. QEM sponsors numerous national research and action programs and convenes briefing sessions on varied issues pertaining to educational equity. QEM also sponsors the "January 15th" Network, a coalition of representatives of educational and scientific organizations, gathered for sharing information, creating dialogue, and developing positions to impact education and public policy.

REACH Center
180 Nickerson Street- Suite 212
Seattle, WA 98109
Phone: (206) 284-8584
Fax: (206) 285-2073
E-mail: reach@nwlink.com
Web site: www.reachctr.org

The REACH Center for Multicultural and Global Education offers training, resource materials and manuals to create multicultural awareness, human relations skills and cross-cultural understanding.

Shomburg Center for Research in Black Culture
New York Public Library
515 Malcolm X Boulevard

New York, NY 10037
Phone: (212) 491-2200
Fax: (212) 491-6760 (but center doesn't respond to fax requests)
Web site: www.nypl.org

A primary source of information on Black history and culture, the center's collection includes articles, publications, materials, and antiquities from all parts of the world where Blacks have resided in significant numbers.

Southern Poverty Law Center

400 Washington Avenue
Montgomery, AL 36104
Phone: (205) 264-0286
Fax: (205) 262-2419
Web site: www.splcenter.org

The Southern Poverty Law Center combats bias and monitors hate groups. It publishes *Klanwatch* and *Teaching Tolerance*, a periodical containing resource information and ready-to-use ideas and strategies for building understanding in classrooms, schools and communities. Several poster sets and educational kits, including videos, are available to schools without charge.

Teachers of English to Speakers of Other Languages (TESOL)

1600 Cameron Street - Suite 300
Alexandria, VA 22314
Phone: (703) 836-0774
Fax: (703) 836-7864
E-mail: tesol@tesol.edu
Web site: www.tesol.edu

A professional organization of teachers, researchers and administrators, TESOL publishes the *TESOL Quarterly* and *TESOL Newsletter* addressing all aspects of teaching English to children, youth and adults who speak a language other than English.

Three Circles Center for Multicultural Environmental Education

P.O. Box 1946
Sausalito, CA 94965
Phone: (415) 561-6580
Fax: (415) 332-9197
E-mail: circlecenter@igc.apc.org

The Three Circles Center is part of the environmental justice movement and works to develop multiculturalism within environmental education, within the curriculum and with strategies for effective environmental education for diverse populations. This nonprofit organization publishes the *Journal of Culture, Ecology and Community*.

United States Committee for UNICEF

Education Department
333 East 38th Street
New York, NY 10016
Phone: (212) 686-5522
Web site: www.unicefusa.org

Publishes and disseminates free and inexpensive print and audiovisual materials with international perspectives.

The Wellesley Centers for Women
Wellesley College
106 Central Street
Wellesley, MA 02181-8259
Phone: (617) 283-2500
Fax: (617) 283-2504

The Wellesley Centers for Women houses an interdisciplinary community of scholars engaged in action, research and training programs and publications which examine the lives of women in a changing world. Components include the Center for Research on Women and the Stone Center, which focuses on studies that have a direct application to policies that affect women, children, families and communities.

2. ELECTRONIC MULTICULTURAL CONTACTS (WEB SITES)

Electronic information has vastly increased the resources available relating to multicultural education and diversity. Web sites exist in varied content areas for various educational levels and communities and from a wide range of perspectives. Web sites frequently change. The thousands of Web sites related to multicultural education which continue to proliferate make a comprehensive, up-to-date listing impossible to provide. This sampling of relevant Web sites offers a core of sites which can lead to multiple links and innumerable resources. The sample listing was current at the time of publication.

The Aframian WebNet
http://www.he.net/~awe/
Centralized listing of links on the World Wide Web which are about or of interest to African Americans and related resources.

African American History Historical
www.msstate.edu/Archives/History/USA/Text Archive Afro-Amer/
afro.html
A comprehensive listing of sites on specific topics related to African American history.

The African American Mosaic
http://www.loc.gov/exhibits/african/intro.html
A Library of Congress Resource Guide for the Study of Black History and Culture. Surveys the variety of collections in the Library of Congress, including books, periodicals, music and film.

African American Site List
http://excalibur.accs.howard.edu/webmaster/african.html

African American Web sites

http://home.earthlink.net%7Earthony/africa/html

A comprehensive listing of Web sites on the Internet related to African American issues.

Allies

http://www.contrib.andrew.cmu.edu/org/allies

Web site with information about support services for gay and lesbian youth.

American Jewish History

http://muse.jhv.edv/press/OCS/ajh/html

Publication of the American Jewish Historians Society, including information on anti-Semitism.

Annotated Holocaust Web Sites

http://socialstudies.com/holosource.html

An annotated listing of more than 30 Web sites related to Holocaust studies.

Arab World and Islamic Resources

http:// gopher://laatif.com

Information about Arab and Islamic culture and events.

Asian American History

http://cwcare.clever.net/cultures/books/asian

Resources on the history of Asian Americans.

Asian American History Links

Extensive list of World Wide Web links to history resources on Asian American history, reflecting many Asian cultures.

Asian American Resources

http://www.mit.edu:8001/afs/athena.mit.edu/ user/i/r/irie/www/aar.html

Extensive list of resources related to organizations and facts about Asian American cultures.

Ask ERIC InfoGuides

http://ericir.syr.edu/Virtual/InfoGuides/

InfoGuides on topics such as migrant education, American Indians and Alaska Natives, gender and ethnic bias in curriculum, Mexican Americans, indigenous peoples, women's literature and Holocaust studies.

Bilingual Education Resources on the Net

http://www.estrelita.com/~karenm/bil.html

A listing of sites and linkages about bilingual education which can be found on the internet.

Black History

http://www.kn.pacbell.com/wired/BHM/AfroAm.htm/

A Web site to support students as they explore topics related to Black history and African American issues. Includes classroom activities for specific topics.

Black History Museum

http://www.afro.am.org/history.htm/

Interactive exhibits for students on African American History prepared by the Afro-American Newspaper Company, Baltimore, MD.

Books about Children with Disabilities
http://www.math.hu.edu/~dmettler/dlit.html
A list for teachers, parents, and students of literature about children with disabilities.

Caribbean Cultural Center
http://www.artswire.org/Artswire/www.caribctr/home.html
Multiple resources about Caribbean culture, activities and educational materials.

Celebrating Our Nation's Diversity
http://www.census.gov/ftp/pub/edu/diversity
Site maintained by the U.S. Census bureau, offering lesson plans on the census and the diverse population of the United States, for teachers in grades K-12.

The Center for the Study of White American Culture, Inc.: A Multiracial Organization
http://www.euroamerican.org/
Descriptions of the organizations, including book listings and references related to building an inclusive society. Includes links related to diversity and antiracism.

Chicano/Latino Net
http://latino.sscnet.ucla.edu/
Information and resources on Latino issues and communities, with particular emphasis on Chicanos.

Children's Literature
http://www.scils.rutgers.edu/special/kay/childlit.html
A list of young children's picture books with positive images of people from a range of ethnic groups. Also lists gender-fair books.

Children's Literature Best Books List
http://www.vcalgary/~dkbrown/lists.html
Numerous recommended book lists, many organized by diversity issues including ethnicity, religion, gender, sexual orientation, and multiracial families.

Clearinghouse for Multicultural/ Bilingual Education
http://www.weber.edu/mbe/htmls/mbe.html
Commercial and noncommercial sources for multicultural and bilingual information, materials and resources.

Cornucopia of Disability Information
http://codi.buffalo.edu/graph_based/
Resources related to services and organizations.

Diversity Webpage of the History/Social Studies Web Site
http://www.execpc.com/~dboals/diversit.html
Part of the History/Social Studies Web Site for K-12 teachers. Includes sections on women's studies, Native American studies, Asian Americans, African Americans, Hispanic studies, disability, and much more.

Diversity Newsroom

http://www.inform.umd.edu/DiversityNews

Developed and maintained by the Association of American Colleges and Universities and the University of Maryland, College Park, with funding from the Ford Foundation. A resource for journalists and other media about varied areas of diversity in higher education including campus access, hiring practices, student admissions, retention, affirmative action and related policies, curricula, with research, statistics, analysis and other current and historical information.

Diversity Web

http://www.inform.umd.edu/DiversityWeb

A project of the Association of American Colleges and Universities, the University of Maryland, College Park, and Diversity Connections at Wesleyan University. Provides an electronic hub linking the diversity work of about 300 institutions of higher education. The Diversity Web was created to "bring people together from across the country to learn from one another, share ideas and generate exciting new approaches to this work."

Edequity Network

To subscribe: majordomo@confer.edc.org
(send message: "subscribe edequity")
To send messages: edequity@tristam.edc.org

An online network/listserv of individuals and organizations working on educational equity issues.

Encyclopedia of Women's History

http://www.teleport.com/~megaines/woindex.html

By and for the K-12 community. Students can contribute biographies to this collaborative effort.

Entirely Too Many Curricular Resources

http://www.trc.org/bookmark.htm

Hundreds of useful Web sites, divided by subject matter. Extensive sections on social studies, languages and cultures.

EQUITY ONLINE/Women's Educational Equity Act

http://www.edc.org/CEEC/WEEA

Resources and information about the Women's Educational Equity Act (WEEA). Resource center providing gender-fair multicultural materials, training and discussion lists.

ERIC (Educational Research Information Center)

http://ericae.educ.edu/search/htm

Lists sites for searching the ERIC database on a wide range of topics, including education that is multicultural.

European American Resources

http://scuish.scu.edu/SCU/programs/Diversity/euros.html

A wide range of Web sites, outlining journals and reference materials about Euro-American cultures, including Italian, Portuguese, Russian, Irish, Slavic countries and Eastern European nations.

European-American Web Links

http://contour.depaul.edu/~diversit/wwweuropean.html

Web sites related to European-American issues and studies.

European History and Culture

http://rmc.library.cornell.edu

Extensive collection of information on American/European history and culture.

Facets of Religion, Virtual Library of Religion

http://sunfly.ub.uni-freiburg.de/religion/remarks.html

Information on religions of the world, including Hinduism, Buddhism, Judaism, Christianity, Zoroastrianism, Taoism, Islam, Sikhism and Bahai.

Famous Hispanics in the World and History

http://www.clark.net/pub/jgbustam/famoss.htm/

A developing site in English and Spanish celebrating Hispanic heritage in the U.S.

GIRLTECH

http://www.girltech.com/

A site with interactive activities related to girls in sports, technology, and Web sites.

Global School Net Foundation (GSN)

http://www.gsn.org

A monthly calendar of online projects related to enhancing global understanding.

A Guide to Children's Literature and Disability

http://ws1.kidsource.com/NICHCY/literature.html

A bibliography of books written about or including characters with a wide range of learning and physical disabilities.

Hispanic America USA

http://www.neta.com/~lstbooks/content.htm

World and United States history information highlighting Hispanic-American contributions. Also lists Hispanic-American resources.

Hispanic CLNET History Sources

http://latino.sscnet.ucla.edu/Test/history.ref.html

An extensive bibliography of references on Hispanic-American history.

Hispanic Heritage

http://www.clark.net/pub/jgbustam/heritage.html

A listing of Web sites related to Hispanic culture and history.

Hispanic Online Latino Links

http://www.hisp.com/tesoros/index.html

Numerous Hispanic education resources and organizations.

Index of Native American Resources

http://hanksville.phast.umass.edu/misc/NAresources.hhtml

A broadly based index of resources about Native Americans.

Intercultural E-mail Classroom Connections (IECC)
http://www.stolaf.edu/network/iecc/
Clearinghouse for K-12 teachers seeking partner classrooms for international and cross-cultural e-mail exchanges. Over 5000 subscribers in 54 countries.

Latino Web
http://www.catalog.com/favision/latnoweb
Resources and contacts of issues related to Latinos in all spheres of interest.

Librarians Information Online Network Multicultural Forum
http://litertynet.org/~lion/forum-multi.html
A listing of several Web sites related to multicultural education for K-12 teachers.

Library of Congress
http://lcweb.loc.gov/catalog/
A catalogue of ways to search for specific content in the Library of Congress Archives. Includes extensive listing of multicultural education topics.

Men's Issues and Support
http://feminist.com/pro.htm
Information about men's groups concerned with gender equity.

Migration to America
http://www.turner.com/+esi/html/migration.html
Activities for students about the Ellis Island immigration experience.

Multicultural listserve
http://multc-ed@umdd.umd.edv
A subscription discussion network to share resources and ideas related to multicultural education. Based at the University of Maryland for NAME, the National Association for Multicultural Education.

Multicultural Organizations
http://curry.edschool.virginia.edu/go/multicultural/sites/orgsites.html
An extensive listing of multicultural organizations nationwide.

The Multicultural Pavilion
http://curry.edschool.virginia.edu/go/multicultural
Resources on multicultural education for the K-12 teacher. Includes a teacher's corner, international project, online discussion board, and links to hundreds of other sites.

Multicultural Publishers
http://www.mpec.org/publishe.html
A constantly expanding list of publishers of multicultural materials.

Multicultural Publishing and Education Council
http://www.quiknet.com/mbt/mpec/mpci/html
National network of African, Arab, Asian, Hispanic, Jewish, Latino, Pacific Islander, Native, and White American publishers of multicultural materials.

Multicultural Resources - Trivia
http://trivadm@dune.srhs.K12.nj.us
Interactive site for students to find out facts related to multicultural history.

National Association for Multicultural Education (NAME)
http://www.inform.umd:edu.8080/NAME
Homepage of NAME, membership organization promoting multicultural research and practices pre-K through higher education.

National Clearinghouse for Bilingual Education
http://www.ncbe.gwu.edu
Links hundreds of Web sites pertaining to bilingual education, bilingualism, language and culture learning.
http://www.ncbe.gwu.edu/classroom/bilschool.html
Site from NCBE which contains information about and links to schools with effective programs in bilingual education.

National Equity On-Line Calendar
http://mdac.ksu.edu/equity/cal
Updated calendar of equity professsional development events.

National Women's History Project
http://www.nwhp.org/
A wealth of information about a wide range of women's history topics and resources.

Native American Homepage
http://www.pitt.edu/~/mitten/indians.html
Extensive listing of Native American resources.

Native American Indian Resources for Teachers and Students
http://www.ncbe.gwu.edu
Extensive educational resources for school use by teachers and students.

Native American Tribes
http://www.afn.org/~native/
A list of federally recognized tribes with connections to tribal homepages.

Native Web
http://www.maxwell.syr.edu/nativeweb/
A variety of resources, including a list of K-12 sites, bibliographies, and organizations.

Notes from the Windowsill
http://www.armory.com/~web/notes.html
Annotated bibliography of multicultural books, including books with gay and lesbian themes and characters, and books with depictions of multiracial families.

Pathways to School Improvement/ NCREL
http://www.ncrel.org

Addresses school improvement issues. Summarizes best practices and research related to specific topics such as multicultural education, search under creative High-Achieving Learning Environments.

Pluribus Unum

http://newlinks.tc.columbia.edu/pluribus/

Maintained by the National Center for Restructuring Education, Schools and Teaching at Teachers College, Columbia University. Focuses on a traditional perspective for studying diversity and pluralism in school and society.

Public Broadcasting Specials

http://www.pbs.org

Infomation about many multicultural documentaries aired on PBS.

The Public Eye

http://www.igc.apc.org/pra/

Site to create understanding about "threats" to democracy and diversity. Addresses issues ranging from racism, sexism, homophobia and anti-Semitism, to issues such as prejudice, scapegoating, and ethnocentrism.

Reference and Research Articles on Multicultural Education

http://ericae2.educ.cua.edu/scripts/webinator.

exe.db=allr&arg=multicultural education

An internet research tool providing abstracts of a wide range of current EMC articles from the ERIC Clearinghouse Database.

RETAnet

http://ladb.unm.edu/retanet/

Internet access to cultural information and contacts for curricular and other resources pertaining to Latin America, the Spanish Caribbean, and the Southwest United States. Maintained by the Latin American Institute at the University of New Mexico, RETAnet is aimed at educators, secondary teachers and scholars.

Rethinking Schools

http://www.rethinkingschools.org

Selected articles from the current issue of *Rethinking Schools* and recent back issues, a complete index of all *Rethinking Schools* articles, information on special publications, and links to other educational and activist sites related to social justice.

Social Studies School Service

http://socialstudies.com/activities/tableh.html

Classroom activities related to multicultural topics, with annotated lists of other sites on issues such as Holocaust studies.

Society and Culture: Sexual Minority Youth Resource Organizations

http://www.yahoo.com/Society_and_Culture/Lesbians_Gays_and Bisexuals/Youth/Organizations

A listing of organizations related to resources for and about gay and lesbian youth.

Southern Poverty Law Center

http://www.sp/center.org

Information from the Southern Poverty Law Center about "Teaching Tolerance" educational activities and monitoring of hate/violence incidents and groups.

UNICEF Cyberspace Bus

http://www.un.org/pubs/CyberSchoolBus/

UNICEF's interactive Web site for teachers and students to promote global understanding.

U.S. Race and Ethnicity Resources

http://www.contact.org/usrace.htm

Numerous links to directories, publications, and organizations which focus on issues of diversity in the United States.

Worldwide Virtual Library of Migration

http://www.rud.nl/ercomer/wwwvl/wwwvlmer.hmtl

Extensive listing on organizations and publications related to the American immigration experience.

WebEd General Links K-12

http://unile2.tisl.ukans.edu/Generic/auxresources/wEdlist.html

Extensive listing of resources for K-12 teachers. Includes several sites related to multicultural education.

Women of Achievement and Herstory

http://www.imageworld.com/istuber.html

Informative calender of events from women's history and information on a CD-ROM Encyclopedia of Famous American Women.

Women's Rights National Historic Park

http://www.nps.gov/wori

Photos, graphic images, and primary documents relating to the first Women's Rights Convention (1848), historic sites related to the movement, and biographies of its leaders.

Yahoo Gay, Lesbian and Bisexual Resources Gays Lesbians and Bisexuals/

http://www.yahoo.com/Society and Culture/

Resources for schools and communities on varied topics pertaining to sexual orientation.

3. FEDERALLY FUNDED ASSISTANCE CENTERS

The U.S. Department of Education supports three types of assistance centers, each serving, or based in, a particular geographic region of the United States. Services to school systems and other educational institutions are generally provided without charge. Print, audiovisual and electronic resources and training or other workshops may be available without charge or at low cost:

A. Equity Assistance Centers—Also known as DACs (Desegregation Assistance Centers), these 10 centers provide assistance in the educational equity areas of race, sex (gender), and national origin, including multicultural education.

B. Comprehensive Assistance Centers—These 15 centers combine the resources and assistance formerly provided separately to help states, school districts, and schools to meet the needs of children served under the Elementary and Secondary Education Act (ESEA). This includes children in areas of high poverty, migratory children, immigrant children, children with limited-English proficiency, neglected or delinquent children, homeless children and youth, Indian children, children with disabilities, and, where applicable, Alaska Native and Native Hawaiian children.

C. Regional Educational Laboratories—These educational laboratories provide a research base for educational policies and practices. Although based in particular regions of the country, particular labs may specialize in specific areas, e.g., urban education, and therefore, can serve as a resource to any region.

A. Equity Assistance Centers

Region I New England Desegregation Assistance Center for Equity in Education
Serves Connecticut, Maine, Massachusetts, New Hampshire, Rhode Island and Vermont
Brown University
144 Wayland Avenue
Providence, RI 02926
Phone: (401) 351-7577
Fax: (401) 421-7650
Web site: www.brown.edu/Research/
The_Education_Alliance/DAC/dac.html

Region II The METRO Center
Serves New Jersey, New York, Puerto Rico and Virgin Islands
32 Washington Place - Room 72
New York, NY 10003
Phone: (212) 998-5100
Fax: (212) 995-4199
Web site: www.nyu.edu/education/metrocenter

Region III The Mid-Atlantic Center
Serves Delaware, District of Columbia, Maryland, Pennsylvania, Virginia and West Virginia
5454 Wisconsin Avenue - Suite 655
Chevy Chase, MD 20815

Phone: (301) 657-7741
Fax: (301) 657-8782
Web site: www.nicom.com/~maec

Region IV Southeastern Desegregation Assistance Center
Serves Alabama, Florida, Georgia, Kentucky, Mississippi, South Carolina,
Tennessee, and North Carolina
c/o Miami Equity Associates, Inc.
8603 S. Dixie Highway - Suite 304
Miami, FL 33143
Phone: (305) 669-0114
Fax: (305) 669-9809

Region V Programs for Educational Opportunity
Serves Illinois, Indiana, Michigan, Minnesota, Ohio and Wisconsin
University of Michigan
1005 School of Education
Ann Arbor, MI 48109
Phone: (313) 763-9910
Fax: (313) 763-2137
Web site: www.umich.edu/~eqtynet

Region VI Intercultural Development Research Association
Serves Arkansas, Louisiana, New Mexico, Oklahoma and Texas
5835 Callahan - Suite 350
San Antonio, TX 78210
Phone: (210) 684-8180
Fax: (210) 684-5389
Web site: www.idra.org

Region VII Mid-West Desegregation Assistance Center
Serves Iowa, Kansas, Missouri, and Nebraska
Kansas State University
Bluemont Hall
Manhattan, KS 66505
Phone: (913) 532-6408
Fax: (913) 532-7304

Region VIII Educational Equity Center at Metropolitan State College of Denver
Serves Colorado, Montana, North Dakota, South Dakota Utah and
Wyoming
1100 Stout Street - Suite 800
Denver, CO 80204
Phone: (303) 556-8494
Fax: (303) 556-8505
Web site: www.mscd.edu/eec_svcs/

Region IX Southwest Center for Educational Equity
Serves Arizona, California and Nevada
4665 Lampson Avenue
Los Alamitos, CA 90720

Phone: (310) 598-7661
Fax: (301) 985-9635
Web site: www.swrl.org/

Region X Northwest Regional Education Laboratory
Serves Alaska, Hawaii, Idaho, Oregon, Washington, American Samoa,
Guam, Northern Mariana Islands, and Trust Territory of the Pacific
101 SW Main Street - Suite 500
Portland, OR 97204
Phone: (503) 275-9507
Fax: (503) 275-9489
Web site: www.nwrel.org

B. Comprehensive Assistance Centers

Overall Web site for all 15 Comprehensive Centers: www.ed.gov/EdRes/
EdFed/EdTechCtrs.html

The comprehensive centers are:

Educational Development Center, Inc. (EDC)
55 Chapel Street
Newton, MA 02158-1060
Phone: (617) 969-7100 extension 2201
Fax: (617) 969-3440

New York University (NYU)
Washington Street - Suite 72
New York, NY 10003-6644
Phone: (800) 469-8224
Fax: (212) 995-4199

George Washington University (GWU)
Center for Equity and Excellence in Education
1730 North Lynn Street -Suite 401
Arlington, VA 22209
Phone: (800) 925-3223
Fax: (703) 528-5973

Appalachia Educational Laboratory, Inc. (AEL)
P.O. Box 1348
Charleston, WV 25325-1348
Phone: (800) 624-9120
Fax: (304) 347-0487

Southeast Educational Development Laboratory (SEDL)
3330 Causeway Blvd. - Suite 430
Metairie, LA 70002-3573
Phone: (800) 644-8671
Fax: (504) 831-5242

University of Wisconsin (U of W)
1025 West Johnson Street - Suite 770
Madison, WI 53706
Phone: (608) 263-4220
Fax: (608) 263-3733

Region VII Comprehensive Assistance Center
University of Oklahoma
1000 ASP - Room 210
Phone: (800) 228-1766
Fax: (405) 325-1824

Intercultural Development Research Association (IDRA)
5835 Callaghan Road - Suite 350
San Antonio, TX 78228-1190
Phone: (210) 684-8180
Fax: (210) 684-5389

New Mexico Highlands University (NMHU)
121 Tejeras, NE - Suite 2100
Albuquerque, NM 87102
Phone: (505) 242-7447
Fax: (505) 242-7558

Northwest Regional Educational Laboratory (NWREL)
101 Southwest Main Street - Suite 500
Portland, OR 97204
Phone: (800) 547-6339 extension 480
Fax: (503) 275-9625

Far West Laboratory and Southwest Regional Laboratory (WestEd)
730 Harrison Street
San Francisco, CA 94107-1242
Phone: (415) 565-3000
Fax: (415) 565-3012

L.A. County Office of Education
9300 Imperial Highway
Downey, CA 90242-2890
Phone: (310) 922-6343
Fax: (310) 940-1798

South East Regional Resource Center (SERRC)
210 Ferry Way - Suite 200
Juneau, AK 99801
Phone: (907) 586-8606
Fax: (907) 463-3811

Educational Testing Service (ETS)
1979 Lake Side Parkway - Suite 400
Tucker, GA 30084
Phone: (800) 241-3865
Fax: (770) 723-7436

Pacific Regional Educational Laboratory (PREL)
828 Fort Street Mall - Suite 500
Honolulu, HI 96813-7599
Phone: (808) 533-6000
Fax: (808) 533-7599

C. Regional Educational Laboratories

Northeast Region The Educational Alliance, Brown University
164 Angell Street - Box 1929
Providence, RI 02912
Phone: (401) 863-2777
Web site: www.lab.brown.edu
Specialty Area: Language and Cultural Diversity

Mid-Atlantic Region Temple University
933 Ritter Annex
13th and Cecil B. Moore
Philadelphia, PA 19122
Phone: (215) 204-3001
Web site: www.temple.edu/departments/1.SS
Specialty Area: Urban Education

Appalachian Region Appalachia Educational Laboratory, Inc. (AEL)
1031 Quarrier Street
P.O. Box 1348
Charleston, WV 25325
Phone: (800) 624-9120
Web site: www.ael.org
Specialty Area: Rural Education

Southeastern Region Southeastern Regional Vision for Education
(SERVE)
P.O. Box 5367
Greensboro, NC 27435
Phone: (800) 755-3277
Web site: www.serve.org
Specialty Area: Early Childhood Education

Midwestern Region North Central Regional Educational
Laboratory (NCREL)
1900 Spring Road - Suite 300
Oak Brook, IL 60521-1480
Phone: (708) 571-4700
Web site: www.ncrel.org
Specialty Area: Technology

Southwestern Region Southwest Educational Development
Laboratory (SEDL)
211 East Seventh Street - Second Floor
Austin, TX 78701-3281

Phone: (512) 476-6861
Web site: www.sedl.org
Specialty Area: Language and Cultural Diversity

Central Region Mid-Continent Regional Educational
Laboratory (McREL)
2550 South Parker Road - Suite 500
Aurora, CO 80014
Phone: (303) 337-0990
Web site: www.mcrel.org
Specialty Area: Curriculum, Learning and Instruction

Western Region Far West Laboratory for Educational
Research and Development
730 Harrison Street
San Francisco, CA 94107-1242
Phone: (415) 565-3000
Web site: www.fwl.org
Specialty Area: Assessment and Accountability

**Northwestern Region Northwest Regional Educational Laboratory
(NWREL)**
101 SW Main Street - Suite 500
Portland, OR 97204-3212
Phone: (800) 547-6339
Web site: www.nwrel.org
Specialty Area: School Change Processes

Pacific Region Pacific Region Educational Laboratory
828 Fort Street Mall - Suite 500
Honolulu, Hawaii 96813
Phone: (808) 533-6000
Web site: prel-oahu-1.prel.hawaii.edu
Specialty Area: Language and Cultural Diversity

INDEX

by Virgil Diodato

Index

Index